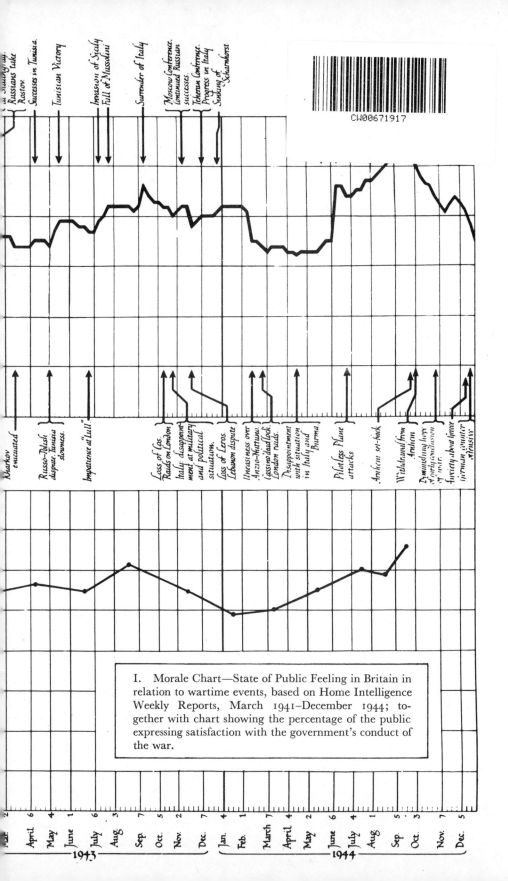

I. Morale Chart—State of Public Feeling in Britain in relation to wartime events, based on Home Intelligence Weekly Reports, March 1941–December 1944; together with chart showing the percentage of the public expressing satisfaction with the government's conduct of the war.

MINISTRY OF MORALE

Ministry of Morale

Home Front Morale and the
Ministry of Information in World War II

by IAN McLAINE

London
GEORGE ALLEN & UNWIN
Boston   Sydney

First published in 1979

GEORGE ALLEN & UNWIN LTD
40 Museum Street, London WC1A 1LU

© Ian McLaine, 1979

British Library Cataloguing in Publication Data

McLaine, Ian
    Ministry of morale.
    1. Great Britain. Ministry of Information – History
    I. Title
    940.54′886′41   D799.G7   78–40848

    ISBN 0-04-940055-X

Typeset in 11 on 12 point Baskerville by Trade Linotype Ltd, Birmingham
and printed in Great Britain
by Unwin Brothers Limited, Old Woking, Surrey

Contents

List of Illustrations

FIGURES

PLATES
between pages 86 and 87

between pages 214 and 215

All the illustrations are reproduced by courtesy of the Imperial War Museum except for the 'Morale Chart' on the endpapers which is Crown Copyright (PRO INF 1/291) and reproduced by permission of H.M. Stationery Office; and for Plate 3 for which acknowledgement is due to the British Library.

Author's Acknowledgements

Without the constant support of Mr John Prest, of Balliol College, Oxford, this book would certainly have never seen the light of day. To Dr David Cuthbert I owe the original suggestion for a study of British civilian morale and Professor Alan McBriar a debt for invaluable comments on the manuscript. John Cornwell also provided a fund of assistance, particularly in matters of style, while my dear friends, Maurice and Juliet Bloye, furnished hospitality and companionship during my visits to Britain. For a perceptive analysis of the shortcomings of the first draft I am indebted to Dr Paul Addison.

I am grateful too to Lord Briggs, Mr Charles Lysaght, Professor Arthur Marwick, Dr Henry Parvis, Professor R. B. Pugh, and Mr A. J. P. Taylor for their willingness to offer expert advice and for directing me to fresh sources.

For allowing me to draw upon their recollection of wartime experiences I wish to thank Mrs Mary Adams, Mr Malcolm Barnes, Professor Michael Balfour, Mr Rohan Butler, Lord Clark, Mr Alan Hodge, Mr Tom Hopkinson, Professor H. G. Nicholas, the late Lord Radcliffe, Mr Bernard Sendall, Mr Peter Smolka, and Lord Taylor. Mr T. W. Tallents kindly gave me access to the papers of his father, Sir Stephen Tallents. I hesitate to single out any individual, but feel I must do so in the case of the late Professor Tom Harrisson: as well as permitting me to range about freely in the Mass-Observation Archive, he was unstintingly generous to me with his personal reminiscences and with his reflections on the nature of morale.

I must also acknowledge the help of The Master and Fellows of Balliol College in permitting me access to the original diaries of Harold Nicolson in their Library, the copyright of which, however, rests with Collins Publishers.

The staff of the Public Record Office, and particularly the officers at the old Ashridge repository, of the Beaverbrook Library and of the Imperial War Museum were unfailingly helpful. Crown copyright material in the Public Record Office appears by permission of the Controller of Her Majesty's Stationery Office. As a research fellow at the University of Melbourne, I was able to commence writing and received much encouragement from the then Chairman of the History Department, Mr Weston Bate. My thanks are due, as well, to Professor Ross Duncan, of the University of Wollongong, for allowing me to make adjustments in my teaching programme during the final period of research and writing.

Glenys, my wife, succeeded in boosting my confidence while applying her mind to the task of seeking flaws in my reasoning and argument; and my children, Meredith and David, exhibited remarkable forbearance in the face of the frequent admonition: 'Quiet! Daddy's working!'.

MINISTRY OF MORALE

Introduction

This book was inspired by the conjunction of two problems. The first is related to the fact that British civilian morale during the Second World War has subsequently assumed the quality of myth: 'myth' in the sense of a story which encapsulates for its believers all the qualities they see themselves as possessing in circumstances of extreme adversity. Since the war the myth has been continually nourished by the tendency of politicians and others to call for a revival of 'the Dunkirk spirit' whenever Britain has faced a threat to her well-being. Unfortunately for the efficacy of such calls, Britain's post-war ills have appeared to be of a far less immediate character than the presence of Hitler's armies across the Channel.

For a subject which appears to occupy so important a niche in the national consciousness, one might almost say the folk memory, surprisingly little has been written about wartime morale. There have been exceptions. Constantine Fitzgibbon, T. H. O'Brien, Angus Calder and, pre-eminently, Richard Titmuss and Tom Harrisson have to varying degrees touched upon the subject, but principally in the course of examining other aspects of wartime life and experience.[1] As if fearing that too close an inquiry might erode the foundations of the myth, many writers have been content to assert that the nation won through because the morale of the population was indestructible. Of course the difficulty for anyone interested in the nature and quality of wartime morale is the very imprecision of the term and, more importantly for the historian, the ephemeral and diffuse character of the sources to which he must turn. The risks of producing a compilation of random impressions and reminiscences are considerable.

The second problem is posed by, and offers a possible solution to, the first. There existed a body, the Ministry of Information, whose prime duty on the home front was to sustain civilian morale. The puzzle is that during the initial two years of war this department was roundly and widely condemned for inefficiency, for comic blunders and for irritating rather than reassuring the public. How could it be that morale was sound and yet the department responsible for it so

1

bad? Did Britain's leaders believe morale could be safely left to look after itself?

In April 1941 an official of the Air Ministry commented on the aloofness of Whitehall, and the service ministries in particular, in matters related to civilian morale:

> I believe the basis of the trouble to be the old 'Service' attitude of mind, founded on memory of when armies conducted campaigns out of England, independent of home control, with slow communications between the field of warfare and the British public, and in a spirit which said that the civilian's job was to ask no questions, to pay his taxes in order to keep up the Armed Forces, to take off his hat when the Colours marched past, and generally to regard himself as a necessary but unfortunate adjunct to the glories of military life which, coupled with fox-hunting, really go to make up England.[2]

This attitude stemmed from a refusal to acknowledge one of the major consequences of a change in the nature of wars between nations. They had, according to one authority, 'come to resemble campaigns in which whole countries besiege one another'.[3] In conflicts in which whole populations were considered – and exhorted to think of themselves – as front line troops, the role of the civilian was crucial. The dependence of the armed forces upon the industrial and organisational skills of the home population had grown in direct proportion to the increase in the technological sophistication of warfare. This development was, moreover, accompanied by an increasing disinclination of the populace to accept uncritically the policies and decisions of government in wartime. The citizen's morale and his willingness to contribute to the war effort had therefore become of decisive military importance – the more so because of the advent between the wars of the long-range bomber, a means by which war could be carried to the great cities of combatant nations. Defeat might flow not from the collapse of armies on a conventional battle-front but from the breakdown of morale at home.

Churchill's modest disclaimer to the effect that he merely supplied the lion's roar, as if to say that limitless courage is integral to the British character, obscures the fact that a great deal of official thought and anxiety was expended by the Ministry of Information on the problem of morale. And, despite the vicissitudes experienced by the department, the officers and their political chiefs stuck to their task as they saw it, systematically making recommendations to government, producing unique, lengthy, detailed and generally accurate weekly reports on public opinion and public spirits, and eventually coming to believe that their actions were of central importance.

By examining the domestic work of the Ministry of Information it is possible to gain an unprecedented insight into the mind of both government and people during the war, and I have sought to answer three broad questions. First, how did a government department, initially constructed as if in parody of Whitehall bureaucracy, assess and set about maintaining morale? Because morale was, and was seen to be, linked with social and political questions – such as the prospect of post-war social reform, the nature of the Soviet regime, and press freedom – the Ministry was necessarily involved in a number of controversial issues. How were these handled and what constraints operated upon the department? Finally, just how sound was morale on the basis of the considerable evidence then available and was it enhanced in any way by the Ministry of Information?

It is ironic, and not a little poignant, that the body charged with sustaining public morale and with maintaining confidence in the government should itself have suffered from chronically low morale and been the object of general ridicule. Unpopular with press and Parliament, with both Chamberlain and Churchill, and with Tommy Handley, the department underwent severe organisational changes, frequent shifts of senior personnel, and a steady erosion of its powers. Since 1945 it has received only slight and slighting references from historians and has gained no recognition in the official history series. It was expertly satirised in Evelyn Waugh's *Put Out More Flags*, first published in 1942. As originally conceived, however, the Ministry was allotted five broad functions whose necessity in time of war few questioned: the release of official news; security censorship of the press, films and the BBC; the maintenance of morale; the conduct of publicity campaigns for other departments; and the dissemination of propaganda to enemy, neutral, allied and empire countries. In the seven months between October 1939 and April 1940 the Ministry's responsibility for censorship and news was lost to the newly created Press and Censorship Bureau. Also lost in October 1939, in this case permanently, was control of propaganda to the enemy, although the department later regained some influence when it was represented on the Political Warfare Executive together with the Foreign Office and the Ministry of Economic Warfare.

In emulation of existing departments of state, whose structures had evolved pragmatically over long periods of time, the Ministry adopted a structure of great complexity. It continually changed shape, now contracting, now expanding, convoluting itself and thoroughly confusing MPs, the press, the public and, not least, the officers of the department themselves. On the outbreak of war, when the Ministry was lodged in Senate House at London University, the fourteen divisions of the department were organised in four groups: censorship, news and press relations; 'publicity' – that is to say, propaganda – covering home, empire and foreign countries; production of publicity material; and administration. In October 1939 the loss of censorship, news and enemy propaganda entailed drastic reorganisation. And before the department had time to settle down another major adjustment occurred in February 1940. The divisions remaining to the Ministry were grouped under a Directorate and a Secretariat. The former, with the Deputy Director General at its head, comprised the Foreign, Empire, American, Religions, General, Films and Broadcasting divisions; while the latter, under the direction of the Deputy Secretary, comprised the Home Intelligence, Communications, Regional Administration, Finance and Establishments divisions. With the re-acquisition in April 1940 of news and censorship, as well as the transfer from the War Office of postal and telegraph censorship, further modification was required.

Remorselessly the process continued. In September 1940 the separation of the Ministry into a Directorate and a Secretariat was abandoned, although the scheme of divisional groupings was maintained: News, Censorship and Photographs; Home Intelligence, Regional Administration, and Home Publicity; Overseas Affairs; Production; and General Administration. Standing outside these groupings were BBC Relations and Commercial Relations. There were to be further refinements, but with the arrival of Brendan Bracken as Minister in July 1941 a measure of stability was achieved. Figure II shows the settled structure as of 1943. None of these reshufflings would have mattered very much had the various divisions been allowed to get on with the job. But this was not the case. On each occasion new lines of authority were laid down and, as the Ministry clung tenaciously to the Whitehall way of ordering things, the personnel – most of whom were strange to the ways of the civil service – were thrown into confusion.

The low fortunes of the department were attributable in part to the choice of the first three ministers: Lord Macmillan (appointed on the outbreak of war), Sir John Reith (5 January 1940) and Duff Cooper (12 May 1940). This sprightly procession of ministers, accompanied by the equally frequent dismissal and appointment of directors-general,[4] prompted the more irreverent officers to chant:

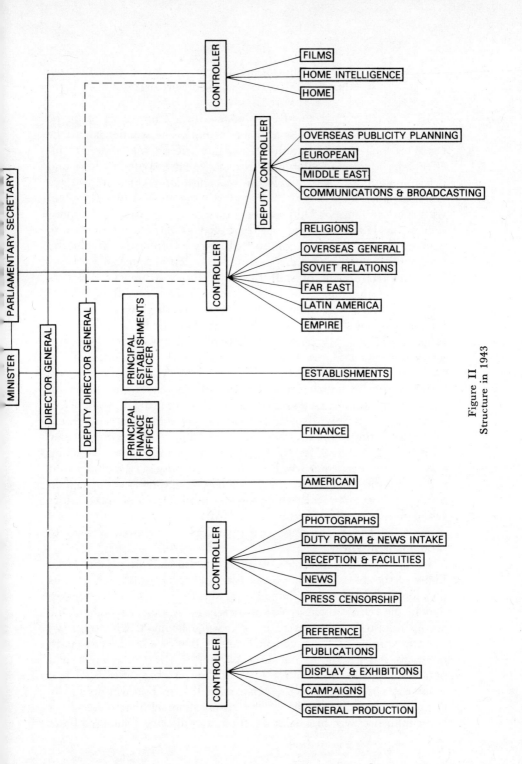

Figure II
Structure in 1943

Hush, hush, chuckle who dares,
Another new Minister's fallen downstairs.[5]

Lord Macmillan, a distinguished judge with a long record of public
service, was completely lost and ineffectual. The wonder is that he
lasted as long as four months in the post. Reith was almost as ineffectual. For a man who had displayed great qualities of drive and
determination at the BBC, Reith was curiously reluctant to force
Chamberlain's hand when the Prime Minister refused to endow him
with more authority. Duff Cooper, though creating a good impression in the House of Commons, managed to alienate the press and,
worn down by attacks upon the Ministry of Information and by
Churchill's indifference, merely wanted to be left in peace.

In the recruitment of staff the cult of the amateur reached its
apogee and the universities, the legal profession and the ranks of
retired admirals were thoroughly scoured. While it was difficult to
find at short notice experts in such nebulous fields as morale and
propaganda, the possession of experience in, say, psychology and
journalism seems almost to have been a positive disqualification for
employment. Representatives of the trade union and Labour movements were also largely ignored. Richard Crossman was taken on
early in the war as a token gesture but the department remained a
Conservative enclave. Parliamentary and press criticism were severe
and unremitting, and in 1940 Beverley Baxter and Norman Riley
each published a book in which the manner of the Ministry's staffing
was roundly condemned.[6] It is hardly surprising, therefore, that
everything the Ministry touched in domestic and foreign propaganda
seemed to turn immediately to dross. In the circumstances critics
found it easy to characterise the department as a behemoth, grossly
over-staffed and swallowing great quantities of taxpayers' money to
little apparent effect.

Unfortunate as the choice of ministers and staff may have been,
many of the disasters which befell the Ministry were not really of its
own doing. The evident bungling of the department in censorship
and in the release of news was in nearly every case the fault of the
service ministries. They were extremely parsimonious with the news
in their keeping and engaged in Homeric battles with the censors in
order to restrict the publication of matter which the press had
obtained from its own sources. As in time of peace, the BBC had
many detractors and since the Ministry of Information was nominally
responsible for the actions of the corporation, although exercising
scant influence over broadcasting, the critics directed their broadsides

against the department. The collection of domestic intelligence on movements in public opinion, a task of considerable importance for the Ministry's forward planning and for the work of government generally, was branded by newspapers as 'snooping' when, in fact, only one person in 200 refused to be interviewed by the department's investigators. In short, the Ministry was a victim of what might be called the Aunt Sally syndrome. If anyone had a grievance, be it about the course of the war or the lack of news or the existence of public apathy, he soon found an emotional release in jibes at the Ministry of Information.

In June 1941 Duff Cooper was forced by the threatened resignation of two senior officers to demand greater powers for his department. The demand was refused by the War Cabinet and shortly afterwards he resigned. His replacement by Brendan Bracken was a master-stroke. Bracken possessed everything his predecessors had lacked: excellent press relations, a very close friendship with the Prime Minister, bustling confidence in tackling the Ministry's adversaries, and a scorn for the exhortation of the British public. Under his – initially reluctant – stewardship, the Ministry of Information became efficient and unobtrusive. As Lord Hood, private secretary to the first three Ministers of Information, remembers, 'Only when Brendan Bracken became Minister and Cyril Radcliffe became Director-General, did the MoI become really efficient and respected.'[7] By 1943 its staff in the United Kingdom numbered 2,824, over three times as many as in the days of ridicule, and yet not a murmur was raised. Also put to rest was the charge that the Ministry granted refuge to dilettantes in search of an easy war, for the 'amateurs' remaining in the department – such as Cyril Radcliffe, the Director-General, and Admiral Thomson, Chief Press Censor – had proved their fitness as administrators and makers of policy. In August 1943 Bracken complained that the House of Commons took no interest in his department. 'We are now', he declared, 'less exciting than the British Museum.'[8]

In spite of the importance attached to the phenomenon at the time, neither the Air Ministry nor the Ministry of Information – the two arms of government most concerned – tried very hard to define civilian morale. In all the Air Ministry's discussions of German morale and how best to break it 'there was hardly any consideration of what exactly was meant by the term'.[9] As for British morale, over two years were to pass before the officials of the Ministry of Information made any attempt to define what it was they were charged with sustaining.

Tom Harrisson, co-founder of Mass-Observation and commissioned for a time by the Ministry to assess the impact of war events upon the people, has stated: 'I am unable satisfactorily to define morale. It is too complex and variable.'[10] But this is perhaps to confuse morale with the factors which form and influence it. While agreeing with the implication of Harrisson's statement that the description and identification of these formative influences are difficult, it is possible to discern a working definition of morale arrived at during the war. Certainly there appears to be a consensus of usage in the contemporary and subsequent literature on the subject. What do the dictionaries say? The Shorter Oxford is rather terse: 'conduct, behaviour; esp. with regard to confidence, discipline, etc.' Webster's offers a fuller description:

A confident, resolute, willing, often self-sacrificing and courageous attitude of an individual to the function or tasks demanded or expected of him by a group of which he is part that is based upon such factors as pride in the achievements and aims of the group, faith in its leadership and ultimate success, a sense of fruitful personal participation in its work, and a devotion and loyalty to other members of the group.

The emphasis is on behaviour and action, as it was in works written during the war. Morale is 'meaningless, or at least ineffective, unless it promotes action';[11] 'it is of value only insofar as it facilitates or promotes favourable action';[12] 'morale pertains to [the individual's] efforts to enhance the effectiveness of the group in accomplishing the task in hand'.[13] The task during war is, of course, the achievement of victory or at the very least the avoidance of defeat. 'Morale', stated another authority, 'is essentially a zest for solving problems. A national emergency forces upon each individual the necessity for solving one overwhelmingly important common problem'.[14] F. C. Bartlett, a Cambridge psychologist who was consulted in a half-hearted fashion by the Ministry of Information in 1940, defined it as 'a lively and not too serious spirit of adventure which meets emergencies clear-eyed and calmly'.[15] But perhaps the most apposite comments were made after the war:

Under whatever conditions, the objective of propagandists in wartime is to maximize social participation among members of their own group . . . Social participation is characterized by concern for the objectives of the group, the sharing of its activities, and the preparedness to accept deprivations on its behalf. High 'participation' is therefore identical with high 'morale'.[16]

8

Morale is obedience to an internal, personal authority . . . which arises out of an ideal or value common to the group, the end sought by the group being defined by the ideal or value. Furthermore, action in obedience to the sense of duty is essentially one of service in a role for the furtherance of the aim of the group in achieving its goal . . . Strong service drive indicates high morale, and vice versa.[17]

As Jacques Ellul has put it, the aim of the morale propagandist is not 'to modify ideas, but to provoke action'.[18]

The utility of seeing morale in terms of action was recognised by Dr Stephen Taylor, Director of the Ministry's Home Intelligence Division, when he wrote in October 1941 that morale must be 'ultimately measured not by what a person thinks or says, but by what he does and how he does it'.[19] Dr C. W. Emmens, of the Research and Experiments Branch of the Home Office, in a report on post-raid morale in English towns expressed agreement, adding:

The definition had best be in terms of behaviour, since whatever may be the psychological and other realities underlying states of high or low morale, we are likely only to observe their effect on the actions of communities.[20]

However, the link between attitude and behaviour was not overlooked in this necessarily pragmatic climate. In 1942 a medical psychologist, P. E. Vernon, pointed to the need for research on the subject and asked, 'For example, does a man who criticizes the present Government actually do less valuable war work than the optimistic supporter?'[21] In a nation of supposed grumblers the question was a valid one. To assert that high morale is founded on 'hope, confidence in oneself and in what the future will bring'[22] is to forget that in the latter half of 1940 the common sense of many British people must have told them that the nation faced defeat. If opinion and conviction are the principal criteria for the assessment of morale, then it might well be concluded that such individuals exhibited very low spirits. But if these same persons, in spite of their fear, continued to work to the best of their ability, to withstand air raids without crying for peace at any price, and to abide by the many tiresome regulations then in force, their morale can be said in the most direct practical sense to have been high. Goebbels, too, recognised this. He distinguished between *Haltung* (bearing, conduct, behaviour) and *Stimmung* (feeling, spirit, mood) and was occasionally prepared to overlook a general depression of spirit so long as the people continued their active support of the war effort.[23]

Was, and is, this too simplistic a view of morale? To say that a person's morale is good when he actively assists the achievement of the nation's goals and bad when he fails to assist or actually retards it is open to the charge of stating the obvious and of neglecting consideration of the factors contributing to his behaviour. But, unlike the situation in peacetime, when there exists a multiplicity of disparate private and community goals, total war imposes a starkly obvious purpose on the nation and the citizen's role is correspondingly direct and simple. There was, in fact, an awareness among officials of the more tangible factors influencing morale, for example, the adequacy of news, the degree of physical safety afforded by the state, a belief in equality of sacrifice and confidence in military and political leadership. These coexisted, however, with numerous less measurable factors and in a rapidly changing war situation it was virtually impossible to anticipate what might emerge as important to morale. The authorities simply had to remain watchful and sensitive to currents of public feeling. They were also obliged to develop a finely tuned appreciation of what it was best to leave alone.

But until the second half of 1941 the propagandists of the Ministry of Information persisted in confusing morale itself with certain of its isolated components. Starting from a bland confidence in the resilience of the public, they swung sharply in the other direction in 1940 and seized upon the slightest grumble, rumour or expression of doubt as symptomatic of alarmingly low morale. Lord Clark, who was then working in the Ministry, remembers it thus:

> In retrospect the only interesting feature was the amount of evidence that came in on how low morale in England was, much lower than anybody has ever dared to say. But there was obviously nothing that we could do about it, except to hope that by some miracle we could win a few battles.[24]

He and his colleagues were projecting their own fears on to the public at large, failing to apprehend the significance both of the people's zealous co-operation in the war effort and the widely reported feeling that the government was prosecuting the war with insufficient vigour.

I shall argue that for nearly two years the measures taken by the propagandists were unnecessary and inept, based as they were on misunderstanding and distrust of the British public which, in turn, were products of the class and background of the propagandists themselves. Even after this period, the consistency with which the Germans were characterised as irretrievably wicked and the care devoted to separating communism and the Soviet war effort in the minds of the public were intermittently prompted by doubts about the people's martial stamina and their devotion to parliamentary democracy. These shortcomings were, however, outweighed by certain achievements. Through stern practical experience the Ministry came to realise the cardinal importance of full and honest news as a factor in civilian morale. The sheer doggedness with which the department fought the service ministries and even Churchill himself over news and censorship was a measure of the strength of this conviction and, indeed, of a determination that, in fighting totalitarianism, Britain should not borrow one of its chief weapons. With the constant and thorough analyses of the Home Intelligence Division as a sure guide, the Ministry also came to regard the British people as sensible and tough, and therefore entitled to be taken into the government's confidence. Possessed of this belief, the erstwhile propagandists became the evangelists of a novel attitude towards the people, furnishing them and the government with the means for a more cohesive national war effort.

I

Preparing for the Apocalypse

In October 1935 a subcommittee of the Committee of Imperial Defence (CID) was formed for the purpose of preparing broad guidelines for the establishment of a Ministry of Information on the outbreak of war.[1] Nine months later the subcommittee had completed its report.[2] The function of the Ministry would be to:

> . . . present the national case to the public at home and abroad in time of war. To achieve this end it is not only necessary to provide for the preparation and issue of National Propaganda, but also for the issue of 'news' and for such control of information issued to the public as may be demanded by the needs of security.[3]

These functions were to be carried out by five principal divisions: News, Control (censorship), Publicity, Collecting (intelligence) and Administration. The Home Office was made responsible for overseeing the planning of the Ministry and for any pre-war legislative and executive measures that might be necessary.

No one is recorded in the documents as having said so, but the example of Goebbels's Ministry of Propaganda clearly played a part in this early decision to create a Ministry of Information. Certainly no comparable body existed in the First World War. There were, rather, a diversity of agencies which – constantly merging and splitting – discharged the various functions relating to morale, news, censorship and propaganda. A Ministry of Information was created in 1918, under Lord Beaverbrook, in order to impose some order on the confusion but it was unable to widen its purview beyond the dissemination of propaganda to neutral countries, despite the strenuous efforts of Beaverbrook.[4] In the records of the shadow Ministry between 1936 and 1939 there are to be found only the most oblique references to the German propaganda organisation, and no mention whatsoever of Goebbels by name, the reasons for which may be sought in a gentlemanly reluctance to appear to be emulating the Nazis. However, an uncomfortable awareness of the evident superiority of Nazi methods was betrayed by the Ministry's chief planner when he stated that 'war, if it came, would be against at least one totalitarian state, i.e. against a state which, by the possession of a fully equipped Ministry of Propaganda, developed in peace but organised in readiness for war, would enter a war against us with a long start in preparedness'.[5] Such was the presumed success of Goebbels's machine that it is scarcely conceivable that the British did not intend fighting fire with fire.

The obligation laid upon the Ministry to sustain civilian morale was not, for all its awesome implications, clearly set down. The CID failed to mention the word 'morale'. It hovered ghostlike between the lines of the recommendations for the functions of the Publicity Division :

> Broadly speaking, the functions of the Publicity Division will be to secure that the national cause is properly presented to the public , . . Various aspects of the national activities will have to be analysed and explained; enemy activities must be examined and criticised; and means must be devised to disseminate the national point of view in a guise which will be attractive and through channels which will ensure that it reaches persons who are likely to be influenced by it.

Since initially neither the CID nor the planners contemplated the creation of a division devoted solely to maintaining morale it seems clear that 'propaganda' was intended to perform the job.

The report was accepted in full and Sir Stephen Tallents, then in charge of public relations at the BBC, was appointed as Director-General Designate and made responsible for the detailed planning of the department.[6] It was a wise choice. Tallents had been a pioneer in the field of government public relations, at first with the Empire Marketing Board and latterly with the Post Office and the BBC, and had created the Post Office's film unit which, among other outstanding productions, made the deservedly famous *Night Mail*.

Tallents was going to need every ounce of his experience and ability. Very little information about the various propaganda, censorship and news agencies of the First World War could be found. The planners were grossly overworked and neglected by government and, worst of all, subject to highly disruptive Whitehall intrigue which led not only to Tallents's dismissal early in 1939 but also to frequent changes in personnel. In the period that elapsed between the decision to set up the Ministry and the outbreak of war, a time of mounting nervousness on the part of government officials at the possible impact of total war on the population, such problems severely hampered preparations for the maintenance of civilian morale.

If the planners were to profit from the precedents of the First World War they needed to know in some detail what had actually happened at that time. This knowledge was not easily gained. And, as planning moved into the late 1930s, the series of international crises that characterised the period lent an edge of desperation to the search. In April 1938 one planner informed a colleague:

> The Record Office tells me that (1) they know nothing of North-cliffe's propaganda records; (2) the records of the Ministry of Information . . . were transferred to the News Department of the Foreign Office and have not yet reached the Record Office; (3) the Treasury have transferred to the Record Office the records of the National War Aims Committee . . . I do not know what this committee did.[7]

Ignorance of this latter body was significant since it was chiefly responsible during the First World War for the maintenance of morale. The elusiveness of the documents persisted and another official, plaintively insisting that 'there must be experts somewhere',[8] was reduced to consulting an article on propaganda in volume 32 of the 12th edition of the *Encyclopaedia Britannica*.[9] 'To produce anything coherent', he told Tallents in September 1938, 'has in many cases been rather like completing a Chinese puzzle, with the key pieces missing.' And he added darkly that it was 'more than odd' that the Foreign Office could not produce documents relating to the old Ministry of Information.

For reasons best known to the government the planners were not released on a full-time basis for the creation of this new department of state and they were simultaneously carrying out work in their own departments. R. W. Leeper pulled out early in 1938, complaining that it was impossible for anyone like himself so busy at the Foreign Office 'to give any real attention to these matters',[10] while another stuck it out but could not help exclaiming, 'It can only be kept moving in present circumstances by a few of us putting in ghastly hours, risking their health, sacrificing leisure, and possibly prejudicing their position in their own Departments.'[11] It is not surprising, therefore, that Sir Stephen Tallents should, in the course of emphasising to the CID the poor rate of progress, comment:

> Our preparations for the conduct of wartime operations of great possible variety and extent in the field of public opinion have no comparable peacetime base, and their planning is dependent on a handful of men, all with one exception very fully employed on other work. Those who have been entrusted with the working of these plans have been impressed at every stage by these handicaps.[12]

Six months later he informed Lord Macmillan, who was to have the misfortune to be the first Minister of Information:

> Not many people feel the urgency and importance of this fourth armament and recognise the severe and practical preparation which its effective use involve. That fact, and the secrecy in which this work has had to be done, have combined to make it an uncomfortably isolated job.[13]

With the exceptions of Tallents and J. H. Brebner, in charge of publicity at the GPO, none of the chief planners possessed specialist qualifications or experience in the field in which he was working. Of the four top men, J. B. Beresford was recruited from the University Grants Commission; another, G. C. North, was an Assistant Secretary at the Ministry of Health; a third, H. E. Dannreuther, was a retired admiral; while the fourth, W. P. Hildred, was Deputy General Manager of the Export Credit Branch of the Customs Department. Able administrators they may have been but expertise in the construction and running of elegant bureaucratic machinery, like patriotism, was not enough.

During a debate on the Ministry in July 1939 Sir Samuel Hoare said he was confident that 'the Press side of the organisation would be able to operate quickly and efficiently'.[14] That this did not prove to be the case is, for the moment, beside the point. Hoare's statement reflected the governmental bias in planning towards press and censorship matters and the almost exclusive concentration upon these aspects of the Ministry's functions exhausted the initiative of the few lonely planners. The speed of external events may have overtaken them, but the CID's insistence on the setting up of the Administration, News and Censorship divisions before thought could be given to the Publicity and Collecting divisions worried Tallents from an early date: 'Unless they [the propaganda and intelligence divisions]

15

are so established, the Government of the day will be liable to charges of neglecting an obvious function and there will be a danger of alternative and improvised measures being forced upon them.'[15]

At the time of the Munich crisis in 1938 the first stage of the Ministry's establishment was put into operation and the personnel earmarked for the Censorship, Administration and News divisions were told to stand by. Midnight on 29–30 September was chosen as the 'zero hour' and, according to Tallents, 'the Divisions concerned would have been ready to function then, if they had been required to do so'.[16] Lord Stanhope, President of the Board of Education and Minister of Information designate, congratulated Tallents on the smoothness of the operation and believed 'we could have given a good account of ourselves'.[17] In view of the fact that only three of the proposed divisions were mobilised, Tallents was unable to share Lord Stanhope's confidence and the expression of his misgivings, as well as criticism of the Cabinet's lackadaisical attitude towards the Ministry of Information, contributed to his dismissal on 2 January 1939.[18]

In a letter to Tallents after the war Lord Reith recalled, 'It is tolerably clear that from the time you left nothing much was done, that is, in the nine months prior to war.'[19] That nothing would be done was guaranteed by the choice of men who succeeded Tallents. Sir Ernest Fass, the Public Trustee, lasted until April 1939 and was replaced by Lord Perth who, said *The Times* somewhat pointedly, had just retired from a 'remarkably long diplomatic career'.[20] These men might or might not have been excellent directors-general if the Ministry had been fully formed and functioning according to well laid plans, but at a crucial stage of the department's formation neither of them appears to have been suitable for the job. Reith, who might have imparted real drive to planning and who was to be appointed Minister of Information in January 1940, was offered the post in April 1939. A strong supporter of the idea was Lord Beaverbrook, who had been advising Sir Samuel Hoare about the shadow Ministry on the basis of his experience as Minister of Information in 1918.[21] But Reith, for reasons not stated in his memoirs, did not accept the appointment and confined himself to writing a perceptive memorandum on the chaotic state of planning.[22]

Not surprisingly, the limits of responsibility between the Ministry and other departments were left in a blurred state, making conflict inevitable and denying the Ministry a foothold from which to defend its authority against powerful adversaries. By August 1939 the original five divisions had increased to thirteen. And although

16

complexity is not necessarily a sign of confusion, especially in a department with so many duties, the absence of a guiding intelligence ensured that the Ministry would come to resemble a Heath Robinson contraption, whose imperfections defied removal until after Brendan Bracken became Minister in July 1941.

With good reason Duff Cooper remembered it thus:

A monster had been created, so large, so voluminous, so amorphous, that no single man could cope with it. Within the mind of the monster there lurked as much talent, as much experience, as much imagination and brilliance, and as much devotion to duty, as could ever have been collected in any one department of state . . . It was tragic to see so much ability, so much goodwill so nearly wasted.

A government department is an organism, not a machine. Man can make a machine but he cannot make an organism, because an organism has life, and the creation of life remains a mystery which baffles science. If I were called upon to create a Ministry, I should select a man, give him an office and a cheque-book and tell him to hire others as the need for them arose.[23]

Whether quite so much mystery surrounds the creation of a government department is doubtful, but certainly if the man with the cheque book had been Tallents or Reith or even, if he had been so minded, Lord Beaverbrook, the Ministry of Information might not have started life in an enfeebled condition.

An overworked planning staff, the priority given to news and censorship, the bulky structure of the department, the intrigues against Tallents – these, while sufficient causes in themselves for the plight in which the Ministry was to find itself on the outbreak of war, do not constitute the ultimate cause: the attitude of Hoare and of the Chamberlain government. Hoare, given the task of overseeing the formation of the Ministry, undertook it with the greatest reluctance, hinting at his lack of enthusiasm in July 1939 when in the course of a debate he said, '. . . it came about a short time ago, as it was nobody else's business, the Prime Minister asked me to look into the questions connected with the organisation of this war-time department.'[24] Fifteen years later he confessed in his memoirs, 'Much against my wish, I had been involved in the Ministry's creation from the start . . . None of my colleagues wished to undertake the work, with the result that the Home Secretary . . . had it thrust upon him.'[25] Thus was the co-architect of the Hoare–Laval pact, having recently been brought back into government after a period of disgrace, given the job which nobody else wanted to touch. What of Chamberlain's attitude? When Reith was asked to replace Lord Macmillan as Minister he discussed the matter with the Prime Minister:

> All most unsatisfactory. One was being told to do a job by a man who agreed that one ought to do whatever one was asked to do; but who could not or would not tell one what the job was; nor what, if any, support he would give. Not only was the Ministry in thoroughly bad odour, it had no terms of reference and no authority.[26]

Chamberlain cared as little for the Ministry as Hoare. Until its 'bad odour' began to permeate the government, it remained on the periphery of his concern and was a victim of the lassitude which characterised the government's preparation for and prosecution of the war.

It was in this context that the planners struggled to produce measures by which the country might be psychologically armed against the anticipated rigours and horrors of total war. Vague though the CID's recommendations were, and evidently subsidiary to the other functions of the Ministry, the problem of morale was accorded signal importance by the planners. Propaganda, or that variant of it essential to the nation's war effort, 'must rank at least equal in status to all measures of offence and defence,' insisted Stephen King-Hall, the noted publicist who was brought in to assist the planners,[27] and who shortly afterwards used his newsletter to proclaim the necessity of setting up the Ministry before the outbreak of war. Writing to Tallents, H. V. Rhodes prophesied that 'Home Publicity during the next war will be of paramount importance.'[28] Nonetheless, the procedure adopted in tackling the question followed a perambulatory and leisurely course.

In 1938 a small body known as the Home Publicity Sub-Committee was set up in order to investigate the objectives and means by which domestic propaganda should be conducted. It first met on 12 July and after six meetings was wound up in September 1938, having submitted two reports. One of the committee's briefs was to consider Tallents's set of objectives for home publicity:

(1) To get British war aims understood, the Government's efforts in pursuance of them, at home and on the fighting fronts clearly interpreted and appreciated in the United Kingdom.

(2) To perform a like service for the aims and efforts of our Allies.

(3) To secure the prompt and wide dissemination of such instructions, advice and reassurance as individual Government Departments may wish to communicate . . .

(4) To prepare the public mind for new measures contemplated by the Government . . .

(5) To prevent panics, to allay apprehensions and to remove misconceptions . . .

(6) Generally to keep the public in good heart.

(7) By the dissemination of truth to attack the enemy in the minds of the public; and to counter enemy propaganda as required.

(8) To reflect in the United Kingdom, as circumstances dictate and opportunity allow, the attitude of neutral countries.[29]

The committee agreed with these objectives, adding only that the material and moral contribution of women had been overlooked, and made a number of recommendations for the machinery and media of publicity which were later adopted in full. Considerable stress was placed on the organisation in each constituency of local information committees, to be formed around representatives of the political parties and co-opting 'leading citizens of every shade of thought'. Also recommended was the appointment in each civil defence region of an information officer who would be responsible for the local implementation of the Ministry's policies.[30] At headquarters a number of divisions would produce and distribute propaganda material. Films, broadcasting, posters, pamphlets, books, public meetings – no medium was excluded from the scope of the Ministry's morale-boosting operations, least of all the provision of 'inside track' information for the powerful and the influential. These comprised MPs, peers, high government officials, judges, magistrates, doctors and editors, and their total was put at the curiously exact figure of 109,422.[31]

In view of the patronising attitude later adopted towards the public, it is interesting to note that the Home Publicity Sub-Committee was disposed to regard the British people as intelligent, well-informed and critical:

We consider that the formulation of some priority programme for the subjects of publicity is essential to a good start . . . It is, for example, useless to waste force on combating war weariness before it has set in. It is a dereliction of duty to omit to advise the public on such matters as air raids, which may take place immediately

19

the Ministry is set up . . . Other reasons are to be found in the relevant changes in modern life. There is the realisation that war now comes directly into the home and that the people will consider they have a right to guidance as well as a liability to duty. There is the greater interest taken in affairs other than local, especially in international affairs. There is the increased importance of women.

Accordingly, the committee strongly recommended that during a crisis preceding war the public should be given a clear statement of the issues involved, expositions of the many regulations likely to be introduced and a reasoned explanation of the necessity for calm, orderly and voluntarily disciplined behaviour. After the commencement of hostilities priority should be awarded to a statement of war aims :

We consider a clear and authoritative statement of these to be imperative right from the beginning. If a full prescription cannot be given, a start might be made on the lines that the war is a war of ideas, and that the enemy's recourse to war does not represent the will of the people but rather reflects the obsessions of misguided leaders.[32]

The shadow Ministry therefore anticipated dealing with a public which, although willing to embark on war, would demand reasons for doing so and a full explanation of their part in it.

In February 1939 an approach was made to the Royal Institute of International Affairs in order that it might make recommendations for the content of domestic and foreign propaganda.[33] Working secretly under the title of the 'International Propaganda and Broadcasting Enquiry', the Institute set up a number of committees which met for the first time on 10 March 1939. The members of the committee concerned with home propaganda organised discussion within the framework provided by the Home Publicity Sub-Committee, but they ignored or failed to comprehend that body's insistence on the capability of the British people to assess a situation realistically and to act accordingly. F. C. Bartlett's comment on propagandists is apposite in this case :

. . . almost all of the principal exponents of political propaganda frequently claim that their practices are based upon a special knowledge of the psychology of the 'masses'. When this knowledge

20

is critically considered it turns out to consist in a number of high-sounding generalisations for which not one scrap of empirical evidence . . . is offered.[34]

From the minutes and memoranda of the inquiry emerges the idea of an Englishman of particular characteristics (the Celtic fringe was not considered). He was, first of all, assumed to be deeply conscious of his class. Rohan Butler reminded his colleagues that 'in concerting means of publicity the importance of class issues should be borne in mind'.[35] They did not need reminding. Their deliberations were based upon the assumption that British society was demarcated by class to such an extent that the matter was never raised as a subject of debate. Arguing that officially-inspired propaganda could best be spread by word of mouth, H. V. Rhodes advised feeding rumours into circulation at the highest social level :

. . . the information should always flow downward, or at least on the same level. Confidential information about the war would not be so weighty if it comes from below. We must, in short, start in a Rolls-Royce way and not in a Ford way.[36]

Similarly it was suggested that the issue of confidential letters to influential persons should be supplemented only at a later date by 'second-grade or third-grade letters . . . to tallymen, commercial travellers, publicans, barbers, etc.'[37] A suggestion for the initial poster, as well as taxing the limits of patriotic iconography, drew very heavily on the supposed class-consciousness of the people :

As to design I would suggest :—
   A long-bowman from the Hundred Years War, standing with his feet outspread (to represent steadiness) and drawing his bow (to denote vigour). Behind him there would be a silhouette of England (in green); one of the man's feet might be in Devon, the other in Kent. At each corner of the picture there would be mailed fists, with knives, clubs, etc., intruding in a menacing manner. The reasons in favour of this design are :—
   (i) The archers, who provided the mainstay of the English Army, were drawn from the lower classes. The dress of the archer should make this point clear.[38]

The propagandists' preoccupation with class distanced them from the public. Instead of asking themselves 'What would *I* want to know in

the event of war?' and endeavouring to answer the question in a simple and honest manner, they proceeded on the assumption that the mass of their fellow citizens would need to be cajoled and wheedled into acceptance of their obligations. The propaganda was framed as if for an alien people. Hence the clumsiness and comic unsureness of touch typified by the 'long-bowman' poster.

'Our masses dislike and distrust argument,' it was asserted;[39] they are 'idealistic and illogical in temperament', added another memorandum.[40] But although the British people were thought unlikely to respond 'to such abstract concepts as Freedom'[41] and had 'never consciously fought for an ideal in the "Liberty, Equality, Fraternity" sense',[42] they were 'at least averagely susceptible to propaganda (more so than the French)' as long as it didn't provoke their sense of the ridiculous.[43] What emerges from these deliberations is a portrait of the Englishman as a bluff, rather dull, no-nonsense sort of fellow, somewhat bucolic in temperament, who could be relied upon to respond to 'simple facts, anecdotes, descriptions and so forth'.[44] Although 'oblique shepherding of opinion' was thought to be required from time to time,[45] the propagandists appear to have had no misgivings about the people's spirit and their qualities of sturdy obedience. Such bland confidence, rooted in an essentially patronising attitude and based on little more than intuition acquired in the great public schools and Oxbridge, took no account of the likely nature of the coming war.

If the Ministry was to preserve morale, then clearly there had to be some sort of machinery for the collection of intelligence on the public's reactions to wartime events and difficulties. Such machinery had to satisfy two broad conditions: the assessment of morale and the supply of information to other departments about the impact of their policies upon the public. The value of domestic intelligence was likely to be far greater than the lazy assumptions and recommendations of the propagandists.

From the earliest days of planning, a Collecting Division – as the intelligence unit was then called – had formed part of the proposed structure of the Ministry. In June 1937, John Beresford, of the University Grants Commission, was appointed provisional director of the unit and made responsible for its planning. The sources of intelligence were originally envisaged as other government departments, the BBC and the Press. This scanty range of sources had by 1939 expanded to include Rotary Clubs, Chambers of Commerce, the Federation of British Industry, Workers' Educational Associations, school inspectors, teachers' organisations, the Ministry's Regional

Information Officers (RIOs), the Labour movement, and even 'Communist cells', the latter contact 'to be explored as discreetly as possible'.[46] Precisely what information was to be derived from this mishmash of bodies and individuals and how it was to be co-ordinated and interpreted no one ventured to say, nor could anyone at the time have done so since it was very much a matter of casting about for possible sources. The planners were working in virtually uncharted territory.

There did, however, exist one body whose work was highly appropriate. It was Mass-Observation, which had been founded in 1937 by Tom Harrisson and Charles Madge in order to study British society, and which used some of the tools of anthropology.* The first cautious approaches were made at the suggestion of Ivison Macadam, Secretary of the Royal Institute of International Affairs. No firm arrangements were concluded with Mass-Observation before the war but interest within the Ministry quickened sufficiently for the Treasury to be informed that the body might be commissioned to undertake work 'on the principles laid down by the American expert, Gallup, to obtain information . . . from typical samples of society',[47] a statement which betrayed ignorance of current social research methods, for Mass-Observation consciously eschewed statistical survey methods. The British Institute of Public Opinion, which conducted polls for the *News Chronicle*, was the body in Britain which used Gallup's techniques and it too was contacted by the Ministry.

A good deal of nervousness attended the discussions about Mass-Observation and it was suggested that the body should be used only if the public were led to believe that its inquiries had no connection with the Ministry, making it necessary therefore to finance its activities from Secret Service funds.[48] What is the explanation of this caution? Officials within the shadow Ministry anticipated that, if the existence of a domestic intelligence machine became known, public controversy was bound to follow. Beresford found himself having to defend his work against Treasury objections that an intelligence division would merely duplicate information about public feeling which could be obtained at no cost from MPs:

> Questions to or correspondence received by members of Parliament would certainly provide some information, but it would be unsafe to rely solely on this source even for the assessment of public

---

* For an account of the early days of Mass-Observation see Charles Madge, 'The Birth of Mass-Observation', *Times Literary Supplement*, 5 November 1976.

reactions to departmental activities. Such representations would not cover the whole ground and whilst they might be considerable in bulk would be sporadic and not necessarily representative. The ordinary citizen does not normally write to his MP. From time to time some grave deficiency is brought to the notice of Parliament, but it would clearly be better for action to be taken before public discontent had reached such proportions.[49]

The jealousy of MPs and of the press at the usurpation by a government department of their sacrosanct role as interpreters of the public mind reached a peak early in the war and the planners were possibly far-sighted in anticipating such a development. But the caution thus induced had an unfortunate consequence. A heavy stress was laid on the necessity for secrecy in the Ministry's intelligence operations, a secrecy which – when broken – imparted to the work precisely that aura of sinister intent that the Ministry had wanted to avoid.

Beresford likened the creation of the intelligence division to 'rolling a heavy boulder up a hill, which has a way of rolling to the bottom at odd intervals'.[50] He was acutely aware of the magnitude of the task: 'I should like to point out that the Collecting Division is an entirely new and pioneering experiment. No division with similar duties as far as I am aware existed in the last war. It is impossible to foresee before the event precisely how it will actually develop.'[51] In the circumstances, such flexibility of attitude was no bad thing to possess.

Although it was not fully perceived before the war, the relationship between the news and censorship functions of the Ministry and the health of civilian morale was strong and direct. The dissemination in wartime of inadequate news and news suspected of being false or over-optimistic fosters anxiety and rumour, and ultimately creates distrust in the government's motives and conduct of the war.

It was therefore just as well that censorship of the British press was to be operated on the voluntary principle. Editors would be invited to submit for the scrutiny of the Censorship Division any matter which they had reason to believe might infringe Defence Regulation 3, which made it an offence to obtain, record, communicate or publish information which might be of military value to an enemy. In the words of an official memorandum, the Press Censorship Division:

. . . will either return [the item to the editor] passed in full, or passed subject to certain details, words or passages being cut out;

24

or it may decide to 'hold' the whole story or picture. If the article or photograph . . . is so published, the Editor is absolved from his responsibility for publishing it, should it subsequently transpire that the article or photograph contained matter of value to the enemy. . . .

An Editor who does not choose to abide by the cuts made by the censorship would not necessarily commit an offence. He has merely asked for expert advice and, if he ignores such advice, it must still be proved against him that he has in fact published matter valuable to the enemy.[52]

In order to assist the press a booklet entitled the Defence Notices was issued. It contained many subjects deemed to be of military value and which fell under the following broad categories:

(a) The number, description, armament, etc., of any of H.M. Forces, vessels or air-craft.

(b) Any operations or projected operations of any forces, vessels or air-craft.

(c) Any measures for the defence or fortification of any place.

(d) The number, description, or location of any prisoners of war.

(e) Munitions of war or anything whatsoever which would or might be of use to the enemy.[53]

Beresford was alarmed at the proposed constraints on the press:

I cannot help having grave doubts whether the Press . . . realise the implications of the drastic and detailed regulations which have been drafted. If they do, all I can personally say is God help them and this country. If they do not, and I shrewdly suspect that they do not, there will undoubtedly be an outcry in Parliament and elsewhere as soon as any emergency begins.[54]

One of Beresford's colleagues, D. B. Woodburn, was also fearful that the Defence Notices left the press with nothing whatever to talk about and came close to instituting compulsory censorship.[55]

It could be argued, however, that it was wise of the government to cover the field as widely as possible and to allow the censoring authority a good deal of latitude in interpreting the Notices in the light of experience. But the service ministries were to oppose a policy of flexibility and throughout the war tended to regard each of the ninety or so subjects listed in the Defence Notices as holy writ, never to be profaned by publication in the press. The successful operation of censorship would depend, first, on the spirit in which the censors interpreted the regulations and, second, on the extent to which the service ministries persuaded the censors to adhere rigidly to them.

The News Division aspired to 'tell the truth, nothing but the truth and as near as possible the whole truth'.[56] As the centre for the distribution of all official news, the Ministry appears to have been in a position to achieve this laudable goal. If, however, it was to be more than a passive channel through which news originating in other departments would pass, two things were essential: the right of access to news and the right of editorship. Of primary importance was the demand of the Ministry that it be made privy to *all* news in the possession of the service departments. Without access to full information about the war the Ministry would be unable either to prepare propaganda policy adequately or to form a judgement as to whether a security objection raised by another department against the release of an item of news was outweighed by the public's right to and desire for information. The other power required was that of deciding the form of words in which news was to be issued. On the well-founded suspicion that the service departments would tend to couch bad news or news of minor successes in euphemistic language, and thus irritate those members of the public who wished to be treated as responsible adults, the Ministry was anxious to secure editorial control over official announcements. Neither requirement was to be satisfied. Despite the priority awarded by the CID to news and censorship, the outbreak of war was to find the Ministry without the power to impose a rational and uniform policy on the issue of official news.

Baldwin's maxim 'the bomber will always get through' expressed a fear which had permeated civil defence thinking ever since 1918. At the onset of war Germany was expected to deliver a massive bombing assault on Britain.[57] The vital prediction, so far as the Ministry of Information was concerned, was that which related to the psychological consequences of bombing. According to a report of a committee of psychiatrists submitted to the Ministry of Health in 1938, the psychiatric would exceed the physical casualties by three to one, which, on the basis of the government's estimates of killed and wounded, would mean between three and four million cases of acute panic, hysteria and neurosis during the first six months of war.[58] People in these states of mind would be the responsibility of the health authorities but the strain on even those people who had not broken down mentally would be such as to cause them to regress to infantile forms of behaviour. In attempting to stiffen the nerve and resolve of a population reduced to such a condition, the Ministry of Information would have a formidable task on its hands.

What, then, was done to formulate measures to keep spirits buoyant and morale steady under air attack? In 1938 Stephen King-Hall insisted that the 'Ministry must be consulted as to the psychological effect of such matters as the bombing of so-called civilians',[59] thus acknowledging the department's responsibility in this sphere and the extent to which civilians would be thought of as front-line troops. But thereafter until September 1939 it is possible to find in the records only one reference to air raids. In a note on poster slogans one of the members of the Home Publicity Enquiry 'emphasised the great importance of maintaining the sense of humour, balance and confidence of the public, whose morale, in urban centres at least, might otherwise be seriously affected by aerial bombardment'.[60]

On the day of Germany's invasion of Poland – 1 September 1939 – the officers of the Home Publicity Division met to discuss what immediate action could be taken to counteract panic resulting from air raids:

1 Lady Grigg said that the most comforting thing – at least where women were concerned – was to have a cup of tea and get together to talk things over.

This was agreed to be a most valuable suggestion. Ways for carrying it into effect . . . were considered. It was decided that some . . . widely spread method was required and that an appeal should be made to householders to supply tea to anyone in their neighbourhood who needed it during or after an air-raid.

Professor Hilton . . . referred to the value of sugar for steadying the nerves.

2 Lady Grigg suggested that sensational newspaper placards should be prohibited, as was done in the last war.[61]

Sensible suggestions, no doubt, but they fell rather short of what might have been expected a day or two before the Luftwaffe was supposed to launch a heavy attack against the country. A few days later the division interviewed J. B. S. Haldane and his wife, who advised on morale in air raids on the basis of their experience in the Spanish Civil War, but little of value emerged from the meeting.[62]

On 13 September the Ministry sent the Home Office a memorandum on the preservation of civilian morale in air raids.[63] Based on consultations with a group of 'experts' (one of whom, J. T.

MacCurdy, was to write a book on morale in 1943), it represented a far more earnest attempt to come to grips with the problem than had previously been made. But in the first section, which dealt with measures considered essential for the creation of sound general morale, the Ministry made two suggestions which were distinctly out of keeping with avowed policy:

> It must be realised that large masses of people distrust the radio and a press which they know to be censored. Hence support for the energetic prosecution of war from those sections of the Labour Movement known to be most opposed to the Government on other matters will have a quite disproportionate effect in raising civilian morale . . . It is not too much to say that . . . their propaganda value will be actually increased if the speakers attack the Government on other points . . .
>
> The people must feel that they are being told the truth. Distrust breeds fear much more than knowledge of reverses. The all-important thing for publicity to achieve is the conviction that the worst is known. This can be achieved by the adoption, publication and prosecution of a policy. The people should be told that this is a civilians' war, or a People's War, and therefore they are to be taken into the Government's confidence as never before . . . But what is truth? We must adopt a pragmatic definition. It is what is believed to be the truth. A lie that is put across becomes the truth and may, therefore, be justified. The difficulty is to keep up lying . . . *It is simpler to tell the truth and, if a sufficient emergency arises, to tell one big, thumping lie that will then be believed.**

This was followed by a list of twenty-eight items of advice relating specifically to air raids. At least two observations proved accurate: it was pointed out that spontaneous leadership would be likely to emerge in air-raids and that people should be reminded that the last war had not seen any increase in the incidence of insanity. Various devices to quell or to channel fear were suggested:

> It is important to evaporate fear by intellectualising it. Much can be done by encouraging people to observe their own reactions to fear and to discuss them with one another, and by rehearsing how to hide the fact that they are afraid . . .
>
> During air raids people should be encouraged to keep themselves

---

* Author's italics.

28

busy by knitting, doing crossword puzzles, playing games etc. . . .
The importance of laughter, which acts as a strong release, is not
to be forgotten. After a raid people should be given as much to do
as possible . . .

Scared people sheltering during a raid should be made to sit
quietly, be told their fear is only natural and given a cup of coffee
after which they should be all right . . .

Prayer or the psychological equivalent of prayer is important,
i.e. relying on something bigger than yourself.

All news of air-raid casualties and damage − short of that which
might aid the enemy − should be given out as soon as possible 'as a
matter of principle', the memorandum urged. This was sound advice,
since the Ministry's later experience bore out the great effect of full
and frank news on people's ability to resist physical danger and
discomfort.

The memorandum was ill-received by the Home Office. E. T.
Crutchley, who had been one of the members of the Home Publicity
Sub-Committee in 1938, commented :

I can only answer that a lot of the material seems to me extremely
elementary and condescending; some of it is misleading, some
contradictory. Generally I think it greatly undervalues the spirit of
our people, e.g. I do not believe that the English want paraded
for their benefit examples of Chinese stoicism as Professor Haldane
suggests . . . The people of this country do *not* distrust the radio
and the Press . . . The suggestion that the propaganda value of a
speaker is increased if he attacks the Government on other than
war points seems to me entirely mischievous and wrong-headed.
Trust in leadership is an enormous factor in maintaining
confidence.[64]

Despite Crutchley's strong reservations, many of the suggestions were
embodied in two circulars sent to Regional Information Officers on
13 and 20 September. The fact remains that they were belated and
ludicrously inadequate in the face of the expected scale and consequences of air attack.

But what more could the propagandists have done? Other departments were providing shelters, issuing gas masks, preparing evacuation
schemes, recruiting and training civil defence personnel and setting
up emergency medical facilities. If, despite these measures, the public
were still expected to be prey to wholesale panic and neuroses, of

what possible use, the propagandist might have anxiously reflected, are any measures I can propose? But why was no real attempt made to confront the problem until *after* the war had started? The marked absence of discussion on air raids seems to have derived from the assumption that the success of general propaganda would engender sufficient resilience to enable the public to withstand the shock of bombing. In the circumstances it was a dangerously complacent attitude.

On the outbreak of war it was proposed to institute certain immediate measures of reassurance: messages from the King and leading members of the Government, an initial pictorial poster, a statement of the duty of the individual citizen, insistence on the certainty of ultimate victory, warnings against enemy propaganda, and publicity about the allies, the dominions and 'benevolent neutrals'.[65] Morale was to be sustained by the propagation of three basic themes: the justice of the British cause, Britain's strength, and the commitment of the whole community to the war effort. As a means of communicating these themes, great attention was paid to posters:

> Much of the Ministry's future practice and usefulness would depend on the initial impression that its work made on the nation. It is important therefore that its first pictorial poster should give no possible grounds for suspicion of exaggeration, distortion of the truth, or of raising hopes or expectations unjustified by facts.[66]

The poster was expected to:

   (i) attract immediate attention and evoke a spontaneous reaction.
  (ii) exert a steadying influence, i.e. the idea of tenacity and vigour.
 (iii) incite to action.
 (iv) harmonise with general preconceived ideas among the public.
  (v) be short.
 (vi) be universal in appeal.[67]

No poster could possibly have achieved all these objectives. One of the propagandists tried to persuade his colleagues that the British people would respond more readily to colloquial and defiantly humorous captions such as 'Say it with guns – to Hitler' and 'Don't worry – you're not in Germany'.[68] He argued that the stress should be laid on an attitude of mind rather than on solemn declarations[69] – in keeping with the agreed conclusion that the British public were suspicious of lofty sentiment and reasoned argument. But his suggestions failed to divert the planners from an inclination towards the wordy and high-flown.

A. P. Waterfield, a career civil servant with no credentials in the field of publicity, wanted 'a rallying war-cry that will . . . put us in an offensive mood at once' and put forward '*Your* courage, *your* cheerfulness, *your* resolution will bring us victory'.[70] Its choice as the initial poster was unfortunate. *The Times* was to comment:

> . . . the insipid and patronising invocations to which the passer-by is now being treated have a power of exasperation which is all their own. There may be no intrinsic harm in their faint, academic piety, but the implication that the public morale needs this kind of support, or, if it did, that this is the kind of support it would need, is calculated to provoke a response which is neither academic nor pious.[71]

The public cynically read into the poster the implication that sacrifices would be made by the many for the few and Mass-Observation's unfavourable report on it[72] evidently made no difference, since the Ministry went on to consider an even more clumsy statement based on the Prime Minister's condemnation of the Germans: 'We are fighting evil things. Against brute force and bad faith. Right will prevail.'[73] Richard Crossman was asked to contact David Low in order to persuade the cartoonist to illustrate posters and leaflets.[74] In view of the high quality and the immense popularity of Low's work, it was a wise suggestion. But, beyond producing a cartoon for inclusion in a news-sheet dropped over Germany, Low – struck with the 'ineptness and futility' of the Ministry – refused to work for it.[75]

The King's message on the outbreak of war was considered even more important than the first poster. It was drafted in the Ministry and after modification by the Home Office was delivered by the King in a broadcast on 3 September. Lofty and quasi-religious in the tone deemed suitable for royal pronouncements, the speech conformed closely to the three basic themes of the Ministry's reassurance propaganda and it is worth quoting in full:

> In this grave hour, perhaps the most fateful in our history, I send to every household of my peoples, both at home and overseas, this message, spoken with the same depth of feeling for each one of you as if I were able to cross your threshold and speak to you myself.

31

For the second time in the life of most of us we are at war. Over and over again we have tried to find a peaceful way out of the differences between ourselves and those who are now our enemies. But it has been in vain. We have been forced into a conflict. For we are called, with our allies, to meet the challenge of a principle which, if it were to prevail, would be fatal to any civilised order in the world.

It is the principle which permits a state, in the selfish pursuit of power, to disregard its treaties and its solemn pledges; which sanctions the use of force, or threat of force, against the sovereignty and independence of other states. Such a principle, stripped of all disguise, is surely the mere primitive doctrine that might is right; and if this principle were established throughout the world, the freedom of our own country and of the whole British Commonwealth of Nations would be in danger. But far more than this – the peoples of the world would be kept in the bondage of fear, and all hopes of settled peace and of the security of justice and liberty among nations would be ended.

This is the ultimate issue which confronts us. For the sake of all that we ourselves hold dear, and of the world's order and peace, it is unthinkable that we should refuse to meet the challenge.

It is to this high purpose that I now call my people at home, and my peoples across the seas, who will make our cause their own. I ask them to stand calm, firm and united in this time of trial. The task will be hard. There may be dark days ahead, and war can no longer be confined to the battlefield. But we can only do the right as we see the right, and reverently commit our cause to God. If one and all we keep resolutely faithful to it, ready for whatever service or sacrifice it may demand, then, with God's help, we shall prevail.

May He bless and keep us all.

Only lack of paper prevented the issue of the speech in the form of a wall hanging to every household in the country.[76] Drafts for a message from the Queen by A. A. Milne ('too Christopher Robinish' according to the Parliamentary Secretary, Sir Edward Grigg) and Godfrey Winn were rejected.[77]

Like David Low, the Labour Party believed that the Ministry's propaganda was likely to be inept. On 4 September Philip Noel-Baker and Will Henderson met the Director of Home Publicity and insisted that the department should have an advisory committee on which the party was represented, 'otherwise there was a danger that fatal blunders might occur in connection with the publicity material issued by the Ministry'.[78] It was then that Richard Crossman was hastily taken on as a member of the Home Publicity Division in order to 'improve the blend':

> Mr Crossman represented a section of current thought which it is considered has not been adequately provided for . . . His appointment is the answer to the demand of the Labour Party that everything we issue must be submitted to the Publicity Branch if we are to assure the Party's co-operation.[79].

This concession did nothing to alter the Ministry's adoption, in A. J. P. Taylor's words, of 'supine confidence'.[80] The danger of over-confident and remote deliberations was not that morale might fail to be stimulated but that the Ministry might bring about the reverse of what it was supposed to achieve. For all the talk of a people's war, the style and content of domestic propaganda seemed unlikely to convince the public that the conduct of affairs was in capable hands.

2

Morale and the Phoney War

In the early days of September 1939 the Ministry of Information noted 'with some alarm that . . . the public is stolidly facing a catastrophe. There is a danger that this attitude may degenerate into defeatism'.[1]

There was certainly no evidence in the period between September 1939 and May 1940 pointing to the widespread existence of defeatism, but reports reaching the Ministry of Information spoke of apathy and boredom, of bewilderment and frustration. Morale appears to have been lower during this period, when the impact of the conflict was relatively slight, than at any other time during the war. Having gone to war ostensibly to defend Poland, the British government, in the opinion of some of its members, seemed to stand by while Poland was crushed by the Germans and as a consequence the public had little idea of what they were fighting for.[2]

The government steadfastly refused to say what Britain's war aims were supposed to be. So inactive were the armed forces that many must have wondered whether the government had any aims at all, except to disengage from a state of war with as little loss of face as decently possible. People were said to be sceptical about the reality of the war and dangerously complacent about its outcome.[3] Perhaps the public could not be blamed for scepticism. Simon's first war budget hardly reflected a national emergency, food rationing did not commence until January 1940 and the take-up of labour into war industries was so slow that unemployment remained at over a million until April 1940. In December 1939 Sir John Anderson, the Home Secretary, reported to the Cabinet:

Criticism of the black-out, the strength of Civil Defence personnel, the emergency hospital scheme, all reflect the same tendency to call in question the need for the precautions which have been taken; and in the present state of public opinion there is real danger that the re-adjustments that have been made to meet present circumstances may be interpreted as an admission that the scale of our Civil Defence measures was out of proportion to any risks to which we are likely to be exposed. At the present moment public opinion is only too ready to discount the risks of large scale air attack, merely because no such attack has yet been delivered; and unless active steps are taken to counter this spirit of false optimism we may well find that, by the time the blow falls, we shall have dissipated the resources and broken the morale which we have built up to resist it.[4]

The lack of news, aggravated by the service departments' unwillingness to release all but the most innocuous bulletins, reinforced the public's impression that nothing was happening. Six months after the outbreak of war Sir John Reith, by then Minister of Information, informed his colleagues:

(a) Among the less informed classes a passive, negative feeling of apathy and boredom is apparent. Associated with this is a reaction to grievances and discomforts. There is a general feeling that individuals do not count in the conduct of the war and that the only thing to do is to live as normal a life as possible.

(b) The 'Bomb Germany' movement . . . expresses a wish held by more active sections of the community to end this negative phase of the war, and to do something, however unpleasant the consequences.[5]

With such gloomy estimations of public feeling swirling about, the Ministry had much to do in this period. Countering the discontent of a people who could be satisfied only by decisive action was daunting enough, but the department found itself engaged in a furious little dispute of its own and perhaps it was just as well for morale that the larger conflict was in a stalemate. Most of the trouble was caused by news and censorship.

The war started tolerably well as far as the news and censorship divisions were concerned. The press were delighted with the facilities provided for them on the ground floor in Senate House, London University. Sir James Grigg of the War Office, in replying to a sharp rebuke for having allowed his department to make an announcement independently of the News Division, proffered an abject apology which promised well for the future authority of the Ministry.[6] This pleasing state of affairs did not last long, however. After a few weeks the confusion and lack of uniformity which characterised censorship rulings made it imperative that the instructions issued to the censors should be more closely defined.

Cyril Radcliffe, who had been recruited from the Bar, studied the Defence Notices and the instructions, and laid down guiding principles which subsequently formed the censors' charter : as Defence Regulation 3 referred solely to information of military value, censors had no right to interfere with opinion, comment, speculation or matter which the enemy might find useful in his propaganda; moreover, censors should not concern themselves with an editor's liability under other regulations, such as the publication of subversive or other material which sought to undermine the people's morale or their will to continue the war.[7] So far so good. The press were assured that there would be no meddling by the Ministry of Information in the expression of opinion. Nor would there be any suppression of facts other than those which could be clearly shown to be of value to the enemy. In both these points was embedded the assumption that public morale could withstand the airing of unpleasant news and adverse criticism. But the defence departments, suspicious of the new and untried ministry, had the final say as to whether a press message was or was not of potential military value.[8]

Why were the fighting services so reluctant to part with news? The Admiralty was the worst offender in this respect and its attitude was succinctly expressed when Churchill, as First Lord, said that 'it was for the Admiralty or other department to purvey to the Ministry the raw meat and vegetables and for the Ministry to cook and serve the dish to the public. If the Admiralty could have had their way they would prefer a policy of complete silence'.[9] G. P. Thomson, the Chief Press Censor and a retired admiral himself, in commenting on the gradual acceptance by the other two services of the value to civilian morale of full news, said of the senior service :

> But the Admiralty never varied . . . it was seldom, if ever, that any
> naval news of real interest or importance was allowed to come out,
> unless from the lips of the Prime Minister or the First Lord of the
> Admiralty, until so long afterwards that any interest in the event
> had vanished.[10]

The situation was not improved by the fact that early in the war an impressive minority of the 350 news and censorship staff were ex-naval men who, according to Francis Williams, treated 'all newspaper men as potentially mutinous naval ratings who should be warned that they would be instantly put in chains if they disobeyed an order'.[11] This autocratic tendency was exacerbated by 'the habit of discipline in the Navy' which meant that nearly all questions were submitted to higher authority[12] and the consequent loss of time invariably infuriated the press. It was perhaps natural that the service departments should regard the escape of even the most innocent piece of news as potentially damaging to military operations. They found it tempting to take refuge from the uncomfortable demands of the Ministry of Information behind a screen of security objections whose importance they did not expect mere laymen to comprehend. There was, too, another reason, one which stemmed from an attitude held by many in government toward the functions of the Ministry. A. P. Ryan, adviser to the BBC on home affairs, accurately identified it :

> Statesmen, civil servants and leaders in the fighting Services, cannot openly say that news is a nuisance and propaganda a cheapjack charlatan game. They know that compulsory censorship is impractical . . . Hence the setting up of the Ministry of Information, and hence also the omission to define its functions or to endow it with recognised authority in its own field.[13]

Mistrust of the Ministry of Information as a parvenu whose doings accorded ill with the august machinery of government was a fertile source of trouble, and was aggravated by the department's insistence that the government should abandon the traditional view that the people should be told only so much as was good for them.

The troubles associated with news and censorship very nearly led to the early demise of the Ministry. In the event they forced one Minister to resign, severely distracted another, brought ridicule on the government generally and resulted in the fragmentation of the department. As one commentator observed, instead of directing activities in the fields of morale and propaganda the ministers and their senior officials 'became obsessed with questions of mechanical organisation'.[14]

The restiveness of journalists at the paucity of news and the growing realisation within the Ministry that only a nominal power was possessed provoked the Chief Press Censor to write on 10 September :

> I think the only way is to take the bull by the horns and get it established that the decision rests with us, and it is for the fighting ministries and the F.O. to keep us properly advised.[15]

Before the Minister had time to consider a course of action his department suffered a blow to its reputation from which it was never fully to recover. On 11 September the radio in Paris announced the arrival of the BEF and, as the Germans could be presumed also to have heard the broadcast, the War Office agreed with the Ministry of Information that the ban on the story should be lifted. Accordingly, the press went ahead and printed the news for release in the morning editions. Just before midnight, by which time the newspapers were on their way to all parts of the country, Hore-Belisha, the Secretary of State for War, ordered the reimposition of the ban because the press were giving more details of the BEF's dispositions than the War Office thought desirable. The Home Office called in the police, who occupied Fleet Street offices and confiscated copies of the early morning editions from trains and astonished motorists. At 2.55 a.m. on the morning of 12 September, after frantic efforts had been made to print new editions, the reimposed ban was lifted and the dazed editors permitted to retrieve the situation as best they could.[16] This was the very stuff of farce and, quite naturally, the fury of the press was directed at the censorship authority responsible which, however much it tried to point out privately that the ultimate power of censorship did not reside where it should, was obliged to bear the blame. But the Ministry did not lack champions. Arthur Greenwood, speaking for the opposition in a debate on the episode, said :

> The real difficulty, as I see it, is that the Fighting Services appear to be a law unto themselves in this matter . . . The absurdities of Monday night were really due to one person, the Secretary of State for War. I say that he has no right to override the Ministry of Information . . . the final responsibility must rest in the hands of one Minister, and he must be the Minister of Information.[17]

Lord Radcliffe recalls that the department was determined not to become a Ministry of Entertainment,[18] but it unwittingly became one when the boredom induced by the phoney war found an outlet in a plethora of jokes and quips at the Ministry's expense. In answer to a question on 26 September, Sir Edward Grigg, the Parliamentary Secretary, informed the House that there were 872 staff employed at the Ministry's headquarters and 127 in the regional offices.[19] MPs were not slow in adding these numbers together and it was to be some time before they tired of conjuring with the magic figure of 999. Underlying this jibe was the more serious accusation that the Ministry was both overstaffed and poorly staffed. There were said to be too many civil servants, too many non-specialists, too many academics and museum curators. To Harold Nicolson (later to become Parliamentary Secretary under Duff Cooper) the Ministry had 'been staffed with duds at the top and all the good people are in the most subordinate positions'.[20] Norman Riley wanted to know why Senate House was a 'dumping ground' for people whose activities before the war were 'never related to anything remotely connected with the general public, the Press and propaganda'.[21] *The Observer* spoke of the 'stupefying absurdity' with which it had been staffed,[22] while some months later the *New Statesman* commented that nepotism was at the heart of the trouble and had resulted in a 'scramble of socially favoured amateurs and privileged ignoramuses into the Ministry of Information'.[23] Malcolm Barnes, who worked in the Censorship Division, has confirmed the view that the Ministry was to a considerable extent recruited through 'the old boy network',[24] although it should be added that many wartime departments had to be staffed in the same fashion. Another authoritative opinion came from R. A. Bevan, the man behind the successful Guinness advertisements in the thirties. Resigning his post as head of the General Productions Division in May 1940, he wrote to the Director General:

> I feel that my own mistake in the months during which I have been Director of the Division has been in trying too much to work in with the existing organisation, which has not been very helpful in the creation of ideas or speed and efficiency of production. There is now a terrific weight of people in authority at the top of the Ministry before one gets down to anybody who has any practical experience of propaganda and publicity. I am not suggesting that these are not men of real administrative ability but their minds cannot work in the same way as that of a man whose life has been spent and whose living has been made in the persuasion of people to do what they do not want to do . . . which is why I am pressing for some change which will enable people who have experience either in politics, journalism, authorship or publicity to have some real say in the determination of policy and its carrying out . . . I am quite convinced that a wrong attitude has been taken towards the expert from the beginning.[25]

Outside observers were also bemused by the Ministry's structure and multiplicity of function. Lord Macmillan himself, in a moment of admirable but startling candour, confessed to the Lords, 'I may say that I have had considerable difficulty in ascertaining what are its functions.'[26] In his memoirs he was equally frank about his failure as Minister of Information and was at a loss to know why Chamberlain appointed him 'to such a controversial political office'.[27]

Less than two weeks after the commencement of war Lord Macmillan informed the War Cabinet that 'the press correspondents in London as a whole, both British and foreign, were in a state of revolt'.[28] According to one American journalist, Quentin Reynolds, censorship at this time was 'petty, absurd, tyrannical'.[29] They complained of receiving little news of value, objected to the apparently momentary whims of censorship officials, and were being improperly forbidden by the Foreign Office to send abroad any stories which might upset relations with other countries.[30] The Minister did not exaggerate the strength of press feeling. Admiral Thomson was in agreement with the journalists about the lack of uniformity in censorship rulings.[31] The system could not cope with the volume of material submitted and in view of the fact that before the war neither instructors nor trainee censors 'had any idea of the working of the press'[32] it is not surprising that their interpretation of the Defence Notices was unsatisfactory. Norman Riley commented, 'In the first two months of this war hardly a newspaper escaped being a victim of one bungle or another due to inexperience of the duties of a censor . . . there was a dull, unattractive uniformity about most papers'.[33] Every journalist had an anecdote about the censorship. John Gunther's, as related to Harold Nicolson, was one of the better stories: on asking for the text of a leaflet which had been dropped in millions over Germany, Gunther was told by a censor, 'We are not allowed to disclose information which might be of value to the enemy.'[34]

On 18 September the Minister presented a grand remonstrance to the War Cabinet. Denied full access to war information and unable to counter the excessive demands for censorship made by the service ministries, the department was powerless to relieve the irritation and boredom of a public starved of real news. Not only was the Ministry suffering for the sins of others but it had to stand impotently by while the Germans revelled in the propaganda advantage brought about by the absence of news from Britain in the neutral press. Two urgent reforms were necessary: recognition of the principle that it was for the Ministry alone to decide what should or should not be published and, lest he became 'merely a postman' delivering to the public letters of whose content he know nothing, the Minister must be fully informed of all relevant war news.[35]

The War Cabinet answered Macmillan's lament with the statement that 'the fundamental cause of the present dissatisfaction lay in the fact that we were not ourselves as yet taking part in warlike operations of the first importance, and that there was, therefore, little information which the Defence Departments could give to the public'.[36] Unwisely building on this excuse, Sir Samuel Hoare told the House that as arrangements for news and censorship had been based on the assumption of widespread destruction on the outbreak of war, the unanticipated calm in Britain had led to criticism of them.[37] He was castigated for this remark by D. N. Pritt, who observed that if the Ministry had failed to work properly in conditions of relative calm it could hardly have been expected to work better if there had been air raids and widespread disruption.[38] 'Is the Minister aware', asked Aneurin Bevan on another occasion, 'that the impression is now universal that if the Germans do not manage to bomb us to death the Ministry of Information will bore us to death?'[39]

Confused and frustrated, Lord Macmillan could see only one way out of the impasse and that was to divest the Ministry of all its news and censorship functions by the creation of an independent press bureau. Drastic though it was, this remedy offered no solution to the fundamental difficulty for, unless there was a shift of authority from the service ministries to the censors, the mere transference of news and censorship would achieve nothing. Given the situation, it cannot be said that Lord Macmillan was 'exceptionally inept'[40] or that 'it would have been hard to find a man less fitted for this particular task'.[41] However, *The Times* was not far short of the mark in observing that he had shown 'greater courage than discretion' in accepting the appointment.[42] His courage failed him on this occasion. The War Cabinet leapt eagerly at his suggestion and on 3 October the Prime Minister announced that the functions of news and censorship would henceforward be conducted by a Press and Censorship Bureau under the control of Sir Walter Monckton, who would be answerable to the Home Secretary. The various departments, as well as having the final word in censorship matters, would now be able to issue news other than through a central agency if they so desired.[43] It was a famous victory for the service departments.

As for the men most affected, a committee representing over two hundred journalists working at Senate House pleaded with Chamberlain not to take this step, pointing out that although they had in the past been critical of the department, 'our complaint has never been against the . . . Ministry but has been directed against the stranglehold of the news exercised by some of the Government Departments'.[44] From the earliest days of planning the issue of news and the operation of censorship had been the *raison d'être* of the Ministry. Now all that remained to it was the framing of domestic and foreign propaganda policy and from this the Foreign Office, taking advantage of the Ministry's low fortunes, seized the dissemination of propaganda to enemy countries. Little wonder, then, that Chamberlain gave serious thought to abolishing the Ministry altogether. On 21 October Lord Halifax told Sir Alexander Cadogan, Permanent Under-Secretary at the Foreign Office, that the Prime Minister was thinking of winding up the Ministry.[45] Just why Chamberlain held back from from the *coup de grâce* is not clear. He may have toyed with the idea of replacing Macmillan with Lord Beaverbrook.[46] Or perhaps he hoped that Sir John Reith, whom he appointed in January 1940, might work the miracle and rescue the Ministry and the government from continuing embarrassment.

Meanwhile Lord Camrose, proprietor of the *Daily Telegraph*, whom Macmillan had appointed as his Chief Assistant, carried out a purge in which a third of the staff were removed. At headquarters sixty-seven were fired, at an annual saving in salaries of £46,000. In his report Lord Camrose stated:

> I am forced to the conclusion that the structure on which the Ministry was formed and the selection of its personnel will stand in the way of its proper functioning unless the Minister can satisfy himself . . . that the members of the staff are fitted for the work required of them, and that responsible heads of Division understand his policy and can be trusted to carry it out adequately.[47]

In the subsequent upheaval the regional organisation was disrupted, many Regional Information Officers losing their jobs and Local Information Committees being suspended or dissolved. At Senate House the interruptions caused by constant reorganisation led to numerous resignations, including that of Professor Ifor Evans, who felt it 'a strong public duty to depart'.[48] The press had a field day with headlines such as '999 at SIXES and SEVENS'.[49]

Sir Walter Monckton embarked on the directorship of the Press and Censorship Bureau in October 1939, acknowledging the limitations placed upon it, namely the ultimate authority of the service departments to decide on censorship and the role of the News Division as a 'post office' which simply transmitted those messages the departments deigned to send through the Bureau to the press.[50] But it was only a matter of days before Monckton began to make demands similar to those made by the Ministry of Information immediately before. On 14 October, five days after the setting up of the Bureau, he could see no alternative to bringing it to an end unless greater co-operation from the service departments could be secured.[51] What was wrong? In addition to the familiar problems, the service ministries aroused the press's old suspicion of the BBC's favoured position by neglecting to co-ordinate the release of their communiqués and thereby allowing the corporation to broadcast news well before the newspapers could print it.[52] The Admiralty refused to abide by the convention which permitted the publication in Britain of news which had already been printed in the neutral press overseas.[53] Stories passed for publication in one paper were stopped in others.[54] And reports which carried no real security risk, such as the accidental crashing of a single aircraft, were completely censored even though they might be common knowledge to thousands of people.[55]

The senior officers of the Bureau shared the anger of the press. Cyril Radcliffe, who had worked so hard to establish an efficient and flexible machine, commented:

> It is *not* an answer to the Press to say 'We censor this because the War Office wanted it out'. This is partly the Departments' fault, because they ask for *much too much* to be kept out. But it is certain that neither now nor later in the war are the Press or the public going to be satisfied with something simply because some department or official in it thinks it necessary in the interests of the war.[56]

So contemptuous of the censorship system did the press become that editors simply ignored rulings and risked prosecution, safe in the assumption that the department concerned would not institute proceedings against them. In such circumstances the collapse of the voluntary system and its replacement with compulsion was a strong possibility.[57]

In spite of the great trust and liking for Monckton that quickly developed among the journalists,[58] he felt so frustrated by the powerlessness of his position that he threatened resignation on no less than four occasions in the space of a month,[59] and it was only the possibility of the Bureau's reabsorption by the Ministry of Information – a suggestion which he himself had made as early as 19 November[60] – which stayed his hand. If Monckton found it impossible to gain for the Bureau all the power he believed it should have, it was not for lack of friends in high places. As the idea of reabsorption gained momentum so did the desire of Chamberlain, Sir Horace Wilson and

Reith to see Monckton installed in the House of Commons as Parliamentary Secretary to the Minister of Information.[61] In a letter to Reith, Monckton gave his reasons for not wishing to do so:

> I can assure you that you will have my loyal and hearty support without promoting me into the House. I know I shall enjoy serving under you on personal as well as public grounds . . . I know . . . my limitations and have no ambition apart from doing my job as well as I can. In other words, you are being too kind and careful about me.
>
> I should advise you to appoint another P.S. and I'll be as happy as a sandboy.
>
> One of my troubles is that I am a rotten politician and no Conservative.[62]

Three months later *The Times* was still regretting the fact that Monckton had not found his way into the House,[63] although he was to do so in 1951 – as a Conservative.

Following some largely unsuccessful bargaining with the service departments over the distribution of power, the Ministry reabsorbed the Bureau in April 1940, Monckton going over with it as Deputy Director General and also as Deputy Under-Secretary of State for the Foreign Office, this latter arrangement being designed to secure greater co-operation between the Foreign Office and the Ministry. But Reith could hardly have been satisfied. Nothing had changed in the basic situation: government departments still had the choice between issuing news themselves or channelling it through the Ministry and the service ministries retained the final say in matters of security censorship.[64] Reith's doleful countenance was well suited to the wearying task he had set himself. Without the backing of the Prime Minister his attempt to wrest back from the Foreign Office control of propaganda to enemy countries was fruitless. The one apparent sign of progress – the transfer in April 1940 of the Postal and Tele-graph Censorship from the War Office to the Ministry – came to be regarded as no more than the acquisition of an incubus. Bracken commented rather unkindly in 1943, 'This grim-faced baby was thrust upon the M.o.I.'s doorstep and warmly fostered by Lord Reith who was apparently a connoisseur of bastard responsibilities.'[65] Reith clearly found his tenure of office debilitating. Writing to Sir Stephen Tallents after the war, he said of the period:

It's a sorry tale. I, of course, had immense trouble when I went there in January 1940, the business having been largely disintegrated by then. It took me three months to collect most of the scattered parts and get some recognisable organisation working, Chamberlain announcing the whole story on April 24th, a week before he was out himself.[66]

Before he had time to achieve much more Reith was unceremoniously dumped from office by the incoming Churchill government.[67]

Amidst all these alarums and excursions the Ministry struggled to develop a policy on morale. Little help was forthcoming from the ministers. Lord Macmillan, in a memorandum on general policy, saw the role of domestic propaganda as 'rousing the whole nation and inspiring them with devotion to the national cause . . . for which no sacrifice is too great', and added:

Great Britain must be represented as fighting Germany on land, in the air, and at sea, ceaselessly, without remorse, with all her armed might, with financial resources, industrial manpower, and commercial assets, with all her idealism and determination.[68]

Such had in fact been the tenor of the Ministry's propaganda since the opening of the war but, if the reports reaching the department were correct, it had had small impact on a bewildered public; and indeed may have induced even more scepticism since Britain was palpably neither fighting nor producing with anything approaching the intensity suggested in Macmillan's statement. He lamely admitted as much: 'If periods of inactivity are strategically necessary, these very periods should be represented as fraught with particular and purposeful significance.' When Sir John Reith succeeded Macmillan, he attempted to recast the Ministry's propaganda philosophy:

1. We shall win the war by our strength; but that includes will and economic power as much as military power.
2. We are making an immense effort, by sea, land and air. Our army, navy, air force are alert and valiant.
3. Our industrial and financial resources are vital for victory. Work for victory; save for victory.
4. Be of good heart; we fight for the right and against evil; we have with us, in growing strength, the free nations of the Empire from the ends of the earth; the French, our allies, are a brave and unconquerable people.

45

5. But no magnitude of strength and resources is in itself enough. There must be a concentration of mind as well. A determination and a will to victory.

6. The greater the will, the greater the effort, the sooner victory, peace and the security of a better world.[69]

This was essentially more of the same, exhibiting little correspondence with reality and sounding distinctly hollow.

Meanwhile the Ministry tried to start the machine which had been so painfully constructed before the war. The Local Information Committees formed an integral part of the regional system and were to be more than mere handmaidens of the RIOs. They were to have:

> . . . as their concern the public morale of their neighbourhoods. They were to have provided a united party platform in all localities, a means whereby the political party machinery of the areas could be concentrated upon the national cause, and they were to have collaborated with the voluntary societies in the holding of meetings, the distribution of literature, and the sustaining of local public morale by every practicable means, including the extensive personal contacts thus assured. They were to have reported on the state of public opinion and on the need for public action to meet any threatened deterioration on the home front. They were to have served as local rallying points throughout the Kingdom.[70]

The scheme, on paper at least, was a good one. By drawing on the British tradition of local government and participation and by bringing in various interests such as political parties, trade unions, business leaders, voluntary societies and the press, the Ministry hoped to harness the zeal and local pride in each parliamentary constituency throughout the country. At the beginning of September a letter was sent by Sir Samuel Hoare to the parties' chief agents, asking them to instruct their constituency managers to co-operate with their opposite numbers and with the Ministry in the setting up of Local Information Committees.[71] After initial reluctance on the part of the Labour Party, for 'fear that their hands might be tied if at a later date they wanted to criticise the Government',[72] the parties agreed to co-operate and, by early October, 23 committees had been formed, a further 100 were in the process of formation and the remaining 500 were waiting on the initiative of RIOs. But Lord Camrose's purge of the Ministry led to the suspension of the regional system and it was not until March 1940 that it began to revive.

Public meetings, too, got off to a slow start. Their purpose, as laid down in a set of instructions to Ministry speakers, was to 'explain to the people the policy of the Government, and the progress of the war . . . the industrial and economic measures which the Government will have to take . . . how the individual can and should play his part by carrying out Government instructions'. The speaker himself was expected to:

(1) inspire confidence in the Government, by enabling people to feel that they are being kept informed . . . of the real progress of the war.

(2) to inspire a sense of collective discipline by helping people to understand the instructions of the Government . . .

Emphasis should be laid on our traditional love of liberty and freedom. This has given us a national unity unparalleled in the history of the country. We have the will to victory and the means to accomplish it.[73]

The early reluctance of the Labour Party to participate in Local Information Committees, which in turn prevented the large-scale organisation of public meetings, was considered sinister by the Ministry when 'a Socialist meeting addressed . . . by Mr Hugh Dalton was packed out'.[74] At a meeting of the Cabinet's Home Policy Committee in November Lord Macmillan brought up the question of public meetings and observed that as the Conservative and Liberal supporters had 'gone off on war service the field had been left open to the Pacifist and Communist elements'. The time had come for a campaign:

At present the Labour Party were getting the best of all worlds and were claiming credit for (1) patriotic support of the war; (2) the defence and bettering of the less prosperous elements in the community while at the same time actively bidding for the support of Pacifist and other defeatist elements. Unless steps were promptly taken there was a real danger that the Labour Party would soon capitalise these advantages in furtherance of their general socialistic policy.[75]

A fortnight later the Minister informed his officials that as a result of his representations the Prime Minister 'had stated his intention of launching an active campaign of public meetings all over the country, "under the auspices of the Ministry of Information",' at which ministers were to play a prominent role.[76] The Labour Party was perhaps justified in regarding the Ministry warily. However, by February 1940, public meetings undertaken by the department were of a strictly non-party nature and were not to be used as a forum for expression of 'controversial' views. To make doubly sure, RIOs were instructed to see that speakers drawn from the Ministry's panel were introduced to audiences as private citizens expressing purely personal views. Which was far from strictly true. Large numbers of 'Speakers' Notes' were produced by the Ministry for the guidance of speakers and conformed closely to the current propaganda line.

In the field of publications the Ministry decided that 'so far as possible the production of literature should be carried on by the normal publishing channels',[77] and arrangements were concluded with publishers such as Penguin and the Oxford University Press, the magazine *Picture Post*, and distributors such as Foyles. The Ministry's power over the release of extra supplies of paper, exercised by recommendations to the Paper Controller, considerably enhanced its ability to persuade publishers to co-operate in joint ventures.[78] As Tom Hopkinson, former editor of *Picture Post*, explains: 'The position was that every periodical tried to think up any excuse it could to get hold of even a ton or two of extra paper . . . In our case at least, this was not a matter of profit – all papers did extremely well during the war; it was the wish to give readers a bit more value, and ourselves to do a slightly less meagre job in covering the war.'[79] The Ministry would suggest an idea to a publisher who might then commission an author to work on it or would provide the raw material for an author who would then seek publication or pass on to a publisher something wholly written in the Ministry.[80] Thus *Can Germany Stand the Strain?* and *The Two Germanies* were given to the Oxford University Press for publication on condition that the name of the department should not appear in connection with them.[81] Whenever possible the Ministry preferred to remain anonymous. Hugh Walpole was commissioned to write a small propaganda treatise which was slipped into each of the 190,000 books issued monthly by Foyles to readers belonging to its book club in Britain and overseas.[82]

The suggestion made before the war of gently coercing *Picture Post* to print propaganda material[83] became superfluous when the magazine offered to produce special numbers on agreed themes, with the proviso that the Ministry met the cost of printing and paper in excess of the normal weekly size of the magazine.[84] In this manner the Ministry gained relatively cheap access to an audience estimated at five million. The editor was congratulated for his co-operation in producing a special issue on 'The Battle of the River Plate' and for undertaking to print an issue devoted to the United States.[85] Collaboration even went as far as the preparation of an article aimed at popularising the unpopular Ministry of Information, although certain precautions were felt to be necessary :

> The words 'Home Front' should be avoided like the plague and the idea would be that the Ministry's objective is to act as a Grand Liaison Officer between the Executive and the people, and not to suggest that it is part of the Executive, cajoling a reluctant populace into a dreadful struggle . . . It should not be difficult to put it over as being a perfectly legitimate channel of helpfulness and explanation much to be welcomed in these disordered and disturbing times. It should not, of course, be hinted that it knows the existence of such a thing as public morale.[86]

In the first weeks of war there was little domestic intelligence activity apart from a report on rumours about evacuation, a survey of peace propaganda and a memorandum on public reactions to the prospect of petrol rationing.[87] The intelligence division had barely got started, however, when it was killed off in October 1939. Lord Camrose wielded a heavy axe and among his victims were the entire staff of Home Intelligence. They were part of the 'massacre of the innocents' deplored by the *New Statesman* : Camrose 'had decimated the ranks of the experts but left safe in their posts most of the "high-ups", who planned the Ministry before the war and ran it into trouble in the first weeks of the war'.[88]

Agitation soon occurred for the re-establishment of intelligence operations. The Cabinet wished to be supplied with daily reports on criticism of the government's wartime control policies, while the Home Office was anxious to have weekly reports on the state of morale and opinion throughout the country. If none were forthcoming from the Ministry, the Home Office proposed to set up its own intelligence system.[89] Inside the Ministry, A. P. Waterfield felt the department should 'assume the responsibility for collecting and collating reports on the state of public opinion at home', adding 'I feel most strongly that without providing means for obtaining information of this kind . . . the Ministry is gravely handicapped in all its undertakings as regards publicity on the Home Front'.[90] Increasing anxiety had been felt at the possibility of allowing the services of Mass-Observation to slip out of the Ministry's hands, for without steady work from government agencies there was every likelihood that it would expire through lack of funds. Accordingly, Mass-Observation was asked to report on the Ministry's early posters and such was the enthusiasm with the results that the Treasury was persuaded to sanction the expenditure of £100 for another piece of research. The British Institute of Public Opinion was similarly engaged. But Lord Macmillan, disturbed by press and parliamentary rumblings about the overstaffing and excessive spending of the Ministry, would not agree to the further employment of the two bodies[91] and, despite entreaties from his officials, refused to reconsider the matter.[92] No less alarming was the determination of the then Director General, Sir Findlater Stewart, not to re-establish Home Intelligence 'in any form'.[93]

John Hilton, Professor of Industrial Relations at Cambridge, a popular broadcaster and Director of Home Publicity in the Ministry, was characteristically undeterred by these setbacks. He approached Mary Adams with an offer of the directorship of the intelligence division. She had latterly been a television producer at the BBC, having graduated from Cambridge with a science degree and become herself a broadcaster in 1925. In December, by which time the climate had eased for the advocates of domestic intelligence, Mary Adams was appointed to the post. On 26 January she presented a paper to the Ministry's top decision-making body, the Policy Committee, outlining her proposals for the structure and functions of the division. It exhibited a sound perception of the difficulties likely to be encountered and incorporated many of the ideas which had been circulating in the Ministry:

> It has long been recognised that a knowledge of public opinion is essential to a democracy, a necessity which in war-time becomes doubly apparent . . . Reliance on guess-work and partial surveys, or on information lodged by interested bodies can be misleading and dangerous. Thoroughgoing opinion studies are therefore vital.

> *Purposes*
> (1) To provide a directive for Home Publicity. A continuous flow of information is required on what the public is thinking in order that publicity measures may be formulated and their effectiveness tested.
> (2) To provide an assessment of home morale. For this purpose it is necessary to study immediate reactions to specific events as well as to create a barometer for the measurement of opinion, on questions likely to be continuously important . . .

Objectives not secret

The *purposes* of an intelligence system should be widely known and receive the approbation of all political parties : it is not, however, necessary to make known the methods by which the system is made to work. It would be a grave mistake to injure the work of Home Intelligence with a suggestion that its activities must be secret.

Difficulties

The creation of a comprehensive intelligence service is not easy. The sources of information already available . . . are inadequate; attitude testing methods are not yet agreed among authorities; Great Britain is backward in the field of social survey; there is no proper understanding of the fundamental relationship between *saying, doing* and *thinking*.[94]

The division's immediate tasks were to supply the Ministry itself with routine monthly and *ad hoc* reports on matters of urgency and on the effectiveness of propaganda. For the Ministry of Home Security it was to furnish a monthly report, supplemented by interim fortnightly reports if they were found to be necessary. By the time the division was set up in March it had acquired additional responsibilities, comprising investigations into food-buying habits for the Ministry of Food, by-election studies, and an investigation into the attitudes of students towards the war. This rapid accumulation of tasks in so short a time indicates a wide demand for opinion studies. Those officials who firmly believed that they were needed were vindicated.

With the increase in demand for specific sorts of information came an increase in the sources employed. Although they were not permitted to canvass opinion directly or to undertake surveys, the RIOs were expected to supply daily reports based on their extensive local contacts. Directly in touch with Senate House were branch managers of W. H. Smith and Sons and of cinema chains, officials of the London Passenger Transport Board, workers in Citizens' Advice Bureaux, and members of such bodies as the Brewers' Society, all of whom responded to the inquiries of Home Intelligence by filling in questionnaires. Another and very valuable source was the BBC's Listener Research unit. Officials of political parties also volunteered information on request and the numerous voluntary societies supplied information relating to the condition and attitudes of those members of the public with whom they came in contact. Considering this veritable beehive of activity, it is a wonder that the existence of the intelligence network remained a secret for so long. There were, finally, two principal secret sources of information: police duty room reports, passed on by the Home Office, and Postal Censorship. From Postal Censorship came frequent and lengthy reports on public attitudes and morale, as culled by the postal censors from outgoing mail. The primary function of this body was the operation of security censorship on mail leaving and entering Britain. But time was found to compile weekly and monthly intelligence reports, the latter often being based on a scrutiny of as many as 200,000 letters[95] – a task presumably made possible by the sheer size of the organisation. In May 1941 the Postal and Telegraph Censorship staff numbered 10,443.

Despite some misgivings, the Ministry placed a heavy reliance on the work performed by Mass-Observation. Mary Adams, who was chiefly responsible for its re-employment, warned that Mass-Observation's methods were not strictly scientific and that care should be exercised in the interpretation of their findings.[96] Richard Crossman, after reading one of Mass-Observation's pilot surveys, observed that in spite of Tom Harrisson's 'astonishing ingenuity' the scientific shakiness and subjectivity of his judgements made it important that the work 'should be accepted only with caution'.[97] This caution was reinforced by a lingering suspicion in the minds of the career civil servants in the Ministry that Harrisson's organisation was heavily inclined towards the left, and Mary Adams was obliged to defend it against such charges:

> What does one mean by 'subversive'? The results of Mass Observation are, not unnaturally, critical of certain social happenings and I do not think that criticism is subversion. The use to which criticisms are put may lead to subversive actions. But it is our business to acquaint ourselves with criticisms and direct the attention of those in authority to the causes of discontent.[98]

Some thirty years later Harrisson said of his dealings with the Ministry, 'There was all sorts of skullduggery and dirty work in this field, and quite a lot of it came our way. At one stage, for instance, certain sections were obsessed by the completely erroneous idea that we were Communist dominated or oriented.'[99]

Nonetheless, Mass-Observation became essential to Home Intelligence. By using the special units maintained in Bolton and Fulham (which had been established in 1937) and by setting up a 'flying squad' which could investigate events at short notice, Mass-Observation was able to supply regular reports on a wide range of subjects, including the incidence of gas-mask carrying, current rumours, the size of shelter populations, shopping habits, and reactions to new films and to the Ministry's propaganda. When asked to do so, it undertook investigations into particular events such as by-elections and the conditions in recently raided towns. It is true to say that in the absence of the speedy and versatile work of Mass-Observation much would have gone unnoticed and unattended – especially in 1940 when Home Intelligence was having considerable trouble in creating its own machinery.

The difficulties associated with Mass-Observation were as nothing compared to those of the Wartime Social Survey. For over a year after its creation the staff of Home Intelligence had to defend the Survey against attacks from almost every quarter. Yet at the time of the reconstruction of the Home Intelligence Division Mary Adams did not envisage the setting up of a statistical survey unit. Such a body, she explained, 'would be fairly expensive to maintain, it would take time to put it into useful operation, and it would be clear that investigators were at work with the name and authority of the Ministry'.[100] But the need was soon felt for some means whereby the 'qualitative' findings of Mass-Observation could be checked by a 'quantitative' method; that is, findings which were the results of observation and overheard conversation were to be set against the findings of statistically verifiable surveys conducted among representative samples of the population.[101] The Survey was placed under the supervision of the London School of Economics in order to avoid the appearance of 'inquisitorial' activity by the Government'.[102]

In the initial stages of planning, the Survey was conceived of as a supplement to the work of Mass-Observation rather than a substitute for it.[103] And, since Mass-Observation's broad task was to assess civilian morale, the Survey was intended to do a similar job with different means:

> Investigators will interview, each month, about 5,000 persons, so chosen as to constitute a representative sample of the total population of Great Britain, and will obtain answers to about ten simple questions designed to test their attitudes to various aspects of the war situation.[104]

A less ambitious aim was imposed on the Survey in its early work: inquiries for the Ministry of Food into public attitudes towards the food supply and for the Ministry of Home Security into the ARP's state of preparedness.[105] These more factual inquiries, impinging on morale only slightly, were in fact to form the basis of the Survey's work for the entire war period. It acted as a barometer of morale for only a short time.

In the absence of a smoothly functioning intelligence division the Ministry adopted the blunderbuss technique of domestic propaganda, firing as much material as possible in the hope of hitting something. The country was festooned with posters: 'Freedom is in Peril – Defend it with all your Might!', 'We're Going To See It Through!', 'Our Fighting Men Depend On You', 'It all depends on me', 'Don't Help the Enemy! Careless Talk May Give Away Vital Secrets'. These injunctions and affirmations, as well as posters designed for other departments, were placed on 24,000 railway sites, in 27,000 telephone booths and on scores of thousands of sites in pubs, shops, factories, service establishments, public libraries, buses and trains. The output of pamphlets and leaflets was no less prodigious. 'Make Your Home Safe', written on behalf of the Ministry of Home Security, was distributed to 7 million households, and, while items of literature aimed at boosting morale were individually less numerous and were often sold rather than given away, they reached a vast audience. By April 1940 the despatch of photographic prints and copies of press articles produced in the Ministry averaged 737,500 each week. Letters to the press, either written in the Ministry or inspired by it, added a more subtle dimension to propaganda. Public meetings had got off to a hesitant start but by April over 200 each week were being held under Ministry auspices. Running parallel with these national endeavours were the local but very widespread activities of RIOs and the Local Information Committees.

Yet on the Ministry's own reckoning morale remained low throughout the period. After some six weeks of war there was considerable anxiety at apparent signs of poor morale: attacks on the wastefulness of the ARP, grumbling about the slowness of government in placing the country on a war footing, and suspicion of official news to such an extent that the public believed rumours 'because they are *not* official'.[106] The prospect of the coming winter assumed a dread aspect. Ifor Evans told the Director General:

If there is no major action on the Western Front and the war of what may be called the 'mental black-out' proceeds, the enemy will attempt to destroy our morale at home in many ways. Further, there will be forces independent of the enemy in this country who are wearied, disillusioned and in many cases ruined.[107]

By February the degree of public apathy and churlishness was thought to be such as to cause the Policy Committee to search for anything that might bring a 'diversion of present public resentment away from domestic affairs towards the enemy'.[108] It seems as if the Ministry of Information was longing for the real war to begin in much the same way as was the public.

But in March 1940 the BBC's Listener Research Department, whose reports always received the closest attention in the Ministry, confirmed the conclusion already reached that defeatist propaganda appeared to be having little effect, discontented though the people were. It was found that at the end of January one out of every six adults listened regularly to German radio propaganda. The regular listener was more politically conscious than the average non-listener and was more likely to agree with certain claims of the enemy, such as the positive social achievements of Hitler, but there was little evidence to suggest that the listener 'would not have held those views in almost as great a measure if Hamburg had never broadcast in English' and he was opposed to Nazism. At the same time hatred of the enemy did not exist. The report concluded:

> If there were widespread social discontent . . . this would be Hamburg's opportunity. It is certain that the impact of Hamburg propaganda should be kept under constant supervision.[109]

Similarly, Reith was of the opinion that despite the failure of anti-war propaganda to make inroads into the public's determination the situation might well become more serious in a population which was already 'bored and uncomfortable'.[110]

The danger to morale of pacifist, and especially communist pacifist, propaganda in Britain was also believed to be potential rather than actual. In February 1940 Mary Adams assessed the situation:

> There is evidence that pacifism, communism and fascism are increasingly active as organised movements. But there is no evidence, as far as I can tell, that these movements have been gaining ground either by securing an increased membership . . . or by an increased circulation of their propaganda organs. It is true that pacifists are very active and it is natural that what they say and do should attract more attention in wartime than in peace-time. In wartime pacifist activities are not in accordance with public policy; even moral sanctions are withdrawn from them. It cannot be too strongly stressed, however, that there are two kinds

of pacifist activity: philosophical and Christian pacifism which is legitimate even in wartime; and political pacifism which in wartime may be actively subversive.

Our Religions Division is in close touch with Christian pacifist movements and is thoroughly aware of their viewpoint and activities.

Political pacifism may conceivably become dangerous in time. There seems no evidence that it is dangerous at present. If apathy and boredom continue, however, we may well expect political pacifism to grow . . .

One comes to the conclusion that counter-measures are *desirable* although not *necessary* in a strict sense of the word. Supporters of the war and of the Government *expect* that something will be done; they are *disappointed* that nothing is done. That does not seem to me any valid reason for doing it![111]

Sir John Reith felt rather more strongly about the communists. In a memorandum of April 1940 he analysed their propaganda:

The policy of the British Communist Party as stated in the *Daily Worker* has steadily changed since the outbreak of war. On September 2nd, 1939, the *Daily Worker* said that 'the Communist Party would do all in its power to ensure speedy victory over Fascism'. On October 7th, a new manifesto was issued reversing this policy and stating that 'this is not a war for Democracy against Fascism; it is a fight between imperialist powers' . . . The manifesto of April 10th is consistent with the support of the enemy against the Allies. There is no indication whatever in the issue of April 10th that the enemy invaded Scandinavia on April 9th. And in a manifesto issued by the Political Bureau of the Communist Party . . . the conduct of the enemy is implicitly defended if not supported.[112]

It was noted that the abrupt turn-around in communist policy had caused a good deal of confusion and doubt within the party, but for his part Reith thought its discipline would triumph. 'Some say', he concluded darkly, 'that with rope the Party may go some way to hanging itself.'

Of greater concern than the open expression of anti-war opinion was the effect of communist agitation in industry and among aggrieved sections of the population. The application of 'Lenin's injunction to "Take advantage of every concrete example of oppression for the purpose of agitation" '[113] was judged to be having some success.[114] But, despite the party's progress 'towards an attitude indistinguishable from that of a supporter of the enemy',[115] the government, for reasons stated by the Home Office three months later, would not take direct action. The communists' advocacy of social reform had elicited great sympathy which would arouse accusations of victimisation if the government adopted repressive measures and, moreover, it would be very difficult to prove that they intended or had advocated giving aid to the Germans. In no country which Hitler had invaded, it was observed, had any evidence come to light showing that the fifth column was drawn from communists. Nor had any evidence been uncovered of organised attempts by the party to slow down or disrupt production in Britain. Having quite 'failed to shake the loyalty of the working people', the communists were not to be singled out for special treatment simply because they professed a certain political creed.[116]

While restraint was the order of the day at Senate House, some regional officers of the Ministry were fairly straining at the leash and anxious reports on communist and pacifist activity daily arrived at headquarters. Not placed at the centre and unable to assess the situation at a general level, the Regional Information Officers tended to magnify local instances of anti-war agitation into symptoms of a seditious, nation-wide conspiracy. The officers in London found themselves having to restrain the regions from taking precipitate action.

In March 1940 Hubert Banner, the south-eastern Regional Information Officer, distributed to editors of local newspapers some 'Confidential Notes on Anti-Pacifist Arguments', in which he suggested a number of points that might be printed. For example :

If the Pacifist bodies are free to preach their creed, similar freedom must be accorded to those who believe they are misleading our young men. They must likewise be free to call 'artificial' conscientious objection by its true names, which are Disloyalty, Treachery and Cowardice . . .

Does the Pacifist realise that, in the event of Britain passing under German domination, he himself would undoubtedly be the first victim of the concentration camp? The Nazis, for all their faults, hate and despise cowards and traitors. If they ruled Britain, they would assuredly not allow people of that kidney to remain at liberty.[117]

Unfortunately for Banner and the Ministry, one of the recipients of this document broke 'the journalistic code by sending that letter to *Peace News*, and the latter has not only printed the whole letter in this week's issue, but even reproduced parts of it in facsimile'.[118] Banner insisted that the culprit be tracked down and *Peace News* threatened with the Official Secrets Act,[119] but the Ministry wisely decided to let the matter rest.[120] Generally speaking, a quiet word from headquarters was enough to prevent the regions from committing blunders. One officer, when asked precisely what it was in the *Daily Worker* that was treasonable, had to admit that he was referring to the unconstructive attitude shown by the paper rather than to statements of a specifically treasonable nature.[121] The antipathy of some RIOs towards communism may be gauged by a report of a meeting in March 1940. Held in Oxford, the meeting was addressed by a housewife who made a 'telling speech' on the difficulties confronting the working-class woman. She was listened to by 'the type which one normally sees at Communist meetings – life's unsuccessfuls with a sprinkling of young men and women who would be all the better for being compelled to do an honest day's work . . . [and] quite a few obviously middle aged spinsters with the look of fanaticism in their eyes'.[122]

When possible – and only if the Ministry was not seen to be involved – action was taken, but it was of an improvised and spasmodic nature, tending to wait upon opportunity rather than conforming to a settled policy. Thus, when in March 1940 the RIO in Wales reported that communists intended capturing a meeting of the North Wales Miners' Federation, the Ministry quickly contacted the *Daily Herald* and the *News Chronicle* in order to pour a 'cold douche' over the scheme by giving it adverse publicity.[123] Film shows, first used as a means of relieving boredom in air-raid shelters, became a device for preventing communists from gaining the attention of shelter populations.[124] Broadcasts by 'certain left-wing leaders who have come round to support the national cause', such as John Strachey and Vera Brittain, were suggested as a means of countering the anti-war propaganda of other left-wing spokesmen.[125] But the relative quiescence on the part of the Ministry is at first sight puzzling. Even the People's Convention, whose supporters were irritably dubbed as 'left-wing psychopaths' in a Home Intelligence report,[126] failed to excite much concern and passed off with no departmental action. However, the policy of 'pushing the War Effort as hard as we can'[127] avoided a possibly damaging confrontation with the communists. And if the fact that the number of days lost in strikes in 1940 was the lowest on record is an index of the success of communist propaganda, and of its impact on morale, then the Ministry acted wisely in playing a subdued role.

As Duff Cooper was to do with equally little success, Sir John Reith urged the government to make 'constructive statements' on the social order as a means of giving the nation something to fight for :

> Propaganda succeeds best when it is directed to a clearly defined object. Vague generalisations are comparatively ineffective . . . In time of war the progressive elements are eager to see the ideals for which the nation is fighting translated into concrete pledges of Government action at home and abroad. No one claims that the present social system is perfect. One effective remedy for possible discontent and disaffection in this country would be the adoption of a striking social policy.[128]

The Ministry had been notably unsuccessful in its declared aim of imparting to the war the flavour of a crusade and of keeping the spirits of the people buoyant. Now, as later, the promise of social reform, however vaguely worded, was expected to come to the rescue when it was judged that all else had failed. Predictably enough, Chamberlain would not oblige the Ministry with such a statement.

What did catch the public's imagination and drew people out of themselves was the Finnish resistance to the Soviet invasion. But after the capitulation of the Finns in March 1940 sympathy for them turned into resentment against the British government. According to a report, compiled from surveys and inquiries conducted by Mass-Observation, the British Institute of Public Opinion and RIOs, there was a general feeling of distrust and depression :

> Although the circumstances bear little comparison with the state of affairs during the Munich crisis, there appears to be every similarity between the state of public opinion then and now . . . There is a guilty feeling that we have in some way shirked the issue . . .
>
> Besides this feeling of guilt, widespread bewilderment arises from the public's knowledge of its own impotence; responsibility for this is laid upon the secrecy observed by the Government and the BBC.[129]

Towards the end of April the public's impression that news was being withheld was powerfully strengthened by the confusion which reigned over reports of operations in Norway following the German invasion of Denmark and Norway on 8 April. People were 'staggered' when the true proportions of the fiasco were pieced together.[130] Reith himself was kept in the dark by the service departments.[131] Some three days after the decision had been taken to evacuate the troops in the Trondheim area in order to assist the British capture of Narvik, officials of the Ministry and Ivone Kirkpatrick of the Foreign Office pleaded with Reith to obtain more information:

> What, in our view, will tell most heavily against any case we can make are the statements of the Prime Minister and M. Daladier that 100,000 men were ready to be sent to Finland, a subsequent statement by the Prime Minister that he had prophesied the invasion of Norway and that events had shown him a true prophet, a recent statement by the P.M. that Hitler had 'missed the bus' . . .
>
> We think that you should make the Cabinet understand clearly that the situation is becoming extremely bad and that it can only be defended with the assistance of drastic action.[132]

Thus it was that at the end of an eight-month period of inactivity the first significant engagement between Britain and the enemy brought defeat and, by the Ministry's reckoning, 'public morale was at a low ebb'.[133] Having been incapable of influencing morale when the war was in a static phase, the Ministry was equally powerless when Britain suffered a – by no means disastrous – military reverse. It was a gloomy augury for the future.

3

The 'Emergency'

The period from May to early September 1940 witnessed a bewilder-
ing and increasingly ominous succession of events. From a concern
with relieving the irritable boredom of the public, the propagandists
of the Ministry of Information had suddenly to switch their attention
to a situation which became much more critical than they, or anybody else for that matter, had bargained for. Few people prior to the
war or during its first eight months had mentioned – or envisaged –
the possibility of the collapse of Britain's strongest ally and the
probability of invasion.

The nature of the war for which morale-boosting propaganda had
been prepared was akin to that of the First World War. The battle
would be fought on continental soil and the British public would
need to be prepared for discomfort and short rations, not for
imminent invasion. True, air raids on a large scale were anticipated
but the Ministry had done little more than dispense vague exhortation as if on the assumption that the Maginot Line was as close as
the enemy would approach to the British mainland. So when, less
than two months after Churchill assumed the premiership Britain
was faced with defeat, the propagandists acted like men confronted
with the inconceivable and behaved with a good deal less aplomb
than that which they were supposed to instil in the public. Indeed,
the panic which Harold Nicolson, the new Parliamentary Secretary,
observed in the senior ranks of the services[1] was not entirely absent
from the Ministry of Information. And despite reports which
generally pointed to a different conclusion, the public's determination
and capacity to see things through were seriously doubted.

In a preface to the first daily report, Home Intelligence summarised
the state of 'public opinion', a term often used as a euphemistic
substitute for 'morale', up to 18 May:

The Norwegian defeat staggered people . . . People came not to believe anything. The BBC suffered less than political leaders and the press, but all suffered. In the early days of May, therefore, public morale was at a low ebb, although there were for the first time signs of psychological healthiness : people were facing facts and were not bathed in phantasy. The early mood of complacency entirely disappeared. Norway was regarded as a defeat. In this situation came the invasion of Holland and Belgium.

It must be remembered that the defence of the Low Countries had been continually built up in the press . . . Not one person in a thousand could visualise the Germans breaking through into France. A certain amount of wishful thinking was still at work, and a relieved acceptance of Mr Churchill as Prime Minister allowed people to believe that a change of leadership would, in itself, solve the consequences of Mr Chamberlain . . .

Reports sent in yesterday afternoon and this morning show that disquiet and personal fear has returned.[2]

Seeing that the Germans were making rapid advances since their breakthrough at Sedan and were threatening to cut off the BEF in the north, it is hardly surprising that the public should have felt some measure of anxiety.

On 22 May a 'Home Morale Emergency Committee' was set up for the purpose of suggesting measures to counter 'the danger of a break in morale'.[3] In view of the presumed urgency of the task, it seems an oddly constituted body. Ivison Macadam – as Secretary of the Royal Institute of International Affairs since 1929 – had perhaps some claim to knowledge of the behaviour of nations in times of international conflict. The Director of the National Gallery and art historian, Sir Kenneth Clark, who had been appointed Controller of Home Publicity by Reith and persuaded to stay on by Monckton, wrote in *The Other Half*, 'We were not ourselves a very war-like body, and I remember one of our number, Harold Nicolson, who was far too civilised a man to be concerned with propaganda, saying several times "All we can do is lie on our backs and hope that no-one will tread on our tummies".' The third member, Nicolson, was a former diplomat, National Labour MP for West Leicester since 1935, journalist and man of letters, in short, a man of varied talents and experience. But a colleague echoed Clark's opinion when he wrote :

He was a wonderful gossip but seemed to know hardly anyone outside Westminster, St James's and Bloomsbury. He was quite ignorant of the habits and attitudes even of the middle classes. As for the working classes he seemed to regard them as barbarians to be feared, admired and placated. Never was there a man who represented so completely in himself the distinction between Us and Them.[4]

However, the committee acted with a speed appropriate to their title and produced reports on each of the two succeeding days, following these up with suggestions to the Policy Committee and presenting a long report on 4 June which itemised the chief factors in a possible 'disintegration of public morale'.[5] These were, they asserted, a fear of air raids and of invasion, the existence of class feeling, and the prevalence of confusion, suspicion and defeatism.

Fear of air raids, at least until the commencement of heavy bombing on 7 September 1940, was not a prominent topic in the Home Intelligence reports. There were some shivers of apprehension when Paris was bombed early in June[6] but nothing to indicate that strenuous counter-measures were called for on the part of the Ministry. Which was just as well. Sensibly enough, the Home Morale Emergency Committee deemed it a matter of some importance to revive faith in the ARP services after the long period during which they had been criticised as a waste of money and manpower and to give the public concrete instructions, if somewhat belatedly, on what to do should water supplies fail and sewers burst. But the other suggestions put forward by the committee exhibited a certain poverty of invention. 'Tell actors', it was urged, 'that they are counted upon to keep people cheerful, lead singing, etc.' At one time the message to be put across was that 'the moral effect of air raids is greater than the physical effect'.[7] At another, the message was one of stoicism in air raids since 'this was a war of wills in which victory would go to the side which endured longest'.[8] However, until September the raids experienced in Britain were comparatively light and reports indicated that not only was morale high in bombed towns but that people actually benefited from air raids, perhaps because at last there was something to be experienced as a relief from prolonged tension :

Intensified raids have not affected morale; rather the reverse : confidence is increased, opinion is stiffer and there is a feeling of growing exhilaration. The spirit of the people in raided areas is excellent.[9]

Apart from fatigue due to lack of sleep – to which people appear to have adjusted quickly – and the shaky morale of 'the lonely woman', the principal causes of concern to the public were confusion over the siren policy and annoyance at the withholding of casualty figures and names of places bombed.

Complaints about the late sounding of sirens were frequent and vociferous[10] and it seems that many members of the public had simply failed to absorb the instructions. On 27 June, George Orwell noted in his diary:

> It appears that the night before last, during the air-raid alarm, many people all over London were woken by the All Clear signal, took that for the warning and went to the shelters and stayed there till morning, waiting for the All Clear. This after months of war and God knows how many explanations of the air raid precautions.[11]

The Ministry's response to this state of affairs was to suggest 'that warnings should only be put out when they were really needed, i.e. in the event of a dangerous mass attack, and that the public should become accustomed to receiving no warning when only a few aircraft were in the neighbourhood, even if these carried bombs'.[12] But with the onset of mass attacks in September recognition of the sirens soon became second nature.

The Ministry argued strongly that news of damage and of casualties caused by air raids should be released as quickly and as fully as possible. There were two reasons for this policy. It was feared that the withholding or delaying of such news would, first, create distrust of official announcements and, second, bring about a lowering of morale because of the public's intense dislike of being kept in the dark. Tom Clarke, Deputy Director of the News Division and ex-editor of the *News Chronicle*, had expressed the Ministry's viewpoint at the very outset of the war:

> Frankness will give all the more emphasis to bulletins announcing our successes. Our civilian population is not afraid of an occasional dose of bad news, and would not be cast into panic by it . . . Detail kills the public distrust of vague announcements.[13]

This philosophy was contested by the Air Ministry and the Ministry of Home Security on the grounds that publication would convey to the enemy otherwise unobtainable facts about the accuracy and effect of his bombing. However, in February 1940 the almost total ban on what little air-raid news there had been was relaxed. The Secretary of State for Air and the Minister of Home Security agreed that extreme secrecy was not practicable:

> Nor is it now held to be desirable, the general view being that unless detailed information is issued promptly and authoritatively when severe raids take place, there is the danger that rumours will grow with such rapidity as to create grave public alarm . . .
>
> We accept this view, and consider that no news of actual air raids or of civil casualties ought to be suppressed or delayed except in so far as this is vitally necessary on grounds of national security.[14]

Henceforward, RIOs would be permitted to put up lists of casualties sustained in their regions, while at a national level the approximate numbers of killed and seriously injured were to be indicated as soon as possible and the names of large towns hit normally given. Certain categories of information, such as the identity of damaged military objectives and the number of British aircraft brought down, would remain secret.

Two principal categories of information were normally suppressed for security reasons. Obviously, the enemy could not be allowed to learn of damage to armament factories, main railway stations, power installations and the like. Except in the case of large cities like London and Liverpool, it was considered undesirable to give the name of a town lest this enable the enemy to correct his navigational techniques. Within these restrictions, Cyril Radcliffe – as Controller of News and Censorship – endeavoured to apply common-sense principles and told the censors to judge each story on its individual merits. He advised, by way of example, that as there had been several raids up and down the east coast, there would be no harm in passing a Hull newspaper story about damage done to a house in which an old lady of eighty-five lived, so long as the city was not named and a description of it not given. On the other hand, a recently published interview with a named clergyman whose vicarage was said to be opposite the place bombed should not have been passed, since it was only necessary to look up his name in *Crockford's* to obtain the exact location.[15] But Radcliffe's wish to strike a balance between the good achieved, or the evil averted, by air-raid news and the possible harm done to security by its release foundered on a Cabinet decision of 3 July 1940. In future, casualties were to be described only in terms of 'slight', 'considerable' or 'heavy'.[16]

Duff Cooper objected that this decision contradicted assurances previously given to the press and would be taken by the public as a sign of the government's lack of confidence in morale.[17] The Air and Home Security ministers agreed with Duff Cooper but, despite the agreement of the departments most vitally concerned, the decision stood.

The most pressing of immediate concerns was the possibility and, after France's capitulation on 17 June, the likelihood of invasion. As early as 20 May it was reported that 'many people have envisaged the possibilities of invasion';[18] and, although fear of invasion had prematurely faded to widespread scepticism by the end of July, the Ministry did not feel the public needed to be warned about the situation. There were, however, two difficult jobs to be done. The first was, in consultation with the services and the Ministry of Home Security, to draw up instructions to the civilian population as to their behaviour in the event of invasion. The second task was to reassure the public that the Germans – so spectacularly successful in Europe – could be thrown back from the beaches or, failing that, routed further inland.

To have issued the leaflet of instructions, *If the Invader Comes*, as late as mid-June, that is to say nearly a month after people had become apprehensive, could be represented as a dereliction of duty on the part of the government. But, while it is probably true that events had moved with too much speed for the authorities, the publication of instructions before the quarter million troops of the BEF had been evacuated might have seemed a counsel of despair and done more harm than good. There was another consideration. Until the fall of France was absolutely certain, Duff Cooper was reluctant to put out instructions in case it appeared that the British were turning their attention 'away from France and concentrating on the defence of this country'.[19] Churchill's half dozen urgent flights to France between 16 May and 17 June made Duff Cooper's reservations all the more appropriate.

Prior to the writing of the leaflet a detailed emergency plan was worked out at the end of May which gives some indication of the sequence of events and the tenor of the announcements that would have been made had invasion been attempted. The keystone of the plan was to be a broadcast by the Prime Minister on 5 June, which, as well as announcing the dangers of possible invasion, was designed to hearten the nation. Presumably Churchill would have written it himself, but the points suggested by the Ministry aimed at a combination of reassurance and a call to sacrifice:

1. Gallantry of the British Expeditionary Force an example to the nation.

2. Moment now come to complete preparations to fight off the invasion of this island (and turn it into a fortress) . . .

3. Note of confidence. Fighting of past weeks proved in actual combat our sailors, soldiers and airmen more than a match for the Germans man to man. 1½ million men already under arms. Local Defence Volunteers in addition. British Navy intact. Command of the seas. Empire's resources.

4. Factories working day and night to produce armaments. Civilian population in factories, in the fields and in the mines, making mighty effort to increase our strength to resist enemy and make sure of final victory of ourselves and our Allies.

5. German losses and German difficulties. New armies to go to France to stand shoulder to shoulder.

6. Mention of men and women who for months have been working to perfect Air Raid Precautions.

7. In calling the nation to arms, the Government will make it clear what part each man and woman will be called upon to play.

8. Words of command not words of comfort. Obey the authorities: the Government, the police, the military authorities, the civil defence authorities and air raid wardens.

9. Message to France: new armies will return to France and stand beside French. Sacred alliance sealed by what has happened in Belgium . . .

10. A great moment in our history. A moment of sacrifice and dedication.[20]

The Prime Minister's broadcast was to be accompanied by a series of announcements on 4, 5, and 6 June, dates so closely specified that it becomes clear how seriously the threat of invasion was taken. On 4 June appeals were to be made to all civil defence personnel to return to their posts and to the public at large for recruitment as nurses, stretcher bearers and special constables. General Ironside, the CIGS, was scheduled to broadcast on 5 June 'with the object of reassuring the public regarding the preparedness of Home Defences' and on the following day Duff Cooper would inform the public of the sorts of instructions which were to be issued by means of the press, the BBC and pamphlets.[21] No plans were made for the fourth or successive days, presumably because everyone would be too involved in beating back the Germans. 'The essential point', concluded the Ministry's draft memorandum, 'is that all the people, whatever their tasks may be, should face the national peril in a spirit of comradeship, for it is this sense of comradeship in a common cause which will do so much to strengthen morale and avert the paralysing effect of personal danger.'[22]

With the successful completion of the BEF's evacuation this scheme was put into abeyance and the Ministry, believing that the Germans were 80 per cent likely to finish off France before turning to Britain,[23] endeavoured to use the breathing space by producing the set of instructions which it had not the time to write late in May. According to Sir Harold Nicolson's diary he was given the job of writing *If the Invader Comes.* In a footnote in his second volume of autobiography *The Other Half* Lord Clark writes, 'I see in Harold Nicolson's diary that he says he wrote it. It is not an honour that I would keenly contest. But as a matter of fact, I did.' After the various authorities concerned had been consulted, a draft was produced which, after Cabinet approval on June 13 was issued as a leaflet to all householders in the country.[24] The ideal citizen under circumstances of invasion was expected to be brave, calm, alert and obedient to higher authority. He was given seven rules to follow:

(1) If the Germans come, by parachute, aeroplane or ship, you must remain where you are. The order is 'Stay Put' . . .

(2) Do not believe rumours and do not spread them. When you receive an order, make quite sure that it is a true order and not a faked order. Most of you know your policeman and your ARP wardens by sight, you can trust them. If you keep your heads, you can also tell whether a military officer is really British or only pretending to be so. If in doubt ask the policeman or ARP warden. Use your common sense . . .

(3) Keep watch. If you see anything suspicious, note it carefully and go at once to the nearest police station or officer, or to the nearest military officer . . .

(4) Do not give the German anything. Do not tell him anything. Hide your food and your bicycles. Hide your maps. See that the enemy gets no petrol . . . Remember that transport and petrol will be the invader's main difficulties. Make sure that no invader will be able to get your cars, petrol, maps or bicycles . . .

(5) Be ready to help the military in any way. But do not block roads until ordered to do so by the military or LDV authorities.

(6) In factories and shops, all managers and workmen should organise some system by which a sudden attack can be resisted.

(7) Think before you act. But think always of your country before you think of yourself.[25]

According to Duff Cooper, the leaflet 'had a good reception, but there is no doubt that people are expecting further instructions. The main points about which they want guidance are (a) whether they – the civilians – are to fight, or (b) whether they may even take steps to protect themselves.'[26]

The more combative members of the public were bound to be disappointed with the essentially passive role assigned by the leaflet to civilians. 'Stay Put' must have seemed merely another way of saying 'Accept the German presence', and yet the leaflet tantalisingly implied that factory and shop workers could engage in some form of fighting to protect their work-places.[27] If the individual was to think of his country before he thought of himself, he was unlikely to feel much sense of achievement by staying put, vital as it was to keep roads clear and the armed forces unencumbered by amateur guerillas. The Ministry of Information was in a difficult position. Recognising, as Nicolson put it, that 'it is absurd to expect people to stay in their homes without telling them what to do',[28] the department was, however, in no position to tell the War Office its job. On 1 July the Planning Committee (the body responsible for initiating and co-ordinating domestic propaganda) agreed to ask the War Office and the Ministry of Home Security to inform civilians that 'they could and should defend themselves or, failing this, need more orders, instructions and reasons for staying put'.[29] Duff Cooper was in full agreement, but a meeting on the same day with representatives of the other two departments proved fruitless. Understandably, the War Office was of the opinion that 'unless there are arms for the whole population, passive resistance was the most that civilians could be allowed to attempt'.[30] The Ministry's finding that 70 per cent of people questioned expressed approval of arming civilians was therefore of academic interest only.[31] The Ministry of Home Security objected even to the encouragement of people to dig trench shelters in their gardens, provoking Duff Cooper into writing to the Minister to point out that trenches would provide greater safety under shell-fire than houses.[32] On 8 July, Anthony Eden, Secretary of State for War, informed the War Cabinet that although his department had been 'inundated with enquiries from all over the country asking for a lead', civilians could not be authorised to 'use lethal weapons'.[33]

After further discussion the three ministers produced a pamphlet which went a little way towards satisfying the anxious inquiries of the public. The emphasis remained firmly on 'stay put' and citizens were told to 'behave as if an air raid were going on' should fighting occur in their districts. 'But if small parties are going about threatening persons and property in an area not under enemy control', continued the instructions, 'and come your way, you have the right of every man and woman to do what you can to protect yourself, your family and your home.'[34] A great deal of obscurity still surrounded the issue. The Ministry had done what it could to force the other departments to recognise public unease as to the martial role of civilians in case of invasion, but what more could be done? Unarmed and untrained, ordinary men and women – as in any war – represented a nuisance to the defending army and the military authorities, no doubt with the lamentable example of France in mind, could only hope they would keep well out of the way.

The apparent unwillingness of the government to respond to insistent public demands for instruction was leading, in the opinion of the Ministry of Information, to a dangerous situation. Earlier reports of a 'desire for definite instructions to be issued . . . about what people could or should do to help the country and themselves'[35] began to assume an urgent tone by the middle of June. From 'the better artisan classes, from the workers, and from young businessmen' came an increasing volume of criticism at the failure of the government to use their services, and the Ministry became apprehensive at the possibility of the formation of private armies.[36] Some people reflected on the nature of the Pétain regime:

> That appreciation has now penetrated the popular mind and the effect of it is to bring to the front those doubts about our own leadership which have been finding expression in criticisms of Government action. There is no escaping the tenor of our reports: leadership is in jeopardy.[37]

This was indeed an ominous statement. But an enduring characteristic of the public during the war was the attribution of weakness and irresolution to the government whenever co-operation was requested rather than ordered. In these anxious months, when the natural desire of the individual was to contribute to the war effort in a tangible way, the evident failure to order total conscription led to frequent reports of intemperate criticism. The Ministry, although incapable of abandoning vague exhortation, insisted 'that what the public wanted were not words of comfort but of command'.[38] 'The difficulty was', Sir Kenneth Clark observed, 'to think up enough

70

technical instructions.'[39] The suggestions of the Home Morale Emergency Committee, such as the collection of waste paper and the inculcation of neighbourliness, were unlikely to satisfy many people; and the slogan 'It all depends on ME', first suggested in the committee's report of 4 June was certain to foster a sense of frustration in those individuals who believed they were doing little to aid the national cause (see accompanying illustration).

A draft Cabinet memorandum, to accompany Duff Cooper's presentation of the morale committee's June report, uttered a stern warning:

> I would emphasise that the authors of the report are not questioning the energy or efficiency of the Government, but merely pointing out that the Government must not only possess these qualities but must also be popularly believed to possess them . . . the public is tired of being left to find for itself ways of helping in the war effort. People want to be ordered about, to have sacrifices imposed on them, to be provided with occupations obviously related to national defence . . . unless the demand for compulsion is met, the public will feel the Government lacks efficiency and energy . . .
>
> I would ask my colleagues to give this aspect of Home Morale the most serious consideration, and, in deciding on the policy of their Departments, to keep constantly on the watch for ways in which this insistent demand for service and sacrifice may be used. I shall find it difficult to carry out the responsibilities entrusted to me unless I can receive from Departments some schemes by which the universal demand for compulsory service can be satisfied.[40]

Duff Cooper's appeal had disappointing results. A number of meetings were held between the Ministry and other departments in order to draw up a list of practical suggestions but one such meeting, held on 20 June, was typically unsuccessful and underlined the problem women posed to the propagandists. It was suggested that women be employed in an increased number of canteens for the forces and possibly train as reserves for the Home Guard; but, as neither was greeted with enthusiasm in the meeting, the representative from the Ministry of Home Security 'emphasised the desirability of reminding the wives of people engaged in war-work that they could not contribute to the national war effort in any better way than by doing all in their power to make things easy for their men-folk'. It was also suggested that anyone with 'a knowledge of musketry' should give instructions in how to shoot.[41] Considering the desperate shortage of small arms and the attitude of the War Office to arming civilians, this was a less than helpful suggestion. It should be remembered, however, that there was a limit to the number of persons who could be engaged on the construction of tank traps, the installation of glider obstacles, the removal of road signs and the like, nor could the Home Guard more speedily absorb the vast number of volunteers who came forward.

On the day of the French capitulation, when Home Intelligence reported that the public were certain to turn defeatist in the absence of immediate leadership and guidance,[42] it was imperative that the people be given a sense of immediate involvement. But instructions were not forthcoming. The Planning Committee thought it essential that the Minister of Information broadcast in the evening 'if only to tell them that it was too early to say anything'.[43] The Prime Minister himself made the broadcast which, although having a steadying effect, failed to stem the tide of criticism against the government as measured by Home Intelligence.[44] The Planning Committee then suggested that the BBC make the greatest possible use of folk tunes and national music and the press be persuaded to emphasise the theme of what Britain means to its citizens.[45] Thus the demand for words of command and clear instructions, noted by the Ministry since the middle of May, was not met at this the most critical day of the war to date. Like the teacher momentarily caught out by a difficult question, Duff Cooper in one of his circulars to influential citizens called for an end to spoon-feeding:

We are continually hearing the demand that people should be told what they have to do, that they are ready enough to do it, but that they are waiting for instructions. Now it is the policy of the Government to give people as full instructions as possible; but at the same time people should be encouraged to think for themselves. All through our history we have been a nation of individualists, full of sturdy independence of mind, acting on our own initiative. We do not want now to become like the Germans or inhabitants of other totalitarian States, who cannot move or think without being told what to do.[46]

If the Ministry was unable to issue sufficient instructions or to persuade other departments of the psychological value of compulsion, it could at least attempt to reassure the public. This it did by the simple expedient of insisting that the invasion would not succeed. How necessary was such an assurance? Although the course of events gave little comfort to the realistic observer, there was reported to be an astounding degree of confidence. At the height of the Dunkirk evacuation the public were said to be 'facing up to the possibility of invasion and many speak of it as certain' but there was nonetheless a strong belief in 'ultimate victory';[47] and, when the prospect of invasion appeared even more certain after the French collapse, people would go only so far as to doubt whether Britain would 'now be able to obtain "absolute victory"'.[48] No doubt many, if not most, people feared invasion and defeat but were constrained to keep such dark musings to themselves, as Harold Nicolson had done in January when he confided to his diary: '. . . at the bottom of our hearts we feel we may be beaten.'[49] Fear of defeat was manifested in a more oblique fashion. People spoke of the 'inevitable Hitler' approaching nearer and nearer and of his almost 'astrological, superhuman successes'.[50] Such talk was common enough for Home Intelligence to recommend its immediate discouragement.[51] As usual, the propagandists were subjected to conflicting advice. A member of the Commercial Relations Division suggested that people should be told:

> This is not the battle of England alone but the battle of civilisation. It does not matter even if, at the worst, Britain herself is crushed. The empire is still there and it will go on arming and fighting until Germany is finally crushed.[52]

This suggestion was wisely declined. For all the reported toughness and determination of the British people, such a theme might have imposed too severe a demand on their capacity for self-sacrifice and, moreover, might have strengthened the current belief of many that the government intended evacuating itself to Canada. The Home Morale Emergency Committee put forward the obvious line: 'In the event of a threat of invasion, steps must be taken to rouse a sense of resistance and to convince the public that a German invasion could be only locally and momentarily successful.'[53]

The collapse of the French armies, especially after their big propaganda build-up, had serious potential implications for British confidence and morale. Even before Dunkirk, Home Intelligence reported a 'great increase and sometimes intense violence of criticism against the French' who were fast becoming scapegoats and for whom there had never been a 'nation-wide feeling of affection and brotherliness'.[54]

73

Nor did the commanders of the BEF wish to hide their feelings. On 27 May, General Mason MacFarlane told Nicolson that the French 'had shown no fighting spirit at all' and he wanted to save the reputation of the British army by putting the blame 'partly upon the Belgians and French and partly upon our politicians'.[55] Any such pronouncement was, of course, out of the question. Instead, the Ministry tried urgently to resuscitate the reputation of the French, although it is questionable whether as late as 4 June a campaign to 'restore confidence in the strength and efficiency of the French armies'[56] was likely to carry much conviction. When Pétain sued for peace, Home Intelligence noted, 'Many people express relief (of a quite unrealistic kind) that at last "There are no more Allies." '[57] Realistic or not, the people were at one with their King, who wrote to his mother, 'Personally, I feel happier now that we have no allies to be polite to & pamper.'[58] In a curious way the French disaster appears to have had no lowering effect upon British morale. Thereafter, the public were said to exhibit an ambivalent attitude towards their former allies: hostility to French servicemen in their midst and yet deep admiration for General de Gaulle, hatred of the Vichy government for betraying the French nation jostling with contempt for the French people. The immediate problem, though, was how to counter the feeling 'If France, why not Britain?'

Many hasty lessons were drawn from the French experience but none more starkly reflected the semi-panic of British officials than what Nicolson described as 'the ill-planned and quite heartless internment of all aliens'.[59] This was a blanket measure aimed at rounding up spies, saboteurs and supporters of the enemy, whose colleagues in France and other occupied countries were presumed to have made Hitler's conquests all the easier. If nothing else, the internment of aliens encouraged the public to believe the country was infested with German agents. Home Intelligence commented on 5 June 'that Fifth Column hysteria is reaching dangerous proportions'.[60] The Ministry itself was not immune from this hysteria. On 23 May, for example, concern was expressed in the Policy Committee at the 'considerable alien element in Broadcasting House' and Ogilvie, the Director General of the BBC, undertook to see MI5 about a review of the staff.[61] In July it was suggested that publicity should be devoted to the fate of quislings and to the shooting of spies in Britain, the latter being recommended as having 'an excellent effect on morale'.[62]

In an issue of 'Speakers' Notes', the fifth column was said to have 'enormously helped' the Germans in their conquests on the continent.

In France, for instance, 'the fifth column worked in high places. It got hold of some important people and through them spread that spirit of defeatism which prepared the way for the Bordeaux government and the shameful armistice.' In the light of the reported fear of some people that the British government would 'sell the pass' to Hitler as the French leaders were thought to have done, this was at the very least an unwise thing to say. The fifth column was supposed not only to 'stealthily gnaw away the fibre of resistance' and engage in acts of sabotage but actually to join with the invading armies in the battle. As for their presence in Britain, the pamphlet warned :

> There is a fifth column in Britain. Anyone who thinks that there isn't, that it 'can't happen here', has simply fallen into the trap laid by the fifth column itself. For *the first job of the fifth column is to make people think that it does not exist.* In other countries the most respectable and neighbourly citizens turned out to be fifth columnists when the time came. The fifth column does not only consist of foreigners . . .
>
> *The Government is doing its duty and is dealing vigorously with the fifth column.* It has rounded up a great many dangerous and suspect characters and it is keeping a constant look-out. *It is not difficult to deal with such people if action is taken in good time and in good order. But it can't be done unless you help. It is up to you to do your duty too.*[63]

Exactly how the citizen should do his duty was not made clear but certainly there was for a while a wave of informing which, together with prosecutions for spreading 'alarm and despondency', produced an atmosphere of suspicion unconducive to national unity. In a sense the fifth column scare was not surprising. The conviction, shared and fostered by the Ministry, that the collapse of so many European nations was due in large measure to a fifth column shielded the believer from the unpalatable fact that the Germans had won because of superior tactics and greater strength. It was now the turn of the victors of 1918 to promulgate a 'stab in the back' theory. And it was but a short extension of this conviction to the comforting belief that if Britain could rid herself of fifth columnists the expected invasion could not hope to succeed.

Insofar as it accorded with the widely reported faith of the public in Britain's defences, the Ministry's dogmatic assertion that the Germans would be thrown back served to buttress an already firm morale. Statements such as the following were placed in newspapers :

This Empire fights on to final victory. We, in this island, working, planning and fighting as one, can never be defeated. Remember, the strongest armed force that can be brought against us can be outnumbered, outfought and utterly destroyed upon our soil. Meantime, there grows behind us, stronger and stronger with every hour, a mightier armament than the world has ever seen. From our Dominions, from America, no less than from our own factories, will flow – are flowing – tanks, guns, aircraft and equipment for the offensive yet to come. Our food, our trade, our credits, are secure. But upon the enemy, who in his turn, must face our attack, the strain of war will take increasing toll. Be of good courage. Work, fight, and we shall win.[64]

This faith was not universal. Early in June the morale committee stated that the 'success of the German armoured divisions and the stories which are being circulated as to our lack of equipment and aircraft should be countered by a campaign reminding people of our resources and mounting production'.[65] The fact was, however, that despite the prodigious armaments drive then under way, it was far from certain whether Britain possessed enough arms to repel a successfully landed German force. But the propagandists can hardly be blamed for putting out information to the contrary, since only a government bent on surrender would have admitted the dearth of arms at that time. Churchill, too, had to exhibit more confidence than was warranted by the circumstances. In a letter to the higher officers of the service and civil departments early in July he insisted :

> . . . there are no grounds for supposing that more German troops can be landed in this country, either from the air or across the sea, than can be destroyed or captured by the strong forces at present under arms. The RAF is in excellent order and at the highest strength it has yet attained. The German Navy was never so weak, nor the British Army at home so strong as· now.[66]

Between 14 and 26 June the Ministry undertook the following programme :

Reassurance
1. The Minister's letter has been issued to 55,000 people;
2. A poster design bearing a photograph of battleships with the slogan 'Mightier Yet', followed by concrete details of the strength of the Navy, has been chosen to succeed the 'Go To It' posters . . .

3. A campaign to remind the people of the resources of the Empire is being planned . . .

4. Pamphlets are in hand on the following subjects:—

The Difficulties of Invasion.

The Work of the RAF in Germany.

'Where Napoleon failed' . . .

5. A special number of 'Illustrated' devoted to Britain's naval power and achievements will appear the week after next;

6. Various steps are in hand to urge on the War Office the importance of providing plenty of bands and marching Troops . . . the BBC has included frequent simple and direct programmes of English, Scottish, Welsh, Irish and Gaelic music, songs, fiddling and piping.[67]

For all the Ministry's exertions, there ran through the internal discussions a note of desperation. A Planning Committee paper of 17 June stated: 'For want of something better we shall have to plug (1) the Navy, (2) the Empire's strength and (3) what a hell of a fine race to build up both.'[68] In his letter to influential people, Duff Cooper showed that the propaganda cupboard was nearly bare:

Moreover it is a great advantage to have our men fighting on their own soil for their own homes. There will for the present be no more Expeditionary Forces with all the anxiety that separation entails. Our loved ones will be near us and we shall have daily news of them. So fighting side by side for the fields and villages and cities that we love we shall have greater confidence, knowing that our cause is just, that the life of our country is at stake and that we shall never surrender.[69]

Specific reassurances, to judge from the tenor of intelligence reports, ceased to be necessary by the middle of July, although it was not known, of course, that on 16 July Hitler ordered invasion preparations to commence. From mid-July onwards reports showed people passing from acceptance of the possibility of invasion[70] through to a tendency to doubt its imminence[71] and then, with the exception of people living near the eastern coast, to a stage late in August when expectation of invasion seemed to have almost entirely receded.[72] There was, however, said to have been a sense of relief with the passing of 15 August – the date which Hitler was popularly supposed to have chosen for his arrival in Britain.[73] The Ministry then proceeded to worry about 'complacency', but in response to intelligence reports abandoned the policy of immediate reassurance and set about devising a long-term programme of sustaining morale.

The designation by the Home Morale Emergency Committee of confusion as one of the disintegrators of public confidence mirrored the government's preoccupation with the supposed destructive power of rumour. Action taken to counter rumour culminated in the Silent Column campaign of July, which not only failed in its object but almost certainly did more harm to morale than the rumours it attempted to suppress.

Rumour was automatically assumed by Home Intelligence to be a bad thing and the daily reports, from their inception in May 1940, were replete with 'dangerous' examples. Princesses Elizabeth and Margaret Rose were said to have fled to Canada, parachutists were landing in specified areas,[74] General Gamelin had shot himself,[75] and the Duke of Windsor was to be the puppet ruler of a Nazi administration.[76] These and numerous other stories dwelt chiefly on the power of the Germans, the cowardly and semi-traitorous actions of highly placed people, gross inefficiency on the part of the government and the weakness of British arms. The reaction of the Ministry was one of alarm. 'Dangerous rumours not to be ignored', enjoined the morale committee.[77] An Anti-Lies Bureau was set up in order to counter rumours and to bring their existence to the attention of the rest of the Ministry. On 17 June, Charles Wilson of the Bureau minuted:

In view of the extremely widespread distribution of rumours that the British Government is preparing to leave for Canada, I consider that some positive counter-statement is urgently desirable.

These rumours take many different forms. Some suggest the Government is contemplating flying to Canada as soon as invasion starts, while others . . . suggest that a shadow cabinet is already being formed the other side of the Atlantic. Further rumours about the imminent departure of the Royal Family and reports that the Royal Princesses have already left help to strengthen these ideas.[78]

A fortnight later the War Cabinet expressed concern at these same rumours and thought it of the first importance to scotch them.[79]

Curiously little attempt was made to investigate the causes of the rumours. In a special report of 24 May, Home Intelligence made in passing a significant observation: 'Rumour during the last few days has tended to emphasise some aspects of our own feebleness and futility . . . This kind of rumour is clearly unhealthy for it is an

78

unconscious reflection of privately held opinion.[80] If rumour is private opinion made manifest then it has deeper roots, especially in a time of crisis, than a mere delight in passing on something akin to salacious gossip. It has been suggested that rumour has part of its origin during a crisis in a demand for more news than can be supplied.[81] That this may have been the case in 1940 was implicitly acknowledged by the Ministry when it tried to persuade the government to release fuller air-raid news because of the encouragement given to fantastic rumours by the absence of sufficient news. In the months between May and September, filled as they were with one sensational and worrying event after another, the public's thirst for news was naturally great, but due to government policy this thirst often went unslaked and people were obliged to improvise their own news.

Suspicion and scepticism developed quickly, especially after the public's loss of faith in the news during the phoney war, and even as late as August 1940 Home Intelligence warned, 'Every day provides us with further evidence of people's doubts about news.'[82] The loss of the *Lancastria* in July, for example, was not announced until many days afterwards and, as the sinking 'was generally known in certain districts and the news had been heard in the German wireless programme', criticism and suspicion were engendered.[83] On 6 August the Scottish town of Penicuik was bombed. The news spread rapidly but the morning news bulletin stated that no air attack had been delivered on the country the previous night.[84] Equally disliked were the euphemisms employed to disguise British reverses. Thus the withdrawal from Somaliland in August provoked the comment, 'We should have recognised the danger signals: first, silence, then inadequate news, then hints that the place wasn't worth defending, then the successful strategic withdrawal.'[85] The Ministry certainly appreciated the situation and did what it could. Harold Nicolson met the leader writers of the press on 27 May:

> I tell them about morale but they are not really interested and when questions come they get back on their hobby horse of censorship and complain bitterly that they are not told any news. I cannot exactly rule such questions out of order since I cannot pretend the absence of news is not having a bad effect on morale.[86]

Such 'confusion' as there was, therefore, was not attributable to rumour. According to Tom Harrisson, 'the most favourable condition for the origin and spread of rumour is undoubtedly dread without knowledge'.[87] Rumour was a palliative used by a public frustrated by official news policy.

The extent to which a rumour is widespread is a measure of the consensus given to it as explaining an otherwise chaotic situation. The rumour of General Gamelin's suicide served to explain in some measure the poor showing of the French armies and, by implication, the desperate position of the BEF. No amount of refutation could have scotched the story concerning the flight of the government and the royal family to Canada because those who believed it were expressing their numerous fears and perhaps preparing themselves for the worst. In some instances during this period certain rumours did correspond to the truth. Churchill was said on 22 May to have gone to Paris in order to stiffen the weakening resolve of the French government.[88] Some days later it was rumoured that the RAF were to be withdrawn from France for home defence purposes,[89] and following the return of the BEF from Dunkirk the soldiers were said to be extremely bitter about the RAF's lack of support and the poor showing of the French.[90] Many such rumours were intelligent deductions from the available scanty facts. Home Intelligence recognised the futility, if not the possible danger, of attempting to smother rumour:

> The rumour situation is becoming so serious that it becomes imperative for the whole matter to be discussed in detail. It is useless to warn people against *repeating rumours*; most people only repeat what they believe to be true and they repeat it because they have nothing more positive to talk about . . . evidence before us at the moment suggests that most rumours are passed on by idle, frightened, suspicious people.[91]

If rumour was to be killed, then the only way of doing so was to prevent people becoming idle, frightened and suspicious. The Ministry of Information could not hope to achieve this. The 'distribution of facts and the interpretation of facts'[92] by the authorities might alleviate the condition but only a change in Britain's fortunes, leading to greater confidence, could effectively abolish rumour. Attempting to suppress it was tantamount to treating the consumptive with cough medicine.

One of the legends to have emerged from the war is the omniscience of Lord Haw Haw. 'Lord Haw Haw', reported Home Intelligence somewhat nervously on 5 June, 'is alleged to have stated that the Darlington Town Hall clock is 2 minutes slow, which in fact it is.'[93] By the spring and summer of 1940, listening to Haw Haw had declined considerably but two other German stations, the New British Broadcasting Station and the Workers' Challenge Station, became the subject of discussion in the Ministry. The Home Morale Emergency Committee advised that 'occasion should be taken to discredit the Hamburg broadcasts and the New British Broadcasting Corporation. In particular an early and renewed effort should be made to dispel the legend of Lord Haw Haw's omniscience.'[94] Charles Wilson wanted the stations jammed.[95] In July the Ministry put out a press warning:

> What do I do . . . if I come across German or Italian broadcasts when tuning my wireless? I say to myself: 'Now this blighter wants me to listen to him. Am I going to do what he wants? . . . I remember nobody can trust a word Haw-Haw says, so just to make them waste their time, I switch 'em off and tune 'em out.'[96]

But statements attributed to Haw Haw relating to the minutiae of British life were the product of rumour. 'In fact, no rumours', it was reported at the Planning Committee, 'could be traced to the NBBS except for those which had been taken up after they had become widespread.'[97] The relationship between rumour and German broadcasts was investigated and the conclusion reached 'that no case has yet been discovered in which Haw Haw or any German wireless made predictions regarding a specific place or announced any detailed facts which . . . could not have been obtained through an explicable channel'.[98] Again, rumour was giving expression to fear, in this case a fear of spies and fifth columnists. Or, as Mass-Observation put it, 'unconsciously people project on to him the phantasy rumours which are produced from fear or despair to explain the facts or expectations of the moment'.[99] The Ministry resisted suggestions that German broadcasts should be jammed on the grounds that such action would draw too much attention to them.[100]

On 5 July, Churchill told the Ministry of Information 'that a wide campaign should be immediately put in hand against the dangers of rumour'.[101] Thus was born the ill conceived and ill fated Silent Column campaign. The Ministry had in fact been discouraging rumours for some time past. A Mrs Watson, for example, of 145 Empire Court, Wembley, had been reported as saying that officers at Dunkirk had fought to be evacuated before their men. The Ministry informed Scotland Yard and 'asked them to send an officer to reprimand and warn Mrs Watson'. However, Harold Nicolson doubted the efficacy of the suggested campaign[102] and Home Intelligence advised against it.[103] But a direct order from the Prime Minister could not be ignored. Sir Kenneth Clark was put in charge of the campaign and, having accepted the advice of an advertising agency as to the aptness of the term 'Silent Column', he made preparations for a large poster, radio and press campaign to begin on 11 July.[104] Despite his hope that it would make people feel that 'they were making a positive contribution to the defence of the country',[105] the campaign's very nature ensured that the public would not take kindly to it.

With a lumbering jocularity, advertisements like the following appeared in the press:

MR SECRECY HUSH-HUSH: He's always got exclusive news, very private, very confidential. He doesn't want to spread it abroad but he doesn't mind whispering it to you.

MISS LEAKY MOUTH: She simply cannot stop talking and since the weather went out as conversation she goes on like a leaky tap about the war. She doesn't know anything but her chatter can do harm. Tell her to talk about the neighbours.

MR PRIDE IN PROPHECY: Here is the marvellous fellow who knows how it is all going to turn out. Nobody but he does. He's a fool and a mountebank.

MR KNOW ALL: He knows what the Germans are going to do and when they are going to do it. He knows where our ships are and what Bomber Command is going to do. With his large talk he is playing the enemy's game.

MISS TEACUP WHISPER: She is a relative of Mr Secrecy Hush-Hush and an equal danger.

MR GLUMPOT: He is the gloom brother who is convinced everything is going wrong and nothing can go right. He is so worried by the enemy's strength that he never thinks of ours. Tell him to cheer up and shut up.

TELL THESE PEOPLE TO JOIN BRITAIN'S SILENT COLUMN!

The sting came in the tail of the advertisement: 'If you know anybody who makes a habit of causing worry and anxiety by passing on rumour and who says things persistently that might help the enemy – tell the police, but only as a last resort.'

The earlier anti-gossip campaign, 'Careless Talk Costs Lives', was aimed at preventing the exchange of information of possible

value to the enemy rather than preventing the spreading of supposedly depressing stories. The campaign, with clever posters
such as 'Keep it under your hat!' avoided browbeating the public.
As part of the same campaign, Fougasse's brilliant posters were,
according to the artist, designed to exploit humour as a 'corrective'
device[106] and their very lightness of touch and aesthetic sophistication
concealed the campaign's tendency to reinforce the prevailing belief
that spies and fifth columnists were everywhere. The Silent Column,
on the other hand, created the impression that the authorities regarded almost any exchange of information or opinion on the war as
unpatriotic and dangerous.

At the same time the government instituted prosecutions against
individuals for spreading 'alarm and despondency'. The public resented the well publicised spate of prosecutions for what was regarded
as grumbling 'in the British tradition'[107] and with equal speed Home
Intelligence conveyed the public's disquiet to the attention of the
Ministry:

> Most serious cause [*sic*] are the prosecutions for defeatist talk and
> for spreading rumours. There is alarm at the coincidence of
> measures which appear to be aimed at the freedom of the civilian.
> The civilian is beginning to feel, and has been encouraged to feel,
> that he is in the front line: at the same time attempts are appar-
> ently being made to undermine his status.[108]

Although the Ministry appears not to have deliberately inaugurated
the Silent Column to coincide with the prosecutions, people could
not be blamed for assuming they were complementary parts of
government policy.

The campaign, as well as producing 'increasing suspicion and
unneighbourliness',[109] was considered 'sinister' when linked in the
public mind with prosecutions.[110] It was decided that in order to
correct the repressive atmosphere caused by the campaign people
should be told that they were allowed to grumble, but there was
no thought of abandoning the campaign[111] and Harold Nicolson
became very concerned:

> There is no doubt that our anti-rumour campaign has been a
> ghastly failure. Altogether the M. of I. is in disgrace again. Partly
> owing to the Press having misunderstood something that Duff
> said suggesting that censorship might become compulsory. Partly
> because Duff is unpopular for having sent John Julius [his son]

83

to America. Partly because our silence campaign and the prosecutions for gossip which have taken place in the country have caused justifiable irritation. And partly because the country is in a bad state of nerves during this lull before the storm.[112]

The Minister endeavoured to soften the harsher edges of the campaign by insisting that he had 'no wish to stop people talking, nor expressing their opinions upon any subject'.[113] On the day that both the Policy and Planning committees were discussing the Silent Column and wondering how it might be kept going without doing further damage, the Prime Minister – without acknowledging his inspiration of the whole thing – announced its abandonment to the House of Commons.[114] And early in August the Ministry, believing that the Director of Public Prosecutions had 'not exercised due discretion' and that magistrates had given excessive sentences for defeatist talk, decided to advise the Home Office to prosecute only in the most serious cases.[115] The prosecutions ceased shortly afterwards.

The effect of the campiagn gave proof enough, if proof were needed, of the foolhardiness of attempting to suppress rumour. Had the government and, to a lesser extent, the Ministry of Information possessed more faith in the public the campaign would not have been mounted. Rumour and gossip would continue to be regarded as undesirable, indeed as morally reprehensible, but in future they would be allowed to go unchecked, save for counter-publicity in particular cases.

Even more distressing than the Silent Column was the Cooper's Snoopers affair. On 25 July, Ritchie Calder, writing in the *Daily Herald*, revealed the existence of a Ministry-sponsored survey team and attacked it on the grounds that the members of the survey were prying around, asking a lot of silly questions about morale and upsetting the public.[116] On the following day the editor of the *Daily Herald*, Percy Cudlipp, wrote a feature on 'Cooper's Snoopers' and delivered a general broadside on the Ministry for its past and present mistakes.[117] Other newspapers, including those of the Beaverbrook press, joined in the attack so vociferously that it seemed to Harold Nicolson that the press were determined to force the Minister's resignation.[118] The Commons took a lead from the newspapers and Duff Cooper was catapulted into a full-scale debate on the Wartime Social Survey. The fuss had been anticipated. 'It must be expected that some M.P. will ask questions and charge us with "snooping",' wrote the Deputy Secretary to the Director General two months

84

earlier.[119] This premonition added to the urgency with which the Ministry sought to ensure, first, that the department could not be accused of needlessly prying into people's lives and, secondly, that the techniques employed were beyond criticism. The planning of the Survey was largely undertaken by Arnold Plant, Professor of Commerce in the University of London. Through the agency of the London School of Economics, the Survey was placed under the auspices of the National Institute of Economic and Social Research, which was prepared to vouch for the integrity of the Survey's aims and techniques. A committee independent of the Ministry was appointed in April 1940 to 'assess the value of the evidence provided by Home Intelligence machinery'[120] of which the Survey was formally part. The Committee included Dr Edward Glover, Julian Huxley, Richard Crossman, Tom Hopkinson, Lord Horder and Tom Harrisson. In order to ensure the anonymity of persons interviewed the Survey was housed away from Senate House, the names and addresses of respondents were immediately detached from the questionnaires when received at Survey headquarters, the replies tabulated and interpreted, and only the final report issued to the Ministry of Information. It is difficult to imagine what more could have been done as an earnest of the Ministry's pure intentions.[121]

On 31 July, the Minister, answering hostile questions in the House, pointed out that the Survey had been set up for perfectly valid reasons and that the anonymity of those interviewed was guaranteed by the destruction of all names and addresses.[122] In an adjournment debate on 1 August, Sir Archibald Southby resumed the attack and gave voice to a number of fears and prejudices held by the press and a minority of his fellow MPs: government surveys of public opinion were not only an invasion of privacy but were unnecessary when the government could call on MPs and the press for information. The public's morale was sound and investigation would only result in lowering it.[123] Duff Cooper could do little but repeat what he had said the day before, adding that the work of the Survey had improved the lot of the people and that the controversy was nothing more than a press 'stunt'.[124] It was a vigorous defence of himself and the Survey and a delighted Harold Nicolson entered in his diary: 'We all go round to Pratt's Club and celebrate what we regard as a triumph.'[125]

But the press continued the campaign under the impetus, according to Nicolson, of Beaverbrook, whom he believed to have been brought into the Cabinet 'as a reward for his campaign against

Duff Cooper. It looks as if eventually he would take on the Ministry of Information.'[126] On the following day he commented, 'The newspapers abate their attack, probably under the instructions of Beaverbrook. The power exercised by that man fills me with alarm. He may well be our Laval.'[127] Nicolson was being unfair. It was attributing too much to Beaverbrook to say that he was the moving spirit behind the press campaign. After all, it was the *Daily Herald* which initiated the attack. There is little doubt, however, that the fuss owed its origins solely to the press.[128] Home Intelligence stated that 'the whole controversy has been well above the head of the man in the street. Reports show that a majority of those who had any opinions about the "snoopers" were in favour of them.'[129] Some eighteen months later the Select Committee on National Expenditure reported 'that the case against the Survey's work was much exaggerated. They find that there was, or is, little objection on the part of the public to being interviewed in this way.'[130] In fact the percentage of interview refusals was usually at or below 0·4 per cent.

The blame for the disruptive affair must be shared by the ministers and the higher officials who ignored the advice of Home Intelligence that the existence of the Survey should not be kept secret. Mary Adams, writing a heartfelt letter to the London RIO, complained:

> I would like you to know that I have pleaded with successive Ministers here for the publication of a frank statement of what we are doing and intend to do; but they have been unresponsive. I agree with you that the press should have been taken into our confidence long ago . . . Only ten days ago I begged the Minister, in answering Acland's question in the House, to say that our methods were not secret and to give a brief résumé of our machinery. But deaf ears were turned . . . We have been having a horrid time.[131]

Notwithstanding Duff Cooper's vindication of the Survey, some thought was given to curtailing and perhaps to abolishing the unit, for August saw a cascade of memoranda seeking to justify the activities of the Survey and of the Home Intelligence Division itself. One paper commented, 'It is necessary to emphasise that the work of Home Intelligence cannot be carried on without the support of responsible objective field work . . . without it there would be no statistical check on the generalisations which are made about "public opinion" as a whole.'[132] Another paper attributed impressive success to Home Intelligence in keeping spirits high and grumbles low on the home front:

YOUR COURAGE
YOUR CHEERFULNESS
YOUR RESOLUTION
WILL BRING
US VICTORY

1. Intended as 'a rallying war-cry that will . . . put us in an offensive mood at once', this poster drew the following comment from *The Times*: 'The insipid and patronising invocations to which the passer-by is now being treated have a power of exasperation which is all their own.'

It all depends on ....

2a. Posters featuring injunctions and affirmations such as 'It all depends on me', 'We're going to see it through', and 'Freedom is in Peril' were displayed on 24,000 railway sites and in 27,000 telephone booths and in scores of thousands of pubs, shops, factories, service establishments, public libraries, buses and trains.

2b/c. Fougasse's brilliant 'Careless Talk Costs Lives' series, and the clever 'Keep it under your hat!' posters (next pages), concealed by their very lightness of touch the campaign's tendency to reinforce the belief that spies and Fifth Columnists were everywhere.

Do you know one of these?

Mr Secrecy Hush Hush

He's always got exclusive information — very private, very confidential. He doesn't want to spread it abroad but he doesn't mind whispering it to you — and others he meets. Tell him to keep it to himself.

Mr Knowall

He knows what the Germans are going to do and when they are going to do it. He knows where our ships are. He knows what the Bomber Command is up to. With his large talk he is playing the enemy's game. Tell him so.

Miss Leaky Mouth

She simply can't stop talking and since the weather went out as conversation she goes on like a leaky tap about the war. She doesn't know anything, but her chatter can do harm. Tell her to talk about neighbours.

Miss Teacup Whisper

She is a relative of Mr. Secrecy Hush Hush and an equal danger. Everything she knows is so important that it must be spoken in whispers and she whispers all over the town. She's one of Hitler's allies. If she does not know that, tell her (in a whisper).

Mr Pride in Prophecy

Here is the marvellous fellow who knows how it is all going to turn out. Nobody else knows but he does. He's a fool and a mountebank. Give him a look that tells him what you think of him.

Mr Glumpot

He is the gloomy brother who is convinced that everything is going wrong and nothing can go right. He is so worried by the enemy's strength that he never thinks of ours. Tell him to cheer up and shut up.

Tell these people to
JOIN BRITAIN'S SILENT COLUMN

the great body of sensible men and women who have pledged themselves not to talk rumour and gossip and to stop others doing it.

THIS ANNOUNCEMENT IS ISSUED BY THE MINISTRY OF INFORMATION IN THE INTERESTS OF NATIONAL SAFETY

3. On July 5, 1940 Churchill told the Ministry of Information 'that a wide campaign should be immediately put in hand against the dangers of rumour'. But the Silent Column campaign created the impression that the authorities regarded almost any exchange of information or opinion on the war as unpatriotic and dangerous.

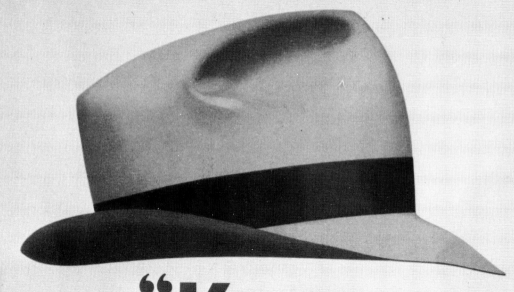

"Keep it under your hat!"

CARELESS TALK COSTS LIVES

PRINTED FOR H.M STATIONERY OFFICE BY S! MICHAEL'S PRESS LT? LONDON. 51-187

"Keep it under your hat!"

CARELESS TALK COSTS LIVES

...TED FOR H.M STATIONERY OFFICE BY ST MICHAEL'S PRESS LT? LONDON. 51–187.

6.   Ernest Bevin used to complain that the Ministry had no one on its staff who could express the working-class mind, although he himself was used in this poster.

7. 'Mightier Yet' fell completely flat as propaganda; and its very bombast must have raised many a hollow laugh from shelterers in the tube stations during the blitz.

8. The only politician whose speeches were more popular than J. B. Priestley's broadcasts was Churchill. The Ministry of Information was quick to exploit this in simple yet effective posters like 'Let us go forward together'.

Subjects of this kind which we have been able to influence are the need for more news of air raid casualties; the laying down of a consistent siren policy; definite statements about evacuation from coastal areas; the treatment of aliens and refugees; the anxieties of parents with children evacuated . . . hardships of allowances for soldiers' wives and dependents . . .

We have also pressed for official statements when we have found confusion and anxiety over official orders and plans. This was the case with overseas evacuation; the free and cheap milk scheme; the tracing of missing men in France and Flanders . . .

We have been able to enlist the attention and sympathy of the War Office in regard to cases of men home on convalescent leave without ration money, causing hardship to their wives when there is little money in the family . . .

The Minister of Labour, at our request, took up complaints at the behaviour of officials in certain Exchanges . . .

Hearing of Group troubles – such as the hunger for Indian news among the Indian community; the isolation of the coloured Colonials in London . . . and that several thousand soldiers in the White City needed entertainment and consideration – we have been able to set in motion ways and means of satisfying these needs.

We act as a Clearing House for news of people's own ideas and efforts to help themselves and the Community . . .

The Government is often accused to being too Olympian, 'Whitehall has no contact with the people' is a common accusation. At such a time when the solidarity and resistance – mental, moral and physical – of the whole people is of vital importance . . . it is very wrong if grievances and hardships should be allowed to fester and go unnoticed. We have built up a system whereby we hope to hear all of them; after which we strive to put them right.[133]

But there remained one official whose heart was untouched by such appeals. H. V. Rhodes proposed that the whole division be transferred to the Ministry of Home Security.[134] It is likely, too, that Frank Pick, the new Director General who had come over from the London Passenger Transport Board to succeed Sir Kenneth Lee in August, shared Rhodes's wish to be quit of the division. Certainly he saw it as his mission to regenerate the Ministry[135] and part of the process involved a decision about the retention of the Wartime Social Survey.[136] The survey was retained but Pick ruled that in future it should undertake work only at the specific request of other departments, thus bringing to an end its excursions into civilian morale.

He also severed the connection between the Survey and the National Institute of Economic and Social Research and with a final flourish reduced the Survey's staff by half.[137]

In view of the Ministry's past record as an advocate of press freedom and its recognition of the relationship between news and morale, there was a curious interlude in 1940 when the institution of compulsory censorship was considered by the Ministry and the War Cabinet. At a meeting of the Policy Committee on 31 May Sir Walter Monckton asked whether it was not time to abandon the voluntary system. He advanced two reasons : the anxiety of the French for the introduction of 'effective' censorship of the British press and the imminence of heavy bombing in London.[138] Preliminary steps had already been taken. Radcliffe had drawn up a scheme which envisaged compelling the press to publish only official news, forbidding speculation and subjecting comment to compulsory scrutiny. Barrington-Ward, editor of *The Times*, had been consulted and understandably expressed the belief that the scheme would have disastrous consequences. The newspapers, he insisted, would be reduced to the status of government propaganda organs, the public in their millions would be driven to listen to the German radio, and the press would no longer have the power of criticism such as brought to light the shells scandal of 1915.[139] The Policy Committee observed that it would be difficult to recruit an additional 150 censors and to apply the scheme to the 900 provincial newspapers. It was also stated :

> . . . there had been few serious incidents arising from the publication in the Press of material which should have been excluded. There had been breaches of the regulations without any serious effect on security but, where security issues have been raised, the indiscretion was not the fault of the Press.[140]

The Committee accordingly decided to advise the Minister to take the powers which would enable him to apply the scheme only when its introduction was judged to be necessary. Three days later the War Cabinet, disturbed by the publication in the *Evening Standard* of a Commons question dealing with places vulnerable to German bombing, asked Duff Cooper to investigate the steps necessary for the compulsory censorship of all stories relating to military affairs.[141]

With the situation worsening in France, the idea of narrowing the latitude allowed the press was contagious. On 9 June the Chief of the Naval Staff submitted a memorandum to the Prime Minister in which he urged compulsory censorship :

Experience has shown that Press Associations and similar combinations of Pressmen, although willing to help, are unable to check the evils that come with an uncontrolled Press. Mischievousness, commercial competition, political antagonisms, professional jealousies and desire of individuals to secure a 'scoop' all play their part in assisting the enemy and retarding the efforts of the Allies. Pressmen are the first to admit this, and the sensitive ones deplore it, but unassisted by a controlled censorship, appear to be unable to stop it.[142]

In a memorandum of 11 June, Duff Cooper underlined the extent to which effective censorship depended not on Defence Regulation 3 but on the goodwill of the press:

Since the war began there has never been a prosecution of a newspaper under Defence Regulation 3. It has been allowed to become a dead letter. This has happened in spite of several urgent appeals from the Censorship authorities to Service Departments that if what they require of one paper is ignored by that paper or another they should support their security requirements by a prosecution.[143]

The Minister put forward three alternative courses. The institution of compulsory censorship, by which all items touching on military affairs would have to be submitted, he judged, however, to be impracticable on administrative grounds. A system known as 'compulsory sources', the second alternative, would require the press to print only official communiqués on defined subjects, but was open to the objection that it would impose a rigid uniformity upon the whole press. Duff Cooper favoured the third course: the setting up of a Censorship Board which, meeting twice daily, would issue legally binding directions to the press on what might or might not be said on war subjects. Such a system, while involving a strong element of compulsion, had the advantage of obviating the need for submissions to censorship and left the newspapers with a certain degree of editorial freedom. But even this mildest of the three proposals represented a severe incursion into the independence of the press; and by early July, Cooper, agreeing with the newspaper men to whom he had spoken that they 'had behaved very patriotically and that comparatively few mistakes had been made', informed Churchill that the proposal to set up a Censorship Board was to be abandoned in favour of tightening up the Defence Notices and making them compulsory.[144] This was hardly in the nature of a concession, as the press realised, and the Minister finally returned to the voluntary principle, although intending to extend the scope of the Notices and make them 'peremptory in form':

> The Press are very sensitive and must either be humoured or completely squashed. The great argument against the latter method would be the shock it would give to public confidence and also the recent and melancholy example of France. It would also shock the United States where the President has so lately made freedom of information one of his all-important Five Points.[145]

It was agreed in Cabinet that the Defence Notices should be extended in scope, while leaving the voluntary system in being, and that the Minister of Information should take the power to compel the press in event of invasion to publish only official communiqués and censored news agency messages. In view of the reluctance of the defence departments to undertake prosecutions, the Minister was made responsible for deciding whether or not a breach of the regulations should be brought to the notice of the Director of Public Prosecutions.[146]

Neither the Cabinet nor the Ministry relished the prospect of the intense opposition that would have been aroused had compulsion been introduced short of the ultimate emergency of invasion. By the middle of July the 'earnest wish' of the French authorities to see the introduction of compulsory censorship in Britain[147] was, of course, no longer a consideration. There appears to have been no good reason for discarding the voluntary system even in the dark days of June and July 1940 since, as the Policy Committee and the Minister observed, the press had given no sign of threatening national security. The flirtation with the idea is a symptom of the panic that occasionally gripped men in government in mid-1940. In his memoirs Duff Cooper attributed the attacks of the press upon him and his department at the time to the 'mistaken belief' that he intended to tighten up censorship,[148] but his discussion with the press could have left them in little doubt of the seriousness with which the government was contemplating the introduction of compulsory censorship.

At no other time during the war did the Ministry of Information, as distinct from the government, consider the extension of its powers to embrace comment, speculation and the expression of opinion. For example, when the Foreign Office objected to articles which were thought likely to disturb foreign relations, the censors would go no further than append to such submissions 'The censorship of this article is advisory only. It represents the views of the Department of Government concerned as to what is undesirable to publish at the present time.'[149] Similarly, nothing was censored on the grounds that it might feed the German propaganda machine. Which is not to say that some officers of the Ministry were never tempted by the apparent advantages of a repressive policy. Sir Kenneth Clark's experience as a member of the Home Morale Emergency Committee led him to appeal to Monckton in June 1940:

> In making a preliminary survey for the Home Morale campaign, I am more than ever convinced that there is no use in trying to turn public opinion in our direction if the Press is perfectly free to turn it in the other. What is the use of our spending vast quantities of ammunition when we do not attempt to deprive the enemy of his ammunition when it is in our power to do so? In other words I would plead most strongly in the interests of home morale for some extension of censorship, not so much the censorship of news as the censorship of interpretation.[150]

Sir Kenneth's notions on the link between press comment and civilian morale no doubt contributed to the fears which gave rise to the Ministry's drastic proposals of June 1940.

The Ministry of Information might not have indulged in overt censorship of opinion but it did seek to influence the way in which events were reported and interpreted. Indeed, it would have been surprising had the government and the Ministry not attempted to persuade the press to see things their way. 'The Press', observed Monckton to Sir Horace Wilson, 'is like a young horse, to be ridden with good hands and a light curb.'[151] One method of leading the press in the right direction was the issue of confidential guidance letters to editors. These were of two types. It was necessary, first, as the war developed, to revise the Defence Notices from time to time so that new subjects of military importance could be brought to the editors' attention. This was an unexceptionable and important function of confidential letters. And if compulsion was to be avoided it was essential that the press exhibit some degree of willing co-operation in matters such as that which formed the subject of the following letter:

> The Ministry of Home Security asks . . . them [editors] to pay particular attention to the need for depriving the enemy of infor-

mation about the effect of repeated bombing of a particular town. Reports indicating marked disorganisation of Civil Defence, health or local government services, or large scale evacuation, or great disturbance of any aspect of normal life in a town, are a direct invitation to the enemy to renew and continue his attacks. They represent the type of information stated by our own Air Staff to be of the highest value to the RAF in its operations against Germany, and likely to be of similar value to the enemy.

If criticism of the Government is thought necessary, let it be printed by all means, but in such a way as not to connect the grounds of criticisms with a particular place, or a particular raid or series of raids.[152]

But requests to editors to refrain from publishing articles on subjects which did not touch on security or to adopt a certain policy slant were in fact issued. Admiral Thomson insists that they were despatched very rarely.[153] This may have been so, but the evidence suggests that many letters sent out in strictest confidence, purporting to sketch in the background to certain events and developments, amounted to an exercise in subtle moral blackmail. If an editor was told in off-the-record terms of the facts behind a news item, none of which could be censored on security grounds, might he not have been reluctant to publish them even if – as must often have been the case – he had prior knowledge from his own sources?

Another means of influencing the press derived from the agility of the News Division. J. H. Brebner, its director, was very proud of the way in which the Ministry turned to advantage the bombing of Buckingham Palace on 13 September 1940:

The 'blitz' was heralded by a devastating attack on the East End . . . Reports were received of the complaints of the people in this district, that 'it is always the poor that gets it' and the ill-feeling arising from this belief began to cause anxiety. Then – Buckingham Palace was bombed, and the opportunity was presented of counteracting immediately the bad feeling in the East End . . . Arrangements were made for more than 40 journalists . . . to visit the Palace to see the damage. The theme 'King with His People in the front line together' was stressed with the journalists . . . The story was front page news throughout countries outside the Axis orbit. It immediately dissipated the bad feeling in the East End, led to remarkable expressions of affection for the Royal Family and aroused intense indignation throughout America.[154]

Brebner may have inflated his achievement here. True, the Ministry did provide access to places and installations normally closed to the public and in this way assisted the press to write up stories from a fresh viewpoint, but journalists were certainly in no need, and probably resented, suggestions from the News Division as to the approach they should adopt.

A third means of influencing the press, and perhaps the most effective, was touched upon by George Orwell. He maintained that the Ministry of Information achieved the suppression of 'undesirable or premature' news and opinion by participation in a conspiracy of the governing classes which had always succeeded in preventing public discussion of anything thought to be uncongenial.[155] To the extent that men such as Sir Walter Monckton, Harold Nicolson, Sir Kenneth Clark and Duff Cooper moved easily in the upper reaches of society, politics and journalism, Orwell's observation was apposite. A quiet word dropped in the appropriate ear at the appropriate place must often have secured a discreet silence on issues judged to be sensitive, as it had before the war on the subject of King Edward VIII's association with Mrs Simpson. But, although press and government agreed that Hitler must be beaten at all costs, there were within the boundaries of this broad consensus numerous issues of policy which divided them and often aroused a passionate response from both sides. Churchill in particular was always ready to accuse critics, even among the ranks of long-established and respectable press proprietors, of seeking to undermine the war effort by sowing discord and lowering morale.

One of the chief disintegrators of morale as perceived by the Home Morale Emergency Committee was 'class feeling'. Because of an increase in class resentment and the likelihood of its becoming more acute in the event of air raids, the committee stated that the problem was one for the government as a whole and that it could offer only a 'minor' suggestion:

> . . . something might be done to diminish the present predominance of the cultured voice upon the wireless. Every effort should be made to bring working class people to the microphone, and more frequent use should be made of left-wing speakers to counteract the propaganda of our enemies regarding imperialism and capitalism.[156]

The officers of the Ministry were not given to defining the terms used in their discussions on morale, least of all in a committee set up to handle an 'emergency', and so it is difficult to say with any precision just what was meant by 'class resentment'. There is little to go on except the reports of Home Intelligence. The level of generality at which class resentment was considered points not to conclusions reached on the basis of empirical evidence but rather to the unspoken assumption that the working classes might be expected to cause trouble in this critical phase of the war.

The ways in which class feeling were thought to threaten the war effort remained largely unspecified as well, but there is no doubt that the Ministry believed the workers' sense of economic grievance might prevent them from contributing to the defence of the country. On the evidence available to the Ministry, however, there was no reason to suppose that such a grave situation existed. Instead, there was reported to be an unprecedented degree of national unity which cut across social barriers. The obsession with class was not to be found among the working population but among the propagandists themselves.

In the eighty-eight daily reports issued by Home Intelligence between 18 May and 7 September, covering hundreds of opinions on a wide range of issues, there are only twelve occasions on which mention is made of class-based resentment. This is a remarkable small tally when it is considered that the period was one of unremitting tension. The grievances uncovered by Home Intelligence may be divided into three categories: a conviction born of a sense of economic disadvantage that a German victory would harm only the wealthy, an upsurge of disappointment at the shelving of the government-sponsored evacuation of children to North America, and a suspicion that sacrifices were being inequitably shared.

The propagandists took fright at reports, rare though they were, of a defeatist attitude towards Hitler: 'He won't hurt us: it's the bosses he's after: we'll probably be better off when he comes.'[157] Members of Parliament passed on anxious letters from constituents to the Ministry, where they appear to have been taken more seriously than intelligence reports. E. C. Cobb, MP, forwarded one such letter:

I should like to point out the following which appears to me to be quite serious. My Char-woman gives me the views of some of the working-class people around here, many of whom, I know, work in the English Electric Aircraft Factory. A remark which is constantly made is 'Well, at any rate, one good thing about Hitler is – he robs the rich to help the poor.' Would it not be possible to arrange for some speakers who would appeal to the masses, such as a North End footballer or some similar 'hero' to counteract this Nazi propaganda. One cannot help feeling that there is much of this sort of thing in the whole of Lancashire.[158]

Attributed largely to the poorer members of the working class, this attitude was nonetheless held to be present 'among lower middle class women and the small "white collar" men'[159] and even, according to Sir Kenneth Clark, 'latent in a large section of the middle class'.[160] But the Home Morale Emergency Committee proposed to aim countermeasures principally at the workers:

> It is important to make it clear to the public that a German victory would not affect the propertied classes alone, but would bring humiliation and misery to the nation as a whole. The Nazi and Communist propagandists are instilling the idea that only the rich would suffer by defeat and that the working classes in this country would actually benefit by a German triumph . . . a concentrated effort should be made to establish the conviction that our defeat would not merely mean the loss of wealth, power and reputation but would also entail enslavement.[161]

Ivison Macadam wished to accentuate this line by stressing 'to the public the fact that the wealthier people realise that they are up against it with everyone else, and are actually taking their share of the burden'.[162] Sir Kenneth perceived certain pitfalls in this approach:

> I am afraid I think it would be very dangerous for us to support any propaganda on behalf of the wealthier classes. It is true that they have made real sacrifices in this war, but their standard of life is still incomparably higher than that of 75% of the community. If we are caught out putting their case there would be a fearful rumpus, especially as the Press is now banking on the support of the poor: 'Voice of the poor against the governing classes', etc.[163]

Undoubtedly there were numbers of people who attempted to assuage their fear of invasion by assuring themselves that Hitler would harm only the better-off and that life for the working class under a Nazi regime would not be insufferable. Such a monumentally mistaken belief was defeatism of the rankest sort. But there was no evidence to suggest that it existed among more than a tiny minority and the Ministry's proposals for counter-propaganda took on the quality of a man preparing to do battle with phantoms of his own imagining.

A short-lived but significant outburst of discontent concerned the children's evacuation scheme. The transport of children to North America was paid for by the government on a sliding scale, involving a means test. After some initial resistance by parents to the idea of sending their children abroad[164] there was an enthusiastic response and a flood of applications. But on 1 July the Prime Minister expressed concern in Cabinet at the way a large evacuation of this kind 'encouraged a defeatist spirit, which was entirely contrary to the true facts of the position'. Shipping space was limited and it was also pointed out that those public schools considering evacuation should be discouraged from doing so, since 'if facilities were afforded to the well-to-do, but not to others, to remove their children, a difficult situation might arise'.[165] The announcement some days later of the decision to abandon the scheme provoked, according to Home Intelligence, precisely that reaction which the Cabinet had wished to avoid:

> There is a great disappointment at the postponement of the plan for evacuating children . . . the results of a statistical survey showed that the parents of approximately 1,000,000 children were prepared for them to go. The effect of a reversal of policy has provoked sharp recrimination against the rich, whose children were enabled to sail . . . The psychological effect of the scheme and its publicity has been bad.[166]

The significance of the episode lies less in the degree of feeling it aroused, strong though it seems to have been, than in its exceptional quality in this period of the war – exceptional in the sense that the working classes seem to have ignored or not noticed the numerous other benefits to be derived from the possession of wealth.

In war as in peace money bought privilege. Good food 'off the rations' could still be had in restaurants and hotels, although the introduction of works canteens and the highly popular British Restaurants did mean that wholesome food was provided at low prices; comfortable houses were leased or bought in safe areas of the country; and domestic help hired while the lady of the house devoted a few hours to the WVS. Those who could afford none of these things, the vast majority of the population, nevertheless responded to the government's call for a total national effort and believed that equality of sacrifice would be imposed. From some, however, certain rumblings of discontent could be heard:

Although the family income of many industrial communities has increased, it is clear that certain regulations and restrictions strongly affect the working classes; practical difficulties, e.g. long hours, high prices, tea rations, are frequently spoken of in illustration of the inequality of sacrifices demanded.[167]

Such reports were rare and the working population appears on the whole to have been satisfied with the impression of equality created by measures such as food rationing.

In none of these issues was the extent of discontent judged by Home Intelligence to be a major cause of concern. In May it was reported that 'working class people seemed to be on the whole rather more optimistic' than other classes[168] and in the scale of anxiety 'middle and upper middle class women' consistently registered the highest level, while working-class men exhibited the least.[169] 'The whiter the collar', it was framed as a general rule, 'the less the assurance'.[170] This optimistic toughness at the lower end of the social scale was attributed to the fact that working people were less well informed, poorly educated and politically ignorant[171] and were unlikely to be affected by peripheral developments such as the internment of aliens which so distressed the 'intelligentsia'.[172] Whatever the reasons for the alleged optimism of the workers – and it is doubtful they were any less capable of grasping the seriousness of Britain's position than their social betters – their loud calls for leadership and aggression certainly indicated a willingness to suppress any grievances they may have nourished.

Why did the Ministry misread the temper of the public? Why did senior officials continue to think in terms of class when all the signs indicated that the bulk of the population had, if only for a brief time, ceased to do so? The answer is to be found in the distance the propagandists maintained between themselves and their audience. As F. C. Bartlett wrote during the war, 'Only those people can compass what is needed who are in sympathetic understanding with the masses of the people they address, who know or can learn about their common condition of life, their common interests and their common hopes.'[173] Harold Nicolson and Sir Kenneth Clark, who at this time were mainly responsible for formulating propaganda policy, did, however, begin to suspect that their backgrounds might represent a handicap. Of Lord Davidson, a former MP and a close associate of Stanley Baldwin who was appointed as Controller of Production after publicising his bizarre view that the Ministry was 'directed exclusively by Communists . . . determined to plan a success for the extreme left at the next general election',[174] Nicolson wrote: 'I can see that he thinks Kenneth Clark and I are too intellectual to get a real nation wide appeal';[175] and when told that Duff Cooper was thinking of putting Davidson in charge of home front propaganda, Clark agreed 'that publicity of the nature we shall now require needs a bull rather than a china collector and that Davidson is probably the best bounder we can get'.[176] Stronger evidence, perhaps, was Nicolson's reaction when he was taken by Sir Kenneth to dine at the refectory at Senate House: 'It is absolutely foul and offers no solution at all. It is run on the cafeteria system and we have got to queue up with trays with the messenger boys. Nor is there any food which is eatable.'[177]

The food and the conditions under which it was eaten were no worse, and probably a lot better, in Senate House than those enjoyed by the mass of the population. If this was the response of a member of the Ministry to sharing momentarily the lot of his fellow citizens, it might well be concluded that, however much sympathy existed for the people, there could have been little real understanding of their lives and mental attitudes. Criticism along these lines came once more from the Labour Party. Ernest Bevin 'complained that the Ministry had no one on its staff who could express the working-class mind'[178] (although Bevin himself was used in the department's posters such as 'Ernest Bevin says – "We must have Exports" ') while Attlee objected to the BBC retaining its class voice and personnel and 'would like to see a far greater infiltration of working-class speakers'.[179] There was, though, a reluctance to take on men associated with the Labour Party. When, for example, Francis Williams was being considered as Director of Press and Public Relations, A. P. Waterfield minuted, 'He is of course a Socialist, and it would be well to make discreet enquiries before we commit ourselves.'[180] By January 1941 Nicolson, for one, had come round to the view that the Ministry needed a greater infusion of left-wing representation, but he saw difficulties:

> The bother is that the left wing people are either Bloomsbury high-brows (who are no more in touch with the people than we are) or else the Trades Union people who are slow, slow, slow.[181]

For all the preoccupation with class, the Ministry failed to create appropriate propaganda. There had been frequent warnings since the early days of the war against couching domestic propaganda and instructions in stiff and incomprehensible language. What seems to have been required was a simple style, uncomplicated and free of allusion, such as 'Go To It', whose success was attributable not only to the way in which Herbert Morrison's slogan echoed the mood of the public after Dunkirk[182] but also to its simplicity and directness. Its successor, 'Mightier Yet', fell completely flat[183] and its very bombast must have raised many a hollow laugh from shelterers in the tube stations a few months later. The poster fell flat because it was too vaguely reassuring at a time when people yearned for something closely related to their individual efforts and because it demanded recognition of an allusion to 'Land of Hope and Glory'. However widely known the song, the slogan required a literary way of thinking to which most people were unaccustomed.

BBC speakers, often supplied by arrangement with the Ministry of Information, were always under attack. Home Intelligence frequently drew attention to the fact that many poorer people 'find wireless voices too impersonal and language too academic to affect them personally'.[184] Hence the great popularity of J. B. Priestley's broadcasts. Nicolson thought him a 'sly demagogue'[185] who, after hinting in his last broadcast that Tory objections were putting him off the air, retired 'in the guise of a martyr whereas if only he had given five or six more talks would have retired in the guise of a bore'.[186] But it was the contrast of Priestley's unpatronising and simply expressed ideas with other BBC speakers, among whom must be numbered the unnamed ministers whom the Ministry wished to take off the air so poor were their speeches,[187] which accounted for his following. The only person whose speeches were more popular was Churchill, a fact which the Ministry were quick to exploit in the production of simple yet effective posters (see accompanying illustration). Yet his language and the form in which it was cast was far removed from the speech of the ordinary people. However, he so patently declined to talk down to the nation and so clearly avoided self-conscious colloquialisms that the public sensed an honesty of sentiment and delivery and responded to it. Churchill spoke as a leader who possessed a deep faith in the qualities of the led. Priestley spoke as one of them. The Ministry could do neither. Not that the need to avoid talking down to the people went unrecognised. At the end of August, Sir Kenneth Clark advised, 'A certain amount of patting on the back for workers is desirable, if a form can be found free of patronage.'[188]

The men of the Ministry felt more comfortable addressing their own kind, that is to say persons whose background and occupations accustomed them to leadership and to whom Duff Cooper directed his confidential letters. In the first of these, he wrote :

99

This is the first of what I hope will be a series of letters that I shall address to you from time to time. People in positions of responsibility such as you occupy are in constant touch with different types of your fellow citizens and it is but natural that they should look to you for information, comfort and guidance in a time such as this.[189]

It has been suggested that in times of crisis people turn instinctively to 'opinion leaders' in their national and local communities, men who because of their position and the respect accorded to them are able to exercise a calming influence on their fellow citizens[190] J. T. MacCurdy, writing during the war, placed this concept in an English context :

> Obedience to authority because it is all part of a system is bred in the Englishman's bones. In an emergency a fortuitous group of Englishmen look about for the squire or for somebody of the squire's class to be their leader. They do not imagine that he is necessarily more intelligent or more intrepid than anybody else, but somebody must lead and an accepted social system decrees that somebody from the upper classes should do so. This is one of the most important factors in the general orderliness of Englishmen.[191]

But while the propagandists clearly possessed such a belief at the beginning of the war, their reading of the public's temper after May 1940 led them to doubt the permanence of the Englishman's instinctive obedience to authority.

There was throughout the period under discussion an uneasy feeling in the Ministry that unless the government made a firm pledge of post-war social reform the people would not be persuaded to give all their energies to the war effort. Even worse, they might succumb to German promises of a better life. Under both Lord Macmillan and Sir John Reith the Ministry had tried hard to extract a statement of war aims and peace aims (the terms were used interchangeably) from the Chamberlain government. From early June the attempt was revived and intensified and pressed so hard throughout the remainder of 1940 that one cannot escape the conclusion that the intention had become bribery. The motive was not entirely base, for as the year progressed there developed within the department an enthusiasm for discussing the post-war future of Britain; but it remains clear that the worsening war situation brought to the surface a conviction that the public were seething with discontent and could be appeased only by the inducement of substantial material improvement and by what has been called the 'manipulation of expectations'.[192]

On 4 June the Home Morale Emergency Committee suggested:

It is for consideration (but far beyond the scope of the Committee's functions), whether the time has not arrived when a statement of peace principles (both external and internal) should not be made. It should not prove beyond the ingenuity of man to draft some statement analogous to the 'Four Principles' of President Wilson such as would affirm our moral attitude without committing us to any precise programme.[193]

Vague as this was, it is the timing that is of significance. Coming hard on the heels of the evacuation of the BEF, the raising of the subject represented no idle wish to indulge in lofty rhetoric. A fortnight later at a meeting of the Policy Committee the Director General 'raised the question whether opportunity should be taken of an all-Party government to make some promise as to social reforms after the war'. Monckton observed, 'Our aim should be to redress grievances and inequality and create new opportunities.'[194] The presence of Labour ministers in the government undoubtedly emboldened the Ministry. It was shortly after Nicolson had agreed to draft a memorandum on the subject that he took note of Attlee's desire for a definite statement about the future:

The Germans are fighting a revolutionary war for very definite objectives. We are fighting a conservative war and our objects are purely negative. We must put forward a positive and revolutionary aim admitting that the old order has collapsed and asking people to fight for the new order.[195]

Fresh impetus was provided by the likelihood of a peace offer from Hitler. Nicolson feared that people might not be able to resist such an offer and the Policy Committee, observing that the terms of an offer would be 'plausible', asked him and Sir Kenneth Clark to formulate a set of opposing doctrines which were to include the abolition of privilege and equality of opportunity.[196]

Doubtless realising that the unenviable task of bringing it before Churchill would be his, Duff Cooper was moved to comment that the Ministry ought 'not to go too far in the matter of proclaiming a "revolutionary" doctrine'. Sir Kenneth doubted the willingness of Cabinet to make a statement[197] and the responsibility for drafting the document was left to Harold Nicolson. He secured the agreement of the Policy Committee for a manifesto calling for socialism at home and free trade and federalism abroad. Duff Cooper, while admitting to Nicolson 'I am myself more Conservative than you are', agreed to present the memorandum to Cabinet.[198] So convinced had the Ministry become of the necessity to promise socialism that the Policy Committee thought it was not 'possible to meet the forthcoming peace offensive' in the absence of radical government undertakings.[199]

How much support did the available evidence give to the view that the British people demanded something more than national survival? In the four and a half months between 18 May and early September the subject of post-war social reform was mentioned by Home Intelligence on only four occasions. The first was a rather worried observation that the 'young people are not content with "We are fighting for our lives; nothing else matters" ',[200] but thereafter those people said to be concerned with the issue were variously described as 'many in authority',[201] 'certain circles'[202] and 'small intellectual groups'.[203] It was further stated that the 'great bulk of the population are satisfied with the present situation and are prepared to leave this matter until victory is in sight or attained'.[204] In other words, the evidence reaching the Ministry did not point to a widespread demand for social reform as the price of co-operation in the war effort. In this, for the moment at least, the people agreed with the Prime Minister that victory was the exclusive goal of the nation. As for the dreaded peace offer of 19 July, Home Intelligence reported: 'On the whole, people have treated the speech less seriously than the press have done. People laughed and jeered.'[205] Two days later references to Hitler's speech were said to have practically disappeared from public conversation.[206]

The memorandum prepared by Nicolson was discussed by Cabinet on 26 July,[207] that is to say a week after Hitler's peace offer had been made when it should have been obvious even to the Ministry of Information that the public were as contemptuous of Nazi overtures as the government. Hitler, the memorandum suggested, might attempt an invasion which would be defeated or might postpone the attempt indefinitely, but he was certain to make offers based on an arrangement whereby Britain would be permitted to keep her empire in exchange for allowing Germany a free hand in Europe. Such an offer would have a wide appeal:

To those suffering from war weariness and lack of vision it would seeem eminently fair and reasonable. People would ask themselves for what it was that they were fighting. They surely could not be expected to continue a world war for the sake of Poland. Still less could they be asked to sacrifice themselves for the small neutral countries . . . As for France . . . few English people would be found willing to make sacrifices on her behalf.

How could these people be convinced that they should fight on? For the internationally-minded the government would promise to work for a united federal Europe, organised on the lines of the American Union, in which armaments would be pooled and trade barriers abolished. As for Britain:

We should proclaim that we intend to make a better world at home in which the abuses of the past shall not be allowed to reappear. Unemployment, education, housing and the abolition of privilege should form the main planks of such a platform. We must be careful not to slip into the error of appearing to be bribing men to fight by the promise of short hours and high wages when it is all over . . . But we can promise in return for labour and sacrifice a greater equality and a more even distribution of wealth.

This was a far cry from socialism even as understood in the Ministry, despite the elasticity of the phrase 'abolition of privilege', but notwithstanding Duff Cooper's disclaimer its intention surely was bribery.

The Minister was asked by the Cabinet to examine further the ideas put forward in his paper.[208] His brief was not to modify the paper in a form suitable for pronouncement but to set up machinery for examination of the whole question: a time-honoured process normally guaranteed to lead a scheme into a bog of subcommittees and memoranda. Duff Cooper, however, set about the task with some urgency. He did not 'want to have a lot of professors, out of touch with realities, thinking brilliantly in an academic void',[209] but wished to 'get a practical scheme within a few weeks'.[210] Why this sense of haste? It was feared still that the public might prefer a negotiated peace on Hitler's terms to a continuation of war, a fear which – even before the advent of heavy bombing – led Harold Nicolson to wonder of the public whether 'a great surge of longing will arise in their hearts for peace at any price'.[211] Another, if less urgent, cause for haste may have been a suspicion that sooner or later there would arise a widespread demand for some statement of post-war domestic reform and the related conviction that it would be as well for the government to take the initiative rather than leave it for seizure by groups whose demands might be less than moderate. Now that the door to a statement on peace aims was at last open, however narrowly, the Ministry wished to put a foot in the door before Churchill slammed it shut.

The presence of Labour ministers in the Cabinet probably lent strength to Duff Cooper's belief that he could arrive at 'something about which political parties and the people of Great Britain can be in agreement'.[212] Nor was hostility necessarily to be expected from those Conservatives who were brought into the discussion. Lord Halifax revealed in a letter to Duff Cooper that things were stirring in his own mind:

> At Winston's request I met last night the Ministers who are not in the Cabinet and, after some discussion about foreign affairs, our talk drifted into a channel, marked in the first instance by Bevin, concerning the kind of economic prospect that we might be able to hold out to the masses in Europe and indeed to our own people here . . . We were all conscious as the talk proceeded of the contrast between the readiness of the Nation, and particularly the Treasury, to spend £9 million a day in war to protect a certain way of life and the unwillingness of the administrative authorities in peace to put up, shall we say, £10 million to assist in the reconditioning of Durham unless they could see the project earning a reasonable percentage. In other words, a good many of us felt that in the future days of peace . . . it was necessary to have greater regard to the human values and not allow them to be smothered by considerations of old fashioned financial purity.
>
> I was interested to see that Woolton, from his industrial point of view, was very much alive to all this kind of thought . . . I asked him whether he did not think it might be possible to get some of the best of his friends to talk it out with the best of the Bevins, and he thought something might be done in that direction . . .
>
> . . . I have not the knowledge to judge how these solutions may be found; but I am quite certain that the human conscience in this country is not going to stand for a system that permits large numbers of unemployed . . . And we must always remember that the necessity for it may be on us quicker than we think.[213]

The important thing to note here is the extent to which men like Halifax and Duff Cooper were preparing themselves for what they regarded as thoroughgoing change. Hitler may have been the spur, as Halifax's concluding remark seems to suggest, but their motives had risen above pure expediency. It was, then, rather unfair of Duff Cooper to tell a gathering of journalists on 7 August that he found it impossible to sell to Halifax the idea that propaganda should be based on a vision of the future.[214]

On 23 August the Cabinet discussed the matter again.[215] Typically, Churchill showed little interest in the domestic side of the problem and launched into an exposition on the shape of the post-war world which is remarkable for its confidence at such a bleak phase of the war :

> In addition to the five Great Powers of Europe, there should be three groups of smaller States – in Northern Europe, in Middle Europe, and in the Balkans. He also looked to see the five great nations and these three confederations linked together in some kind of Council of Europe. There should be a Court to which all justiciable disputes should be referred, with an international air force. There must be a scheme for a fair distribution of raw materials. It was also important that there should be no attempt at a vindictive settlement after the war.[216]

Accordingly, a committee – comprising Duff Cooper, Bevin, Halifax, Attlee, Chamberlain and Sinclair – was invited 'to make suggestions in regard to a post-war European world system, with particular regard to the economic needs of the various nations, and to the problems of adjusting the free life of small countries in a durable international order'. They were also asked 'to consider means of perpetuating the national unity achieved in this country during the war through a social and economic structure designed to secure equality of opportunity and service among all classes of the community'.

These were tasks of some magnitude, to say the least, especially at a time when the ministers concerned were fully stretched in their own departments. And when Chamberlain, the chairman of the War Aims Committee, fell ill, the scheme languished until fear of another peace offensive revived it late in the year under Attlee and Halifax.[217] Chatham House, despite Duff Cooper's aversion for academics thinking in a void, had previously been brought in, with Arnold Toynbee attending meetings of the committee. A discussion paper was produced which, although highly tentative and posing more questions than solutions, showed how far along the road towards agreement on basic social problems Labour and Conservative ministers could travel at this time.[218]

The opening paragraph embodied a compromise between the gradualist philosophy of moderate Conservatism (anticipating the ethos of the Beveridge Report) and the redistributive impulses of Labour :

> The creation of a social and economic structure designed to secure equality of opportunity and service among all classes of the community implies acceptance of the principle that there should be assured to each of its members a minimum of what is needed for health, efficiency, and self-respect. The National unity achieved during the war will create a favourable atmosphere for post-war reconstruction on these lines. On the other hand the period will be one of stress and difficulty, and a policy far-reaching enough to meet the legitimate demands of various classes of the community for reform must involve very large state expenditure. Much of this expenditure will ultimately be remunerative from the point of view of the community as a whole, but it will involve heavy immediate sacrifices by certain classes. The attached paper does not include any discussion of the financial measures (e.g. a capital levy) by which a social and economic programme of this magnitude could be carried out.

The body of the paper leant heavily towards the notion of the state as guarantor of basic minimum living standards and of greater social equality. Family allowances, it was affirmed, 'need not be confined to wage earners'. In asking whether there should be a fairer distribution of health services, the paper suggested that 'it may be desirable for the state to extend its medical services or to assume control of medical services as a whole'. Privilege and patronage in government service, particularly that which assisted 'the undue influence of social advantages', should be replaced by a system of open competitive entry. In education it was suggested that state assistance for public schools be conditional on their 'greatly widening the social field' from which students were recruited. State-coordinated housing and town and country planning schemes were envisaged, as were tighter control of capital investments and the provision of much larger funds for the arts and public leisure facilities.

Many of these suggestions looked forward to the flood of white papers and bills which during and shortly after the war laid the foundations for Britain's welfare state. The detail, the obvious hard work and, no doubt, the bargaining between Labour and Conservative representatives that were contributed to this paper cannot reasonably be described as the deliberations of men intent on offering shallow bribes to the public. On an interpretation least charitable to Halifax and Duff Cooper, it may be said that the presence of Attlee and Bevin made sure of that. A well disposed observer might conclude that the experience of working with Labour ministers and of helping the state to intervene to an unprecedented degree in the economic and social life of the nation led moderate Conservatives to the belief that carefully controlled state intervention in peacetime might not be such a bad thing.

But the Ministry of Information had not been transformed overnight into a Trojan horse packed with socialists. A declaration of peace aims in the face of Churchill's opposition to specific statements of post-war intent would, at this stage of the war, have been platitudinous and if used as a basis for morale propaganda could only have appeared as yet one more item of vacuous exhortation. The public neither required inducements to continue the fight nor, for the moment at least, demanded promises for the future.

4

Air Raids and Morale

The Ministry of Information's responsibility for the morale of the population implicitly embraced the formulation of measures designed to ease the psychological consequences of air raids. Very little had been done in preparing suitable measures, chiefly because no one knew what to do. It is difficult to make plans for the apocalypse. But air raids on Britain before the beginning of intensive bombing on 7 September 1940 caused little concern in the Ministry. With only some 300 civilian casualties up to 10 August and with no sign of crumbling morale after the intensification of attacks from this date until early in September, the tone of the intelligence reports was sanguine.[1] So too were the observations of the Ministry of Home Security. On the eve of the Luftwaffe's heavy strike on the East End it was reported, 'Morale continues to be excellent even in heavily bombed areas, and Chief Officers of Police in all parts of the country comment on the calmness and courage which the public are showing, in some cases to the point of foolhardiness.'[2]

However, the scale of bombing on London between September and November 1940 and on the provinces and ports, lasting from the end of the year to May 1941, was to resurrect pre-war expectations of universal panic. These expectations were confounded. Writing in May 1941, after Britain had suffered nine months of heavy raids, Dr Felix Brown of Guy's Hospital echoed many of his colleagues when he stated: 'The incidence of genuine psychiatric air-raid casualties has been much lower than might have been expected; the average previously healthy citizen has proved remarkably adjustable.'[3] The question therefore arises: was the morale of the civil population assisted in any way by the Ministry of Information? The answer being in the affirmative, further questions are raised. What was the nature of the department's assessments of morale under raid and post-raid conditions? What use was made of the knowledge acquired about people's reactions to air attack? How was the Ministry integrated into the whole network of relief services?

The Ministry's assessment of civilian morale in London during the early months of the blitz was very much an empirical procedure, for there were no precedents to follow and the Ministry had to improvise and learn from immediate circumstances quite as fully as the public were forced to readjust their lives to conditions of unremitting danger, discomfort and anxiety. British, not to say human, behaviour as shaped by the attack on London of an average of 200 bombers for 57 consecutive nights was an entirely new phenomenon, at first entirely unpredictable in its principal features, and it was to be some time before the Ministry's observations could be worked up into a body of data by which morale might be tentatively predicted. The department was not staffed by scientists seeking to test a hypothesis. Rather it was composed of civil servants and wartime recruits from academic and professional life, none of whom could lay claim to expertise in the behaviour of a community in a crisis. As for those who did claim such expertise, P. E. Vernon, in the course of a survey based on the observations of fifty social psychologists, psychiatrists and doctors, admitted in 1941 that they had failed to anticipate correctly how people would react to raids.[4] The officials of the Ministry could only sift anxiously through the intelligence reports, hoping to perceive signs that the public were not unduly affected by sustained bombardment. The aim of intelligence work in these early months was threefold: to assess morale generally, to discover how people reacted and adapted to bombings, and to bring to the attention of other departments shortcomings in their relief services.

Morale, according to the early reports, was extremely volatile, 'high' one day and 'strained' the next, 'cheerfulness' co-existing with a conviction that 'in a few months time there will be little left of London or its people'.[5] In general, however, the London public were said to be possessed of a determination to 'see it through' and to 'go on to ultimate victory'.[6] Confirmation was again forthcoming from the Ministry of Home Security, whose intelligence branch reported on 19 September: 'Out of some 50 confidential reports from Chief Constables . . . it is noticeable that in no single instance is there any suggestion of the least faltering in public courage.'[7] But the optimism of the reports circulating through Whitehall belied more private reflections within the Ministry. While the intelligence report could say of the East Enders after their terrible experience of 7–8 September that 'there has been little sign of panic and . . . increased determination to "see it through" ',[8] Harold Nicolson stated in his diary that everybody in the Ministry was worried about the feeling in the East End.[9] By 1 October, morale, he observed, 'is rather shaken, especially in the London suburbs' and a 'very dangerous situation may develop unless we are active and alert'.[10] Later in the month, at a time when the Ministry was asserting officially that people were cheerful,[11] Sir Kenneth Clark expressed serious misgivings to Nicolson:

> He feels that if the Germans make a good peace offer after having bombed our cities rather more and taken Egypt we shall find that the popular Press take the offer up and that we shall be in great difficulty. I agree that the spirit of London is excellent but it would take little to swing this courage into cowardice.[12]

Why was there such a disparity between the confident tone of the officially circulated reports and the conclusions reached by the Parliamentary Secretary and a senior officer? After all, the effects upon morale of continuous bombing were far less serious than had been anticipated and, even allowing for the possibly over-rosy picture painted by Home Intelligence, there was a distinct sense of surprise, almost of amazement, at the 'extraordinary resilience' of the Londoners.[13] Leaving aside the question of their own morale, it may well be that Nicolson and Clark, no doubt weighed down by their sense of responsibility, looked forward with anxiety to, say, a year of continuous raiding on the same or on an increased scale and concluded that no city could sustain such punishment without crying for peace or surrender.

Important though it was to assess the general state of morale, it was of no less importance to observe specific aspects of public behaviour since future policy on a great number of matters would depend on them. There were scores of things to observe under such radically altered conditions of life. Some bulked larger than others. An enduring characteristic of people in severely bombed areas was first noted in the East End – 'an aimless evacuation to what are believed to be safer places'.[14] Despite the Ministry's belief that 'this exodus is caused by greater fear than the actual circumstances justify',[15] very many people sensibly continued as a matter of routine to move out of London or to seek shelter at night deep underground.

Raids on provincial towns were later to produce the similar phenomenon of 'trekking' among the inhabitants of towns which lacked the vast capital's power to absorb punishment. For those denied access, for whatever reason, to safety outside London the underground stations represented as safe a refuge as could be found in the city. The nightly trip to the tube was not halted by official objections and the Ministry noted this characteristically stubborn refusal of the public to be deterred by unconvincing official requests not to shelter in underground stations.[16] The Government wisely decided not to insist on closing the stations to shelterers. 'People are orderly', commented the report of 21 September; 'officials humane',[17] and although much remained to be done to render the stations sanitary and reasonably comfortable the London people displayed from a very early date a talent for improvisation and for co-operation with their fellows.

Morale might remain steady, but the physical fatigue induced by sleepless nights was seen as a danger to the individual's capacity, especially that of the civil defence worker, to continue working.[18] Hence the urgency with which the Ministry recommended short breaks for key personnel from blitzed areas.[19] As for the public's comprehension of its place in the total situation, Home Intelligence commented that there 'appears to be very little relationship between "the bomb at the corner of our street" and the war as a whole'.[20] Perhaps it was only by localising his experience that the individual could come to terms with it. Certainly it seems true that within a very short time people came to accept the bizarre conditions of daily life as routine, even after the loss of their homes :

> A special study of the attitude of those whose homes have been destroyed shows 'an astonishing degree of readjustment, providing they were in a shelter and that none of the family were killed. After a short period of great depression and shock, they wash their hands of past responsibilities and think about starting again, unless they are weak types.'[21]

The tendency of the Ministry occasionally to ascribe 'weakness' to persons who failed to behave normally, not to say stoically, indicates how quickly what was at first regarded by the authorities as surprising resilience came to be thought of as normal behaviour. By early November, when the Germans switched their heavy attacks to the provinces, it had become 'increasingly evident' to the Ministry that the public accepted raids as 'part of war-time conditions' and were determined to continue to regard them as such,[22] a judgement echoed by the Home Secretary in a special report on the London raids.[23] That is not to say that the public did not devoutly wish for a cessation of bombing. A tremendous fillip was given to morale by the great AA barrage on the night of 11 September[24] and hopes were

111

high for an effective defence against the night bomber. Churchill himself was confident.[25] Unfortunately, at this stage of the war there were no means of bringing down more than an insignificant proportion of the attacking force and the public were not slow in observing that the din and clatter of the AA guns brought little reward. The situation was made worse by optimistic official statements and inspired press stories. In November comments were reported 'on the "harm done by premature and optimistic announcements" of our progress in methods to defeat the night bomber; Churchill and Joubert are both criticised for "raising false hopes" '.[26]

Although the proportion of fatal casualties was only some seven per cent of the expected total, the extent and degree of physical damage was very much greater and the central and local authorities had accordingly failed to anticipate the problems of the homeless. The Ministry therefore found itself obliged to report the shortcomings of post-raid relief – much to the displeasure of other departments – and to make recommendations for their eradication. 'The first line of air-raid services – ARP, AFS, etc.', the Ministry pointed out in October 1940, 'work admirably, but the second line has not received the same consideration.'[27] This was a considerable understatement of the actual situation, in which thousands of homeless people were crowded into too few and inadequately equipped rest centres from which they were hurriedly ejected after a short stay with little prospect of alternative accommodation. In this general situation there were numerous faults in organisation, trivial in themselves but which added to the distress of raid victims. At many centres no records were kept to show who had passed through and where the homeless intended finding accommodation;[28] feeding provisions were in many cases entirely lacking;[29] and local authorities proved unequal to the task of co-ordinating action with other authorities and agencies in finding temporary accommodation and transport.[30] Compounding the sense of chaos was the absence of central information bureaux in each district.[31] A special report by Julian Huxley stated that : 'Too many agencies are concerned in re-billeting, house repairs, compensation, evacuation, pensions, etc. and there is not enough co-ordination between them.'[32] Things began to improve after Herbert Morrison became Home Secretary early in October but complaints of 'appalling delays in relief'[33] were still being received a month later in London. It was this muddle rather than the fear induced by bombing which may have contributed to the impression gained by some officers of the Ministry and by Herbert Morrison that morale was in danger.[34]

112

It was not until May 1941 that the Ministry actually distilled its observations in a special report.[35] The period of heavy raids was nearly at an end but no one could have anticipated this at the time and the summary of the constituent factors of morale was of value to the Ministry itself and to other departments, insofar as it was within the power of the authorities to foster conditions in which factors leading to poor morale might be checked. Not that the Ministry was above stating the glaringly obvious: 'The sight of severe casualties or sudden death, the loss of friends or relatives, "near misses", temporary entombment, or the loss of one's home, has a definite "unnerving" effect.' However, the other material factors in the summary were of greater use:

1. *A secure base* . . . the way civilians stand up to continuous raiding depends largely on their having the feeling that there is a safe refuge *somewhere* . . .
   In the London raids, the factor is less important than in the provincial towns . . . [where] not only does the proportion of homeless following a series of severe blitzes exceed the capacity of the rest of the town, but the homeless themselves often do not regard the rest of the town as a 'secure base' . . .
   2. *Fatigue* . . . As raid succeeds raid, night after night, not only does the general population become 'stunned', but Civil Defence and other key personnel . . . decline in efficiency . . . after a few nights of unbroken sleep, there is considerable recovery. Complete recovery, however, seems to take about a fortnight or three weeks.
   3. *'Conditioning'*. Other things being equal, populations which have been subjected to gradually increasing raids take heavy raids better than those who experience a sudden heavy raid without previous 'conditioning' . . .
   4. *Food* . . . is of equal importance to the 'secure base'. Hot cooked food is much more valuable than tea, cold bully beef and bread and butter.

Four non-material factors were said to assume suddenly exaggerated significance in heavy raids. First, people would put up with very great hardship so long as they were convinced that all sections and classes of the community were suffering and enduring equally. 'Indignation against "unrationed rich at the Ritz" ', observed the report, 'has remained within bounds while there is still an occasional "cut off the joint" at the public house.' Second, trust in leadership at all levels of government was seriously jeopardised if muddles occurred or the

113

local authority was believed to have mismanaged its post-raid services or if news was clearly 'doctored' or withheld. Third, the loss of confidence in ultimate victory was not the cause but merely a sign of bad morale, thanks to the British tradition of 'always winning the last battle'. A fourth, more general, factor was belief in a better post-war world. Paradoxically, a large section of the population was said not to have held such a belief and yet morale was still judged to be sound.

As the result of observations made over an eight-month period of intensive bombing, this report was as comprehensive a summary of the causal factors relating to morale as probably could be made at the time. But it should be asked what signs, what modes of behaviour, were taken by the Ministry as indicative of low morale. A reading of the reports for the period between September 1940 and May 1941 reveals no single instance of a community having lost its spirit, so perhaps the question need never have been asked. Or did the Ministry fear to ask it? If so, it is possible that morale did break occasionally and yet went unacknowledged. At least one qualified observer was of a different opinion:

> . . . there were failures of morale and a definite tendency for it to deteriorate, particularly in areas which had a number of heavy raids with long periods of calm between them. Deterioration of morale was shown by unauthorized and unnecessary evacuation, general depression about the War, and criticism of the Government.[36]

Some towns, though, were judged by the Ministry to have been seriously affected by heavy raids. In Coventry, following the extremely heavy raid of 14 November 1940, 'there was great depression, a widespread feeling of impotence and many open signs of hysteria'.[37] Later in November the poorer people of Bristol indulged in 'much talk of having been let down by the Government, and of the possibility of a negotiated peace'.[38] Portsmouth and Southampton became 'severely strained' after continued raids in March and April 1941,[39] while a special report on Portsmouth in May noted that although the inhabitants' spirit was unbroken, 'their nerve had gone'.[40] And yet in Plymouth, subjected to five heavy attacks in the space of nine days in April, morale 'appeared to be good',[41] despite Herbert Morrison's impression that the contrary was the case.[42] As far as the Ministry was concerned, then, it appears that morale, though endangered from time to time, never actually sank below the level at which it could be said to be basically sound.

114

It is possible, however, to glean from the Ministry's reports certain commonly reported phenomena which were assumed to be symptomatic of lowered morale. These were, first, the expression of particular attitudes: despair about the future of the bombed town allied with personal fear and anti-war feeling, the fastening of hostility on to popular scapegoats, and especially Jews, and grumbling about the performance of the local authority in the discharge of its emergency functions. Second, particular modes of behaviour: hysteria, trekking, and action, such as looting, which threatened to erode that sense of community and corporate spirit so essential to effective passive resistance against air raids and to the rebuilding of the town.

Did these symptoms in fact justify a diagnosis of lowered morale? It was not uncommon for people to be reported as saying immediately after a heavy raid that the town was finished, that it could never be rebuilt;[43] but this understandable reaction to the sight of physical devastation was invariably short-lived, as people busied themselves with their numerous post-raid tasks, be they personal – such as finding alternative accommodation – or public – clearing debris and assisting the rehabilitation of essential services. Even more common were statements by individuals of doubt about their ability to take any more nervous strain and fear. Of some groups in the community this was expected, for example 'the middle and upper middle class hotel dwelling ladies'. 'A feeling that "they can carry on no longer" ', observed one report rather unsympathetically, 'is not a new thing in this group.'[44] But when this state of mind was noticed in whole communities the situation was clearly more worrying, as in the case of Hull following a heavy attack of 18 July 1941: 'One could frequently hear comments by people of all different social types, which indicate that they would find it impossible to stand the strain any longer.'[45] Similarly with Norwich as late as 1942, when its inhabitants were seen to be noticeably more shaken by the raid of 26–27 June than by earlier and more severe attacks.[46] But the fact was that when people suffered further raids they did 'take it', either because they knew there was no alternative (if they had not left the town) or they underestimated their own capacity for endurance.

The most infrequently reported attitude associated with air raids was that of defeatism or, to put it another way, of anti-war feeling. This was what the Ministry feared most. And with good reason, for if the enemy could succeed in battering the civilian populace to the point at which they no longer believed that continuing the war was worth the price of their suffering, the nation would have been on the edge of defeat. But there were only three references to this most dangerous of reactions to continuous raiding. In Coventry, after six air raids in October 1940 but before the bludgeoning of 14–15 November, factory workers were said to be ready to 'support any plausible peace proposals',[47] though it is important to note that after the big raid Mass-Observation reported the existence of no anti-war talk.[48] After the Southampton raid of 30 November 1940 it was anticipated that 'young women' would turn defeatist in the event of continued bombing[49] and following the two heavy attacks on London of 16 and 19 April 1941, in which 1,180 and 1,200 people were killed respectively, people were quoted as saying, 'A few more nights like this and it would be all up with us.'[50] That such reports were extremely rare must have given great comfort to the authorities. Badly shaken and afraid, as were the people of Portsmouth in May 1941, the British public were time and time again said to be determined not to give in.

A second state of mind interpreted as a sign of low or sinking morale was the tendency to fasten on to groups, and especially Jews, and to accuse them of various forms of anti-social behaviour. Such was the reported intensity of feeling in the East End in September that Home Intelligence went to some pains to point out that stories of Jewish cowardice and selfishness were without foundation:

> A certain amount of anti-Semitism in the East End still persists, but this is not so much on account of a marked difference in conduct between Jews and Cockneys, but because the latter, seeking a scapegoat as an outlet for emotional disturbances, pick on the traditional and nearest one. Though many Jewish people regularly congregate and sleep in the public shelters, so also do many of the Gentiles, nor is there any evidence to show that one or the other predominates among those who have evacuated themselves voluntarily through fear or hysteria.[51]

On Merseyside similar reports were made in July 1941. Jews were supposed to have fled to the safest billets and to have avoided fire-watching duties. Liverpool's rich mixture of races and nationalities provided ample scope for 'distrust of foreign elements': Greeks and Chinese were singled out for insults and Free French sailors occasionally subjected to 'rough usage'. Again, the situation was attributed to a 'need to have someone to blame, and someone to act as scapegoat to work off the people's own fears'.[52] By itself, however, anti-semitism – though it may have increased in intensity during and shortly after air raids – was not a significant index of low morale, since it was widely reported in areas not bombed and would continue to be reported for the rest of the war.

Finally, what is to be made of the large volume of grumbling, sometimes passing over into bitter accusations, about the ineptitude of local authorities in the discharge of their post-raid functions? Janis asserts that the 'one outstanding generalisation' that may be made about all nations subjected to air attacks during the war is the frequency with which air raids aroused hostility not against the enemy but against the home authorities.[53] But as Titmuss has pointed out in the context of Britain, 'damage to homes, and the search for shelter and rest, were among the most serious – if not the most serious, consequences of air attack on the civilian population'.[54] With very few exceptions, praise for the personnel of the vital services during air raids was high, but when, with the coming of dawn a dazed population emerged from shelter only to find that hot food was not available, that they were packed into poorly equipped rest centres and that little provision had been made for temporary accommodation, it was little wonder that they should count the inadequacy of the responsible authority as a highly unwelcome addition to their sufferings.

Home Intelligence invariably bracketed reports of grumbling with evidence justifying the specific allegations of shortcomings. Of primary importance after a raid was the provision of information on the location of various agencies offering relief services. This was more often than not either entirely lacking or spread bewilderingly about the town, which was in any event distressingly unfamiliar and dis-orientating after a heavy raid. Having found a rest centre, raid victims – as in Manchester – might be 'bundled off in a highly nervous state, and dumped into empty rooms, where they have to spend the night, cold and over-crowded, and where little preparation has been made to receive them'.[55] Communal feeding arrangements were often found to be poor.[56] Evacuation plans and co-ordination with authorities in the surrounding districts were often lacking, and yet at the same time there was active discouragement of trekking, which for many raid victims was the only form of escape. The lessons of the London blitz were lost on provincial cities, even when imparted by Ministry of Health inspectors, and it seems that each city and town had to experience a major attack before making adequate plans for the relief of the community.[57]

Certainly the Ministry of Information uncovered a surprising degree of complacency. In May 1941, for example, the reports on

Plymouth and Portsmouth, both of which had suffered heavy bombing early in the year, castigated the local authorities. 'The pre-blitz preparations of the Plymouth Local Authority', said a report of 7–14 May, 'appear to have envisaged nothing on the scale of what actually did happen. The authority was carrying on, on an expanded peacetime basis, rather than on the expectation of being a front-line headquarters.'[58] Observing that the communal feeding arrangements were poor in Portsmouth, Home Intelligence commented :

> The attitude of the official in charge appears largely responsible for the policy. Apart from a personal horror of communal feeding, he expressed the opinion that it encouraged parasitism and laziness and he did not see why 'workers probably earning more than I do should be encouraged by the Government'.[59]

However justified the complaints of the public, there was little evidence linking the intensity of grumbling with low morale. Towns where spirits were reported to be high and determination unaffected by raids were often the sources of bitterest complaint. In October 1941, Dr Stephen Taylor, Director of Home Intelligence, wrote that in dealing with the British public it was important to remember that 'admirable behaviour is often coupled with a veritable wail of grumbles'.[60] His judgement was supported by a study undertaken by Dr C. W. Emmens of the Research and Experiments Branch of the Ministry of Home Security. Submitted in June 1943, the study was made for the Air Ministry in order to discover whether certain factors influenced the morale of one town's population more adversely under the impact of bombing than another's and thus aid the Air Ministry's selection of targets in Germany. Dr Emmens investigated the morale, and the best means of assessing it, in six towns : York, Exeter, Norwich, Canterbury, Bootle and Clydebank. Part of the study was concerned with the relationship between the intensity of local press criticism, as reflecting the views of the community as a whole, and the state of the town's morale. He concluded that 'marked and frequent press comment on ARP shelters, post-raid services and of the local and central authorities', among other things, 'is not in itself an indication of bad morale but may reflect the normal course of events in a town which has been badly hit'.[61]

If even the most depressed or critical attitudes voiced by victims of air raids were no guide to morale, what of people's behaviour? Throughout the war Home Intelligence paid the closest attention to

118

the attitudes of the public on a host of matters and seemed to assess morale according to how people were said to feel on particular issues. However, as we have seen in the Introduction, Taylor himself defined morale as 'the state of conduct and behaviour of an individual or a group' and added that morale 'must therefore be ultimately measured not by what a person thinks or says, but by what he does and how he does it'.[62] The definition employed by Dr Emmens was, in his own words, 'virtually equivalent', which gave him 'some confidence in the comparability of Home Intelligence estimates of morale with those derived from statistics of absenteeism, etc.' The important point here is not that attitudes can never provide indications of morale, but that so far as the Ministry's intelligence reports are concerned there is an absence of correlation between the two. Both Taylor and Emmens appear to have thought that in wartime it does not matter what a man thinks or says so long as he continues to perform his allotted task to the best of his ability. When he fails to do so – or, more importantly, when large numbers or key sections of the community fail to do so – morale can be said to have broken down. It remains, then, to ask whether in the post-raid behaviour of bombed populations the Ministry noted significant indications of such a breakdown in morale.

Hysteria, the most palpable form of behaviour suggesting a break in morale, was rarely to be observed. Fear, 'jittery' behaviour and occasional panicky action were in evidence, naturally enough, but the scenes reported by Mass-Observation in Coventry were atypical.

> There were more open signs of hysteria, terror, neurosis observed in one evening than during the whole of the past two months, together in all areas. Women were seen to cry, to scream, to tremble all over, to faint in the street, to attack a fireman, and so on.[63]

There is no reason to suppose that similar behaviour did not occur in towns subjected to heavy attacks but if it did, Home Intelligence failed to report it. It seems likely that hysterical outbursts were insufficiently widespread to merit comment as a significant aspect of the responses of people to air raids. The finding in Germany 'that fear and terror in the presence of bombing bore no relation to the practically more important aspects of morale, such as willingness to surrender'[64] applied equally to Britain. Neurotic conditions, possibly because they were more the province of the clinician, were also absent from the reports, although the Ministry of Health's findings were included in the Home Intelligence report of 12–19 February 1941 :

119

Only 5% of all people incapacitated by air-raids were suffering from 'nervous shock'. Some of these were probably physical in origin, the result of blast. The great majority had recovered within a week or two. In December 1940, the number of civilian neuroses due to air-raids requiring admission to special psychiatric hospitals was: London 25, rest of England 3. In January there were still fewer cases . . . At out-patient clinics, the number of new cases seen in 1940 was below that of 1939. Following the Coventry raid, the number of neurotic out-patients was the same as usual.[65]

The reference to Coventry seems to contradict the Mass-Observation report but it might well have been the case that hysterical behaviour during and shortly after an air raid, like despair for the future of the town, quickly subsided and was not translated into the medical statistics on neuroses, either because the initial experience of bombing produced subsequent toughness or because those people who could not control their fear left the area for safer parts of the country. Although he raises the important question of the long-term psychological effects of bombing, Titmuss tells us that not only is there no evidence to suggest that neurotic illness or mental disorders increased during the war, but that during the raids of 1940–41 there was a decrease of such admissions to hospitals and clinics.[66] Again, the German experience was similar.[67]

An aspect of air-raid behaviour very commonly reported was trekking, the term applied to the nightly private evacuation of townsfolk to supposedly safer areas in the immediate district. The typical features of the phenomenon were described in a report on Portsmouth :

By 6 p.m. an observer will see that all traffic is moving northwards. The movement begins at about 3.30 p.m. and continues until dusk; at the peak period, there are long queues at every bus stop along the route. The people are making for the bridge on the main road out of Portsmouth, in order to sleep in the northern suburbs, the surrounding hills or in towns and villages within a radius of 20 miles. On one night after a bad blitz, it was estimated that 90,000 left the city and now, after a raid-free period, there are said to be still some 30,000 trekkers, half of them being men.[68]

Far from being a panicky mass flight, trekking was normally a very orderly procedure but Home Intelligence, like officialdom in general, tended to regard it as an alarming symptom of sinking morale. In

April 1941, eight months after the practice had first been noted, the Ministry delivered itself of the following analysis :

> It is known that there is a section of the population, estimated at a maximum of one-tenth, who are of a weaker constitutional mental make-up than the rest. These people react to different situations in two ways – either by a cowardly retreat, or by a neurotic mental breakdown . . . The potentially neurotic section of the population takes to the roads each evening and seeks safety in dispersal. In London, however, they have what they believe to be an equally safe escape in the tube shelters. So the problem of the nightly trek is in London only the problem of the trek to the tubes.[69]

There is a glimmering of understanding here : by linking the motives of tube shelterers with those of their fellow citizens in the provincial towns, Home Intelligence mentions the desire for escape. Escape from what? From the real possibility of sudden death and from constant noise. The desire to enhance one's chances of survival and for a good night's sleep was of itself no indication of poor morale, as, indeed, was verified by reports of excellent morale in towns which nonetheless had had large proportions of their populations trekking each evening. In the words of a Ministry of Home Security study, 'Temporary evacuation or nightly trekking . . . is a most valuable safety valve.'[70] The important question is whether the trekkers return-ed in the morning. Except for those whose houses had been destroyed or badly damaged and who therefore had to take time off from work, they did.[71] The 'problem' was not one of morale. Such problems as were associated with trekking consisted in the inability of local authorities to arrange sufficient accommodation for the thousands of persons who left raided towns each evening, many of whom were obliged to sleep as best they could in the open.

'On all sides', wrote the Ministry's observers in Portsmouth, 'we hear that looting and wanton destruction had reached alarming pro-portions. The police seem unable to exercise control . . . This seems another illustration of the lack of community spirit. The effect on morale is bad and there is a general feeling of desperation as there seems to be no solution.'[72] Looting was mentioned on very few occasions and then only in passing, but its incidence was almost cer-tainly greater than Home Intelligence suggested.[73] The very fact that Dr Emmens established a relationship between criticism in the press of looting and the degree of damage in a town suggests that it was by no means an isolated phenomenon.[74] Such anti-social behaviour was surely as serious in implication for morale as defeatist feeling. But, although looting may have been more common than the Ministry allowed (even among the disciplined Germans it was reported to be the most common type of crime following a raid[75]), it was of a petty, unorganised nature for the most part and therefore of little significance in the absence of other indications of communal dissolution.

If none of the factors considered above, both attitudinal and behavioural, was sufficient in itself to lead the Ministry to conclude that morale had broken down in a particular place, what of the situation in which a number were present? Merseyside, second only to London in the weight of bombs sustained in the period from September 1940 to May 1941, was raided on seven successive nights at the beginning of May 1941 and suffered severe physical damage and some 1,900 persons killed. A special report,[76] embracing the Liverpool, Bootle and Birkenhead areas, opened rather inauspiciously:

To the visitor, Liverpool has a depressed and sordid atmosphere. This is partly due to its blackness and the number of very poor seen in the streets, and is enhanced by the blitz debris . . . The mixed population of the city is a special feature. There are small colonies of Chinese, Arabs, Greeks, West Indians, transient seamen of all nationalities and a large settlement of Irish, reported to be of a poor, even primitive type.

The local authorities were judged to be 'too easily satisfied with the provisions made and are inclined to ignore public opinion . . . [and] to be on the defensive and unwilling to discuss difficulties'. Described by some of the public as 'apathetic and moribund', the local officials had failed moreover to promote co-ordination with the voluntary bodies and between police and wardens. Although emergency measures were said to have improved since earlier raids, many problems persisted: dispersal, particularly of elderly people, was poorly organised, as was the distribution of food, and there were many accusations against the authority of forcing people to remain in the city during bombing. The condition of many shelters and rest centres was 'indescribable'. An estimated 50,000 people trekked from the area each night. Looting was reported. Anti-Semitism was said to be present and growing. And yet morale 'in general', despite a strong undercurrent of anxiety, was assessed very favourably. This judgement was confirmed by Dr Emmens. Taking the number of man days lost in production as his basic index of morale and relating it to the extent of damage suffered, he concluded that Bootle's average of from 2·8 to 3 days lost per worker compared well with towns such as York and Canterbury which suffered much less heavily and whose morale was 'excellent'.[77] Of 17,000 houses in Bootle, some 14,000 were affected, 14 per cent either totally destroyed or seriously damaged. Considering all that the householder had to do in seeking new accommodation and, if possible, in repairing his house, some three days' loss of work could hardly be interpreted as a sign of poor morale.

The absence of defeatism and the remarkable capacity of people to keep alive a sense of community (assisted in the case of Merseyside by the family solidarity of the Catholic population) overcame those disintegrating influences which might otherwise have brought about a faltering of spirit. It may be concluded, therefore, that on the evidence available to Home Intelligence the Ministry did not err in proclaiming the resilient qualities of the British. In October 1941, Stephen Taylor was moved to comment:

There is, at present, no evidence to suggest that it is possible to defeat the people of Britain by any means other than extermination.[78]

In the light of the nervous suspicion with which the propagandists had earlier regarded the public, Taylor may perhaps be forgiven this patriotic rush of blood to the head.

Perhaps on the assumption that German morale was more brittle, the government chose to ignore the Ministry's findings when the RAF's bombing policy was revised.[79] Instead, a special study was commissioned. In October 1941, Dr Stradling of the Ministry of Home Security was asked by the Air Ministry to investigate the effects of bombing on production, transport and morale in Hull and Birmingham. The Air Ministry wished to form an opinion 'as to the possibility of bringing about a decisive breakdown in morale in urban districts', as part of the deliberations which led to the directive of February 1942 that Bomber Command's chief object was the destruction of German morale.[80] The Air Ministry's summary of the subsequent report[81] stated that production was affected only to the extent of 5 per cent in Birmingham and, under the impact of more concentrated bombing, Hull was scarcely worse affected. The effect on the morale of the populations, reflected both in findings on the return to work rate and as directly measured by the Wartime

Social Survey, was 'not decisive'. Unless their houses were destroyed people did not vacate them nor were they persuaded either by lesser damage or by fear of further raids to leave the towns for more than a short period. Raids of the order of five times greater might 'be a different matter' but, it was stated, 'we are still without definite knowledge of the point at which air raids become insupportable'. Under 'Practical Application' the following recommendations were made:

> To attack industry it still appears . . . to be best to concentrate on causing direct damage to factories, although attack on a population largely consisting of war workers must have an indirect effect on industry; thus if industrial areas adjacent to congested housing zones can be selected for attack, the two effects can be combined.
>
> To attack the population, houses must be destroyed, and for this it is most economical to attack the densest zone, which is invariably in or around the city centre, that part of the town which is most vulnerable to fire. Thus in the attack on people, our present technique of firing the city centre to provide a beacon on which later arrivals carrying H.E. can concentrate is perfectly correct.[82]

This technique was to culminate in the devastating attack on Dresden towards the end of the war,[83] but it is difficult to understand how these recommendations could have flowed from the evidence adduced for them, unless the Air Ministry decided that Bomber Command should be allowed to seek the threshold of insupportability by means of much heavier bombing than had hitherto been experienced in either country. The attempt was made and was largely unsuccessful. The morale of the German work-force, like the British, was not significantly impaired.[84]

Prior to September 1940 there had been a reluctance in the Ministry to formulate any set of principles which might guide their actions in the event of heavy air raids. True, the devastating attacks expected at the beginning of the war did not materialise but the Luftwaffe's absence could not be taken to mean that the blow would not fall. The truth was that no one had any real idea of what could be achieved in the face of a situation conceived in terms of mass panic and near total community breakdown. When the heavy attacks did come and their consequences were seen to be less horrific than expected, the Ministry of Information found itself performing tasks of an almost mundane nature, chiefly in support of the post-raid services of other departments and therefore of most importance at regional and town level. Given the past record of the propagandists, there was surprisingly little direct exhortation and inspirational publicity. Intelligence sources made it quickly apparent, for example, that, while the public appreciated due recognition of their resolute qualities, they resented too great an emphasis on the stereotyped image of the Britisher in adversity as a wise-cracking Cockney. They were irritated by propaganda which represented their grim experience as a sort of particularly torrid Rugby match. Hence the Ministry's abandonment of the slogan 'Britain Can Take It' in December 1940 and the Planning Committee's anxiety at its continued use 'in spheres outside the Ministry's control'.[85] Its air raid work may be considered in three aspects: information and advice, the preparation and dissemination of publicity for other departments and the activities of the RIOs.

The early Home Intelligence reports did not in fact disguise the existence of faults in the organisation and services of other departments. This frequently aroused annoyance. In January 1941 the full Mass-Observation report on the Coventry raid on 14 November came into the hands of the Ministry of Home Security and provoked an official to write to Herbert Morrison:

> It may be remembered that when what was called a 'Daily Morale Report' was being circulated by the Ministry of Information, based I think on the same sort of organisation . . . it was found by this Department that whenever criticisms of the Department were examined and evidence required, it was found that the criticisms were ill founded.[86]

Such was the typical reaction, based on a misunderstanding of the nature of the Ministry's reports, in Whitehall. Mass-Observation was even less inclined than Home Intelligence to pull its punches and statements such as that suggesting the authorities had not learnt the lesson of the East End blitz were hardly likely to be received warmly by civil servants, already harrassed and overworked. However, the Ministry's reports examined the consequences of air raids not from the point of view of a government department but, insofar as it was possible, from the worm's eye view of the ordinary citizen. If the citizen, as in the case of Coventry, was distressed by lack of hot food, accommodation and information and if the surface shelter in which he took refuge was damp and structurally unsound, no purpose would have been served if the Ministry had ignored his distress for fear of offending other departments. The same anonymous official presumed that the Coventry report had been written 'by what are known as the "intelligentsia" and I think they would be very much better employed in doing something useful for the community'.[87]

Notwithstanding the friction caused by circulation of the intelligence reports, they had a considerable value which stemmed from the comprehensiveness of view which the Ministry could bring to bear on the problems of Britain's shattered towns and cities. The Ministry's general morale-assessing duties, as they devolved at the local level, obliged the RIO and his staff to maintain regular contact not only with hundreds of citizens in all walks of life but also with local authorities, voluntary bodies, representatives of other departments, the press and the Regional Commissioner. This, of course, did not guarantee infallibility, but whereas the local representatives of, say, the ministries of Health and Home Security were necessarily closely involved with their own functions after a raid, the RIO was in a position to survey the picture as a whole. He indicated gaps in the highly complex net of raid relief, identified the points at which co-ordination was necessary and somehow tried to bridge the gulf between raid victims and the sometimes inevitably remote relief services. As Harry Stack Sullivan has pointed out in a broader context, demoralisation is likely to occur when one is obliged 'to depend for security or satisfaction on a person or group which is perceived to have no respect or affection for one'.[88] It was important, therefore, that the Ministry did all in its power to reduce the impression of raid victims that they were mendicants begging for aid from a distant and unsympathetic bureaucracy.

Much of the RIO's work could be carried out locally – a phone call to the Regional Commissioner, conversations with the mayor, advice to the editor of the local paper and to voluntary societies such as the WVS. When some semblance of normal life had been established, he summarised his observations and recommendations on paper and a few days afterwards they were incorporated in the Home Intelligence Report, which in turn was circulated throughout Whitehall. Precisely how much attention was paid to the report it is difficult to say, since liaison between the Ministry of Information and other departments merited only the scantiest reference in their records. There was in the Ministry a conviction that considerable benefit accrued from its intelligence work. As early as August 1940, that is before the period of intensive bombing, it was stated:

We, in Home Intelligence, act as a bridge between the ordinary people and the Government. Grievances and hardships reported to us can be remedied or explained; misapprehensions can be overcome; matters concerning other departments brought to their notice . . . we make strong representations on national issues of vital importance and press for a new policy, in many cases more in line with the needs and will of the people.[89]

The overwhelmingly positive response to a survey conducted in 1943 of the usefulness of the intelligence reports to other departments indicated that they were read with interest and, where possible, acted upon.[90]

As the channel through which the bulk of government publicity passed, the Ministry of Information was concerned with the preparation of instructional material relating to desirable public action and behaviour before, during and after air raids. It also undertook research into public reactions to such material, which often involved a lot of work for the broad-shouldered RIOs. On Sunday 2 March 1941, for example, an advertisement appeared in the press giving instructions on the handling of fire bombs, and RIOs were asked to supply answers to a number of questions:

1. Did the Sunday newspaper advertisements succeed in reaching the vast majority of the public? . . .

2. Were the broadcast announcements successful in drawing attention to the advertisements?

3. Was there much opposition to the exclusive use of this medium by people with religious or other scruples?

4. In your opinion was there need of additional publicity for these instructions? If so, what kind?

5. Is there evidence that people cut out and pinned up the instructions as they were requested to do so?

6. Does the public consider the instructions complete and clear? If not, what difficulties have been raised?

7. Is the method of presentation (pictorial) considered a good one? Are there any errors in the presentation?[91]

The Ministry was not an entirely passive agency for government publicity, believing as it did that it was useless undertaking work of this nature if the administrative measures which were to cope with the desired change in public behaviour were not fully prepared or if the intention was to raise spirits in the face of strongly adverse circumstances. Asked in October 1940 to conduct propaganda in order to raise the morale of public shelterers, the members of the

Policy Committee agreed that 'the difficulties and discomforts being experienced by people taking shelter in the Tubes and elsewhere could not be primarily the business of the Ministry. The most that could be done . . . would be to examine the bearings of these difficulties on morale, and to circulate to the various Departments affected reports on this question.'[92] Later in the month the Policy Committee again refused a request for publicity from the Ministry of Home Security, this time on the ground that propaganda about shelter behaviour and 'help for the homeless' would be fruitless in the light of the poorly co-ordinated arrangements for assistance to raid victims.[93]

In April 1941 the Ministry of Home Security, wishing to overcome the deep public distrust of brick surface shelters, asked the Ministry to 'popularise' the shelters, adding that only those meeting the strictest inspection would be passed as safe. The Ministry of Information was reluctant to undertake the campaign and agreed to do so only on condition that a frank statement be made about the surface shelters' past faults and that the inspection of them was sufficiently thorough to justify the claims that would be made for them.[94] At times, however, the Ministry's thinking is difficult to understand. Having prepared a list of instructions and advice in the pamphlet *After the Raid*, it was decided to issue only one million copies instead of the 7 million requested as it was thought to 'be a waste of time to distribute these to people before they had been bombed'.[95] The Civil Defence Committee of the Cabinet dissented from this decision and ordered the printing and distribution of 15 million copies.[96]

The Ministry's experience enabled it to give valuable advice to the BBC early in 1941, and the episode well illustrates the extent to which the Ministry had endeavoured to understand the feelings of air-raid victims and to persuade the press, the BBC and government departments to take these into consideration. A broadcast given after the raids on Swansea of 19 and 20 February 1941 annoyed Mary Adams:

'But there are the usual smiles; even those who have lost friends and relatives are not really depressed and their stories are told in a subdued manner but with a sense of pride . . . But the only effect on the spirit of the people has been to raise it higher than ever . . . I saw some elderly men and women running through the streets clutching small cases and parcels in their hands. These were all they had left in the world. Many of them raised their hand and gave us a cheery greeting.'

This particular talk was given after the second night of the blitz and the comments of the inhabitants after the third night I leave to your imagination.

It seems to me that it would be far better to rule out broadcasts of blitzed towns altogether if there is no other way of eliminating such mistakes.[97]

Ivison Macadam suggested, and Radcliffe agreed, that such broadcasts should cease forthwith,[98] but instead Mary Adams prepared a memorandum summarising the evolving reactions of raid victims and made appropriate suggestions to the BBC. It is worth quoting at length:

1. Immediately after the raid, people are dazed and in a condition of mild shock. They are surprised and thankful to be alive. They feel *important* and are inclined to exaggerate the experiences through which they have passed. Those who have suffered loss are feeling sad and depressed. A few feel hopeless. All are tired. There is a considerable degree of isolation, both physical and psychological. There is a craving for attention, sympathy and encouragement.

2. During the first day after the raid, people are mainly concerned in making plans for evacuation (temporary or permanent), in deciding on shelter for the following night, getting and cooking food, making enquiries about missing relatives and friends, or thinking about salvaging their furniture and possessions.

3. People seem unable to absorb information easily: many wireless sets are out of action: the written word seems not to have the usual effect. They seem unable to bestir themselves in order to acquire information. Advice is best conveyed by word of mouth.

4. Rumour circulates suggesting the possibility of a return attack. People are abnormally sensitive to this possibility.

5. People are primarily interested in damage, and there is a natural inclination to exaggerate.

6. There are various signs of tension. Those who remain in the town often show a considerable amount of 'cheerfulness' which is often thought to be synonymous with 'high morale'. Joking is common.

7. There is pride in local efficiency but at the same time inefficiency and failure (whether in administration, fire-fighting, the conduct of rest centres, demolition and so on) becomes known very rapidly.

8. Authorities of various kinds, conscious of the many difficulties they have faced, are abnormally sensitive to criticism.

9. There is an initial tendency to look back, to think in terms of the past history and associations of the town, and, in view of the obvious damage, to consider the town 'done for', 'without a future'.

These considerations make it possible to offer the following advice in the preparation of the broadcast.

1. The broadcast, as far as possible, should be confined to eye-witness accounts : hearsay evidence should be very critically examined before it is included.

2. Generalisations on the state of morale should never be given. It is inevitable that many people listening will find themselves an exception to any generalisation.

3. Morale should never be over-played. The raid will have made many people frightened and far from 'heroic'. They will resent a standard being set up which they know to be impossible.

4. Damage should never be minimised. This applies particularly to industrial damage. It is widely thought that the Germans will take advantage of an official statement which suggests that the raid has been relatively ineffective.

5. Examples of local efficiency should be praised, but deficiencies should not be deliberately concealed. Concealment is likely to be recognised and lead to mistrust of official news. It is possible to enhance confidence by mentioning failures in a constructive way.

6. Local leaders should be mentioned by name only if there is certainty that they are not the subject of criticism.

7. Government aid is provided, but individual initiative is always possible and can generally be illustrated, so can neighbourliness which offsets isolation.

8. Useful pieces of information might find a place in the broadcast, e.g. what happens at a rest centre, where the homeless go for aid, what arrangements are made for evacuation and transport. This can be done indirectly, e.g. describing what was broadcast from loudspeaker vans . . .

9. Controlled evacuation is official policy and although it varies in different regions, most towns will have been given an opportunity of profiting by it. Indirect reference to those successful previous plans might be effective. Any description of people moving out of the town during the raid should be avoided : Government advice shows that people are safer in shelters during the raid.

10. Opportunity should be taken of pointing out that this particular raid . . . is an incident on the whole war front. The raided town courageously endures its experiences in common with others: all make their contribution to the general war effort.

11. Reference to the future, to rebuilding, reconstruction, replanning, shift attention from the present to the future. The future will be better than the past.[99]

In addition to gathering intelligence on post-raid conditions, the RIO or one of his deputies was responsible for providing and co-ordinating information services, often under difficult circumstances. The provision of information to the victims of bombed towns was of the utmost importance and it is a pity therefore that so little survives in the Ministry's records of the detailed implementation of this activity. The files containing the individual histories of the work in the regions are closed for fifty years,[100] and the one published account by an RIO of his experiences does not succeed in filling in the gaps.[101]

The fundamental problem facing the RIO after the emergence of people from shelters was their need for information on a host of subjects. In view of the vast amount of instructional literature which the citizen was asked to absorb in wartime, it was likely that such information as was given before the raid had been forgotten or never learnt in the first place. If steps were not taken to redress this ignorance a situation similar to that described in Coventry was likely to follow:

> *Ordinary people had no idea what they should do, and* this help-lessness and impotence only accelerated depression . . . Those citizens who were able to walk about were left to themselves. There were no signs of any official mobile canteens, there was no use of loudspeaker vans, of Information Committee notices, special announcements, or anything of that sort.[102]

Even if the citizen did know where to go, the likelihood was that the various relief agencies administered by local and central government and by voluntary bodies, were scattered widely throughout the locality, some of their premises having been destroyed by bombing. In an article for *Local Government Service* Tom Harrisson described the difficulties faced by a raid victim.[103] He took as his hypothetical model a sailor's wife who runs a small shop in Plymouth, one of whose three small children is killed and whose shop and living quarters are destroyed by a direct hit:

131

1. You have to eat. You have to get new ration books. You go to St Bartholomew's Hall, Milehouse.

2. In the meanwhile, you have to find a communal feeding centre for the children. You go to the girls' high school.

3. You have to try to get tinned food and other stuff in your ruined shop salvaged. You should go to the city treasurer's office, whose last address, given in the M.O.I. Leaflet, is the Guildhall, but that got bombed on the previous night.

4. You are also supposed to report the presence of some contaminated food . . . You would contact the medical office of health, Beaumont House . . .

5. You are already beginning to be faced with the problem of your surviving children as you trek around. You have to find a rest centre and those in your area are destroyed. You find another and leave them there for the time being.

6. But one child is dead. You have to locate the body. Then you have to enquire about the death certificate at the information bureau in the Technical College.

7. Since you cannot afford a private burial, you must apply to the war deaths department in the information bureau.

8. Now you are faced with the problem of extra clothing, especially for the children. The address is 18 Addison Road, Sherwell.

9. You are advised to put in a claim for compensation for clothing, furniture, etc. So off to Mutley Baptist Church, the Assistance Board.

10. They are able to give you a cash advance, but that is necessarily limited. They advise you to apply for extra help from the mayor's relief fund, situated in Morley Chambers, Morley Street.

11. As it is hopeless to get any alternative accommodation locally, you desire to apply for free travel vouchers for the homeless. The address is 'Seven Trees', Lipson Road. Or a child evacuation form can be obtained from the education offices, Cobourg Street.

12. Having lost the family identity cards, you apply for new ones to 13 Thorn Park, Mannamead.

13. Then to get new gas masks. Off you go to the Corporation Surplus Stores, Mill Street.

14. Of course, you have lost your 'Navy Book', and to get another you go off to Pennycomequick Sorting Office in Central Park Avenue.

15. Having got all these Plymouth matters in hand, the problem of your billet in the country arises – a terrible problem for the good citizen who has stayed put until actually bombed out. Here the Chief Billeting Officer, Lipson Road (no address given in the M.O.I. leaflet) appears to be involved.

16. Finally, being a good citizen, you decide to avail yourself of the advised post-blitz measure of typhoid inoculation. The good citizen goes to the Prince of Wales Hospital, Green-bank.

In circumstances such as these the provision of widely-spread, clear and simple information was at the top of the RIO's priority list.

Even allowing for extensive pre-raid publicity, the RIO would have to anticipate the necessity for widespread placarding on the morrow of an attack. Normally, local facilities such as printing presses were employed, but where these were inadequate Ministry head-quarters were called upon to assist the production of posters and placards. In January 1941 some 50,000 copies of each of the follow-ing were printed for a number of towns:

Bring your cans here for water.
You can get drinking water at . . .
Drink only boiled water and milk.
Cancelled.
Rest centres are at . . .
Transport for . . . will leave . . .
For help and information, go to . . .[104]

These are very basic items of information but people's needs after a raid, both physical and psychological, were basic in the extreme and, as Mary Adams pointed out, people were often so dazed that it was essential to instruct them in as simple a manner as possible.

Rather more difficult was the task of persuading all the relief agencies to centralise their advisory services in one or more conven-ient places. Just how successfully this was accomplished it is difficult to tell, although it was such an obvious step and the Ministry from the earliest days of the blitz repeated *ad nauseam* its necessity that it must be assumed the practice gradually gained acceptance. In the larger provincial towns and cities the Ministry put a number of loudspeaker vans in use. They toured the locality, broadcasting advice and instruction and answering queries. Besides the usual questions concerning the location of canteens, clothes stores, fresh water, accommodation and the like, the van's crew – a driver and an announcer – frequently found themselves assisting people to trace missing relatives or even taking casualties to hospital.[105] Much of the work bore little relationship to the strict role of dispensing information but in post-raid circumstances the agents of the Ministry were looked upon by frightened and distressed persons as all-purpose Samaritans. Having organised these activities as matters of first priority, the RIO would set about assisting the local press. Indeed, it was a vital task to revive the press, where its plant had been damaged or its personnel injured, and to bring into the area the national newspapers, since it alleviated that sense of isolation to which inhabitants of heavily raided communities were susceptible. It was part of the RIO's job, as it was the Ministry's at a national level, to help people to realise that society had not collapsed, that the authorities were capably handling an apparently catastrophic situation. There was a risk, however, of creating irritation. Unless the city was very large or it was clear that the Germans were in no doubt of the places they had bombed, censorship would not permit the press to name the town until a considerable period afterwards and its inhabitants would therefore feel aggrieved at the evident lack of interest shown in their ordeal.

Tom Harrisson threw serious doubts on the efficiency of the Ministry's post-raid information services:

> . . . working with a unit of skilled investigators, we have almost invariably found that the worst breakdown was in the information services. Only in one case, Sheffield, could they be called anywhere near adequate to the situation. And there is relatively little sign of improvement after nine months' experience. In Plymouth, after the April blitzes, the situation was much the same as ever. And in Greenock, after its May blitz, it was so bad that the loudspeaker van announcers could not get enough accurate information to disseminate about the elementary social services of the area.[106]

It is more than coincidental that in the case of Plymouth, Home Intelligence came as close as it ever dared to say that morale had gone, and Greenock was judged by Dr Emmens to have had significantly lower morale than the other towns included in his study.[107] Harrisson attributed the poor quality of information services to a number of reasons. Although the 'regional M.O.I. officers have done excellent work in this war, and have shown a grip on local problems', the staffs were far too small and consequently much of the responsibility for post-raid information fell on the Local Information

Committees, who were simply incapable of discharging it. Thus posters were clumsily prepared, poorly sited and written in confusing language; loudspeaker vans were badly deployed; and basic information was almost impossible to obtain for dissemination. A contributory factor, and one which reflected on the Ministry as a whole, was the nation-wide absence of educative publicity regarding the availability of relief services.

Harrisson painted a very sombre picture whose chief elements consisted of a distressed populace wandering aimlessly about their desolated town, while in the background officials myopically busied themselves with their own tasks, oblivious of the distress of those whom they were supposed to assist. It is true that both local authorities and Local Information Committees placed obstacles of considerable bulk in the path of the Ministry. The air attacks of 1941 made a mockery of British local independence and civic self sufficiency.[108] The consequences were to be seen in information services no less than in the physical relief organised by local government. The RIO could not assume precedence over the local authority even in those duties specifically allocated to him by the Ministry,[109] for his was, in theory at least, a supportive and advisory role; and if local officials failed to prepare information or were obviously doing it badly he could not call upon executive authority, but had to rescue the situation as best he could by whatever influence he possessed. Again, so far as Local Information Committees were concerned, the tradition of local self-help and autonomy bedevilled the Ministry. Of necessity, the RIO relied upon their assistance, especially if his region suffered two or more simultaneous raids, but they could not be ordered to carry out a particular line of policy and were often of poor quality and riven with internal feuds and jealousies. An editorial in *Local Government Service* commented: 'These committees have in many cases been an abject failure; and . . . it is doubtful whether they can be relied on for adequate measure of post-raid help even when they are alive.'[110] No doubt local government officers viewed these committees with suspicion as centres of competing administrative power, but they were a source of more trouble than assistance to the Ministry of Information.

Within these constraints the RIO achieved much. Things should and perhaps could have been better. To have made them so, however, might have meant the abandonment of local government and of local autonomy. The British people had already accepted a degree of restriction and direction unthinkable before the war and the total administration of services from the centre, even if possible of achievement by a grossly overworked government, might not have seemed to many people to be worth the price of greater efficiency. Muddling through air raids imposed a heavy price in terms of confusion, discomfort and distress, but perhaps it was preferable to Britain assuming at least the form of that totalitarian structure of government which was one of the 'evil things' the nation was fighting.

To say that the part played by the Ministry in air raids was a subsidiary one is not to minimise the role but rather to place it in perspective as the lubricant of the whole machine of civil defence.[111] Indeed, it seems to have been awarded an even lesser role within the department. What is to be made of the remarkable fact that discussion of air raids, including related matters such as pre-raid instructions and shelter publicity, occurred in the department on less than twenty occasions in the period under review? Possibly the chief executive officers were content to allow the machine to tick over and to let the ministries of Health and Home Security get on with the really heavy work of raid relief. A more fundamental explanation may lie in a changed attitude towards the public. After a period of two or three months from the commencement of intensive bombing, during which time Nicolson and others were anxious about morale, there dawned in the Ministry the realisation that morale would not break. The British people were sturdy after all. There was no mass panic, no call for peace at any price, no querulous demand for material reward in return for a continued war effort. It quickly became apparent that the individual, by dint of a complex of irrational and realistic attitudes and reactions,[112] possessed reserves of strength more than sufficient to withstand the weight of attack of which the Germans were then capable. And although the propagandists toyed with plans for morale-boosting campaigns throughout 1941, they would never again question the nation's determination and courage. The air raids between September 1940 and May 1941 tested the British as never before and they judged themselves as having passed the test heroically, if one is to take seriously the mythology of the blitz which seems to serve as the most recent example of the British people's greatness. They were not to know that those servants of the government employed, among other things, to extol their heroism were at the same time breathing hearty sighs of relief that the task had not been to stem a tide of panic and defeatism.

5

'*The Same Old Hun?*': Anti-German Propaganda

In war it is almost axiomatic that the peoples of the combatant nations must be taught to hate each other. This applied to Britain no less than it did to Germany in the Second World War. Writing before the war, Hans Speier stated, 'In modern war, in which mass opinions count, the enemy has to be wholly identified . . . with the principle of evil, so that one can mobilize the power of right for one's own cause.'[1] As if with the Ministry of Information's propaganda in mind, Joseph Geoghegan observed during the war that the enemy was denied any shred of justification:

> He so blatantly represents the negation of all good, he so deliberately runs counter to every law of God or man, he carries with him such a foul string of barbarities that it becomes only right and proper to smite him hip and thigh.[2]

While the Ministry saw it as a prime duty on the home front 'by the dissemination of *truth* to attack the enemy in the minds of the public',[3] it became clear as the war progressed that statements made about the enemy represented a deliberate attempt to manipulate public opinion and attitude. 'All propaganda is lies', wrote Orwell in 1942, 'even when one is telling the truth.'[4] The validity of this paradox is borne out by an examination of the Ministry's use of the 'truth', for the propagandists did select facts to serve ends and they did offer as truth statements which at best could be described as convenient assumptions. On one issue – the nature of the RAF's bombing strategy in Germany – they were not above stretching the truth to the threshold of lying.

A contemporary psychologist, E. H. Henderson, suggested that

137

the aim of the propagandist is to inculcate certain attitudes by means which prevent critical thinking.[5] That the Ministry of Information attempted to accomplish this should cause no surprise. What is worthy of comment, however, is the fact that the Ministry simultaneously attached great importance to releasing simple, unadorned news and tried to persuade other departments to limit their requests for censorship strictly to matters of security. The ambivalence in departmental attitudes cannot be attributed to poor co-ordination between one division and another, since on the same day a senior officer might berate the Admiralty for witholding unpleasant news and then suggest at a meeting that the public should be induced to regard the Germans with hatred as a means of sustaining morale.

Propaganda policy was formally considered in two committees. On the Policy Committee sat the Minister and his chief executive officers, their task being to formulate and to approve departmental policy over the whole range of the Ministry's domestic and overseas functions. Below it was the Planning Committee, whose job was to work out means for carrying out domestic policy and to recommend courses of action to sustain civilian morale. The arrival of ideas and problems at these committees was a somewhat random process. Some emerged from the numerous divisions of the Ministry, some came in the form of directives from Cabinet, while others were contained in the reports of the Home Intelligence Division; but as often as not the senior officers entered Senate House each day with preoccupations fostered by what they had heard in the club the previous evening or on the train in the morning. Anxiety and irrationality are given ample scope in the shaping of propaganda policy and even a man of the intellectual capacity of Harold Nicolson was unable to escape their influence. We are fortunate in having access to his diaries, for they show the shifting fears and anxieties of a man who was at the centre of policy making during the worst days of the war. Patently honest, he was nonetheless forced into considerable mental contortions in order to carry on his job. He, rather than the soulless apparatchik, should be visualised as the typical British propagandist.

To judge by the resources, man hours and thought expended on telling the public what attitudes they ought to adopt towards the enemy, the Ministry considered the matter to be one of cardinal importance. Surprisingly, the War Cabinet took very little interest in this aspect of the department's work. In spite of his prodigious capacity for interfering in the minutest detail of government, Churchill allowed the Ministry to go its own way and rarely intervened on any matter relating to domestic propaganda about the

Germans. The explanation may reside in the fact that he possessed a much stronger faith in the people's determination than was ever displayed by the propagandists, who were – until the advent of Brendan Bracken – constantly reading into the flimsiest of evidence the imminent breakdown of Britain's martial spirit.

On one of the infrequent occasions on which Churchill ordered something specific to be done he allowed himself to be overruled. The Nazi newspaper *Völkischer Beobachter* stated that Germany's war aim was to reduce Britain to 'degradation and poverty' and Churchill told Nicolson to see to it that the statement was plastered over every wall in the country.[6] Duff Cooper and his senior advisers, presumably on the ground that such a poster might alarm rather than steel the public, successfully vetoed the Prime Minister's order. On another occasion, following a bitter attack on the Italians by Duff Cooper in a broadcast of 10 June 1940, Churchill intervened on a point of historical accuracy:

> I could not express full agreement with what you said about Caporetto, and I have not met one single person who did not think it a mistake. First of all, I do not think the Italian army was much to blame for Caporetto. The great bulk had no opportunity of fighting at all, and were locked in a hopeless traffic jam for five or six days between the mountains and the coast, without food, orders, or the possibility of action. I have expressed these views publicly on several occasions. Secondly, it is a well-known rule of war policy to praise the courage of your opponent which enhances your own victory when gained.[7]

In April 1943 Churchill was irritated by a report in the press of chivalrous German behaviour on the Tunisian front. He wrote to the Resident Minister in Algiers:

> It is a mistake in this stage of the war to pay these kinds of tribute to the enemy, and one is never quite sure that behind such messages is not some preparatory peace propaganda . . . These beastly Huns are murdering people wholesale in Europe and have committed the most frightful atrocities in Russia, and it would be entirely in accordance with their technique to win a reputation for treating British and American soldiers with humanity on exceptional and well-advertised occasions.[8]

On certain major issues it was unnecessary for the Minister of Information to receive detailed instructions from either the Prime Minister or the War Cabinet. For example, the disinclination of both Chamberlain and Churchill to declare Britain's war aims clearly prohibited the Ministry from putting out any such declaration of its own devising, however strong the impulse was to do so. On other major issues the Cabinet should have been consulted. The critical question as to whether the German people were to be characterised as incorrigibly aggressive was left for the consideration of the Ministry. Yet this matter, so closely related to a post-war settlement, should have merited the Cabinet's closest attention. Unlike its operations in censorship and the issue of news, the Ministry was virtually unconstrained by higher authority in pronouncements on the enemy.

In July 1938 Stephen King-Hall insisted:

> We must go into the war with a conviction in the minds of the people that it was forced on us and that we did all that was honourably possible to avoid it . . . The danger would appear to be that in a crisis which may arise very suddenly we shall have public opinion in a muddle in this country . . . we may find ourselves in the dangerous position of the Cabinet having issued threats and being committed to action for which public opinion is unprepared and might not support.[9]

In the event, it was the public that clamoured for a firm declaration of war when Chamberlain appeared to waver after the Germans attacked Poland. Having prepared a considerable amount of material, the Ministry adopted a historical, almost scholarly, emphasis in explaining the causes of the war. In a pamphlet of some 6,000 words, D. A. Routh, the historian, reached deep into German history to expose the roots of her latest act of aggression and, while not sparing the nation from charges of wickedness, concluded:

> . . . the tragedy of Germany is the tragedy of a great people who, through lack of political experience and for reasons lying far back in their history, have twice failed to prevent their national power from falling into the hands of violent and ambitious rulers . . . The overthrow of National-Socialism is the one hope for the future of the German people.[10]

In *Assurance of Victory* it was argued that Britain had striven to ameliorate the harsher provisions of the Versailles Treaty and to integrate Germany in a peaceful Europe but, misled by Hitler, the Germans had insisted on supporting a treacherous foreign policy. There was now no recourse but to prevent Germany from trampling on the rights of other nations, a policy 'which British Governments have consistently pursued in the face of the attempts of any Power to dominate Europe by force'.[11] So strong was the wish to exculpate the German people from blame that one of the Ministry's pamphlet writers was moved to state:

> National-Socialism began as an honourable experiment. Its leaders started with many fine ideals and the German people had every right to expect that they would be realised. Ideals and expectations have been disappointed: both have been sacrificed to the ends of war . . . This is the tragedy of National-Socialism.[12]

The Ministry's apology for the moral decline of Nazism was one of the more bizarre statements it made during the war and is symptomatic of the extent to which the spirit of appeasement still pervaded the Chamberlain government.

Once the British were at war there was little sign of reluctance to pursue a struggle 'quietly accepted as inevitable'[13] and as a consequence the Ministry's long-winded statements about its cause became superfluous. A source of greater concern – and one that would continue well into 1941 – were reports of public confusion about Britain's military aims. It was one thing to know who had started the war but quite another to know what victory was meant to achieve or, indeed, whether the government would stop short of the complete defeat of the enemy.

The longer the nation appeared to be only nominally at war the less likely did it seem that the government was utterly determined to defeat, in Chamberlain's phrase, 'the evil things'. Lord Macmillan cautiously went a little farther. He stated that his department's propaganda was based on the restoration in Europe of '(a) The sanctity of absolute values. (b) The sanctity of the individual and of the family. (c) The comity of nations'.[14] Although he affirmed Britain's intention to 'destroy the rule of the Nazis', the vapid nature of the statement was unlikely to satisfy those people who wanted to know just how far the government intended taking the fight. Sir John Reith gave promise of more vigour. While expressing approval of the principles enunciated by Lord Macmillan, he asked the Cabinet whether they 'considered that sufficient emphasis had been laid on arousing a positive will to defeat and destroy'.[15] His subsequent memorandum contained a good deal of Reithian pith but the statement of war aims was only slightly less vague than Macmillan's restoration of 'sanctities':

5. Victory means:
    (a) Release of Germany's victims.
    (b) The right to live, think, vote, talk, worship God as you choose.
    (c) That the new world which must arise from the war will be Christian and not Satanic, spiritual and not material.
6. A compromise peace with an unbeaten Germany would be defeat in the long run.[16]

Even this was too much for the Chamberlain Cabinet. Reith's warning against a compromise peace was felt to be 'liable to misinterpretation' and it was agreed that in its place should be inserted: 'No peace could be justified which does not secure these things'.[17] It is perhaps too slight a piece of evidence to bear the full weight of the charge that Chamberlain was amenable to the idea of a negotiated peace, but it does show how difficult government policy – or lack of it – made the job of those propagandists who sought to utter a call for the complete destruction of the Nazi regime.

As long as the government cherished the forlorn hope that the Germans might overthrow their leaders the Ministry of Information was unable to tell the British people they were pitted against a ruthless enemy. Reith might inveigh against them in Cabinet: 'You are fighting the German people – 80 million of them . . . The Germans have been taught to be ruthless and to hate the British. They are merciless.'[18] Publicly, however, the Ministry continued to maintain that Germany was a sort of international miscreant who could be brought to his senses by a sharp rap over the knuckles. But the impulse to relieve the German people from blame lasted only as long as the German armies confined their attentions to Eastern Europe. When the war moved closer to home and it was realised the fight was on in earnest the tone of the propaganda underwent an abrupt change,[19] a process greatly hastened by Churchill's accession to the premiership on 10 May.

As British troops were being evacuated from Norway, the Policy Committee agreed that the separation of the German people from Nazism should in future be avoided.[20] And after Dunkirk:

The Director General asked whether it was thought that the Ministry should now begin to stir up people's more primitive instincts. After discussion it was considered that we should now pay more attention to stirring up people's anger . . . It might be merely sufficient to impress the people that they were in fact angry.[21]

142

Two weeks later a paper setting out proposals for an 'Anger Campaign' was circulated at the Policy Committee.[22] It is one of the more remarkable documents of wartime government, not merely because it illustrates the mood which gripped the propagandists themselves but also because it demonstrates the extent to which they were capable of misunderstanding the British public.

The public, 'patient, long-suffering, slow to anger, slower still to hate', were believed to be 'harbouring little sense of real personal animus against the average German man or woman [and] accepting with amazing phlegm bitter reverses without overmuch recrimination'. This placidity must be replaced with 'personal anger . . . against the German people and Germany'. This raises two difficult questions. First, what justification was there for thinking that the people felt no anger towards the Germans? And second, was anger necessary 'as a factor in increasing the war effort and preparing the British public for every emergency'? Such evidence as was available to the Ministry suggested that there was nothing approaching the almost hysterically bellicose mood of the British in the early months of the First World War,[23] which is not to say that in the middle of 1940 the public regarded the Germans with equanimity. What did the Home Intelligence reports indicate? Hitler's discomfiting ability to realise his military predictions aroused apprehension but it was Italy rather than Germany which earned the anger of the British after Mussolini's declaration of war on 11 June.[24] Not until September 1940 were there any reports of bitterness against the Germans, and even then they were said to have been aroused not by Nazi ideology or German victories in Europe but by direct air attacks on Britain.[25] 'It is so strange', observed Harold Nicolson, 'that in this moment of anxiety there is no hatred of Hitler or the Germans.'[26]

Granted, then, that the Ministry had good reason to suppose that the people did not hate the enemy, what justification was there for the deduction that this represented a danger? It is too easy to be wise after the event. We know that the British people displayed resilience and determination, though in no greater measure than German civilians later in the war, but we must avoid the anachronism of imputing that knowledge to the propagandists in June 1940, when invasion seemed a distinct probability. Nevertheless, stolidity and phlegm might just as easily have indicated a sober realisation of the trials that lay ahead and a determination to withstand them; whereas anger of the semi-hysterical sort the Ministry wished to inculcate might, if spontaneously present, have revealed a certain brittleness and instability far more worrying than outward placidity.

143

It was the opinion of contemporary psychiatrists and social psychologists (whom, for the most part, the Ministry studiously avoided consulting) that hate is a poor basis for morale.[27] The emotion, asserted one authority, prevents discrimination between good and bad individuals among the enemy, blinds one to historical realities and may, if continued into peacetime, affect post-war settlements and lay the foundation for another war.[28] If the reasoning then current in the Ministry is followed, where does it lead? The public were not angry. They were, therefore, either not aware of the danger of the situation or were unwilling to construct for themselves good reasons for standing up to the Nazis. In consequence they were incapable of resisting whatever lay ahead.

So in order to 'change the attitude of the most stolid and unvengeable people in the world' it was proposed to mount a massive and, at first, clandestine campaign. Photographs, cartoons, posters, film, radio, leaflets, speeches, exhibitions, window displays – all were to be put at the service of 'the modern art of propaganda – all pervasive, subtle and persistent'. The Ministry should be seen to enter the campaign only after non-official propaganda had succeeded and the people were beginning to feel stirrings of anger. The methods of Goebbels had not been overlooked, for, as the paper averred with a hint of admiration, 'it is exactly upon these intensive lines that propaganda has succeeded in creating the militant Germany of to-day from a battered, helpless nation'. The officials of the Ministry were urged to regard themselves as 'a small group of expert propagandists . . . in a position to tap and colour and guide every source of public expression'. The 'total attack' was to have as its principal weapon the co-operation of the twenty or thirty most influential journalists of the national press who, in consultation with the Ministry, would write a 'stream of carefully worded features' based on certain themes. In suggesting one such theme, 'The German Character', the paper stressed the importance of tailoring the style and content to the class of the reader. For the broad mass the emotional appeal was felt to be most suitable :

EUROPE'S GANGSTERS RAMPANT

THE RECURRING MADNESS OF THE GERMAN EMPIRE

HUNS, GOTHS AND VANDALS

GERMAN LUST FOR WORLD DOMINATION

1870 – 1914 – 1939

'THEY DO NOT CHANGE'

BLOWS ARE ALL THEY UNDERSTAND

144

FREDERICK – BISMARCK – WILHELM – HITLER

THEY SHALL NOT PASS

WHY THE KAISER CALLED THEM 'HUNS'

THE ROUT OF THE GERMANS IN 1918

THE GERMAN IS *NOT* INVINCIBLE

THESE BULLIES CAN BE BEATEN

THE LESSON OF THE AIR FORCE

INFERIORITY COMPLEX – THE ROOT OF GERMAN AGGRESSION

The 'sophisticated and educated classes' were to be given 'more restrained and factual' evidence:

The fundamental 'rottenness' of the German character – historical analysis.

German writers on the Germany bully complex – Nietzsche, Treitschke, etc.

Detailed instances where Germans have crumpled up.

German weaknesses.

Germany's 'case' torn to shreds – refutation of Versailles Treaty attacks, etc.

Events since the war have utterly confuted the weak-kneed apologists for Hitler. His 'lebensraum' is the whole world. His 'culture' the death of every other race.

The middle classes – 'still not mentally at war' – had to be convinced that the Germans intended to rob them of their incomes and culture; the professional classes 'told of refugee professional men, of how they have been hounded and put to menial tasks – like washing dishes and cleaning lavatories'; and shopkeepers, businessmen and industrial workers disabused of the idea that 'things might go much the same way under Hitler'. While being careful to emphasise that stories of German brutality should not be allowed to arouse fear rather than hatred,[29] the Ministry insisted that atrocity stories are believed and are effective. Thus another Nurse Cavell story was to be found and news of German ruthlessness treated so as to illustrate triumphant courage 'such as the woman in Bruges in 1914 who slaughtered two Germans who had killed her son'.

The smaller touches were not omitted. Nazi leaders, it was recommended, should never be mentioned without an appropriate label: 'Hitler – the Arch Gangster', 'Jew Baiter Streicher' and 'Lie Minister Goebbels'. The BBC must be persuaded to cease referring to 'Herr' Hitler and 'Signor' Mussolini. A rather more drastic suggestion was that 'a few death sentences on traitors would have a great effect in heightening the public temper against the enemy'.

Hitler posed a very difficult problem. Later in the war it would be possible to make a joke of him but in 1940 it was not easy to counter the impression of his political and military omniscience, and all that could be done was to suggest somewhat feebly that the opposite was the case :

> It cannot be too strongly emphasized that Hitler's success is engendering a legend of infallibility which is immensely powerful . . . THIS LEGEND MUST BE DEFEATED. It must be made clear that the little countries Hitler has invaded were lying defenceless at Hitler's door for generations. Even in France he is only making headway by sheer weight of metal. Hitler is personally fallible, despicable, cowardly . . . He is important only as the embodiment of the German lust for power in the most evil guise it has ever taken.

This latter assertion contains the essence not only of the Anger Campaign but of the tenor of domestic propaganda for the rest of the war, namely that there can be no distinction between a German and a Nazi. Nazism is but the latest and most virulent manifestation of the inherent wickedness of the German race. Stephen King-Hall's propaganda theme of 1938 – 'we reluctantly destroy German bodies in order to save the souls of the rest'[30] – had been hastily jettisoned. The new orthodoxy, suggested the propagandists, should be embodied by a famous writer such as J. B. Priestley in a short wall text to be issued in millions :

The Secret Beast

In the middle of a great civilised continent, far from the sea which brings a breath of the outer world to freshen men's minds, a secret people dwell.

Ever and again they become crazed with a spell of hero worship. A leader arises among them who tells them that they are greater than the other peoples of the world. Knowing nothing of the world's vastness and of the seas which link land to land, they believe – and march out to slaughter and destroy.

The secret people of the Germanys are worse than fools in their folly. When their madness comes upon them, out leaps a primitive, barbarian beast-like instinct. They kill without pity, rejoicing in blood, as animals kill. They know no law, as animals know no law.

146

They are Europe's secret beasts, roused to senseless fury. It is all Europe's mission to cower them and cage them today, as all Europe has had to do before.

The Hun is at the gate. He will rage and destroy. He will slaughter the women and the children. But in the end, he will run from the men as he has always run in the past.

Out then and kill . . . the extermination of the wild animal let loose on Europe is the plain business of Europe's citizens.

By these and other means a fundamental change of public attitude was to be wrought. The wish was very much father to the thought. No evidence was forthcoming during the brief life of the Ministry to support the belief that public opinion and emotion were so malleable, and just how seriously the proposed campaign was regarded in the department it is difficult to tell. The men responsible for approving it were well educated, intelligent and worldly and it is barely conceivable that they could contemplate treating the British public as a body of credulous simpletons. Moreover, in proposing a reversion to the crudest type of First World War propaganda, were they not aware of the scepticism which the falsity and unscrupulousness of that propaganda had engendered between the wars? The explanation must be tentatively sought in the states of mind of the propagandists themselves. They knew what the public could only strongly suspect – that the threat to Britain was imminent and grave – and the Anger Campaign seems to have been devised to stir up their own 'primitive instincts' as profoundly as those of the people at large. The Ministry saw about them a dangerous complacency whose cure it was their urgent duty to prescribe. While other men produced the munitions and manned the beaches the propagandists probably felt the need to do something which could be interpreted, if only by themselves, as of equal importance to the nation's defence. It was at this time, too, that the Ministry were advocating the imposition of compulsory censorship, but this departure from the liberal attitude with which censorship was normally exercised was soon abandoned. Not so the new propaganda. For, although the Anger Campaign was not implemented on the heroic scale originally contemplated, its principal themes were embodied in the Ministry's public attitude towards the enemy for the rest of the war.

One facet of the belief that the public were insufficiently hostile towards the enemy was a conviction that there existed little comprehension of the consequences of German occupation. In the early months of the war it was the working man who was thought to be in most need of stiffening and he was accordingly referred to the plight of the German worker, whose liberation could only be achieved through the crushing of Nazism by his British counterpart.[31] By 1940 this allusive propaganda was dropped in favour of the blunt approach. It was observed in a pamphlet, *What Would Happen if Hitler Won*, that some people believed that Hitler 'would not bother much about ordinary people like you and me : they think that everyday life here . . . would carry on pretty much as usual'. On the contrary :

> If Hitler won you couldn't make a joke in the pub without being afraid that a spy may not get you run in or beaten up; you could not talk freely in front of your children for fear that they might give you away (in Germany they are encouraged to); if you were a worker you would be at the mercy of your employer about hours and wages for you would have no trade union.[32]

To leaders of opinion Duff Cooper wrote :

> It is most important therefore that people of influence such as yourself should do all in your power to fight against such dangerous opinions. People should be reminded that Hitler has sworn to destroy both France and England and that he will never be content until he has carried out this purpose. In the first place he would take away all our liberties which we have fought for so many centuries to obtain. His secret police would dominate not only our public but also our private lives. It would not be safe to make a joke about our masters either in public or in private. In Germany children are encouraged to spy upon their parents and to repeat any chance remark they may hear which criticises the Government. Trade Unions would be abolished here as they were in Germany, and everyone would be compelled to work for whatever wages and during whatever hours the State laid down. Worse than that, whole portions of the working population would probably be transferred to foreign countries where they would be compelled to labour under the lash, separated from their wives and families, and treated as slaves . . . This is a matter upon which great stress should be laid in giving guidance to people at the present time.[33]

On 22 June, Mary Adams informed the Planning Committee that 'the most notable development was a fear that the British leaders would sell the pass to Hitler as the French leaders were thought to have done'.[34] So, while the public were reported to suspect that certain of their leaders would betray them as Pétain and Laval had betrayed the French people, the Ministry nervously entertained the idea that the people might go the way of the French masses and simply crumple in the face of a resolute enemy. As we have seen in Chapter 3, Duff Cooper in July 1940 tried unsuccessfully to persuade the Cabinet to hold out a promise of post-war economic and social reform in exchange for a total war effort. Denied the opportunity of making promises for the future, the Ministry could at least discredit those made by the enemy. This was not always easy. When J. M. Keynes was asked by Nicolson to broadcast a rebuttal of the economic proposals of the New Order, he replied:

> . . . your letter seems to suggest that we should do well to pose as champions of the pre-war economic *status quo* and outbid Funk by offering good old 1920–21 or 1930–33, i.e. gold standard or international exchange *laissez-faire* . . . Is this particularly attractive or good propaganda? . . . obviously I am not the man to preach the beauties and merits of the pre-war gold standard.
>
> In my opinion about three-quarters of the passages quoted from the German broadcasts would be quite excellent if the name of Great Britain were substituted for Germany or the Axis . . . If Funk's plan is taken at face value, it is excellent and just what we ourselves ought to be thinking of doing. If it is to be attacked, the way to do it would be to cast doubt and suspicion on its *bona fides*.[35]

Nicolson was not disappointed by Keynes's response: 'I am delighted. I hate sham propaganda.'[36]

There was in the Ministry's anti-German propaganda a certain element of defensiveness, perhaps aggravated by the veto on statements about domestic reform, but stemming chiefly from the belief that the frenetic 'dynamism' of Nazi ideology was not unattractive to the British people. Two and a half years after the outbreak of war Home Intelligence observed:

> The public has no clearly worked out conception of the purpose of the war. The Russians have a clear-cut purpose: they have a way of living that they think worth fighting for and which enables them to fight well. The Germans are believed to have

a purpose. We have only vague conceptions, fluctuating between ideas of holding what we have got and ideas of right and wrong.[37]

The tone of the report echoed the stale, even bored, mood of the public in the first half of 1942, a period which witnessed considerable parliamentary and public dissatisfaction with the government's conduct of the war. Britain seemed to be having a minimal impact on the course of events and, having in 1940 achieved the supreme feat of thwarting Hitler's invasion plan, the public could now only set before themselves the distant prospect of victory. The Ministry appears to have believed that the British people, observing from the sidelines the fierce struggle of two nations fighting for opposed but compelling ideologies, yearned for a set of ideas that might invest their sacrifices with a greater significance than the preservation of national sovereignty.

An ideology of sorts was proclaimed by the Ministry of Information. Although used principally to discredit specific aspects of Nazism, it was supposed to represent something worth fighting for. Diffuse, vague and lacking the immediacy of Nazism and communism, it nonetheless reflected the sincere ideas of men forced by circumstances to articulate their convictions. These may be conveniently examined in terms of what the propagandists had to say about the past, the role of Christianity and the future.

The Ministry contrived to stretch a Whiggish interpretation of history back to the pre-Christian era. As part of that civilisation whose 'ideal of a good life men have created through 2,000 years',[38] Britain had contributed the latest ideal :

> . . . human history has been marked by certain definite phases of advancement, each one of which produced its own special contribution to the improvement of Man (e.g. Greece : the freedom of human intelligence. Rome : the sanctity of contracts. Middle Ages : chivalry. France : intellectual sincerity. Britain : fair play).[39]

While the concept of 'fair play' may be deeply embedded in the British consciousness[40] and was possibly a factor in the people's dislike of German behaviour, it was hardly a stirring call to action. Nicolson preferred to speak of Britain's past record in achieving social justice while at the same time preserving the rights of man.[41] The conjunction of the ideas of Britain as a pioneer of freedom and justice, against both domestic and foreign tyrants, and of balanced, gradual social improvement was central to the propaganda, for the Ministry

150

could simultaneously combat the supposed attractiveness of Nazi social promises and represent the country as the defender of Western civilisation. RIOs were therefore asked to preach the following social philosophy :

Evolutionary revolution as distinct from revolutionary revolution is the characteristic British method of ensuring political, social and economic progress. The difference between our method and that of the Germans should be emphasised. One results in forward progression : the other in a reversion to systems long abandoned by the democracies.[42]

Whereas distant times buoyed up the propagandists, the very recent past weighed heavily on their shoulders – indeed it might be said to have haunted them. Lord Macmillan, in speaking of the Nazi and Communist revolutions as 'morbid systems' of a larger social change[43] feared for the immutability of English liberal democracy. Hence the rather desperate grabbing by the Ministry at the half-baked Fabianism of 'evolutionary revolution'. That which they defended and pointed to as Britain's liberal inheritance seemed in danger not merely from the direct military challenge of Hitler or the corrosive effects of communist ideology but from deeper forces of historical change. The glorification of the past was therefore both an invocation of simple patriotism and a call to the people to affirm their belief in the principles upon which the state supposedly rested.

Germany's claim to be the sole bulwark of Christian Europe against Bolshevism was reason enough for the Ministry to insist that a true reading of the situation pitted Christian Britain against pagan Germany. But the constant theme of Britain as a Christian nation, and a nation of Christians, also derived from the received opinion which stated that belief in Christianity informed the country's secular virtues. There seem to have been few qualms about pressing religion into the service of propaganda. Pausing only to observe that the churches should 'not be suspected of being used as channels of propaganda',[44] the senior officials set up the Religions Division, whose purpose at home was to impart 'a real conviction of the Christian contribution to our civilisation and of the essential anti-Christian character of Nazism'.[45]

'God is on our side' has ever been the cry of nations at war and the Religions Division, although aware of the dangers in resurrecting it, comforted themselves with the knowledge 'that the Nazi regime has openly derided Christianity and announced that it is setting up a new religion. The Christian issue has therefore become much

151

more important than in previous wars, when both sides invoked the same creed,'[46] Organised in Protestant, Roman Catholic and, later, Orthodox and Jewish sections, the division worked chiefly through contacts in the churches. It encouraged public meetings, distributed printed material such as a weekly series called *The Spiritual Issues of the War*, stimulated the religious press and put out direct propaganda to the wider public on religious matters. John Betjeman, who was then the press attaché in Dublin, was not a member of the Ministry but corresponded with the Religions Division on the extremely delicate matter of British propaganda in Eire – addressing officers of the Division as 'Brother' and occasionally concluding his letters with 'Yours in Calvin's name'. The Sword of the Spirit, founded by Cardinal Hinsley as a body to proclaim the Church's hostility to Nazism, received a greal deal of assistance from the Ministry of Information, a fact which the Religions Division was anxious to conceal.[47]

The word 'crusade' sprang easily to the lips of the propagandists, since it was very tempting to cast Britain in the role of a Christian warrior opposing the forces of darkness. In September 1939 Lord Macmillan addressed a meeting of church leaders at Lambeth Palace and asked them to issue a joint manifesto declaring their attitude to the war, taking care to emphasise that the Ministry wished to appear in no way connected with the statement.[48] A joint declaration was issued but it was not published until 21 December 1940 and, although exploited for propaganda purposes, could hardly have pleased the Ministry. Signed by the Archbishops of Canterbury, York and Westminster and the Moderator of the Free Churches, the statement made no mention of the enemy and, instead, dwelt on the religious and ethical foundations of a future peace, going so far as to recommend the abolition of material inequality and a fair distribution of the earth's resources.[49] Clearly the leaders of the churches were not going to be drawn into a 'crusade' inspired by a government department.

But Duff Cooper had no reservations about characterising the conflict as a 'religious war'.[50] Nor did the members of the Religions Division, although in a slightly more qualified fashion :

> . . . to speak of a Christian crusade is dangerously misleading. But our civilisation is based ultimately on Christian principles . . . You cannot spread Christianity by the sword, but you can defend a society in which Christian principles are allowed scope and in which there is freedom of thought and worship.[51]

Thus the Ministry turned its affirmation of Britain's Christianity into an attack on Nazi Germany. And almost anything could be and was interpreted as an affront to the spirit of Christianity. The persecution of German clerics such as Pastor Niemoller and Bishop Galen and of churches throughout occupied Europe, the practice of euthanasia – these more obvious crimes were supplemented with accusations of paganism, sexual immorality, Fuhrer-worship and the perversion of children's education. British Catholics were sternly warned :

> No true Catholic can watch with a clear conscience the holocaust of his co-religionists in Nazi-occupied Europe. There can be no compromise or indifference in the realms of the spirit. Those who are not actively against Nazism must ask themselves whether by their passivity they are not actually for Nazism.[52]

The imperative tone of such pronouncements was as strong as that found in the department's general statements about Germany. But, staffed by clerics and working largely through the churches, the Religions Division adroitly sidestepped the potential embarrassment to the Ministry of a situation in which religion was seen to be a creature of propaganda.

Full use was made of symbols designed to fashion an image of the Briton as a tolerant, peaceable, home-loving family man – as opposed to the Germans who, because they found 'it difficult to credit the individual as such with dignity and worth . . . tried to acquire them by huddling into rigid hierarchies and disciplined formations, by reverencing rank and drill'.[53] Furthermore, they 'are dead – dead to joy, dead to decency, dead to thought, dead to reason, virtue and to freedom, dead to themselves, to that humanity which makes men men'.[54] At the same time, propaganda sought to bolster the prestige of the British political system by underlining the relationship between the people's social impulses and those institutions which enshrined them. Francis Williams put it thus :

> The principles of Democracy do not simply affect our political system . . . They are reflected in our family life, in our attitude to children, to marriage, to all personal relationships . . . in little things, in the way a tennis club is run or a village club or a Women's Institute, or a free and easy discussion in the corner pub. They are to be found throughout our Friendly Societies and our Trade Unions and in the principles of collective bargaining honoured by employers and workers alike. They are woven inextricably into the texture of our daily lives.[55]

Having painted this picture of the best of all possible worlds, the Ministry found itself in some difficulty over its propaganda about the future. Because of Churchill's antipathy to public discussion and speculation about post-war Britain, the Ministry could only throw out incidental hints about better material things to come. There were exceptions to this restrained policy, such as Bracken's decision to publicise the Beveridge Report. And some statements accidentally slipped through the net. In a pamphlet on the contribution of women to the war effort a surprisingly radical sentiment was expressed:

> Women can see a new regime developing as they watch. Through their participation in factory and production committees, and through the ever-increasing control exercised by the community on the methods of production and trade, they can see the system of private ownership changing before their eyes. New juridical forms are appearing in social relations between people. The profit motive is fast losing the important place that it had as an incitement to work.
>
> Private interests . . . are giving way more and more to those of the community. There is no longer room for privilege and class interests.[56]

Generally speaking, however, propaganda about the future was couched in vague, if apologetic, terms:

> Nobody would pretend that our lives are perfect. There is room for improvements, and improvements are steadily being made.[57]

> We realise that freedom was not always evened out between . . . class and class, man and man. Now we ought to do better. And so first of all we are out to win the war.[58]

The propagandists turned with relief to the less sensitive theme of national regeneration. Building on the hoary idea of war as a crucible in which the individual and the nation are cleansed of dross, the Ministry in the pamphlet *Faith in the Fight* strove to impart that sense of purpose which was thought to be missing. In a surreptitious blow at those who wanted something more concrete, it appealed for a new charity of spirit, 'deeper and more real than any amount of social legislation', and a personal discipline 'more wholesome and more effective than that which any laws or state-authority could possibly enforce'. Apparently no Homes for Heroes, but something better:

154

The new life would be tingling in our veins so that merely to be ourselves we should be up and doing – going out to meet the future with zest and exuberance . . . Only if every one of us sets about giving a practical, personal vindication of our spiritual inspiration, in peace as in war, in private as in public, shall we be winning a lasting victory over the forces of evil and thrusting forward to the nobler destiny of man.[59]

The dissemination of this sort of propaganda, almost rivalling fascism in sheer vacuity, betrayed a lack of understanding, amounting to lack of confidence, in the British public. Though harmless in itself, it is highly improbable that the Ministry's hazy and essentially conservative ideology had any impact upon a people who, for a complex of practical and idealistic reasons, had demonstrated no lack of willingness to continue the fight.

Vansittart's broadcasts late in 1940 and the publication of his *Black Record*, in which he tried to show that the Germans since earliest times had been violent and aggressive, enjoyed considerable public attention and provoked much controversy. Not that his views were novel. At a meeting of the British Psychological Society in March 1940, Dr H. G. Barnes referred to Jung's description of the periodic madness of the German people as 'furor teutonicus':

It must be assumed to be a latent potentiality of the German unconscious which has remained concealed like an underground mine since barbarian times. When the civilised Christian superstructure was undermined by defeat in war, physical deprivation, and a deep and galling sense of inferiority, 'Wotan' swept the nation away like a whirlwind. The individual man is hunted back into a herd collectivity by a daemonic spirit which Hitler himself identifies with Antichrist, and which has devoured Hitler's own individuality.[60]

At a later meeting of the same society, Professor T. H. Pear put an opposing view. He condemned *Black Record* for its distortion of 'history, ethnology, sociology and social psychology in a manner which Dr Goebbels has made familiar', and added: 'No responsible social psychologist . . . would claim that the Germans have a special innate tendency to cruelty, possessed by members of no other nation.'[61] Although Vansittart's beliefs accorded with the Ministry's indiscriminate anti-German propaganda, there took place a debate as to whether quite the correct emphasis was being given to it. At a

Planning Committee meeting in January 1941 the question was posed whether the line 'Germans will always be Germans' should be continued and Sir Kenneth Clark was asked to prepare a memorandum on the subject.[62] His paper, entitled 'It's the Same Old Hun', asked :

> . . . firstly, if the Germans are really incorrigible, what can be the outcome of the war? Are we hoping to exterminate 80 million people or to keep them in continual subjection? The question is often in the mind of the average thoughtful man, and creates a feeling of hopelessness. Secondly, the comparison of this war to the last must have a depressing and disillusioning effect on anyone old enough to remember the post-war period. It would seem in our interest to stress the very great difference between the Germany of 1914–18 and to-day, by pointing out how in the last war all the best elements of German culture and science were still in Germany and were supporting the German cause, whereas now they are outside Germany and supporting us.[63]

His argument is difficult to follow. To say that Germany was much worse than it had been in the Great War, and to demonstrate the thesis by reference to the fine men who had fled the country, was unlikely to reassure those people who despaired of ever seeing a peaceable Germany. However, in explaining his paper, Clark said, 'The emphasis should . . . be on the deterioration of the German character since 1918' adding, 'The problem of what to do after the war with the Germans if they were really unteachable should be passed over in silence.'[64]

Evidently the 'average thoughtful man' would continue to be troubled. But there appear to have been few of his kind. According to Home Intelligence, large numbers of people felt 'that no peace can be considered which does not ensure that Germany will *never* again be able to declare war on England . . . Many . . . want to exterminate, or at least ostracise, the whole German race'.[65] Reports of this kind reached a peak during the period of intensive bombing. With its passing there were remarkably few expressions of bitterness and ruthlessness towards the German people – grim satisfaction and even exultation at the bombing of enemy cities, but little reported desire for a Carthaginian peace. Some people, indeed, were said to be concerned lest the 'effect of Vansittartism might . . . eventually hamper an equitable and reasonable settlement when the war is over'.[66] But the Ministry continued to lay stress on the moral delinquency of the Germans :

Had it been any other nation that unleashed the present horrors upon the earth, one might well despair of twentieth-century civilisation, and feel that mankind is doomed to perish in a holocaust of ritual hatreds, brutalities and attempts at self-extermination. But the fact that for a second time in one generation it is Germany, and Germany alone, who has done these things – that, surely indicates beyond doubt where the evil lies ... In 1914 the cry was this: 'Remember Belgium!' Now, all who revere justice and honour have still blacker crimes to remember.[67]

Vansittartism was fully embraced:

As for history – 'The Germans possessed a fine culture when Greek culture was in its infancy and Rome was not even founded' (Wilhelm Roediger, Berlin school director). Tacitus, who lived nearer to the time, held a different opinion, stating in his book on [*Germanica*] that the Germans left agriculture to slaves and women, while the men occupied themselves only with war and hunting. But Tacitus was merely a Roman writer of genius, and not a National Socialist.[68]

The Roosevelt–Churchill declaration of August 1941 – the Atlantic Charter – and the magnanimous implications for Germany of Article 6 raised afresh the problem of the depiction of the German character. Evidently feeling some measure of responsibility for the material they produced, the members of the Publications Division asked on 28 August whether in view of the Atlantic Charter it was right to continue propaganda along Vansittart lines.[69] On the following day the Deputy Director General issued a prompt and definitive statement:

We cannot combine a promise of peace and prosperity to all States, including the vanquished, with a quenchless feud against Germany. Nor can we regard 'Hitlerite Germany' as equivalent to Germany under all conditions. Nor can we equate the 'destruction of Nazi tyranny' with the destruction of Germany.

It follows that it is not our public aim to ostracise Germany in perpetuity. If it is not, it cannot be good propaganda to enlarge upon the theme that the Germans are a race which has no future in civilisation. What good can that do? It does not help to divide or weaken Germany: on the contrary. It does not encourage support in the USA whose people discern nothing but an age-

157

long feud which they can neither mend nor end. Its only legitimate use would be to dissipate sentimental Germanizing in this country. I do not think the public stands in any need of such a correction to-day.

This can be taken as Ministry policy.[70]

This was the very matter touched upon by Sir Kenneth Clark early in the year. But in the intervening period the rhetoric of hate had become, if anything, even more shrill. Legitimate targets for criticism – Nazi education, the evils of occupation, racial persecution, the idiocy of Nazi ideology – did come under attack but were so uniformly drenched in emotional language as to leave the impression that everything German was and always would be abhorrent. That the future dangers of such a policy were appreciated in the Ministry is clear from the Deputy Director General's statement. Why, then, was the policy not changed? In the absence of minutes and memoranda relating to the debate (if, indeed, it reached the proportions of a debate) the explanation can only be guessed at. Possibly the sheer momentum of the propaganda brushed aside any alternative. There is no evidence to show that such themes as were employed from the Anger Campaign had had any effect. Neither had there been objections to them. The end of the war seemed a long way off late in 1941. And it was no doubt easier for the Ministry to condemn the Germans wholesale than to embark at such a time upon what to many might have appeared as an over-refined nicety of distinction between the people and their Nazi leaders.

In this context it is instructive to examine what was said about the Japanese. For reasons which were closely related to the public's attitude to the war in the Far East, the production of anti-Japanese propaganda was a peripheral activity. The Pacific war was remote to a people preoccupied with the European conflict and after the fall of Singapore it was regarded as very much an American sphere of responsibility.

The Japanese, described in terms appropriate to a newly discovered zoological species, were objects of amused contempt:

Smoking chimneys, policemen and traffic lights, taxis hurrying little men in black coats and bowler hats to offices that might well be in New York, bear witness to Japan's modern technique and disguise her primitive heart.[71]

Although undoubtedly brutal, their courageous devotion to bankrupt and hollow ideas made 'these mediocre people assume the stature of

158

tragedy'.[72] Their defeat would present the allies with a political and social *tabula rasa* : once the Japanese could be taught to exercise 'self control', their institutions would undergo a drastic remoulding along democratic lines and the old, inferior customs and habits of thought would be destroyed.[73] Japan, in other words, knew no better. Whereas Germany did :

> Japan was ahead of Germany in the follow-my-fuhrer danse macabre, but was also tremendously influenced by Germany. Amazing though the parallel between them is – in pseudo-religions, tribalism, aggression, brutality, false-swearing, density about other mentalities, contempt of women, contempt of freedom, contempt of the human spirit and negation of God – it is not complete. Germany is a heretic, relapsed from universal standards that Japan has never known.[74]

German barbarity for its very wilfulness was therefore all the more reprehensible and, by implication, could not be easily – if ever – extirpated. To say that the Germans had once conformed to a universal standard of civilised behaviour cannot, of course, be reconciled with the Vansittart line that they had never been truly part of European Christendom, but logic is ever the least regarded component of propaganda.

Because of the government's insistence that British policy was directed solely at knocking out enemy war production and internal communications, the Ministry was rather more circumspect in its propaganda about bombing than in other issues involving Germany. A delicate path had to be picked out between the propagandists' desire to show that German civilians were suffering heavily and the obligation to proclaim the essentially strategic nature of Bomber Command's operations. But after February 1942, when the decision was taken to direct the main weight of the RAF's attack against German civilians, the Ministry did more than exercise discretion. It lied. Noble Frankland has written of the Air Ministry's publicity : 'The damage to the residential and central areas, which were in reality the main aim of the area attacks, was ascribed to what could unfortunately not be avoided if the factories and so on were to be hit.'[75] The Ministry of Information was party to the deception.

Although not wishing in 1940–41 to adopt a 'vindictive note',[76] it was nonetheless thought wise to hint at the fact that Germany was sustaining civilian casualties :

Since May 10th [1940], the RAF have carried out widespread raids on Germany . . . For a number of reasons it does not pay us to adopt indiscriminate bombing for its own sake or as a measure of retaliation. The crippling of the enemy's industry and war machine is likely to lead to far more conclusive results in a shorter space of time. Some of the targets which we have attacked are, in fact, situated in thickly populated towns and districts . . . and, consequently, the enemy civilian population has by no means gone unscathed.[77]

In April 1941 RIOs were instructed to 'stress the point that we cannot afford to divert our striking power from the main military and other kindred objectives to actions of a secondary nature'.[78] Indignant at the implication that Britain desisted from bombing German civilians for strategic reasons only, the London RIO asked, 'Must Government always shirk the moral issue? Have we not the courage to say that to take reprisals is wrong in itself, unethical, unchristian and unworthy of the British people?'[79] There was a distinctly uncomfortable reaction to this protest but, at the same time, a strong reluctance to antagonise the public by saying that enemy civilians were being spared on moral grounds. 'Sir Wyndham may be right', observed one official. 'Fortunately it is not for us to say. Perhaps we are not all Christians?'[80] The matter was hastily referred to higher authority for decision, although sufficient qualms existed for the BBC 'to be asked to avoid describing bombs as "beautiful" '.[81] There is no indication in the records to show whether the matter was considered by the War Cabinet but as the policy underwent no change it may be assumed that the Ministry's avoidance of moral entanglements earned the government's approval.

News of heavy attacks was greeted by the public with enthusiasm, despite the knowledge of severe losses sustained by Bomber Command,[82] and by 1942 the earlier veiled hints of civilian casualties had become heavy nudges. Of the extremely heavy raids on Cologne of 30 May 1942, the Ministry commented in a pamphlet: 'Ninety minutes bombing created devastation over an area eight times the size of the City of London . . . Steadily the storm will increase in violence.'[83] No one could mistake the fact that an attack on this scale had no purpose other than to destroy large areas of civilian housing. That there were, in fact, no illusions is clear from the Home Intelligence report following news of the Cologne raid:

. . . nothing has given such a lift to public confidence for many
months as the raid on Cologne. The public's astonishment and
awe appear to have been almost as marked as their elation and
satisfaction . . .

Some regret has been expressed, 'particularly by older people,
that women and children should have to suffer from our bombing :
but no one has been heard to suggest that we should limit our
attacks on this account', and 'even the most soft hearted' feel that
it is 'the only way, however distasteful, to drive home to the
German people what their airmen have been doing in other
countries'.[84]

A debate which took place late in 1943 between Sir Arthur Harris,
Commander-in-Chief, Bomber Command, and the Air Ministry
had profound implications for propaganda policy. In a letter of 25
October, Harris objected strongly to publicity which encouraged the
view that Bomber Command's operations were 'in the nature of an
experiment or side-show' and which misrepresented the situation by
stating that the intention was not 'the obliteration of German cities
and their inhabitants as such'. Harris demanded that the 'aim of the
Combined Bomber Offensive . . . should be unambiguously stated
[as] the destruction of German cities, the killing of German workers
and the disruption of civilised community life throughout Germany'.[85]

Sir Archibald Sinclair, Secretary of State for Air, circled warily
around the problem by declaring that no attempt had been made to
conceal the immense devastation caused by area bombing but that
the emphasis had been laid 'on the fact that our prime objective is
German war industry and transport'. These were not the primary
objectives, as Sinclair knew, but he drew back from admitting the
truth, not wishing to 'provoke the leaders of religious and humanitarian opinion to protest'.[86] The Air Ministry looked hard at Bomber
Command's general directive : 'The progressive destruction and
dislocation of the German military, industrial and economic system,
and the undermining of the morale of the German people to a
point where their capacity for armed resistance is fatally weakened'.[87]
In reply to Harris the Air Ministry told him that the directive 'neither
requires nor enjoins direct attack on German civilians as such',
although it was recognised that attacks on military and industrial
targets entailed the virtual destruction of German cities and heavy
civilian casualties.[88]

At first sight, this seems to have been an extraordinary situation.
For eight months Bomber Command had been carrying out a policy

which was the result of a gross misinterpretation of the original directive. Harris, although placing rather more emphasis than his superiors on 'undermining the morale of the German people', could hardly be blamed for finding the Air Ministry's reply 'ambiguous'. Observing in a rather chilling way that it was not his policy to attack children, invalids and old people since they were a handicap to the German war effort, he stated :

> This, however, does not imply, as the Air Ministry seems to assume that it does, that *no* German civilians are proper objects for bombing. The German economic system, which I am instructed by my directive to destroy, *includes* workers, houses and public utilities, and it is therefore meaningless to claim that the wiping out of German cities is 'not an end in itself but the inevitable accompaniment of all-out attack on the enemy's means and capacity to wage war'.[89]

In an almost Byzantine fashion, the Air Ministry conceded that Bomber Command had in fact been pursuing the right operational policy :

> Thus, while in the case of cities making a substantial contribution to the German war effort, the practical effects of your Command's policy cannot be distinguished from those which would accrue from a policy of attacking cities as such, the Council cannot agree that it is impossible to draw a clear distinction between these two policies. This distinction is in fact one of great importance in the presentation to the public of the aim and achievements of the bomber offensive.[90]

What appears to have been a serious policy disagreement, with fatal consequences for thousands of Germans, was, after all, a mere difference of view on what should be said publicly about the RAF's air raids. And Harris left the Air Ministry in no doubt that he felt free to bomb 'any civilian who produces more than enough to maintain himself'.[91]

The Ministry of Information was thus spared an extremely inconvenient change of direction. Having condemned the Germans' use of terror bombing for three years, the propagandists could not easily have manufactured reasons for Britain's use of the same tactic persuasive enough to overcome the inevitable moral objections from important sections of the community. For everyone concerned it was much more convenient to continue the lie.

162

In any event, it was unnecessary to tell the truth. The reports of Home Intelligence strongly indicated widespread public knowledge of the nature of British bombing policy. In the first place, little interest was shown in attacks on specific industrial targets, unless they were of a spectacular nature such as the destruction of the German dams in May 1943.[92] In the period July–August 1942, for example, the public were said to be disappointed at the apparent failure of the RAF to carry out the destruction of German cities one by one:

. . . 'in the light of the statements made on our policy to bomb Germany with ever increasing ferocity' these raids are neither regular enough nor sufficiently drastic. It is asked why the 1,000 bomber raids are not materialising . . .

There is a renewal of hope that with the longer nights, 'the RAF will blow a bloody big hole where Berlin is'.[93]

Repeated calls for thousand-bomber raids were, in fact, calls for the destruction of whole cities since few people could have been in any doubt that attacks on such a scale were aimed principally at housing and civilians. The press maintained the official fiction that Bomber Command had no such intention, although what were people to make of statements such as that which appeared in the *Daily Telegraph* in October 1943: 'Hamburg has had the equivalent of at least 60 'Coventrys', Cologne 17, Dusseldorf 12, and Essen 10'?[94] The evocation of Coventry, of course, could only bring to the minds of most people a devastating attack on the thickly populated centre of a town.

Secondly, the public were reported to link their exultation at news of heavy raids with the supposed effects upon German morale,[95] not upon industry and the general war effort as such. Similarly, demands for the bombing of Italy, and Rome in particular, seem not to have arisen because of concern about enemy war production but because the Italians were believed not to have suffered enough:

The news of the bombing of Italy is said to have been received with enthusiasm – 'the really bright spot of the week'. It has given particular pleasure as 'there has been a feeling for some time that the Italians are getting off too lightly – possibly for political or religious reasons'.[96]

Occasional expressions of sympathy for the German population and doubts about the impact of bombing upon enemy morale appear to have been founded on the knowledge that civilians were the principal targets of British air attacks. One report mentioned 'some feeling against the bombing of Berlin, on the grounds that there are targets of military importance which do not involve so much bombing of civilians';[97] another spoke of ' "A tinge of pity" for the women and children and horror at their suffering, but acceptance that "civilians must suffer" ',[98] and a persistent minority continued to wonder how decisive an effect the raids were having on German morale 'in view of the effects of the German air offensive on this country'.[99] Significantly, another minority were said to favour the restriction of bombing to military targets, because "they don't believe the mass raids destroy morale" '.[100]

The evidence from Home Intelligence is fragmentary but there seems to have been little that was not known in broad outline of the nature and intention of Bomber Command's raids. It is equally clear that the public enthusiastically endorsed them. This throws a different light on the policy of deception practised by the Ministry of Information. It should, perhaps, first be asked just how much was known in the department. Bracken, as one of Churchill's circle of close acquaintances which included Lord Cherwell, the chief architect of terror bombing, must have been aware of the policy and its development after February 1942. And in view of the arrangement made in July 1941 between Radcliffe and the Air Ministry, under which the Ministry received a secret daily summary of air operations and intelligence,[101] the senior officials were in possession of detailed information regarding area bombing and its effects. There can be no doubt, therefore, that the Ministry attempted to mislead the public. Statements of the following kind continued to be made until the end of the war:

British bombing of German war production centres has, during the past two years, become steadily heavier and more concentrated. Inevitably, damage to civilian life and property has increased in proportion. But incidental damage of this type, heavy though it may in fact be, is a very different thing from the deliberate terror-bombing of civilians . . .

During the autumn and winter of 1943–44, Berlin received a series of paralysing raids – raids designed not to terrify the civilian population, but simply and systematically to eliminate Berlin as the focal point of the German war effort.

164

Luftwaffe offensive against Britain — R.A.F. offensive against Germany
· A COMPARISON ·

	THIRD QUARTER 1940	THIRD QUARTER 1941	THIRD QUARTER 1942	SECOND QUARTER 1943
BOMBS ON BRITAIN	18,900 TONS	1,600 TONS	600 TONS	700 TONS
BOMBS ON GERMANY	2,750 TONS	8,800 TONS	15,600 TONS	36,700 TONS

. . . Many thousands of Germans will owe their lives after the war to the fact that, given ample opportunity and provocation, BRITAIN CONTINUED TO SET HER FACE AGAINST TERROR BOMBING.[102]

The high moral tone, shunned earlier in the war in favour of the argument from expediency, apparently satisfied the Ministry and the public, between whom there was a tacit conspiracy to pretend that Britain declined to use the methods of total war.

As the Anger Campaign paper proposed, the Ministry of Information did exploit stories of atrocities committed by the Germans. But for most of the war they were incorporated in the general propaganda about unscrupulous enemy methods rather than selected for special treatment: thus Germans were said to 'blast and bomb their way across the homes and bodies of human beings, machine-gunning even the sick in hospital and children in the playground'.[103] Much of this material had a perfunctory feeling, as if the Ministry were going through the motions and taking over where their predecessors had left off in 1918. 'But the Nazis now prove', read a pamphlet of 1941, 'by their deeds that no infamy is too foul for them to commit – that bullying, massacre and slavery are things in which they frankly rejoice.'[104] Was there no one in the Ministry who feared that this sort of material would eventually devalue the language of outrage? Apparently not, for the propagandists did not cease stressing the theme that there was nothing of which the Germans were not capable. Of a disturbingly large number of Germans this was true. But the language of hate was too exhausted to describe the enormity of what had been done in occupied Europe when it became known.

In July 1941 the Planning Committee considered whether atrocity stories should be lifted out of the context of general propaganda and given more emphatic treatment as part of a campaign to combat apathy. Sheer horror stories, it was suggested, repel the normal mind:

> In self-defence people prefer to think that the victims were specially marked men – and probably a pretty bad lot anyway. A certain amount of horror is needed but it must be used very sparingly and must deal always with treatment of indisputably innocent people. Not with violent political opponents. *And not with Jews.*[105]

It was not until late in 1942 that news of the true fate of European Jewry began to trickle out of the occupied territories, but certainly it had been known for a long time that the Nazis were systematically persecuting Jews of many nationalities. According to Andrew Sharf, 'Few facts of Nazi anti-Semitism were left unstated by the British Press'.[106] Why, then, was the Ministry reluctant to employ in its propaganda the facts that were known, even after the publication by the Inter-Allied Information Committee in December 1942 of a detailed account of Nazi extermination procedures? For example, the propagandists placed much greater emphasis on the persecution of Christian churches in Europe, whose members did not suffer as the Jews suffered.

Again, there is little to go on owing to the complete absence of minutes and memoranda relating to this issue. It cannot be doubted, however, that the Jews were regarded in the Ministry as 'indisputably innocent' victims of Nazism. Nor can it be doubted that there were any reservations about exploiting a crime of this magnitude as a means of demonstrating what had been said of the Germans since mid-1940. The Ministry almost certainly hesitated because of the widely reported prejudice in the British community against Jews. First reported in June 1940 – when Jews were supposed to be fleeing from Britain to the United States[107] – and reaching its first peak at the time of the East End Blitz,[108] anti-Semitism became such a regular subject that it was placed in Home Intelligence's 'Constant Topics and Complaints' at the end of each weekly report together with such matters as poor transport and shortage of crockery. Jews were said to control the black market, to display ostentatious wealth, to avoid war work and military service, even to force their way to the heads of queues and to exhibit truculent behaviour.[109] A report of May 1942 stated:

'The growth of anti-Semitism is reported from widely separated areas', according to the North Midland report. Infringements of the rationing orders, dealings in black markets and 'deliberate cunning evasions of measures instituted by the Government to meet war-time conditions' are said to have aroused strong public feeling.

Allegations are made of 'enormous' numbers of young Jews boasting of evading the call-up; the expression of 'open indignation' is feared unless measures are adopted 'to bring home to this race that they are inviting a similar revulsion to that which they have experienced in other countries'. This view is confirmed in another Region, whence the comment is reported that 'one thing Hitler had done is to put those damned Jews in their place'.[110]

167

After falling off in the months between early August and December 1942, when there were only three reports, anti-Semitism appears actually to have been revived by the authoritative disclosures of the Nazis' systematic massacre of European Jews. Although there was 'extreme horror'[111] and 'widespread indignation, anger and disgust'[112] at the news, there took place a recrudescence of feeling against Jews in Britain and Home Intelligence came to the conclusion 'that "as a result of the publicity, people are more conscious of the Jews they do not like here" '.[113] The Bethnal Green tube disaster of 3 March 1943, when 173 persons died in a crush on the stairs leading to a shelter, was widely blamed on panicking Jews[114] – an accusation confirmed in many people's minds by Herbert Morrison's decision not to release the findings of the subsequent inquiry.

It is difficult to estimate how accurately these reports reflected the degree and extent of British anti-Semitism during the war; but their frequency was such as to suggest that the propagandists drew back from giving the plight of European Jews more prominence than that of other groups and nationalities under Nazi domination. A Jewish Section was set up in July 1941 as part of the Religions Division. It was not allowed to touch 'political problems' – chiefly because of the Zionist controversy – and was therefore confined to disseminating propaganda to the Jewish community and explaining Jewish religious life to Christian citizens.[115] It did not function as a centre for the compilation and distribution of material revealing the situation in Europe.

In February 1942, Robert Fraser, head of the Productions Division, issued a warning against the use of unverified atrocity stories:

> It must be remembered that the twenty years between the two wars were occupied by a well conducted campaign against atrocity propaganda, and that some people are contra-suggestible to atrocity propaganda. I do not know whether there was a 'corpse factory' or not. But most people believe there was not.[116]

On the whole it appears the majority of people were ready to believe reports of German brutality,[117] especially if they concerned victims geographically close such as the Dutch and the French, but there was a sufficiently large minority sceptical both of stories and of photographs to act as a restraining influence on the Ministry.[118] Another constraint was the evidence reaching the Ministry of the public's hard attitude towards the enemy. 'Hatred of Germany – "enemy No. 1" – is expressed', read a report of February 1943, 'as well as

168

a hope that the Russians get to Germany before we do, "as they're more ruthless".[119] A survey conducted by the British Institute of Public Opinion in April 1943 showed that 41 per cent of the sample thought the German people, as distinct from the Nazi government alone, were the chief enemy. In September 1939 the percentage stood at 6, although it had risen to a peak of 50 per cent at the height of the blitz.[120] The public often displayed impatience at any suggestion of a less than implacable attitude on the part of political and military leaders. In November 1942, for example, a photograph appeared in the press showing Montgomery entertaining one of the defeated Afrika Korps generals, von Thoma. It aroused 'extreme annoyance' and distaste, for the spectacle of the British 'treating him as if he were the captain of an opposing cricket team' was said to be universal.[121] Such reports were undoubtedly instrumental in persuading the Ministry that atrocity propaganda was unnecessary.

In September 1944 *A Catalogue of Crime*, a pamphlet of some 5,000 words, documented extensive and authoritatively verified evidence of the Nazi extermination of Jews and other peoples, its unusually dispassionate and concise form of presentation making the facts all the more horrific. The introductory section reviewed German history since the time of Bismarck and endeavoured to show the gradual process by which Germany had irrevocably advanced towards these latest outrages. In conclusion it was stated:

> The German people have accepted from the nineteenth- and twentieth-century leaders of German thought and action, and have fully supported, the principles and practice of glorification of war; pursuit of world domination; and total ruthlessness in method.[122]

Why, at this late stage, were the German people still identified inextricably with Nazism? Having for so long insisted on the wickedness of the enemy, perhaps the Ministry could not help but regard the discoveries of the allied armies in Europe as final proof of the allegation. If there had been any question of reversing the policy, the prospect of drawing a distinction between Nazism and the German people was simply too daunting to be undertaken. Bracken was certainly in no mood to do so:

> Most of the victims appear to be foreign slaves, and if the German people did not endorse the conduct of the people whom they put in power, then the German people must remember that they have to accept the consequences of the government . . . In this war,

the Germans have shown themselves to be very good in organised fighting, and let me warn the House that they will be equally good in organised whining![123]

But Churchill, despite his wish to have war criminals summarily shot within six hours of their capture[124] and his brief flirtation with the Morgenthau plan (by which Germany was to be reduced to a pastoral nation), was no advocate of a harsh peace settlement. The continuance of the Ministry's propaganda represented, therefore, an implied contradiction of the government's magnanimous intentions towards a defeated enemy and might have served to complicate the task of the peace makers. But the British people were long since inured to the Ministry's propaganda. They did not pursue it to its logical end by calling for the perpetual subjection of the German nation. Nor did they even clamour for simple revenge. As Lord Taylor remembers, 'They were not interested in vengeance. They *were* interested in *no repetition*. They did *not* want to have to do the job again.'[125] The unremitting concentration on the 'same old Hun' underestimated both the common sense and the martial stamina of the British people.

6

Morale and the Prospect of Reform

In 1941, as defeat gradually became less likely and as the British people lifted their heads to look beyond the struggle for survival, increasing thought was given to the shape of post-war Britain. With the passing of the invasion threat and the possibility of a break in morale due to air attack, it also dawned on the populace that the war would be protracted and would demand of them a long, slow and grinding effort. It was from this point – rather than at the time of the crises of 1940 – that the hopes for the future might be expected to influence the actions of the present.

The Ministry of Information's involvement in the debate on post-war reform was judged harshly by a contributor to the *Political Quarterly*:

> The Ministry has shown constant timidity in giving the British public information about anything which has an element of a new order . . . Speakers of the Ministry lecture about the Empire, America, France, war-time cookery, the horrors of Nazi rule and Hitler's new order, but they do not talk about *our* new order. There is, in fact, no recognition of the war of ideas or of the social revolution through which we are living . . . Anything like discussion of new ideas or of a new society is dangerous. It might lead to some demand for a change in the existing state of things.[1]

It is, Daniel Lerner has stated, 'beliefs about the future – *the structure of expectations* – which propaganda attempts to modify on behalf of policy goals'.[2] The Ministry of Information certainly wished to modify such beliefs, but was confronted with a fundamental problem. How was it possible to buoy up the post-war aspirations of the nation while simultaneously bowing to the Prime Minister's desire for silence on the subject?

What became of the work of the War Aims Committee? A draft memorandum prepared by Lord Halifax was judged both by Duff Cooper[3] and Harold Nicolson to be unsuitable, the latter calling it 'a very unctuous statement about God the Father of All and that sort of thing'.[4] Towards the end of 1940, Nicolson, far from deriving comfort from the stoicism displayed by the public under intensive air attack, feared that the blitz might break the will of the people[5] and he tried unsuccessfully to persuade the committee to adopt a statement accepting the necessity for socialism.[6] This was, perhaps, a measure of the anxiety felt within the Ministry of Information, for it could scarcely have been hoped that Churchill, and for that matter the backbench Tories, would have tolerated the publication of such a statement.

The substance of the committee's discussion paper was embodied in a memorandum written by Arnold Toynbee.[7] Duff Cooper much preferred this draft[8] but, as the Foreign Secretary's paper could hardly be ignored, the two were merged to form the final Cabinet memorandum.[9] In the process nearly all the points made by the committee were omitted, leaving a rather watery broth of platitudes. Of twenty-two paragraphs, only three were devoted to social and economic reform at home :

20.   In the economic field at home we can no longer tolerate the existence of abject poverty and unemployment. If through causes which cannot be overcome, such as the loss of overseas markets, unavoidable unemployment should arise, we mean that this should not be a curse but an opportunity. The man who cannot obtain work is as much a member of the community as the man who can.

21.   Just as in order to achieve victory in war we are mobilising all the resources of the nation, so in peace it will be our aim to develop on an orderly plan both town and countryside, not only to produce wealth, but to afford to all the surroundings in which happy lives may be lived . . . we shall allow no vested interests to stand in the way of making Britain in every way worthy of her heroic citizens. Even in the midst of war we shall seek to apply to our national life the principles on which we hope to build peace.

22.   Already the war has broken down many old barriers and prejudices. The social conscience of the whole people has been aroused. These testing days are bringing to the front numbers of energetic and daring men and women drawn from all classes and sections of the community, determined that this great oppor-

tunity shall not be missed. The younger generation to-day is virile, imaginative and alert. We must use the qualities of youth as well as the experience of war-time to overhaul our economic, social and educational practice, in order to secure for all a reasonable standard of life.

On 20 January 1941, after Halifax had been replaced as Foreign Secretary by Anthony Eden, the memorandum was given brief attention when Cabinet discussed what answer should be made in the Commons to a question on war aims:

One view put forward was that any statement which confined itself to generalities would not strike home. (In this connection it was suggested that the draft statement . . . while admirable in many respects, would not, in its present form, impress public opinion). On the other hand any statement which put forward specific proposals would be bound to give rise to difficulties.[10]

Nicolson was downcast: 'Winston refuses to make a statement on war aims . . . Thus all those days of work have led to nothing.'[11]

The link between civilian morale and proposals for post-war domestic reform was explicitly recognised in April 1942, when it was stated that the Minister of Information is 'concerned to promote discussion and publication of the Government's reconstruction programme in so far as it contributes to home morale; conversely it is his duty to prevent the ventilation of topics which might impair it'.[12] Therein lay the rub. Deciding what was and what was not likely to bolster morale became a very delicate process, since the whole issue of peacetime reconstruction was riven with controversy and demanded the most careful handling. Above the Ministry, overshadowing any promptings there may have been to open public discussion, loomed the Prime Minister. At the same time there was an awareness of the extent to which national unity had been exposed to erosion since the critical days of 1940. The simultaneous re-emergence of class feeling, the widespread expectation of post-war unemployment and demands for concrete pledges of reform brought an uncomfortable realisation in the Ministry that debate could not be stifled indefinitely.

In January 1941 Professor Charles Webster, of the Royal Institute of International Affairs, suggested broadcasting a series of debates on peace aims. The fate of this proposal well illustrates the constraints operating on the Ministry. Harold Nicolson enthusiastically supported

173

Webster's proposal and, despite reservations about the inability of the Ministry and the government to disclaim responsibility for 'what could be described in many quarters as a "leftish tendency" ', urged Duff Cooper to go ahead.[13] Sir Richard Machonachie, BBC Talks Director, agreed to arrange the broadcasts on the condition that the Ministry backed the Corporation against criticism from MPs and 'vested interests'.[14] Attlee was also in support of the scheme.[15] Duff Cooper sought the approval of Arthur Greenwood, Minister without Portfolio in charge of reconstruction problems.[16] Greenwood was nervous. He told Cooper that the proposed broadcasts were premature, 'having regard to the Prime Minister's present views', and suggested that the BBC should concentrate on educating the public about the immense difficulties posed by Britain's post-war problems. This had already been raised in the Ministry but would certainly not have added much to the morale of the public. In the early months of 1941 there were problems enough to ponder on without having them increased by schoolmasterly warnings about the difficulties of the post-war world.

The Minister decided to press ahead with the broadcasts. In answer to a question in the House on 8 April, he said that he would be prepared to support discussions of peace aims on the BBC and had 'considered such a scheme, even to the drafting of a programme'. However, the prospect of spirited radio discussion dimmed visibly when he added, 'We can say in a general way, that there will be greater opportunity for all and a more equal distribution of wealth. These are the kind of vague promises which can be made, but I am not sure that they are very much good to anyone.'[17] Churchill's 'known views' inhibited plans for any but the most anaemic of broadcast debates. 'The difficulty has been the objections entertained by the Prime Minister,' Greenwood wrote to Cooper on 1 July. 'It is plain that we must get his imprimatur on any scheme we propose.' Greenwood had nevertheless become rather more enthusiastic and suggested a series of talks in the autumn 'on lines to which he [Churchill] would take no exception'.[18] Even under these conditions the Ministry did not wish to push the matter any further and on 22 July the plan was finally shelved.[19]

If the Ministry could not initiate public discussion of post-war reconstruction, then it certainly did not wish to see outsiders doing so and, indeed, did its best to discourage them. This was reflected most clearly in the change which occurred in the department's relationship and dealings with *Picture Post*.

In November 1940, when the Ministry was advocating a statement

174

of peace aims, Sir Kenneth Clark suggested and *Picture Post* took up the idea of a special number devoted to 'the Britain we hope to build when the war is over'.[20] The issue came out on 4 January 1941 and touched a deep chord in the public, over 2,000 letters being received by the editor on the subject.[21] Thereafter relations began to cool. In February, Clark – as the go-between – undertook to point out to Edward Hulton, the proprietor, that the friendly tone adopted by the magazine towards the People's Convention 'whose professed aim was to stop the war was hardly consistent with the normal and declared policy of the paper'.[22] By March, when the strength of Churchill's opposition to discussion of post-war aims had become clear and the Ministry no longer saw any need to bribe the public, the official response to *Picture Post*'s wish to build on public enthusiasm was distinctly colder.

Tom Hopkinson, who had succeeded Stefan Lorant as editor,* proposed another and bigger edition centred on 'A Plan for Britain' which would carry a report based on extensive consultations with experts and interested readers. He promised to include 'any special subject' suggested by the Ministry.[23] The initial reaction, at least from Robert Fraser, was cautiously favourable :

We could say that it seems to us that they could have the paper if they satisfy us :

(a) The issue will not present a programme or present a policy which would be broadly agreeable to one political party and broadly rejected by another. For then it would be in effect party propaganda.

(b) The aim of the issue must be to create pride in existing democratic achievement and hope and courage for future construction; not dissatisfaction with existing conditions leading to Left wing agitation for reforms.

(c) It should concentrate on comparing the bad old times with already achieved reforms, and these with future possibilities, not on exposing existing deficiencies.

(d) It should have a definite note of 'All this depends on beating Hitler' . . .

---

*Stefan Lorant left Britain for the United States in the middle of 1940. A vigorous anti-Nazi since arriving in Britain from his native Hungary in 1934 and founding editor of *Lilliput* and *Picture Post*, he was unable to persuade the Home Office either to naturalise him or to lift the irksome restrictions imposed on his movements by the wartime aliens regulations – despite the representations made on his behalf to Sir John Anderson by Attlee, Leo Amery, Duff Cooper, Archie Sinclair, Herbert Morrison and Bracken.[24]

The effect on most people, I think, of reading 'A Plan for Britain' itself is to infuse them with a fresh enthusiasm for their country, stimulates and livens up their pride, and is both an antidote to war weariness and a stimulus to effort.

[But] . . . The articles are written for the most part by a Left wing group.

It doesn't present its case in a setting of war effort. It doesn't say 'Beat Hitler or you get none of this.'[25]

Fraser wanted it both ways. He hoped for a treatment which would excite the public about the future and yet would avoid condemning the mistakes of the past and present. Lord Davidson would have none of these theological niceties and, conveniently forgetting the Ministry's past allocation of paper to *Picture Post* (which had been in breach of an unofficial agreement with the press that no publication would receive favourable treatment), he stated that 'there is no justification for any departure from the gentleman's agreement with the Periodical Proprietors' Association'.[26] *Picture Post* went ahead anyway and 'A Plan for Britain' aroused an even greater response than the first issue devoted to post-war reconstruction.

For all its reluctance to encourage debate, the Ministry could not help but be conscious of an emerging public interest in the post-war world which, while proceeding in fits and starts, had gathered considerable momentum by 1941. It was accompanied by reports of a much increased prevalence of class feeling. There were many cynical, occasionally bitter, observations by the less well-off of the ways in which wealth and influence softened the impact of war. As early as October 1940 a 'striking trend' was ill-feeling generated against the 'upper classes' for being first to leave bombed districts and to find the best places in evacuation areas.[27] This compounded the general problem of evacuation, a notable feature of which was the apparent reluctance of people with large country houses to billet the poor from the cities.[28] It was reported by RIOs that many billeting officers, usually local residents, hesitated to use their compulsory powers for fear of incurring the wrath of locally powerful people.[29] More durable than grumbles caused by evacuation was the widespread annoyance at the apparent ease with which certain people evaded the military and civilian call-up, particularly officers' wives who, like other married women, could not be conscripted into industrial work but who, unlike the wives of ordinary working men, were observed 'sitting about in hotels of coastal and country towns'.[30]

Similarly charged were 'well-to-do women and those of the upper classes' who were said to undertake voluntary work, especially in the WVS, in order to avoid genuine war work.[31] The numbers of race-goers and families with domestic servants were also cited as flagrant examples of wealthy people failing to contribute to the war effort.

The greatest ire appears to have been aroused by the evident inequality in the distribution of food, the most basic commodity and one which obsessed most people most of the time. The alleged ability of the rich to purchase almost any type and quantity of food, particularly unrationed meals in restaurants, reached a peak in the six months between January and July 1942, when on no less than twenty occasions food was mentioned by Home Intelligence as a major source of grievance. Having welcomed the government's proposal to set a ceiling on the price of restaurant meals, working-class people were said to be angered and amazed at the maximum permissible charge and they continued to regard it as a 'farce' for weeks after the regulation had been introduced.[32] Home Intelligence's observation of May 1941 to the effect that indignation against the rich remained within bounds so long as there was a cut off the joint in the public house[33] no longer applied:

> There is growing evidence of a feeling among certain sections of the public that 'everything is not fair and equal and that therefore our sacrifices are not worth while'. In particular, there is some belief that the rich are less hit by rationing than 'ordinary people' for the following reasons: .
> (a) They can eat at expensive restaurants.
> (b) They can afford to buy high priced goods in short demand, such as salmon and game.
> (c) They can spend more on clothes and therefore use their coupons more advantageously.
> (d) They receive preferential treatment in shops, as 'people giving large orders are favoured and the poorer people wanting "little bits" are refused'.
> (e) They receive preferential treatment as regards petrol rationing.[34]

Grievances were occasionally expressed in very bitter terms. Amidst the chorus of sympathy that followed the Duke of Kent's death in an air crash in August 1942, someone was heard to remark, 'The Duchess won't have any difficulty with *her* pension.'[35]

If the antagonism aroused by the subject of food can be regarded as symptomatic of the rising tension between the classes in wartime Britain, it is possible, by examining the subject more closely, to arrive at a more balanced picture. The crucial sentiment was that reported in March 1942 : 'It seems clear that "people are willing to bear any sacrifice, if a 100 per cent effort can be reached, and the burden fairly borne by all".'[36] With regard to food there existed a deep conviction that the government was doing everything in its power to see that rationing produced as near to an equitable situation as possible. Praise for Lord Woolton, the Minister of Food, and the rationing system, often infused with a sense of wonderment, was high – not merely for working the miracle of giving everyone enough to eat but for operating the system fairly. It was most important, therefore, that the government was seen to function disinterestedly in those areas impinging closely on civilian life, and reports of grievance over food inequality assume much less significance when set against the overwhelmingly more frequent reports of satisfaction with the rationing system. Much the same might be said for other instances of class resentment. As long as the government appeared to be doing its best to impose the burdens of war equally upon all sections of the community, expressions of discontent did not threaten to coalesce into a serious danger to morale and national unity. An increase, or perhaps the resumption, of class consciousness may be attributable more to the propagandists' insistence on the reality of 'equality of sacrifice' – which focused attention on breaches of the doctrine – than to glaring instances of privilege. The implementation of a state philosophy of egalitarianism, while making people acutely sensitive to its failures, gave the temporary sensation if not the abiding substance of equality.

Perhaps the most important single reason for the failure of class resentment to assume threatening proportions was its absorption into the public's post-war aspirations. The Ministry of Information closely charted the upsurge of public interest in post-war reform and in April 1942 its principal characteristics were summarised in preparation for a meeting between Brendan Bracken and the Paymaster-General, Sir William Jowitt, who had taken over from Greenwood responsibility for the study of peacetime problems :

(1) There is a widespread feeling that 'things will never be the same again' coupled with a widespread **fear** that 'unless the Government take steps before the end of the war, they may be as bad as they were last time'. These two opinions, though contradictory, are often held by the same people.

178

(2) There is a declining belief in political parties, party programmes, and even Parliament itself. Feeling about reconstruction does not seem to divide itself on recognisable party lines.

(3) The main positive aspirations voiced are (a) 'No more unemployment . . . no more dismissal without notice or without reason . . . adequate sickness and old age pensions for all', i.e. occupational and economic security. (b) Levelling up of income with higher minima and lower maxima. (c) An equal chance for all children.

(4) There is little interest in international reconstruction.

(5) The above opinions appear to be fairly widespread amongst the more reflective members of all classes throughout the country, not least the members of the Armed forces.[37]

Fear of unemployment was by far the most commonly reported phenomenon associated with people's expectations of post-war Britain: it was mentioned in almost every report and implicit in others. Although it appears that older men, with sharp memories of the twenties and thirties, were more pessimistic,[38] they were at the same time 'determined that their sons shall not suffer as they did, and many young men seem to have taken to heart the lessons of that period'.[39] Together with this determination not to allow things to be as they had been there was a sinking feeling that they would in fact be so,[40] a feeling which sometimes amounted to dread.[41] The Ministry took these forebodings seriously. Brendan Bracken informed the Cabinet in October 1942 that 'post-war conditions seem to be more a cause of anxiety as to what they may bring to the individual in the shape of unemployment and distress than of hope for the blessings that they may bring to the nation at large'.[42] But, apart from the bogy of unemployment, public expectations were high. Not until Beveridge, that is over three years after the outbreak of war, was there much official intimation of interest in reforming Britain after the defeat of the enemy. Moreover, the experiences of the working classes after the First World War gave scant vindication of the theory – or fond wish – that the Second World War would bring about profound changes in British society, but it seems true nonetheless that many people refused to believe that they could go through the violent discontinuity of war and yet find themselves back in the 1930s at its conclusion.

What was the content of these expectations? At a minimum level, it consisted in 'the provision of certain essentials such as shelter, food, clothing, education and a more adequately protected old age'.[43]

The more optimistically inclined looked forward to better social services, increased old-age pensions, a state medical scheme, and greater equality in education,[44] although people did not usually express themselves in such specific terms. There was, rather, a somewhat nebulous longing for 'levelling of class distinctions',[45] 'redistribution of wealth',[46] and 'less privilege and more responsibility based on service'.[47] It would be wrong, however, to conclude on the evidence of the Ministry's intelligence findings that these half-articulated aspirations issued from socialist conviction, although care must be taken with the Ministry's use of the term 'socialism' since it often meant in the Tory manner no more than 'Labour' or what is understood as a mixed economy. True, there were calls for full-blooded socialism[48] and for an end to 'the system which has given so much power to so few people'.[49] But, despite the Ministry's characterisation of these as the opinion of 'the more irresponsible sections',[50] they had little affinity with socialism as defined in the classical Marxist sense. What was wanted, in fact, was a half-way house to socialism in which most people would be content to reside. As Mass-Observation commented in 1943, 'Post-war expectations were increasingly based on compromise within the present framework, the continuation of some measure of state control, better social services based on war-time experiences.'[51]

Calls for a government statement, if only of principle, became more and more insistent, although subject to fluctuation according to the progress of the war. 'The argument that we must concentrate upon winning the war', commented one report in December 1941, 'before considering these problems cuts little ice',[52] but for three weeks following the fall of Tobruk in June 1942, an event which depressed the public as much as any in a war of reverses, there was a marked decline of interest in post-war reform. 'We must think of winning the war first, or we shall be reconstructing ourselves into defeat' ran one typical remark.[53] After Tobruk there were no further dramatic defeats and the growing likelihood of victory probably assisted the increasing strength of demands for an authoritative pronouncement on post-war conditions. The insistence with which these demands were being put may be judged from a note to headquarters from Sir Arthur Willert, the Southern RIO:

It is difficult to exaggerate the growing force of the demand for guarantees that 'privilege' be not allowed to lose the next peace, as it is generally felt to have lost the last one; individualistic capitalism must yield place to 'controlled' capitalism; we ought to be told what we are fighting for, etc. Remarks like this can be heard wherever working men gather together.[54]

In June 1942 the Director of the Reference Division informed the Director General of the steady increase in the already 'constant demand' by Ministry speakers and others for material on the government's post-war plans.[55] But, clearly aware of the situation as they were, the senior officers of the Ministry made no attempt to loosen the gag. Ministry speakers were warned late in 1942 not to engage in 'unsanctioned prognostication of future policy and legislation' and, more specifically, to avoid 'subjects about post-war reconstruction'.[56]

Yet, while the Ministry appeared to be studiously averting its gaze from post-war reconstruction, in December 1942 there suddenly burst forth from the department a blaze of publicity for the Beveridge Report. 'A large Press Conference was arranged for Sir William', writes Francis Williams, then Controller of Press and Censorship, 'a summarized version of the plan with diagrams was rapidly prepared and issued in large numbers . . . As a result the Beveridge plan swept the country and indeed the world.'[57] There is, unfortunately, not to be found in the Ministry's records a single mention of the Report or of the preparation of the publicity accompanying its publication. Nor does Francis Williams tell us who instructed the Ministry 'to do everything in its power to make the plan widely known and appreciated'.[58] Angus Calder believes that Bracken, 'by permitting the initial spate of publicity, had fathered this one-man plan on the whole Government',[59] but Bracken did not proceed without the permission of the Prime Minister.[60] The publicity was almost certainly designed to act as a weapon in the propaganda war with Germany. The enormous public response took the government by surprise, suggesting that most ministers had no idea of the eagerness with which the Report was awaited.

In March 1943, Sir John Anderson wrote to Bracken:

At the meeting of the Home Front Ministers on Monday, there was some talk about the extent to which, in matters of post-war reconstruction, the field of public discussion had been left open to extremists.

It was pointed out that on various post-war topics extreme views seem to be catching the public imagination; and it was thought to be high time that the balance should be redressed by gaining a hearing for more moderate and realist views.[61]

Well might Anderson have been concerned at the drift of public feeling which followed the government's inept handling of the Beveridge Report. The War Office's withdrawal of an Army Bureau of Current Affairs pamphlet summarising the plan, the long delay before Parliament debated it in February 1943, and the die-hard Tory opposition to Bevin's Catering Trades Bill aroused suspicion, which turned into frank dismay when government spokesmen appeared to be less than enthusiastic about the scheme.

Even before these events took place public cynicism underlay the initial excitement. One old soldier was quoted as saying, 'This new plan for social security makes me laugh, I don't forget the Land fit for Heroes of the last war.'[62] In the week following the unveiling of the scheme there was, according to Home Intelligence, 'a very real anxiety that the plan will not materialise' because of 'vested interests' such as the insurance companies and the BMA.[63] This fear was reported every week until the parliamentary debate occurred and was reinforced by the banning of the ABCA pamphlet: 'If the Forces are not allowed to discuss such far reaching and important documents what are they fighting for?'[64] The significance of public reaction to the plan – said to be supported by ' "the working classes", Liberals, Labour and the Left, a proportion of the middle classes, and . . . a number of the rank and file of the Conservative Party'[65] – was the way in which it symbolised the end of the bad old days and, in a sense, sanctified the nation's wartime sacrifices. The plan gave meaning to the war beyond a struggle for survival, heralding for many people that change which they felt in their bones ought to be an inevitable outcome of the harsh experience of war. The government's response was therefore all the more disappointing to the great majority :

> . . . it is feared that the Government does not realise that it 'has become a religion to some people'. By such, the Report seems to be regarded as sacrosanct, 'like the Ark of the Covenant', quite apart from the actual benefits it promises.[66]

The scheme was far less revolutionary than the enthusiasm aroused by it suggests. The contributory basis of social insurance remained unchanged and it embodied no process by which social levelling could occur. These and other shortcomings were criticised by some people who suggested that the plan did not go far enough,[67] but they were swamped by the enthusiasts, many of whom believed it too good to be true.[68] Their descent from near-euphoria to depression and anger following the government's cool reception of the plan was great. So great, indeed, that the old fear of unemployment was revived afresh and the cynical pessimism about post-war Britain reinforced.[69] Prior to the parliamentary debate there were reports of an ominous character unprecedented in Home Intelligence experience. If the plan was not implemented, 'things will be damned unpleasant for whatever government is in power . . . there will be hell to pay'[70] was the tenor of a number of recorded verbatim comments. But such threats of retribution seem quickly to have given way to a sort of passive despair. Five months after the publication of the Report pessimism was still the reigning emotion.[71] Perhaps it was just as well that there was much encouraging war news at the end of 1942 and during the first half of 1943.

After the February debate there issued from the government, including the Ministry of Information, a deafening silence. Little else could have been expected in view of Churchill's Cabinet memorandum in January:

> . . . Ministers should, in my view, be careful not to raise false hopes as was done last time by speeches about 'Homes for Heroes', etc. The broad masses of the people face the hardships of life undaunted but they are liable to get very angry if they feel they have been gulled or cheated . . . It is for this reason of not wishing to deceive the people by false hopes and airy visions of Utopia and Eldorado that I have refrained so far from making promises about the future.[72]

The ban on the ventilation of post-war topics by Ministry speakers was, therefore, extended to include the Beveridge Report, although no way could be found of insulating speakers from audience questions on the subject.[73] Nor, indeed, could the Ministry avoid preparing publicity on post-war topics for other departments and agencies. One poster 'YOUR BRITAIN – Fight for it NOW', commissioned by ABCA, put in striking visual terms an undertaking which the Ministry was reluctant to proclaim on its own or the government's behalf.

R. H. Parker, at a meeting with representatives of the Reconstruction Secretariat, stressed the urgent need to:

> . . . convince a suspicious and highly sceptical public opinion that the Government was in earnest and that, in spite of the blanket that had been put on the discussion of the subject, a great

183

deal had, in fact, been done and was being done . . . The belief that little or nothing was being done by the Government, and that, in fact, the Government were not particularly interested in reconstruction, or that their interest was simply stimulated for political purposes, was likely to have dangerous consequences.[74]

These dangerous consequences embraced both morale and a feared public drift to the left. That part of the Minister's brief which allowed him to 'prevent the ventilation of topics which might impair' morale had been exercised and had failed in its purpose. If anything, the Ministry's 'blanket' served to depress the spirits of those members of the public who might otherwise have derived pleasure from speculation about the future. It was now proposed to initiate publicity in an effort to rescue the government from obloquy. The propaganda conformed closely to Churchill's notions of post-war economic and social priorities. A booklet published in June 1943, intended for use by journalists and speakers, gave considerably greater prominence to the Prime Minister's four-year plan than to the Beveridge scheme, which Churchill did not even mention when he unveiled his plan in a speech on 21 March 1943. Emphasis was laid on the interdependence of national security, the revival of trade, and domestic reconstruction :

1. After victory international security is the first consideration.

2. The re-establishment of Britain's export trade with a view to maintaining a high level of employment in the country is the second consideration.

3. The success of any measure for home reconstruction will be conditioned by the success achieved in dealing with problems of international security and restoration of trade.[75]

Unexceptionable though this hierarchy of priorities may have been, it was hardly gratifying to the many people still possessed of the bleak conviction that the future as seen by Beveridge was illusory.

At the request of the Ministry of Reconstruction, a special intelligence report was made nearly a year later, in May 1944, and consisted of parallel inquiries by Home Intelligence and the British Institute of Public Opinion into public attitudes towards the Beveridge proposals. Their findings showed 'a high level of agreement' (which Home Intelligence was always quick to proclaim because it validated their 'qualitative' methods). The public remained unconvinced of the government's sincerity :

There is widespread suspicion of the government's attitude to the Beveridge Plan. A great many, perhaps the majority, are convinced that it will either be shelved, mutilated, or whittled away, or else an inferior substitute put forward instead . . .[76]

Cynicism spilled over into reactions to the White Paper on a national health service, published in February 1944, and to Butler's Education Bill, shortly to go on the statute books. According to a special report of March 1944, many working-class people regarded the national health scheme as 'an excuse for not accepting the Beveridge proposals' and, although welcoming the Education Bill, doubted whether education would in fact be improved.[77] The Ministry's publicity had clearly been ineffective. There was little more the propagandists could do without appearing to be protesting too much about the government's pure intentions.

7

Stealing the Thunder of the Left

The problems posed by communism after Hitler's attack on Russia proved scarcely less intractable than those associated with post-war reform. Before considering the consequences for domestic propaganda and morale of this momentous event, it is necessary to investigate the Ministry's policy towards communism in the period that elapsed between the end of the phoney war and June 1941. It will be remembered that during the first eight months of war a cautious policy of non-confrontation was practised. This strategy was to be continued and may be demonstrated by reference to three matters: the reluctance with which the department undertook an export ban on communist publications, its muted disapproval of the *Daily Worker*'s suppression by the Home Secretary, and the futility of the more vigorous anti-communist activity adopted in Scotland.

In press matters the Ministry of Information exhibited nearly as much solicitude for communist publications as it did for other newspapers and, in spite of a marked hostility towards communists, it was strenuously maintained in the department that insofar as their publications expressed opinion – as distinct from printing facts of military value – they were entitled to as much freedom as other sections of the press.

Much against its wishes, the Ministry was compelled by the Home and Foreign offices in March and April 1940 to assume responsibility for banning the export from Britain of undesirable publications.[1] A somewhat Kafkaesque order was promulgated to this end: published matter could not legally be sent abroad other than by post and it was made illegal to send by post otherwise than by permit, which, it was stated, would not be granted 'while these papers remain what they are'. In May and June the *Daily Worker*, several lesser publications and Claud Cockburn's newsletter, *The*

186

Week, were banned for export. Duff Cooper believed that an adequate case had not been made out for bringing the latter publication under the prohibition.[2]

For three months the Ministry chafed against the accusations of illiberality levelled at it by the left-wing press, and in September Radcliffe declared:

> . . . I have always been against such a policy in respect of a publication which is legally produced in this country. The proper remedy if any particular country objects to the circulation of such a paper within its own borders is for it to impose an import ban.[3]

The Director General, supporting Radcliffe, explained to the Policy Committee that as France was occupied by the Germans there was no longer any reason for the export ban (the objections of the pre-Vichy government being the original occasion of the scheme). 'As we are fighting for liberty,' he added, 'all unnecessary restrictions of it are undesirable.'[4] But the Ministry could not so persuade the other interested departments. The Foreign Office, no longer able to point to the sensitivities of the French, expressed concern at the possible effect of the communist papers on relations with Spain, Portugal and the United States.[5] MI5 voiced astonishment at the Ministry's failure to appreciate the link between the British communists, the Soviet Union and the Comintern,[6] an attitude largely irrelevant to the matter at hand but one shared by Lord Swinton's Committee on Communist Activities, an interdepartmental body which monitored the doings of British communists.[7] And the Home Office, wishing to have communist literature suppressed in Britain, viewed the export ban as the next best thing and refused to reconsider its earlier advice.[8] The Ministry had to try another tack. Radcliffe sought the opinion of the Treasury Solicitor on the legality of the order and reported back:

> The method that we have adopted of announcing that [the publications] cannot be sent except under special permit but that we are not prepared to consider the granting of such a permit is indefensible : and that it is our duty to consider each issue as it comes out and see whether we are prepared to stop it or not.[9]

It was therefore decided to advise the government either to suppress the offending newspapers or, failing this, to make a new regulation if export was still to be prohibited.[10] The Ministry's subsequent efforts to clarify the situation must be seen in the context of the government's attitude towards communism. Lord Swinton himself wished to follow up the recent decision to ban the *Daily Worker* and *The Week* by proscribing the communist party as an illegal organisation and interning a small number of its leaders.[11] Ernest Bevin pointed out, however, that communists had not had a serious effect on the output of war industry[12] and he was strongly opposed to action being taken against communists on the shop floor:

> There were many branches of industry where the conditions of work and the general lack of amenities lent themselves to exploitation by agitators. He had been endeavouring to deal with these grievances at their source, by improving the conditions of work, e.g. in the ship building industry and in the docks at Liverpool and elsewhere. In his view no action should be taken to deal with Communism in the work shop until the new agreements on labour conditions had been fully worked out.[13]

But, characteristically, Bevin saw no reason why the 'intelligentsia' should not be dealt with in summary fashion.[14] Herbert Morrison doubted that the House of Commons would approve the use of Regulation 18B to intern communists whose propaganda was not in itself unlawful.[15] As the minister responsible, his view prevailed.

Nevertheless, in such a climate of opinion Duff Cooper could scarcely expect that his appeal for reconsideration of the export ban would have much success. Morrison, having suppressed the *Daily Worker* and *The Week* on 21 January 1941, naturally objected to a relaxation of the export ban on other communist publications lest it appear inconsistent with the rigorous action so recently taken. He was supported by Sir John Anderson, who made an observation which, if they had known it, would have given scant comfort to French resistance fighters: 'Indications had been received from abroad that our Government was suspected of lending support to Left Wing activities in France.'[16] The ban remained in force and the committee asked the Minister of Information, the Home Secretary and the Attorney General to consider the terms of a new regulation conferring wider powers over the export of publications.[17]

Powerless to alter the situation, the Ministry could only expostulate to the Home Office:

The Government has frequently announced that its policy with regard to the Press is to allow freedom of opinion, and to use its censorship powers for the sole purpose of preventing information reaching the enemy which will be useful to him in the conduct of the war.

Papers and periodicals whose objectionableness consists in saying things which are thought to endanger our relations with foreign countries or things which are thought to misrepresent the true nature of the country's war effort at home do not fall under the category of censorship.[18]

However, the Ministry had a long struggle ahead before it could be said that censorship was politically colour-blind. Following a series of vigorous clashes with the Foreign Office, the Ministry succeeded in having the ban lifted in August 1943, nearly a year after the *Daily Worker* was allowed to resume publication in Britain.[19]

In a process similar to that which made the service departments regard almost all information as of military value, the War Cabinet often viewed criticism of its policies as destructive of morale and therefore of the nation's war effort. Although the Ministry of Information pleaded that its sole concern was with security censorship and could thereby avoid entanglement, it is remarkable that the department which was responsible for maintaining morale and which had by far the greatest contact with the press and public should have been consulted so rarely by the War Cabinet on matters concerning the relationship between morale and press comment.

In the discussion preceding the suppression of the *Daily Worker* in January 1941, the Ministry was not asked to furnish a report on the public impact of this newspaper. Had the War Cabinet requested such a report they would have found little evidence to support the contention that the *Daily Worker* and *The Week* were successfully fostering opposition to the war. A reading of the Ministry's Home Intelligence reports reveals a marked absence of comment on the effect of communist propaganda. They show that far more serious in implication for civilian morale was the lack of news, a situation brought about by the government's own policies. Nor was the Ministry able to discover in the *Daily Worker* the presence of overt anti-war propaganda. In September 1940, Mary Adams noted:

During recent months the Daily Worker has concentrated largely on domestic policy and has urged the provision of deep shelters, more highly developed ARP services, better compensation, commandeering of large houses and West End premises and large private shelters . . .

It should be remarked that a number of other papers have now taken up the plea for deep shelters, notably the News Chronicle, the Daily Mail, the Daily Herald, the Evening Standard and the Star, as well as many of the other suggestions put forward by the Daily Worker.[20]

Early in July 1940, Sir John Anderson raised the question of suppressing the *Daily Worker*. A number of ministers pointed out that action might have to be taken against other newspapers including, presumably, *The Times*, in which there had appeared articles which 'represented an attempt by influential people . . . to prepare the country for the suppression of the Civil power and the handing over of the control of affairs to the Military authorities'.[21] On this occasion, therefore, the *Daily Worker* was merely warned.[22] The principle underlying the behaviour of the goverment at this time was enunciated by the permanent head of the Home Office in an instruction sent to Regional Commissioners. 'Action', he said, 'should not be taken against the Communist Party or against members of the Communist Party because they are Communists.'[23]

For five months the Cabinet scarcely referred to the *Daily Worker* or to communism, but in December 1940 the decision was taken to suppress the newspaper. Herbert Morrison presented a memorandum to the Cabinet in which he advised suppression under the power granted to him in Regulation 2D.[24] This stated that action could be taken against a newspaper if the Secretary of State were satisfied that it was systematically publishing matter 'calculated to foment opposition to the prosecution to a successful issue of any war in which His Majesty is engaged'. Morrison catalogued the ways in which the *Daily Worker* was presumed to have attempted to hinder the war effort. These included criticism of the government's civil defence policies and its attitude towards the suffering and hardships of the people, as well as the more general charge that the war was a capitalist venture designed to rob the workers of hard-won privileges. The closest the newspaper appears to have come to fomenting opposition to the war was the statement that Britain might find it impossible to win. Having said all this,

Morrison was unable to strengthen his case by demonstrating that the newspaper's propagation of such ideas was lowering the nation's confidence. 'In fact, however,' he continued, 'little or no evidence can be found that Communist propaganda is having any appreciable effect on the morale of the nation as a whole.' While Regulation 2D did not make it a condition of suppression that a newspaper, as well as systematically publishing anti-war matter, should also be judged to be damaging morale, it could be argued that it was in keeping with the government's stated solicitude for freedom of speech that Morrison should have proved that the *Daily Worker* was undoubtedly having such an effect. If anyone's morale was adversely affected by the *Daily Worker*, it was the War Cabinet's.

Why wasn't Regulation 2C used instead? This regulation possessed the apparent advantage for the government of court procedure. If a publisher ignored a warning to cease printing matter which fomented opposition to the war, the government could prosecute him and thus avoid the accusation – of which the War Cabinet was apprehensive – that it had resorted to autocratic methods. But the Home Secretary was required to demonstrate to the court that 'serious mischief' might have resulted from the publication of the matter objected to, which implied an obligation to prove that the nation, or an important section of it, had been adversely affected by the newspaper. In the case of the *Daily Worker* it is doubtful that he could have done so. Regulation 2C also stated that it was a defence 'that there was no intention to foment opposition to the prosecution of the war or that there was no reasonable cause to believe that the publication was calculated to foment opposition'. And, as Morrison admitted in his memorandum, the *Daily Worker*'s defence in court would have given it 'a good opportunity for propaganda against what it would describe as the Government's effort to "gag" the Press'. The only solid reason advanced by Morrison for the newspaper's suppression was that whereas other papers attacked the government in the general context of furthering the war effort, the *Daily Worker* never contained 'a note of real encouragement'. A sin of omission rather than of commission.

At least two senior members of the Ministry of Information were disturbed by the War Cabinet's action. On 27 January 1941, Harold Nicolson noted in his diary:

191

Cyril Radcliffe comes in. He is worried about the suppression of the Daily Worker and fears that we may be driven thereby to advance step by step to ban the Communist Party. He is sure (as I am) that this would be a mistake.[25]

As for the public, Home Intelligence reported: 'There was little indication that people thought that the Daily Worker and/or the Communist Party were engaged in sabotage or subversive activities.'[26]

If the Ministry played a relatively subdued, even a restraining, role in countering communist activities in England and Wales, such was not the case in Scotland. For many years a rich recruiting ground for communism, the factories and shipyards of Glasgow and Clydeside and the Scottish mines, were sources of deep concern to the RIO in Scotland, N. F. McNicoll. The communists were reported to be causing trouble not only by seeking to discredit the British cause but by exploiting rises in the cost of living, dissatisfaction over working conditions and disputes between unions[27] – all said to be aggravated by the 'supine' attitude of the Scottish TUC.[28] A high-powered group consisting of the Regional Commissioner, the Lord Advocate, the Solicitor General, Lord Rosebery and McNicoll drew up a scheme for an 'Industrial Areas Campaign', whose principal aim was to secure the co-operation of the trade unions and to persuade them to come out openly against communist influence on the shop floor. 'In present circumstances', McNicoll informed headquarters, 'propaganda is a large part of civil defences in Scotland; it has to do much of what bombs are doing in parts of England.'[29]

By February 1941 some progress was believed to have been made. The Scottish TUC asked twenty-seven unions to state their attitude towards the communist-dominated Shop Stewards' Consultative Conference and only one refused to deny this body official recognition. Shop stewards of the AEU were warned that disciplinary action would be taken against anyone attending meetings of unauthorised bodies in his official capacity. Leaflets, pamphlets and broadsheets were distributed among workers, Ministry speakers given union auspices and propaganda films shown in works canteens, but McNicoll was as yet unsatisfied.

Some trade unionists say that Communists are now on the run. This, we think, is putting it far too high . . . The grumbling and whispering campaigns, and particularly the exploitation of

192

apparent defects and deficiencies in the war effort, continue to be serious.[30]

At the time it was recognised that grievances were more than 'apparent'. The cynicism of Scottish workers about the war was attributed in large part to their memories of the depression and, although the majority were believed to have repudiated communist doctrines, the language of communism graphically expressed their discontent.[31] This was especially noticeable in the mines:

> In the mines these men do not act as Communists. They are genuinely, in almost every case, miners with grievances; their communism being a clear cut set of dogma which give an impressive and an inspiring background to the particular grievance . . .
>
> It would be a mistake to attribute the miners' attitude of hostility to the owners and indifference to the war to Communist machinations. On the contrary, these disruptive elements are relatively more effective among the miners than among other industrial workers precisely because wages, working conditions and industrial relations give them more scope.[32]

The alleviation of industrial grievances was the province of Ernest Bevin, and the Ministry of Information could do little more than tinker with a malaise whose cause was deeper than communist agitation.

Complaining that the most articulate 'among the workmen on the Clydeside are those who are dominated by Marxist theory and class war ideas',[33] McNicoll urged headquarters to allow him to employ the services of one William Roberts, a resident of Clydebank who had spent two years at an adult education college and was currently taking a diploma in social studies at Glasgow University.[34] Roberts was given a roving commission which took him into factories and pubs, where he struck up conversations and invited individuals to small meetings whose purpose was to discredit communism. To judge by the volume of correspondence that flowed between Roberts, McNicoll and Senate House, an extraordinary degree of confidence was placed in the success of this venture.

Roberts' reports of his encounters invariably described the communists fleeing in disarray from the field of battle, either because of his own skills at disputation or because he gave to hitherto inarticulate people the ideas and courage to attack party members. After explaining the purpose of communist tactics to a small group in Clydebank, Roberts observed a woman rounding on the communists:

> You are trying to let Hitler win so that you'll be able to save us. What a bloody traitor you are and anyway who the hell are you to think you could save us from Hitler. You threw out your weight for years about how lousy the Nazis were and what you and your bloody tuppence halfpenny party would do, and here when we are at war with them you now want them to win so that you'll be able to save us. Yes we need saving alright, but it's from bloody fools like you who have the gift o' the gab.[35]

After a few months of activity Roberts became convinced that the Communist Party could 'be practically knocked out' by a concerted push by the Ministry[36] and he was pleased to report of his erstwhile opponents:

> They have begun to avoid me, e.g. when some of the men and particularly the Young Communist League are talking with me it invariably happens that an older fellow comes along and says to them, 'Come along, we're going for a walk.'[37]

In spite of high praise of Roberts's work by McNicoll, it is highly improbable that either he or the Industrial Areas Campaign had much impact on an area where, as the Ministry had tacitly admitted, industrial grievances and class bitterness of long standing provided communism with ready-made recruits. And although the Ministry was able to report with some relief 'a striking absence of reference to the "capitalist bosses" ' after the heavy air raids on Clydeside in March 1941,[38] there was little that could be achieved by such superficial methods. The sudden cessation of reports from Scotland towards the end of June 1941 was brought about not by the success of the Ministry's campaign but by an event which occurred 1,500 miles to the east.

Before June 1941 the British communist was regarded as a tiresome opponent of the war but he was not thought by government to be especially dangerous. When he became the most vociferous supporter of the war effort, the authorities took fright and looked upon him as a sort of red-clad Pied Piper intent on leading a gullible populace towards bolshevism. Indeed, to the

194

extent that it was believed that Nazism would die with the defeat of Germany, communism was perceived as the greater long-term threat and the profound change undergone by Anglo-Soviet relations failed to modify the hostility which governing circles in Britain had for long felt towards Russia and her ideology. As a consequence, a not altogether distasteful obligation was laid upon the Ministry of Information – both as propagandist and guardian of public morale – to develop a set of policies almost Byzantine in deviousness and complexity.

There was clearly some inkling within the Ministry of an impending German attack on Russia. On 17 June Harold Nicolson anticipated that a war between the two countries would pose weighty problems for domestic propaganda :

(1) In view of the emotions associated with the general concept of Soviet Russia, it will not be possible to treat Russian belligerency with the same evasiveness which we for so long applied to Abyssinia.

(2) The question will be immediately asked whether we regard the USSR as an Ally or whether we do not. Certain symbols of association and disassociation will at once be seized upon as matters of controversy. Should Maisky be admitted to the St James Palace group? Should the Red Flag be played on Sunday evenings? Should the Communist Party be recognised and admitted to the TUC?

(3) We ought not to be wholly unprepared. From such information as I possess it would seem that in the event of hostilities we are ready to welcome the USSR as a full Ally. If once we have a complete assurance on that point we can give press guidance when the moment comes.[39]

The urgency with which the question was discussed, and a request sent to the War Cabinet, indicates that the possibility of war between Russia and Germany was regarded as likely by senior members of the department. The Ministry complained frequently about not receiving news of important developments from the Cabinet and from other branches of government, but it is barely credible that the Minister was not informed of the intelligence (the actual date of the Nazi attack) which was at that moment being sent to the Soviet government. There can have been few major developments in the war which called for as much thought and preparation on the part of the propagandists.

In reply to the Ministry's request for guidance, Churchill said that 'Germany should be represented as an insatiable tyrant, that had attacked Russia in order to obtain materials for carrying on the war.'[40] Which was all very well, but what was to be said about Russia? Perhaps it did not matter very much what was said, for few people expected that Russia would long be able to resist the German armies. Nicolson thought she would be 'bowled over at a touch'[41] and the public were equally pessimistic:

> There is little confidence in Russia's military capacity, which is judged by her performance against Finland, and a large section of the public feel that the most that can be hoped for is that she will hold out long enough to give us some real advantage.[42]

The Prime Minister's swift and wholehearted declaration of support for the Soviet Union on 22 June made it imperative that the Ministry adopt a similar attitude in domestic propaganda but, again, Churchill's directive was too broad to be of much use to those who were obliged to explain the nuances of the changed Anglo-Soviet relationship to the British people. Anthony Eden, the Foreign Secretary, however, gave a strong indication of the drift of government thinking in a note sent to Duff Cooper summarising a discussion with Maisky, the Soviet Ambassador:

> The Ambassador would understand how deeply was the dislike of Communism rooted in this country. Nothing could be more unfortunate than if the impression was ever to get abroad that, in a desire to promote better Anglo-Russian understanding . . . H.M. Government were lending itself to the popularising of Communist creeds, to which in fact it was strongly opposed. M. Maisky said that he fully understood this point . . . It was rather of the literary and artistic plane that he spoke. Also he thought that it would do the British public no harm to be given some information about the nature of the peoples that made up the Soviet Union, their ways of life, their traditions and so forth. I replied that as long as we vigorously eschewed political propaganda I thought there might be some advantage to such a course.[43]

Duff Cooper agreed with Eden and, indeed, exhibited an even more cautious attitude: 'It is difficult to see how we could boost modern Russian culture without implying some approval of the experiment that has been going on there for these last 24 years.'[44] Hence the emphasis in much of the Ministry's subsequent propaganda on pre-revolutionary Russian cultural achievement.

Nothing more aptly illustrates the government's nervousness about Russia than the decision not to allow the playing of the 'Internationale' in the BBC's popular Sunday broadcasts of allied national anthems. As early as 26 June it was suggested that the national anthems should be replaced by national songs, thereby avoiding the embarrassment of playing all the anthems except that of the Soviet Union.[45] Harold Nicolson observed that it was 'an idiotic question to occupy so much time but in fact it is the symbol of something much more important'.[46] The solution agreed by everyone at a big meeting held at the Foreign Office was 'to play the Internationale next Sunday . . . and then to abolish all national anthems thereafter'.[47] Evidently the government would grit their collective teeth during the rendition, comforted by the knowledge that they would not have to endure it again. But this decision was not carried out. Instead, Duff Cooper tried to persuade Maisky by a rather convoluted argument that the Kutosof 1812 March should be played. Maisky was not so persuaded :

> He said that nothing could replace the 'Internationale' which was the only Russian national anthem. I suggested to him that to call the 'Internationale' a national anthem was a contradiction in terms and that I should have thought that the Russian people would prefer Russian music. He was, however, quite firm on the subject . . . I rang up the Prime Minister last night to see whether he would reconsider his decision about the 'Internationale' but he remained quite firm.[48]

Meanwhile the public, already beginning to suspect the sincerity of the government's vows of support for Russia, were reported to be condemning the failure to play her national anthem.[49] It took six months for the Ministry to change the Prime Minister's mind.[50] Nicolson was right in saying the affair was symbolic : it stood for the government's – and especially Churchill's – lingering distaste for communism and the Soviet Union.

Nicolson was perturbed at the inaction of the Ministry with regard to the formulation of a policy on Russia and confessed to an equally perturbed Walter Elliot that 'we are being slack and optimistic about it, we have not even got a Russian section'.[51] There

197

were others in the Ministry who shared this sense of unease but from Duff Cooper no leadership was forthcoming. The Ministry did, however, ask the Foreign Office to discover whether Sir Stafford Cripps, then Ambassador to Moscow, had any advice to offer. On 24 July Sir Orme Sargent passed on a note to Monckton which had been cabled by Cripps to the Foreign Office. Written by Alexander Werth, a Russian-born journalist working for the British press, and said by Cripps to be an accurate reflection of his own views, the note made a number of important observations and suggested the chief foundations upon which the Ministry's propaganda about Russia might be based.

'It would be well to suggest', Werth recommended, 'that Russia is a Communist country only in name; and that it is, essentially, a Russian patriotic, nationalist country' whose leader 'is not interested in the international aspects of Communism; and certainly since the Spanish war . . . has done very little to foster it.' With this in mind the British worker could be made to understand that his Russian counterpart was fighting not to preserve the regime but to prevent a German conquest of his native soil. The British middle classes, their minds at ease with the knowledge of Stalin's indifference to international revolution, would respond best to Russian music, art and literature. Werth considered it important to stress that the courage and endurance of the Red Army was that of a national army inspired by the military heroes of Russia's tsarist past. And as a concluding suggestion:

> For the harmonious working of this kind of propaganda, it is best that the whole issue of Communism be kept out; and that people like Pollitt should be shut up – preferably by Moscow, which might perhaps also be asked to instruct the British C.P. to go all Union Jacky, just as the French C.P. went all drapeau tricolore on the Kremlin's instructions in 1935, after Laval's visit to Stalin.[52]

The general tenor of these recommendations was followed by the Ministry in its domestic propaganda, although the advice was probably superfluous in at least two respects. The propagandists required no prompting in playing down communism and emphasising the nationalist, rather than the ideological, motivation of the Russian people in their struggle. Nor was the Ministry slow to devise methods aimed at reducing the influence of the Communist Party.

198

R. H. Parker, Director of the Home Publicity Division and known as 'Judge' Parker because of his judicial career in India, had a penchant for long memoranda to which he gave full rein when developing the argument which became the rationale behind subsequent action. 'The great danger that lies before us at the moment', he told Monckton in July 1941, 'is that the popularisation of Russia (or its popularity) must, if it is not interfered with, equally popularise Communism as a method of political living.' The Ministry's inability to brand the Soviet regime as inefficient, in the event of its surviving the German attack, and the socialist measures of wartime control taken by the British government represented to Parker a dangerous combination: 'If we allow the situation to drift for more than six months it will, in my view, be entirely beyond control.'[53] A month later he returned to this theme. Since the First World War the idea of state control, accelerated by the provision of unemployment benefits and the acceptance by the Conservative Party of 'many articles of pure socialism in its programme', had become entrenched in the minds of the British people, so that even 'the intelligent middle class know that it is ruined, and has nothing to look forward to except from the state'. The USSR, 'instead of collapsing as a cranky political machine based on illogic and phantasy . . . should', is now observed to be the first nation to resist the Nazis vigorously. This, together with the public's habituation to state control, would lend communism a spurious aura of efficiency, even of superiority. What was to be done? As well as stressing the virtues and advantages of British democracy, Parker suggested that 'we need not tell the public again that as Hitler has his Gestapo so Stalin has his Ogpu. But we need never let them forget it.'[54] At the same time, he hoped that the Englishman's material comfort and lack of idealism would arm him against the attractiveness of communism:

. . . he hates Nazism and can be brought to hate Communism, because of their interference with his peace, his privacy, his comfort . . . So long as there is a chicken in the pot there is no revolution in the State: and a man who is sure of a chicken next Sunday, and all Sundays, will not raise the Red Flag to make the chicken a turkey. The Englishman is not an idealist and is, therefore, not politically minded.[55]

While Parker's interpretation of the situation was overdrawn, not to mention the unlikelihood of a chicken in the pot every

Sunday for most Englishmen, it found a measure of agreement both within and without the Ministry. Desmond Morton wrote to Churchill on 30 August 1941:

> . . . the excellent weekly report of feeling in England, produced by the Ministry of Information, confirms my personal impression that there is considerable confusion of thought on this subject.
>
> This matter was raised at Lord Swinton's weekly Security Meeting and my view strongly upheld. [It was] pointed out that it would be disastrous if the enthusiasm of the people of England for the excellent Russian defence drifted into an enthusiasm for communism . . . the Communist Party of Great Britain was alive to the possibilities and using all means to increase this confusion of thought for the purpose of promoting communism, sympathy for which was . . . beginning to grow in alarming fashion.
>
> Should not the Minister of Information be invited to consider this with a view to counter-propaganda on the lines of educative talks and articles?[56]

Some days later the Policy Committee was informed 'that the Prime Minister had asked the Minister to consider what action was required to counter the present tendency of the British public to forget the dangers of Communism over the resistance of Russia'.[57] Bracken assured Churchill that the 'propagandists ought not to hesitate about emphasising the divergence between our own political conception and Communism' but for the present he thought it wise to place the stress on 'the enduring value of our democratic way of life' rather than on criticism of Soviet ideology.[58] There were those who took a more sanguine view of the likely consequences of the public's admiration for Russia. In a note to Monckton, A. P. Ryan said that the people had no illusions about the oppressive nature of the Soviet regime but, in view of Russia's stiff military resistance, they were asking with some justification why they had been told in the past that the Soviet system was inherently incompetent. The Ministry could not afford to respond to the public's curiosity about Russia by appearing to approve of critical comments on Soviet affairs. Ryan asked:

> Can we, again, without upsetting the Kremlin, remind people that Communism is as oppressive and as alien to our ideals of right and wrong as is Nazism? I submit that, with the battle still raging, the public are in no need of such a reminder. Their

200

reaction would be 'You're telling us. We know all about that and we don't care. If the devil out of hell came to fight the Nazis just now, we would cheer him and all his fallen angels, and you needn't worry that our cheers would mean that we were turning devil worshippers..'[59]

If Ryan was correct, and Home Intelligence largely confirmed his reading of the public mood, then the British people thought in much the same fashion as Churchill when he said '. . . if Hitler invaded Hell I would make at least a favourable reference to the Devil in the House of Commons'.[60]

What emerged from this period of discussion? Broadly speaking, the Ministry's policy bore two principal aspects: first, praise of the Russian ally with as little mention of communism as possible, and second, sabotage of the British communists' publicity for Russia. It was hoped that such a policy would simultaneously fulfil the government's wish to appear as Russia's stout ally and deny the communists any reflected glory from the Soviet war effort, thus circumventing the seductive appeal of communism to the British people.

The official policy was set out in a memorandum written by H. P. Smollett, head of the Anglo-Soviet Liaison Section which was established in August 1941. The aims of propaganda were to:

(a) Combat such anti-Soviet feeling in Britain as might jeopardise execution of policy defined by the Prime Minister, June 22nd. Counteract enemy attempt to split national unity over issues of Anglo-Soviet Alliance.

(b) Attempt to curb exuberant pro-Soviet propaganda from the Left which might seriously embarrass H.M.G. Anticipate Communist inspired criticism and prevent initiative from falling into the hands of C.P.

It was agreed that in order to ' "steal the thunder" of the radical Left propaganda', the Ministry should promote publicity for Anglo-Soviet co-operation so energetically that it would both outshine the left and rebut accusations of government indifference to the fate of Russia. The delicate matter of political differences between the two nations would be publicly referred to in the following terms:

While both Russia and Britain fully maintain their very different ideals about future forms of society and remembering clearly that they differ fundamentally over their attitude to religion, among other things, they both realise that neither can pursue their own ideals while Hitler and Germany is unbeaten. They therefore wish to pursue the joint war effort against the enemy most energetically and to let each other's populations draw as much inspiration from their Ally's effort as possible. In order to do so the Ministry encourages and assists the distribution of factual information about Russia in Britain and about Britain in Russia.[61]

Much of the success of this policy would depend on the attitude of the Soviet authorities towards the British Communist Party. Smollett was sure that the Soviet government – 'realist to the point of cynicism'[62] – would stick to a bargain suited to their temporary convenience. In support of this conviction he quoted a statement made to him by the Soviet press attaché to the effect that the embassy 'were prepared to disinterest themselves completely in the fate of such organisations as the Russia Today Society, the Friends of the Soviet Union, and the newspaper *Russia Today*'.[63] What did the embassy stand to gain by disowning British communists? It was tacitly understood that the Ministry would not engage in anti-communist propaganda and as an earnest of this intention promised not to employ 'White Russian' speakers on its platforms. More positively, the Ministry planned to distribute posters and, in conjunction with the embassy, to arrange exhibitions around such relatively safe themes as Russian youth, womanhood and agriculture. Facilities were to be provided for the distribution of Soviet press releases, photographs and films. The Ministry would encourage publishers to bring out translations of Russian literature, allow the BBC to broadcast programmes with a Russian content, arrange visits for Soviet workers and soldiers, and generally disseminate publicity about Soviet life and the war effort as widely as possible. The embassy undoubtedly regarded its 'disinterest' in the British communists as a small price to pay for the British government's unprecedented service of publicity on behalf of the Soviet Union, stringently non-political though it was. For their part, the Russians were expected to share some of the considerable costs entailed and to agree not to lend their auspices to any publicity venture unless the organisation concerned met with the Ministry's approval. They also agreed to allow the British to attempt 'to persuade the public in the USSR that Britain was a friendly ally'.[64]

In discharging its side of the bargain, the Ministry exerted itself prodigiously. In the month of September 1943, for example, meetings were organised for 34 public venues, 35 factories, 100 voluntary societies, 9 schools, 28 civil defence groups and one prison. Scores of exhibitions toured the country and by the end of the following October it was expected that the film *USSR at War* would have been seen by a total factory audience of $1\frac{1}{4}$ million. During the month the BBC broadcast thirty programmes with a Russian content to home listeners.[65]

Russian soldiers and civilians were constantly held up as embodiments of various wartime virtues: a poster produced for the Ministry of Labour and National Service, for example, exhorted factory girls to emulate their Soviet counterparts. And even in posters in which no reference was made to the Soviet Union there was injected more than a dash of heroic socialist realism. A vast meeting at the Albert Hall in February 1943 was arranged by the Ministry to celebrate the twenty-fifth anniversary of the Red Army. Attended by leading politicians from all the major parties, the meeting was treated to a massed choir and to readings by John Gielgud and Laurence Olivier. The Ministry's motives were not purely magnanimous since this and subsequent celebrations were organised to prevent the Communist Party from taking the initiative and to dispel lingering public suspicions that the government was not fully behind the Russians.[66] Home Intelligence reported that Red Army Day was greatly enjoyed:

> Although some people believe it was 'all done with our tongue in our cheek', the majority appear to feel 'it has done much to dissipate a suspicion that the alliance between Britain and Russia was artificial'. There has been some amused comment at seeing Red Flags hanging where not so long ago it would never have been thought possible.[67]

In espousing the new orthodoxy, part of which demanded the suppression of even the faintest criticism of Stalin and the evils of his regime, the Ministry went so far as to advise George Orwell's publishers against bringing out *Animal Farm*.[68]

Meanwhile, the Soviet embassy studiously avoided giving offence, going so far as to decline the Ministry's request for speakers from the embassy staff on the ground that they might appear to be intruding in domestic politics. The accommodation between the Ministry and the embassy was a happy – if starkly expedient – arrangement for both parties.

Stealing the thunder of the left entailed more than conspicuous co-operation with the Russian embassy in publicising the Soviet war effort. The Ministry adopted an equally active but clandestine tactic. The very great admiration of the public for the Soviet Union found practical expression in numerous local and national campaigns and 'Aid to Russia' weeks. As the communists were now in the vanguard of those calling for all-out production – albeit to the annoyance of some of their fellow workers who remembered their attitudes before June 1941[69] – so they were the most active in organising publicity and fund-raising ventures on behalf of the Russians; which is precisely what the Ministry had feared as the party's 'attempt to cash in on the courage of the Russians'.[70]

The most easily accomplished part of countering the danger was complete non-cooperation with the Communist Party. In September 1941, Harry Pollitt offered to provide speakers for the Ministry's campaigns for increased production and received the following reply:

> I am to inform you that, having regard to the Communist Party's previous attitude towards the national war effort, the Minister does not feel that it is open to him to invite speakers drawn from the Communist Party to participate in this proposed campaign for increased production.
>
> Mr Bracken will, however, keep the possibility of collaboration under review, and I will inform you if, at any future time, it can be profitably discussed.[71]

The Ministry had absolutely no intention of collaborating with the party at this or at any other time in the future: a policy which even embraced a refusal to give to the communists printed propaganda material which might have been distributed with efficiency and zeal by this most newly patriotic group of citizens. Organisations were classified according to their degree of acceptability to the Ministry. Thus at the top of the ladder, enjoying active Ministry co-operation, came the British Council and the Anglo-Soviet Public Relations Committee; the TUC, the British Association and the Royal Society were given *ad hoc* co-operation; the Society for Cultural Relations with the USSR was recognised but received no co-operation; 'prudent discretion' was exercised in dealing with the International Council of Students and the International Youth Council; and at the bottom of the list, receiving no co-operation whatsoever, were the Women's Parliament, the Anglo-Soviet Friendship Committee, the Russia Today Society, the Joint Committee for Soviet Aid, the National Council for British-Soviet Unity, and the Women's Anglo-Soviet Committee.[72] On Local Information Committees communists were unwelcome, but where there was a strong communist element in a particular locality the Ministry was prepared to consider allowing an individual with left-wing sympathies to join a committee so long as he did so in a personal rather than a representative capacity.[73]

As with so much else of the Ministry's activities, the RIOs became the work-horses in discharging the policy on communism. They were instructed to inform headquarters of any projected campaign in their regions so that the Ministry, if possible in tandem with the Soviet embassy, might take over and advertise it as a joint Ministry of Information–Soviet Embassy venture. The RIOs were expected to use considerable initiative in taking over local campaigns started by communists and to render them politically harmless by bringing them under the – sometimes secret – control of the Ministry, a procedure which was facilitated by the RIO's local contacts and influence. As 'a good example of what a sensible RIO can do without previous direction', his colleagues in other regions were informed of the action taken by the North-West Information Officer in October 1941. Having heard that a local Anglo-Soviet committee was preparing to launch a campaign in the Manchester area, the officer persuaded the lord mayor to give it his blessing and then to disband it in favour of a strictly non-party committee called the 'Lord Mayor of Manchester's Anglo-Soviet Friendship Committee'. This body raised money and conducted publicity for Russia and also took over from the communists a meeting at the Manchester Hippodrome. The communists were no doubt aware of what was going on, but they responded with docility to the intrigues of the Ministry :

> Meanwhile, Mr Pat Devine, representing the Manchester Communist Party Branch, wanted to arrange at short notice a poster parade and a mass meeting. RIO explained that Lord Mayor and Civic leaders were thoroughly co-operative and that Party activity would hinder rather than help. He took a reasonable line and said that he would be very sorry to do anything to interfere with the movement. He has not been heard of since.[74]

In an unnamed town in the south-west the information officer had difficulty persuading the lord mayor to lend his support to a left-wing campaign and to take it over by forming an 'All Citizens

205

Committee', but the Ministry had already secured the co-operation of the Soviet embassy and together they ran the campaign.[75] Another officer was told to 'follow the "stealing the thunder" policy and to get into the picture' after reporting the intention of the trades council in Huddersfield and to hold a special exhibition.[76] In London a more settled procedure was followed:

> In the London Region we have had nearly 50 requests for help in connection with Anglo-Soviet efforts . . . The procedure adopted in relation to each has been identical. The closest possible enquiry is made by responsible officers into the standing and political complexion of applicants for help. In the case of some organisations (i.e. purely Communist Party) we have found it prudent discreetly to indicate why we could not help sectionalised efforts. In other cases we have, through our Committees and the Mayors, paraded a civic all-Party effort which has taken the place of a projected sectionalised effort.
>
> In no case have we rendered help unless we have been completely satisfied:
> (a) That the head of the effort is the Mayor . . .
> (b) That all parties are thoroughly represented on it;
> (c) That Communist influence has been eradicated, at all events as a live factor.[77]

In February 1942 Parker informed the RIOs: 'The first stages of our work in sponsoring Anglo-Soviet publicity and "stealing the thunder" of the Left have progressed as well as could be expected under very difficult circumstances, and we have every reason to be satisfied with the results achieved.' He judged, however, that the stage had been reached where, instead of taking over activities already begun by left-wing groups, information officers should take the initiative themselves by arranging campaigns before the communists had a chance to do so. Not a moment should be wasted. 'We are', Parker warned, 'dealing with activities of a minority which might well do incalculable harm to the democratic cause if it is not prevented from making capital out of a heaven-sent opportunity.'[78]

Insofar as the Communist Party had for years been thoroughly disliked in Whitehall and Westminster it is hardly surprising that the government fostered such activities. But the theory advanced in support of the action taken was that there existed a real danger of the public transferring their admiration for the Soviet Union to a longing for the introduction of its political system into Britain. To what extent was this fear justified on the basis of the evidence available to the Ministry?

There is little doubt that the Communist Party, though sincere in calling for greater effort in aid of Russia and the allied cause generally, welcomed the chance to gain for itself some long-denied respectability and political advantage. And indeed from 12,000 in June 1941 the party increased its membership to 56,000 by the end of 1942.[79] Anyone predisposed to regard the popularity of Russia as a dangerous phenomenon might well have been alarmed at the reports of Home Intelligence. Month after month there were reports of which the following is typical:

> Russian successes continue to provide an antidote to bad news from other fronts and there appears to be growing confidence that the advance is permanent. 'Thank God for Russia' is a frequent expression of the very deep and fervent feeling for that country which permeates wide sections of the public.[80]

By far the most common manifestation of sympathy for Russia was the accusation that Britain was not doing enough to assist her ally. Colonel Moore-Brabazon's statement to the effect that Germany and Russia should be allowed to destroy themselves 'strengthened the suspicion current in certain circles of the continuance, in high places, of a feeling towards the Soviet Union scarcely conducive to effective co-operation'.[81] There was, too, a 'tendency to compare Russian successes with British and American failures'[82] and invidious comparisons continued to be made until the victory at El Alamein.[83] But more worrying than these reactions, which flowed essentially from people's pleasure at hearing of the military successes of an ally, were those which touched more closely on politics. Initially, the public were reported to believe that they had been misled in the years preceding the war about the inefficiency and incompetence of the Soviet system[84] and this led in turn to an intense curiosity about all things Russian. The almost 'unanimous belief that the success of the Russian armies is due to the political system in that country'[85] bred a demand for information about Soviet political practices – a demand which the Ministry was loth to satisfy. The juxtaposition of curiosity about Soviet ideology, widespread admiration for Russia and the growth of the conviction that 'after the war things cannot be as they had been'[86] seemed to give substance to the government's apprehensions.

But the same reports available to the Ministry carried evidence of a not wholly indiscriminate enthusiasm for Russia. There was, first of all, much confusion, some of which the BBC's Listener Research Unit uncovered in September 1942:

A significant feature of the replies was the revelation of the public's bewilderment about Russia – a state of mind hardly to be wondered at, considering the many contradictory and often sensational factors by which opinion about the U.S.S.R. has been influenced since the revolution. The 'terrorism' of the Bolsheviks: the 1924 Anglo-Russian treaty: the Zinoviev letter: the Moscow trials: Russia's entry into the League of Nations, and her support for collective security: and more recently the Nazi-Soviet Pact, the occupation of Poland and the war with Finland, all caused wide fluctuations in feeling about Russia.[87]

But admiration for the Soviet Union, observed one report, 'appears to arise less from a liking for Communism than from a "conviction of our inefficiency, resulting in an increasing degree of admiration for efficiency wherever it is found" '.[88] The transfer of sympathy for Russia to the British communists was, on the whole, not in evidence[89] and, despite the relief which greeted the way in which they had reversed their policy and were now throwing their weight behind the war effort, British communists could not entirely dispel the suspicion with which they were regarded 'by the majority of the people'.[90] In its agitation for a second front the party irritated many people, some of whom believed that the communists were 'quite willing for us to lose a million men if it will help Russia to force Communism on the rest of Europe'.[91] In March 1942, RIOs were asked to investigate the prevalence and causes of 'home-made socialism'. Although linked to Russian military success, it was said to be 'vague' and 'rather inarticulate', lacking any organised political basis and 'groping towards an unofficial and non-party type of social policy'[92] – hardly the stuff of which revolutions are made. There was nothing to show that the public at large desired a radical alteration in the political system. The reception accorded to the essentially gradualist Beveridge Report was proof enough that the people hoped not for full-blooded socialism, but for a greater responsiveness on the part of the political system to their needs and wants.

Russia's popularity reached a peak at the time of the great victory at Stalingrad:

People talk in superlatives of Russia but that doesn't really express how much they admire her achievements.[93]

However successful or even sensational the news from other quarters may be, the eyes and hearts of the majority are turned towards 'our great Allies'. The victory at Stalingrad is said to have aroused more 'intense admiration than any other Russian exploit', and it appears that the admiration and gratitude of the majority have never been higher.[94]

Thereafter enthusiasm gradually declined, perhaps swamped by the Anglo-American defeat of the Axis forces in North Africa and a growing apprehension about the territorial intentions of the Soviet Union. 'Will Joe stop at the Channel?' people were overheard to remark.[95] In March 1943 a special report was made on the subject :

Russia's intentions in the post-war world remain a matter for speculation and apprehension. People want to know if 'the policy of political interference in the internal affairs of other nations has been finally abandoned'. Particular reference is made to the Russo-Polish frontier dispute . . . to her 'religious policy', and to 'possible plans for bolshevising the world'. Two reports refer to comments on the activities of the British Communist Party. There is concern at 'their continual boosting of the Russian system'.[96]

Unfortunately, Home Intelligence rarely quantified their assessments of public opinion and it is difficult to judge the extent to which enthusiasm for Russia was said to be giving way to promptings of hostility. But it is of greater significance in the present context that from June 1941 until the end of the European war the public's comments on British communists were reported by Home Intelligence only very occasionally and even then they were usually derogatory.

In November 1941, Desmond Morton suggested to Lord Swinton that the Ministry of Information's propaganda should separate the Soviet Union and the Comintern in the minds of the people and thereby be free to attack the British communists while publicly supporting the Russian war effort :

For many years to our despite the Soviet Government insisted venomously that it had nothing to do with the IIIrd International. Hyde was not responsible for the acts of Jekyll. Now that it suits us to accept this argument, we are mad if we fail to take advantage of Joe Stalin's past when attempting to ensure our own tranquillity for the future.[97]

Morton advanced the same argument to Churchill, adding that the Ministry should appoint an expert on the Comintern in order to attack it and the Communist Party more effectively.[98] Passing the letter on to Bracken, Churchill noted: 'Mr. Bracken. Please read and digest this. It looks like the right course.' The suggestion, not surprisingly, received the full support of R. H. Parker.[99] But to have criticised the Communist Party in terms broad enough to have had a public impact while simultaneously avoiding criticism of Soviet ideology would have been extremely difficult. S. G. Gates, commenting on the proposal to Radcliffe, voiced an additional objection. While recognising that it was the Ministry's duty to prevent the British communists from obtaining prestige from Russia's resistance, Gates put forward the view:

> We must on the other hand realise that in dealing with Russia we are in a region where the impact of events is too powerful to be substantially deflected by propaganda. If the Russians succumb, Communism will be discredited with them. If they succeed, Englishmen will inevitably contrast their resistance in this war with their collapse in the last and conclude that a 'Communist' system (however obnoxious in some respects) conduces to greater efficiency than the Czarist regime. But it would be a profound mistake to think that distant admiration of this kind implied conversion to Communism. That danger will never come through admiration of the achievements of another country, but only through dissatisfaction with our own – dissatisfaction savage enough to cherish a revolutionary programme.[100]

Radcliffe agreed with this analysis,[101] which – bearing a similarity of attitude to A. P. Ryan's – spoke for the views of those men in the Ministry who possessed more understanding of the British people than to believe that their admiration for Russia would result in calls for a communist government at Westminster. The hotheads, among whom Churchill must be numbered, were prevented from launching an anti-communist crusade.

Nevertheless, the policy of 'stealing the thunder' remained in being and in 1944 one of the Ministry's officers questioned the moral probity of withholding co-operation from the party, pointing out that all members of the community deserved equal treatment at the hands of a government department.[102] By 1944 any illusory danger which had existed had long since evaporated. The real, if unstated, reason for the maintenance of the policy lay in the government's antipathy for communism. Part of the Ministry's activities thus slipped into a twilight world in which the resources of the state were employed to serve political ends which could not be publicly avowed.

The religious dimension of Anglo-Soviet relations posed a peculiarly delicate problem. To the extent that British domestic propaganda proclaimed the war as a defence of Christianity, the alliance with Russia appears to have struck many people as a betrayal of one of the cardinal principles for which they were contributing to the war effort. According to a BBC Listener Research survey, the subject of religion in the USSR was the chief barrier to British understanding of that country:

> It seems that the British public is completely confused on this issue. More than any other problem, it has been a cause of misunderstanding and deep mistrust . . . The main question seems to be 'Is there freedom of worship?' and: 'Is the government hostile, or merely indifferent, to religion?' The feeling among the majority was that this question of religious toleration was one of the first that must be cleared up before any real understanding could be reached.[103]

But a debate which took place in the Ministry eleven months before Russia's entry into the war foreshadowed the determination of the department not to antagonise the Soviet regime for the sake of mollifying religious, then chiefly Catholic, opinion. In July 1940, Richard Hope, head of the Roman Catholic section, submitted a paper to the Policy Committee in which he warned against the dissemination of propaganda appearing to support 'the democratic counter-revolution against the Nazis and Fascists' in occupied Europe. After insisting that English and European Catholics had a dread of revolution and therefore feared bolshevism as much as, and in some cases more than, Nazism, Hope made four recommendations:

211

1. Britain's war aims should be kept on a broad and high level, and should not be identified with Popular Front governments, still less with revolution. We should make it quite plain that the political and internal future of France is for Frenchmen to decide and we should refrain from condemning the Pétain *internal* programme in France.

2. As revolution is particularly dreaded by Catholic populations, and famine is the road to revolution, we should counter the impression that we are responsible for the lack of food in Europe . . .

3. If conditions with the Soviets improve the matter must be handled with care as an uncomfortable necessity as turning the tables on the Nazis.

4. We should continue to use Papal utterances in our propaganda in conjunction with those of President Roosevelt and our own statesmen, particularly Lord Halifax, to convey the sense of a huge common moral front uniting the Catholic Church, the Empire and the United States in a moral alliance against Nazidom.[104]

During discussion of the paper – which, to judge from the minutes, must have been unusually acrimonious – Sir Walter Monckton stated that Hope took too short a view of the Ministry's propaganda policy and had overlooked 'the revolutionary spirit which he regarded as manifest in every belligerent country'. More outspoken, Radcliffe declared that the recommendations were 'very dangerous' and added :

. . . for millions of people militant Socialism was a religion. It was therefore erroneous to say that broad and high levels could not be achieved without adopting a position contrary to that of militant Socialism. For this reason he thought the first recommendation should be condemned. He thought that the second recommendation was a commonplace and that the third would be ruinous and alienate Russia good and for all. The fourth he considered wholly satisfactory if it were possible to persuade the Catholic Church, the Empire and the United States that they were actually in a moral alliance against Nazidom, and that Russia was not excluded from it.[105]

As Monckton was Director General at the time of Germany's attack on Russia and Radcliffe was to succeed him, their attitudes could be expected to prevail over Richard Hope's wish to give the preponderant weight to Catholic – even Vichy Catholic – opinion in propaganda.

Following the German invasion of Russia the Ministry of Information, and the Religions Division in particular, was placed in a considerable quandary. On the one hand, owing to the government's support for Russia, the division was anxious to avoid condemnation of the state atheism of the Soviet Union and to muffle criticism from other quarters. On the other hand, the Ministry did not wish to appear indifferent to the fate of Christianity in the Soviet Union. In the circumstances the Religions Division did well to resolve as best it could these conflicting demands of policy by early July, although the exercise involved some uncomfortable contortions.

> Aggression is aggression even when committed against an atheist state.
>
> We have not altered our opposition to Communism. We lend our aid not to Communism but to the Russian victims of Nazi aggression. The policy of the Government defined by the Prime Minister can be wholeheartedly accepted by Christians. Our business partnership with Russia is strictly limited; it has one aim only: the defeat of Hitler.
>
> What remains of our claim to be fighting for Christian civilisation? The claim remains as before. We are fighting to retain the spiritual heritage of the West. Although many feel, especially on the Continent, that this spiritual heritage is threatened by Communism, there is no doubt that it is actually threatened at the moment by Nazi Germany.[106]

Notwithstanding the latent hostility in this statement of policy, the Ministry was so anxious to place Russia in the best possible light that Sir Stafford Cripps was asked whether he had observed any relaxation in the Soviet government's religious policies. His reply contained little that was encouraging.

Although the anti-God campaign was not actively in progress, there was, according to Cripps, no real indication of a popular religious revival in Moscow and the Soviet regime would certainly not welcome British propaganda designed to show that its anti-religious principles were undergoing revision.[107] Noting Cripps's observations, the Religions Division in a modified statement of policy sounded a note of mixed hope and regret:

213

If at any time the Soviet Government felt able to relax restrictions on the teaching of religion this would be a real item of news worth disseminating, although to do so now might suggest that Russia was only doing it in desperation.

Religious circles in Britain are prepared to stand by Russia and hope that a better day will dawn for religion. They do not wish to cash in on Russia's military emergency to extract relaxations under duress.

It must be realised, however, that the whole spiritual presentation of our case is hampered by the Soviet record (especially by the officially favoured anti-God movement).[108]

There the situation rested for a year. The Ministry's celebration of Russia's achievements had perforce to remain secular.

The attitude of Catholics continued to worry the authorities. One of the principal concerns of the Religions Division was the accusation levelled against Catholics that they wished to see Russia's defeat. But Hope's response to reports of rumours which spoke of the 'hidden hand of Rome' against the Soviet cause was itself rather less than enthusiastic for the same cause :

As far as I am aware there is no propaganda amongst Catholics against giving aid to Russia. They regard this as an obvious necessity if the war is to be won. On the other hand Catholics have reacted against the general and often irrational enthusiasm for Russia which is apparent in England at the present time. Their tendency, therefore, is to keep alive opposition to Communism. As this tendency runs counter to general popular opinion it is of course liable to misinterpretation.[109]

In September 1942 the Foreign Office received a cable from Russia containing a proposal by the Metropolitan of Kiev for an exchange of visits between clerics of the two countries. An almost exactly similar proposal had been made by Smollett eleven months previously when he suggested extending an invitation to Patriarch Sergius, Metropolitan of Moscow, as a means of strengthening the impression of Anglo-Soviet co-operation.[110] But, in view of the surprise with which the Russian invitation was greeted in the Ministry, it is not possible to say whether the proposal was engineered by the department. However, the opportunity to bring off something of a propaganda coup was grasped eagerly by the Religions Division.

9. 'YOUR BRITAIN—Fight for it NOW'—was a poster commissioned by ABCA (Army Bureau of Current Affairs) which put into striking visual terms an undertaking which the Ministry was reluctant to proclaim on its own or the government's behalf.

COVER YOUR HAIR
FOR SAFETY

YOUR RUSSIAN
SISTER DOES !

Issued by the Ministry of Labour and National Service and produced by the Royal Society for the Prevention of Accidents, Terminal House, 52, Grosvenor Gardens, London, S.W.I.

Printed by LOXLEY BROS. LTD.

10. Russian soldiers and civilians were constantly held up as embodiments of various wartime virtues, such as in this poster produced by the Ministry of Labour and National Service.

11. Although no reference was made to the Soviet Union, more than a dash of heroic socialist realism was injected into posters such as 'Women of Britain—Come into the Factories'.

12. Since the débâcle of the 'Silent Column' campaign the Ministry had approached rumour and gossip very gingerly, adopting a lighter, if occasionally sexist touch in such slogans as 'Keep Mum, she's not so dumb!' and 'Be like Dad: Keep Mum' which was well received by the public but earned the displeasure of Dr Edith Summerskill

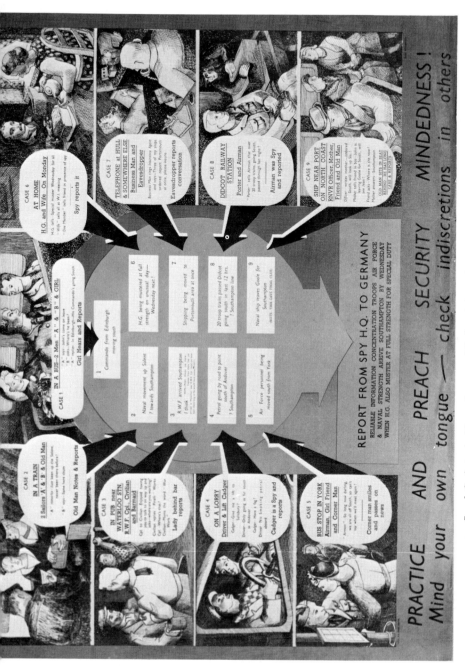

13. Lord Swinton's Committee on National Security agreed that 'there was little evidence of careless talk and less evidence that it was put to good use by the enemy'. Nonetheless heavily didactic posters like 'Practice (sic) and Preach Security Mindedness!' continued to be produced.

Britain develops new desert tactics. Tough, well-trained infantry clear the way for tanks in North Africa

BACK THEM UP!

14/15. Although the arrival of Brendan Bracken at the Ministry coincided with the decline in their belief in inspirational propaganda, he did not halt the celebrations of Britain's war effort in such posters as 'Back Them UP' and 'and the NAVY goes on'

and the NAVY goes on

Great Britain will pursue the WAR AGAINST JAPAN to the very end.

WINSTON CHURCHILL

16. According to the Ministry's Far Eastern War Committee, public interest in and knowledge of the Japanese war remained low early in 1944. In November 1944 Leo Amery and the service ministers recommended that 'a campaign of indoctrination be started'. Bracken pointed out that a campaign, of 'explanation' rather, had been in progress for a year.

Analysing the possible reasons behind the Soviet government's permission to allow such a proposal to be made, H. M. Waddams of the Religions Division surmised that the regime had a threefold purpose : recognition of an upsurge of religious feeling in Russia, a desire to soften foreign hostility towards its religious policies, and a determination to blunt the edge of the Nazi claim to represent Christendom against Godless Russia. In spite of misgivings about the motives of the Russians, Waddams advised strongly that the exchange of visits should proceed since they would bring about the first contact to be made between Christians of the two countries since the Revolution.[111] The Ministry laid down two conditions. The English clerics should visit Russia first lest the Soviet authorities, having allowed representatives of the Orthodox Church to visit Britain, should find some reason for obstructing the completion of the exchange. And the arrangements should appear to be a semi-private affair between the two churches with no public interviews and only agreed statements issued.[112] The Foreign Office approved these conditions and then left matters entirely in the hands of the Ministry.

The Archbishop of Canterbury agreed with the Religions Division that the visits should proceed and delegated the Archbishop of York, Dr Garbett, as the Church of England's representative.[113] Dr Garbett would undertake the journey only on condition that no other denomination was represented. He also insisted on keeping the matter secret until his arrival in Moscow and would countenance no suggestion of discussing reunion between the Anglican and Orthodox churches.[114] Archbishop Temple, reflecting on the purpose of the exchange, commented, 'I have no doubt that from the standpoint of the Russian Government their interest in any such visit will be primarily political . . . There must be no doubt that *our* interest is primarily religious.'[115] That may have been the interest of the Anglican Church but it certainly did not fully apply to the motives of the Ministry. Although the officers of the Religions Division – many of them ordained clerics – were doubtless sincere in wishing to bring about a re-establishment of contact between the two churches, the Ministry did not undertake all the arrangements and the subsequent publicity merely in order to further the cause of religious brotherhood.

In a long statement of policy issued to RIOs, the Home Division illustrated with numerous examples the way in which the Soviet authorities had recently eased their restrictions on religion. It was considered vital not to exaggerate the extent of these concessions, since interested Christians were very well informed, but RIOs were assured that they would not be running counter to policy if they informed the public that religious services were once more permitted, that Russian Christians were fully behind the war effort and that the regime had officially recognised the place of the Church in Russian history. 'In the long run', RIOs were advised, 'an important way of countering enemy propaganda about Godlessness in the USSR, and our own implication in it, is to put out material showing that Britain still stands by the European cultural tradition in law and religion.'[116]

After the many arrangements were completed by the Ministry, the Archbishop and his party made the visit to Russia in late September and early October 1943. On his return, Dr Garbett gave a press conference at Senate House in which Russia emerged very well. The Archbishop had observed during his visit that worship was fully permitted and that the vast crowds filling Moscow Cathedral were composed mostly of young people. In response to the deeply religious strain in the Russian people, Stalin – 'a wise statesman' – had clearly put an end to anti-religious propaganda, as well as closing the anti-God museums and permitting the printing of religious publications. Dr Garbett concluded by stating :

> However much we may condemn some of the methods used during and after the Revolution, and I think we should all condemn some of them, we should now watch with sympathy the working out of a great social and economic experiment, even though we may feel much of it may be inapplicable to our own country.[117]

It is doubtful that the Ministry found this statement congenial (Garbett regarded himself as an even more dangerous reformer than Archbishop Temple[118]) but his visit and the subsequent publicity went a long way towards satisfying the Religions Division's wish to have Britain seen as associating with a not entirely Godless Russia. A return visit was made by the Metropolitan Nikolai in June 1945, after the end of the European war. According to the Religions Division, it was remarkable not only 'for the extreme warmth of sentiment expressed on both sides' but also for the freedom with which the Soviet embassy allowed the delegation to conduct its eleven-day visit.[119]

8

The Decline of Exhortation

To the extent that the Ministry of Information ceased actively meddling in morale in 1941 and came to regard the British as a common-sense, calm and courageous people, George Orwell was correct in his comment of 1944 that 'the Government has done extraordinarily little to preserve morale : it has merely drawn on existing reserves of good will'.[1]

The Ministry continued to take the nation's pulse, however, and exhibited a good deal of confidence in the validity of its diagnoses by committing them to paper as a chart (*see endpapers*). The troughs and peaks of 'public feeling' are related to military and diplomatic events and not in a single instance to matters of domestic significance. The Beveridge Report is omitted, for example. But it was in partial recognition of the fact that the progress of the war and what was called 'the propaganda of events' had a far greater impact on morale than even the most strenuous exertions of the propagandists that the Ministry gradually, and not without reluctance, disengaged from exhortation. This was far from being a wholly negative process. The vehemence with which the new attitude came to be expressed within the department, and to others in government, was a measure of the sheer novelty of the idea that the British people could be trusted to act rationally and ought to be allowed to do so without constant hectoring and wheedling. The application of this doctrine worked something of a minor revolution in the relationship between government and people.

No one had the courage to say so at the time, but it is clear that towards the end of 1940 some Ministry officials were beginning to doubt the value of the department to civilian morale and to the war effort generally. Lord Clark remembers it thus : 'It was a perfectly useless body, and the war would have been in no way affected if it had been dissolved and only the censorship retained.'[2] He may be,

217

indeed probably is, correct if this assessment is applied to much of the period up to his resignation in August 1941. Lord Taylor, who as Dr Stephen Taylor joined the department early in 1940 and remained throughout the war, is of a different opinion. For morale, he maintains, 'domestic explanation and education did a lot. The Government campaigns in the spheres of food, cooking, health, fuel saving, relations with overseas troops etc. etc. did excellent work – both subjectively and objectively.'[3]

But great difficulties were experienced during the latter half of Duff Cooper's stewardship. In July 1940 the War Cabinet had decided to restrict description of air-raid casualties to 'slight', 'considerable' or 'heavy'. This provoked an outcry both from the public and the press when the intensity of raids began to increase.[4] So far as the naming of raided towns was concerned, some progress was made when, on 25 November 1940, the Ministry of Information, the Air Ministry and the Ministry of Home Security agreed upon a working principle.[5] No mention was to be made in such a way as to identify a place until at least 28 days after an attack, unless it was of exceptional interest or of propaganda importance (such as Buckingham Palace). Moreover, in order to confuse the enemy, the elapse of time between a raid and identification of the town concerned was to be deliberately varied.

But the situation late in November 1940, Duff Cooper told the Air Minister, 'is so ludicrous that it can hardly be left where it is'. He explained that in the preceding fortnight, Coventry, Southampton and Bristol had all been heavily bombed and although it was obvious that the Germans must have known they had located and raided these cities, only the name of Coventry had been released. Having enforced the prohibition on the naming of the other cities, in the face of considerable press annoyance, the Ministry of Information was made to look ridiculous when Air Marshal Joubert broadcast full details of all the raids to the United States. Duff Cooper concluded his expostulation by rounding on the Air Ministry:

It seems to me plain that we cannot go on in this way if the public . . . are to retain any respect at all for the official attitude towards news and that those responsible for this branch of the matter at the Air Ministry must be led to take a more realistic and less impracticable attitude.[6]

This entreaty had some effect. A little over a month later Sir Archibald Sinclair, worried about morale and the prevalence of wild rumours, urged the Home Secretary to persuade Churchill to permit fuller publication of air-raid news.[7] Sinclair and Duff Cooper had been heartened by Churchill's agreement in November to allow the release of detailed information about the bombing of certain large towns. This had been achieved when Churchill was shown that the unsanctioned release of news on the Coventry raid had given Britain a propaganda coup in America and even in Germany itself.[8] But it was not until March 1941 that the three ministers reached agreement on the content of a joint letter to the Prime Minister.[9] They requested that casualties should be promptly disclosed and much fuller raid information given to the public. In reply, Churchill stated that although he had no objection to the matter being discussed again by Cabinet, he had not observed any depressing effect on morale resulting from the present policy and would strongly deprecate its abandonment.[10]

Duff Cooper's top officials were not mollified. On 20 March 1941 it was agreed at a meeting of the Planning Committee:

> . . . that the situation regarding air-raid communiqués was most unsatisfactory. The morale of the majority of the public, who were not in a position to know the truth for themselves, depended upon the amount of confidence which they were prepared to give to official statements and this in turn depended on the extent to which men in the street, when in a position to place any check upon official statements, found them reliable. Air-raid communiqués provided the most frequent opportunities for checking, and the impression gaining ground that these were by no means accurate threatened to undermine confidence in all official statements, and to open a wonderful opportunity to German propaganda.[11]

Duff Cooper had by this time been worn down by the cares of office and lacked the courage to tackle Churchill again. Thus it was that the reporting of the single most important manifestation of the war for civilians continued to be attended by confusion, ignorance and rumour.

The bizarre arrival of Rudolf Hess in Britain on 10 May 1941 presented the Ministry of Information with an unprecedented opportunity for lifting public spirits and winning a propaganda victory over Germany. Of all news items during the war, this was one of the most appropriate for the Ministry to handle and in concert with the press to turn to Britain's advantage.

Harold Nicolson, realising through bitter experience that the department might be denied any influence, was anxious to establish a claim over any news that was to be released about the reasons for Hess's arrival: 'I feel that we should make it quite clear that whatever value Hess may be as a prisoner of war, he is fifty times more valuable as a propaganda carrier. He ought to be our bird before he is anybody else's bird.'[12] Equally worried, Francis Williams wanted an agreed story to be put out as soon as possible, 'as otherwise, if a free rein is allowed for some days to two or three or possibly more conflicting theories, the full propaganda value of Hess's flight, both at home and abroad, will be largely dissipated'.[13]

Churchill, however, after drafting a press statement with Duff Cooper, changed his mind and decided that it would be better to allow the press to speculate.[14] Ronald Tree, Duff Cooper's Parliamentary Private Secretary, has suggested that Britain missed a golden opportunity since before anyone could be found to positively identify Hess the Germans put out their own announcement.[15] But, as Churchill was anxious for a British statement to be made even after the Germans had broadcast their version of the news,[16] this hardly seems an adequate explanation. It was, admittedly, difficult to make much sense of Hess's stated reasons for his mission but within a day or two of his arrival it became apparent that the Deputy Führer wished to discuss peace proposals. Angus Calder maintains that the government deliberately kept quiet lest the public respond favourably to a German peace offer.[17] It is unlikely, though, that such a consideration carried much weight with Churchill. He, of all members of the government, possessed the greatest faith in the public's morale and singleness of purpose. Nonetheless, the uncharacteristically hesitant Prime Minister allowed himself to be persuaded that it would be best to keep the Germans guessing.[18]

There was an overwhelming public demand for an official explanation.[19] But five days after Hess's flight, Churchill informed the Cabinet that there was 'no pressure for an early statement' and confined his actions to a demand that the press be reminded that Hess's record was 'as bloody as that of any of the Nazi leaders'.[20] According to Nicolson and Cecil King, it was Beaverbrook who first persuaded the Prime Minister to adopt a policy of silence.[21] Bracken, too, appears to have taken a hand in the management of the government's strategy.[22] In the meantime, the Ministry of Information had been jostled out of the way. Duff Cooper was not even told of Hess's arrival until two days afterwards and his chief contribution was to ask Churchill's permission to have the prisoner photographed 'in not too flattering a light'.[23]

'Hess has already received so much attention in the Press', it was stated at the War Cabinet on 19 May, 'that public opinion would favour giving the topic a rest. The absence of a statement was also calculated to maintain the anxiety of Nazi leaders.'[24] No doubt there was an orgy of nail-biting in Berlin but the suspense in Britain was barely less acute, for far from losing interest in Hess the public's curiosity was reported to be growing:

> No theory has been too fantastic to put forward, from the idea that he was in love with Unity Mitford and had flown here to see her, to the fear that he had come to assassinate the Prime Minister . . .
>
> It was felt from the first that Hess was the 'answer to a propagandist's prayer'. Now, several days later, the view is being expressed that the news might have been handled with greater effect.[25]

The public were never told the reasons for Hess's arrival. Stalin, some years later, argued with Churchill in Moscow and 'steadfastly maintained that Hess had been invited over by our Secret Service',[26] a belief which was not markedly more fantastic than others which had been allowed to flourish at the time.

For the Ministry there were to be more distressing consequences. Three days after Hess's flight and still without an official explanation, the press, according to Sir Walter Monckton, 'were in a state of fury such as neither I nor Ridsdale, the Head of the Foreign Office News Department, had seen before during the war'.[27] Knowing little more than the journalists, Monckton consulted the Foreign Office and on 14 May told the press and the BBC:

> It can now be disclosed that Hess had made an attempt to communicate with the Duke of Hamilton by letter some months previously. The Duke immediately placed the letter in the hands of our Security authorities and Hess got no reply.[28]

This statement was made in an attempt to exonerate the Duke of Hamilton from suspicion following the German allegation that Hess's reason for going to Scotland was to establish contact with the duke, with whom he had previously corresponded. The latter half of Monckton's statement was not true. A letter to the duke, dated 23 September 1940, had been sent through Lisbon from a 'Dr A. H.' – Albrecht Haushover, an associate of Hess – and was intercepted by

Postal and Telegraph Censorship on 2 November and passed on to MI5.[29] Someone in the Ministry must have known that the duke had not received the letter. E. S. Herbert, Director of Postal and Telegraph Censorship, was in daily contact with the Ministry and sat on some of its committees and it is highly unlikely that he failed to inform the higher officials of the interception of such an interesting document. That Monckton's statement was less than honest is confirmed by the Ministry's admission to Sir Archibald Sinclair that it was made because it was felt 'less likely to give rise to suspicion' of the duke's conduct to say that he had received and passed on the letter rather than to say it had been intercepted.[30]

Publication of the announcement infuriated Sinclair:

> There is no truth whatever in this story. The Duke has assured me personally that he had never received the letter from Hess. I feel surprised that your Department should have given currency to a story that affects the reputation of a serving officer in the RAF without consulting me. I feel sure I can rely upon you to give instructions which will prevent such a thing happening again.[31]

On 22 May, Sinclair, in reply to a question in the House, denied that the Duke of Hamilton had ever corresponded with Hess or had received a letter from him.[32] It was now the turn of the press to be angry. The *Evening Standard* commented:

> On May 15 there appeared inspired statements that the Duke *did* receive a letter from Hess and handed it over to the Security Department.
> Can some statement be made by the Ministry, please, to exonerate the newspapers from the imputation that they published an untrue statement.[33]

A question was put down for 27 May and it became obvious that the only way out of the mess was for the Ministry to admit that a mistake had been made. This was too much for Monckton and he submitted his resignation.[34] Duff Cooper tried to dissuade him from resigning and, rather unfairly, added, 'I consider that the Air Ministry have behaved with their customary boorish stupidity, and I shall write a strong letter of protest to Sinclair.'[35] In the Minister's absence through illness, Nicolson answered the question and stated that the information supplied to the press had 'since been found to be erroneous'.[36] On the following day, in an attempt to tie up the loose ends of the unfortunate affair, he asked Bracken to persuade the Prime Minister to tell Monckton – who was acting 'like a wounded Prima Donna' – not to be so silly.[37] Churchill's disregard, not to say contempt, for the Ministry of Information's claim to primacy in the handling of news had forced it into a hasty action which soured relations with the press, angered the Air Ministry, strengthened public scepticism of official news and ruined what little chance remained of making capital out of Hess's mad venture.

One of the last attempts to sustain morale by inspirational methods was the Empire Crusade of late 1940. Largely the brainchild of H. V. Hodson, an Oxford don and Director of the Empire Division, the scheme was meant to educate the public about the empire and the commonwealth, and in so doing convince them of the moral superiority of Britain's way of ordering the world. Furthermore :

> . . . if the public is fully apprised of what it is fighting for in preserving the Commonwealth, the comparatively negative senti-ment of 'defeating Nazi Germany' will be reinforced by a positive and dynamic faith. A nation in arms, possessed by such a faith, becomes irresistible.[38]

Harold Nicolson, although an inveterate worrier about morale, was far from convinced :

> It is to run for ten weeks and will cost pots of money. I was opposed to it since I do not think we should spend large sums on anything which is not essential. The public do not want at present to be told about New Zealand or the Lugard system.[39]

Duff Cooper also wondered whether the campaign was necessary[40], but he and Nicolson were in a minority and the campaign began early in October. The endeavour to impart a 'dynamic faith' to the British people was couched in the following terms :

The Greatest Crusade.

We, who are members of the British Commonwealth, hold in our hands the future of the world.

By fostering the spirit of liberty we are building self-reliant nations of free men.

We are the builders at grips with the destroyers. We stand for healthy unhampered growth, fighting the disease of tyranny . . .

Tyranny is the oldest disease of the human race. For thousands of years men have been tempted by visions of world conquest to sell their souls to a tyrant. Under the thin disguise of new catch-words, the Nazis have started the old futile game of building a slave empire.

The British Empire is exactly the opposite. There has been nothing like it in the world before; it is a commonwealth, a family of free nations – linked together by a loyalty to one king. It stands for progress; it is the hope of the future.[41]

This ponderous language was employed in all the newspaper advertisements: in *The Times* and *Daily Mirror* alike.

Half-way through the term of the Crusade, Hodson reviewed progress. He expressed disappointment at the poor response of the press and the public but, believing that 'certain observers' had been 'somewhat hasty' in concluding that the campaign was a failure, urged his colleagues to agree to a much bigger and more comprehensive operation.[42] It was, however, allowed to run its course and then to expire decently. Mass-Observation found at its conclusion that less than a third of a large sample was aware of the campaign, and of these only one in twenty could recall the content of the press advertisements. Nor had there been any significant improvement in the number of people who were aware of the difference between a dominion and a colony.[43] One observer, already irritated at the 'hopelessly amateurish' propaganda of the Ministry, pointed to a fundamental oversight in the campaign's presentation:

The main criticism lies in the fact that it lacks emotion in its appeal and simplicity in its approach. Its objective, and the media selected, indicate that it aimed at people of all income groups. Three-quarters of the population . . . live in families with incomes of less than £4 per week . . . the copy is difficult for the under-educated to understand, it is stiff reading for anyone who does not take in the *Spectator* . . . The whole thing could not be duller to anyone who does not happen to be intellectually interested in one or other of the countries.[44]

The campaign failed in both its educative and morale-boosting objectives.

A venture undertaken with the greatest reluctance in 1941 was anti-gossip publicity. In February, when memories of the Silent Column were still painfully fresh, the Prime Minister ordered the department to put out 'a lot of anti-gossip material'.[45] Since the débâcle of the Silent Column the Ministry had approached rumour and gossip very gingerly, adopting a lighter – if occasionally sexist – touch, and carefully selecting highly specific target audiences such as lorry drivers and railway workers.[46] One of the slogans – 'Be Like Dad: Keep Mum', coined by Jack Beddington of the Films Division – was well received by the public but earned the displeasure of Dr Edith Summerskill, who thought it 'in the worst Victorian music-hall taste'.[47] Nicolson and R. H. Parker protested that a new gossip campaign would do more harm than good, but the Ministry was obliged to go ahead. Planning commenced, subject to the provisos that the inculcation of 'spy-mania' and an 'unnatural degree of discretion' should be avoided at all costs.[48]

The campaign was prepared with a good deal more care than was shown in the Silent Column, although the fact that it aimed solely at information of value to the enemy made the task easier. Emphasis was to be placed on educating the public in the type of information of military value and how it might reach the enemy. Despite the relatively inoffensive nature of the proposed campaign, considerable opposition developed against it in the Ministry – not least because of the £100,000 cost involved in a six-month campaign. Sir Kenneth Clark summarised the views of those opponents of the scheme who feared it might harm morale:

> They urge that most people want to talk about their work, and that to stop people talking was likely to cause irritation and gloom. Gossip was a kind of lubricant without which the normal machinery of human intercourse would blow up . . . the harm done to the spirit of the country by prohibiting gossip would greatly outweigh any advantage which the enemy might gain by the repetition of valuable information.[49]

Lord Swinton's Committee on National Security agreed that 'there was little evidence of careless talk and less evidence that it was put to good use by the enemy'[50] but the campaign went ahead: and heavily didactic posters like 'Practice (*sic*) and Preach Security Mindedness' continued to be produced. It was improbable that the publicity had much effect but at least, according to intelligence reports, it seems not to have aroused hostility.

The impulse in government circles to lecture at the public was misplaced. It is true that in 1941 people were dispirited when British arms suffered reverses, tired and crotchety after long periods of hard work, and depressed at the nation's seeming inability to defeat the

Germans on land. It is equally true that defeatism was not in evidence. In December 1940 a committee of the Ministry's Duty Room reported on 'the present decline in public confidence'.[51] Citing as the major cause the public's realisation that the war would be long, the committee put forward a number of contributory factors: war weariness; anxiety about air raids, food prices and the labour position; discontent over evacuation, news presentation, shelter and blackout conditions; and the prospect of another winter of war. But how could anyone possessed of a modicum of common sense be other than dispirited at the end of 1940? Insofar as it was possible to alleviate certain difficulties, then the public might have benefited from action taken by the Ministry of Information; but it was not within the power of the department to cause air raids to cease or to bring about sudden improvements in shelter conditions and food prices. Such measures as were suggested by the Duty Room committee – military processions, plenty of bands and flags, discreet propaganda about the prospect of victory and an explanation of the 'ethics' of evacuation – could have had no more than a fleeting effect on preoccupations so firmly grounded in the realities of wartime life.

Harold Nicolson, exemplifying the tendency in the Ministry always to take a gloomier view of morale than was warranted by intelligence reports, continued to express anxiety until mid-1941. Early in March he believed that sheer exhaustion might tempt the public into accepting another offer of peace from Hitler[52] and in April he urged Sir Kenneth Clark to prepare 'a detailed plan ready to launch if morale here fails'.[53] Noting that the public had not responded with their usual enthusiasm to a speech by the Prime Minister, Nicolson observed, 'What they did not like was "conquer or die". They have no desire to die in the least and they don't see how on earth we are to conquer. I must say that when I consider the position in Egypt and Iraq I feel a bit wobbly myself.'[54] Five days later he commented, 'I fear that as before people will jump at any escape which makes cowardice appear respectable'[55] – surely a reference to Munich, since there had been nothing to show during the war that 'cowardice' was prevalent. When told in June that the Prime Minister believed the gloom of the Commons did not reflect the mood of the country, the Ministry of Information strongly dissented and insisted that the country was 'deeply anxious and shocked'.[56]

With so much doubt and pessimism hanging over Senate House it is surprising to discover that in 1941 no large-scale morale campaign was launched. On 3 July the Minister assured MPs that 'at home we have little need for proving that our cause is right – nobody doubts it – or that we shall eventually win'. This was not meant to imply, he added, that the Ministry 'ought to leave the morale of the people to look after itself, which is rather like telling the doctor who asks after your health to mind his own business'.[57] Duff Cooper did not know what had taken place in his own bailiwick. In the first place, the two major campaigns under discussion in the first half of 1941 were designed to assure the public that Britain would win the war and that her cause was right; and, secondly, notwithstanding the work that went into planning these campaigns, it had already been tacitly acknowledged within the Ministry that overt morale-boosting propaganda was ineffective and undesirable.

The first of the two projected schemes was suggested by Harold Nicolson. Feeling in the marrow of his bones that Britain would win in the end but realising that his faith was not based on 'reason or calculation',[58] Nicolson was troubled as to how this conviction might be communicated to the public:

> From the propaganda point of view all that the country really wants is some assurance of how victory is to be achieved. They are bored by talks about the righteousness of our cause and our eventual triumph. What they want are facts regarding how we are to beat the Germans. I have no idea at all how we are to give them those facts.[59]

The problem troubled the Planning Committee as well, and Nicolson was asked to formulate some ideas.[60] Putting them before the committee, he suggested that in order to counter the prevalent mood of hopelessness the public should be told that by 1942 the Germans would be forced to the conclusion that by dint of the overwhelming quantity and quality of British arms they were mathematically certain to lose the war. 'If this doubt were driven home', Nicolson concluded, 'by widely organised raids . . that sense of doom to which Germans are so susceptible would spread throughout the population and with wise political handling a possible peace settlement could be achieved.'[61] Before the entry of the USSR and America into the war such a public statement would have been no more than an unsubstantiated declaration of Nicolson's faith, based as it was on a gross underestimation of the German people's capacity to resist the impact of air raids and military reverses. The suggestion was, however, approved by the Policy Committee and steps were taken to plan the campaign in detail. But it was not put into operation, principally because of its absorption into the more comprehensive scheme of Francis Williams.

Williams wished to convince the public of Britain's eventual triumph by:

> . . . getting into people's minds a conception of Democracy as . . . an essential next step in human history. We want, in other words, to create this feeling that all attempts to block the onward sweep of Democracy by Dictatorship are doomed to failure since Democracy is a great historical force which cannot be permanently checked.[62]

To this teleological appeal Williams added an emotional component:

> The appeal to the emotions must convince men and women that victory is deserved. It must bring to them the burning conviction that they are fighting in a crusade so momentous and so noble that war's misery and hardship, the risk of wounds and death, are small things compared with it.[63]

Almost everything was gathered up into Williams's attempt to construct a convincing case for the British cause: Christianity, democracy, the virtues of the population, liberty, justice and the glorious future. A more intensely exhortative and high-flown campaign it would be hard to imagine. It was precisely the sort of thing Nicolson had in mind when he said that people were bored with righteous talk. The paper was praised as 'admirable' and was sent to RIOs as a general guide and to the production divisions for translation into practical form.[64] The campaign did not see the light of day. According to Michael Balfour, it was worked on throughout the summer of 1941 but after the entry of the Soviet Union and America into the war it was kept as a background document which, Balfour recalls, 'almost – but I think not quite – amounts to saying that it was put on the shelf and forgotten'.[65]

The shelving of these campaigns is attributable in some measure to the 'propaganda of events'; however, from the beginning of 1941 there was considerable doubt about the efficacy of vague reassurance and ideological-cum-patriotic exhortation. In January an unofficial committee composed of public relations officers attached to the defence departments urged upon the Ministry a campaign to make the public 'front-line minded'. Noting that some bus men refused to drive during raid alerts, that factory workers spent too long in shelters, that the public clung to peacetime food habits and that a number of other bad practices persisted, the committee concluded that the war effort was therefore seriously handicapped. They suggested 'Forty Million Fighters' as the theme of a massive national campaign aimed at intensifying the 'team-spirit' of the British.[66] The Ministry responded brusquely :

Sir Kenneth Clark explained that these proposals meant a revival of something on the lines of the Home Morale campaign, and it was agreed that the useful elements in any such campaign would be explanations of facts and the arrangements made by various Government Departments for the well being and guidance of the people. The other part of any such campaign would be mere exhortation, which in the Ministry's experience, would be useless and even aggravating.[67]

But the antipathy to exhortation had not at this time fully crystallised. Nicolson echoed the departmental uncertainty in a report written on his return from an extensive tour of the regional offices :

It is inevitable that the problem of morale should be approached with a certain hesitancy. On the one hand the British public resent attempts to dragoon opinion and are sensitive to any suggestion that the state of their nerves is being maintained by a Government Department. On the other hand the condition of public opinion is at the moment healthy and it may be wiser to postpone all intensive campaigns until the time when defeatism becomes an actual menace.[68]

Yet in March 1941, barely a month after counselling against an intensive morale campaign, Nicolson suggested to Sir Kenneth Clark that they should prepare material 'on a scale five times larger than any campaign we have launched before' in anticipation of a great wave of war weariness brought on by food shortage, heavy bombardment and a possible succession of military defeats.[69]

One senior officer, at least, had no doubts about what the Ministry should be doing. Writing to an information officer, H. V. Rhodes stated :

My own reaction to this morale question is never just the yes or no, namely – is morale good or bad. I always prefer to look at it in terms of the war effort. I don't think the point is at all whether the

229

population is patriotic, satisfied and willing, and doing its bit. In my view the point is has the population been screwed up to the highest possible voltage in the cause of democracy. If it has not, it is nonsense for us to sit still.

But do you suppose I can get my masters to act on a doctrine like this?[70]

His masters were not only beginning to doubt the wisdom of their own exhortations but were also determined to discourage those indulged in by others, including ministers. In May 1941 the Planning Committee, noting that ministers were the 'most outstanding offenders' in constantly delivering 'pep talks' over the radio, agreed to ask Duff Cooper whether he would ask his colleagues to confine their broadcasts solely to 'informed explanations of the work of their Departments'.[71]

This concern for the adverse effect of clumsy broadcast propaganda not only made the Ministry reluctant to use the BBC as an instrument of domestic exhortation but led to action, which may be described as masterly inaction, that actually protected the corporation from a government take-over. On the outbreak of war, responsibility for the BBC had been transferred from the Postmaster General to the Minister of Information, but despite pressure from many quarters the Ministry refused to terminate the BBC's charter or to abolish the Board of Governors.[72] A week after becoming Prime Minister, Churchill wrote to Duff Cooper: 'I should be glad to receive some proposals from you for establishing a more effective control over the BBC. Now that we have a Government representing the Opposition as well as the Majority, we should have a much freer hand in this respect.'[73] In reply, the Minister said that the BBC, as in the past, 'will bow to our decisions after having made their observations'.[74] This did not prove to be the case. A series of arguments, principally about news presentation, caused Lord Hood, Duff Cooper's private secretary, to comment that the Ministry's 'defence of the BBC wears very thin'[75] and to recommend eradicating its 'fear of propaganda and desire to maintain a purely impartial and objective attitude'.[76] Frank Pick departed even further from the Ministry's protective policy. He suggested the appointment of a Political Director who, as a member of the Ministry of Information, would ensure the BBC's compliance in all 'political' and even 'entertainment' programmes.[77] The implication was total government control. Steps were taken in this direction but, as Sir Walter Monckton succeeded Pick as Director General, they were taken so gently as to be barely noticeable. With the appointment in February 1941 of Ivone Kirkpatrick as Foreign Adviser and in the following month of A. P. Ryan as Home Adviser to the BBC, the Ministry appeared to have implemented the take-over – especially as they were to 'exercise supreme control in all matters connected with the conduct of the war, which means all political matters'.[78] The BBC fought a vigorous rearguard action but, as an official of the Ministry made plain, they were in fact struggling against their own saviours :

> Things are quiet at the moment but Parliament and public opinion will never let the Minister divest himself of responsibility for such a vital instrument as the BBC on its non-entertainment side while we are fighting for our existence . . . I think Mr Ogilvie and Sir Allan Powell are shortsighted because the next time the Prime Minister or the House is moved to wrath there will be no half measures and no face saving. They and the 'independence' they are fighting for will go in the night, probably never to return. The greatest enemies to the restoration of our liberties after [the war] are perhaps those who use them too obstructively during the war.[79]

Sir Kenneth Clark let the cat out of the bag when at a meeting of the Home Defence (Security) Executive he admitted to representatives of the many other departments present that the Ministry had 'no control whatsoever over the BBC : they were supposed to have power to issue directives to the BBC but, even if directives were issued, the BBC would pay no attention to them'.[80] Endeavouring to retrieve the situation, Monckton wrote to Lord Normanbrook, personal assistant to the Lord President of the Council, Sir John Anderson, that Sir Kenneth had expressed himself loosely and, in any event, 'was unlikely to remain much longer in the Ministry'.[81] The fact remained, however, that under the protective custody of the Ministry of Information the BBC continued to enjoy a large measure of independence, while for its part the Ministry, cognisant of the substantial contribution the BBC was making to morale, was content to leave well enough alone. Under Brendan Bracken the department continued to act as a shield between the corporation and the occasional eruption of demands for its subjugation, as Cyril Radcliffe made clear : 'The BBC has not been, I think, a grateful body as far as this Ministry is concerned : but I doubt if they realise to what extent the mere existence of this Ministry with formal responsibility for Government relations with it protects it and strengthens its hand.'[82]

231

While the Ministry was moving hesitantly towards a new conception of its role in sustaining morale, the mood of frustration fostered by the government's lofty disregard for the department's functions and skills turned into something more purposive and, at the same time, more desperate. 'Either we are responsible for the handling of news', Nicolson insisted, 'or we are not. If we are not, we had better dissolve the Ministry. If so, then we must have greater authority.'[83]

Given the attitude of the Prime Minister to the Ministry of Information, and particularly his apparent inability to grasp the direct relationship between news and morale, it is not surprising that the situation continued to worsen. By 1941 erstwhile critics of the Ministry, such as the *New Statesman*, had become more sympathetic:

> The Ministry demands to be told the news and to have the most important say in what shall be published. Against the Service Departments they have an unanswerable case . . . In nearly two years of war the Ministry has at least learnt certain lessons. It has some understanding, which the Service Departments seem not effectively to possess, of the nature of the present British public, which is more alive to humbug and more insistent on honest statement than any public has ever been before.[84]

The need for explanation and publicity applied no less to the armed forces than to other aspects of the war effort, especially at a time when, in the view of the Ministry, the public were under the impression that Britain was doing singularly little to bring the war to a successful conclusion. In April 1941 Duff Cooper complained to the Air Minister:

> Even in the days of defeat we should not be reduced to the humiliation of being compelled to print German photographs in British newspapers for the sole reason that there are no British photographs available. I can supply all the photographers and journalists necessary in order to tell the story of the war, but unless the Services are prepared to make use of them and to attach them to men-of-war, to regiments and to aircraft, they will only waste their time at the base . . .
>
> PS The Air Ministry, between ourselves, is *far* the most helpful of the three.[85]

232

Cooper's *cri de cœur* met with a warm response in the Air Ministry. Pointing to the old-fashioned attitude of the services and Whitehall, Air Vice-Marshal Peck commented, 'They think that Home Morale, Empire enthusiasm, confidence abroad and prestige among neutrals are all fixed stars in a British heaven.'[86] But although the Air Ministry was ready to co-operate, neither of the other services appears to have been alive to the situation. Early in June 1941 Nicolson complained bitterly about the attitude of the services regarding the impending Syrian action:

> I say that never in military history has there been an operation in which propaganda was so important. We are about to invade the territory of a former ally and to create a war between France and the Free French. At the same time there is the question of Arab independence. Yet the one person who is not brought in on this is Duff Cooper.[87]

Before the Ministry could marshal its forces in a fight for greater authority, Duff Cooper's sinews required stiffening. He had been 'delighted' at his appointment[88] and had started in office promising to centralise the control of all sources of information in his department.[89] But the difficulties of the job, the personal attacks directed at him by the press, and, most discouragingly of all, the Prime Minister's lack of support induced in the Minister a fitfulness of purpose which hampered forthright action. As early as June 1940, Cecil King – who had tried unsuccessfully since the beginning of the war to get a job in the Ministry – observed that 'Duff Cooper seems thoroughly despondent, suspended between a War Cabinet who obviously do not believe in propaganda and are out of touch with public opinion, and a staff in whom he has little confidence.'[90] Three months later King noted that Duff Cooper 'has no idea what to do . . . He just wants the Ministry of Information to be left in peace'.[91] Harold Nicolson arrived at a similar judgement: 'Duff is not really on very good terms with the P.M. And does not wish to press difficult requests on him. He hopes to live from day to day without trouble authority'.[92] In April 1941 Nicolson bemoaned his chief's lack of 'fire, and inspiration. We need a Cromwell and a Milton, inflamed with puritanical passion.'[93] And after the war Francis Williams recalled that Duff Cooper 'preferred talking over lunch to doing anything . . . he was almost wholly ineffectual'.[94]

Sir Walter Monckton and Cyril Radcliffe came to the conclusion that only by threatening resignation could the Minister be persuaded to take action. They delivered an ultimatum in May 1941 whose terms represented a condition of their continued service with the department. Building their case on the premise that propaganda was vital to morale and to victory, they stated that:

> Its raw material is news and information. But the Ministry of Information is so constituted by the Government that it has no control over either of these. It can decide neither *what* to make public nor *when* to make something public nor *what* line or shape to give such information as is made public . . . The only function left to it is the purely administrative one of the distribution of Government news, a task of the same order of importance as those assigned to the Post Office or the Stationery Office.[95]

The situation could be corrected by the Ministry's assumption of three powers: authority to direct the form, timing and treatment of official news; the right of access to all information available to the service departments and the Foreign Office; and the control over propaganda to enemy countries. 'From time to time', the paper concluded, 'there has been widespread dissatisfaction with our news and propaganda. There is great dissatisfaction at the moment; and it is largely justified . . . Change the personnel, while maintaining the system, and you will only get the same results. There exist defects which can only be removed by changing the system itself.'

This imperious call to action did not arouse Duff Cooper sufficiently to satisfy Monckton and, ever the man for exploiting influential contacts, he busied himself by gaining the support of Lord Beaverbrook. To Beaverbrook he indicated that his threatened resignation was no mere tactical device:

> I have been in this place for twenty weary months and Radcliffe for only one less, and we are both sincerely convinced that we are wasting our time and are bound to be defeated in our mechanical efforts by Goebbels and his Ministry. We both want to hand over to others . . . unless we can be given the changes which our paper sets forth. For your own private information, I would much rather get out for myself in any event, as I have had more than enough of this place. I like the people, loathe the job.[96]

The Hess imbroglio provided Monckton with an occasion for submitting his resignation and Duff Cooper, in successfully dissuading him from carrying it through, revealed his own thoughts about the department:

234

I have long known that the M.O.I. is a misbegotten freak bred from the unnatural union of Sir Horace Wilson and Sir Samuel Hoare (considering the progenitors I wonder the offspring is not even more revolting) but I have tried to straighten the freak's limbs and make it serve some useful purpose . . . I believe that in the last twelve months there has been a real improvement and I hoped that you agreed with this view. If you do, why desert us now? . . . The P.M. is not really interested in propaganda and still less in information but if we could secure Max as an ally we ought to be able to achieve something. I really don't know what would become of the Ministry without you.[97]

Brendan Bracken's support was also recruited and he told Monckton, 'I agree with every word you say, and I hope that your Paper will secure the reforms you desire.'[98] With two of Churchill's intimates committed to the reforms, the Ministry might have allowed itself a certain degree of optimism. Duff Cooper's lethargy and timidity remained, but he could not refrain from action with the threatened resignation of the Director General and the Controller of News and Censorship hanging over his head. On 6 June he wrote to the Prime Minister, reiterating the substance of their complaints and adding:

I have persuaded the officials . . . to carry on pending a decision. I should find it very difficult to conduct the Ministry without their assistance. I would urge, however, that all the functions of this Ministry should form the subject of further enquiry and some decision should be taken which will place in the hands of a single authority the responsibility both for foreign propaganda and the presentation of news.[99]

Leaving no stone unturned, Monckton saw the King who offered to help in the Ministry's 'war for news'.[100] Precisely how the King intended assisting Monckton, who had tendered advice and friendship to his brother during the abdication crisis, is not clear. Monckton also indulged in a little intrigue by suggesting to Bracken that Duff Cooper should be replaced by Lord Cranborne and that Nicolson – 'not of sufficient calibre' as Parliamentary Secretary – should be transferred to the directorship of the Ministry's Overseas Publicity Division.[101] According to Cecil King, Monckton was under the impression that Churchill was considering moving the department into Beaverbrook's orbit.[102]. If the Ministry had previously been the despised and neglected offspring of wartime government it was at least now the subject of much correspondence and scurrying about in Whitehall, Westminster and Bloomsbury.

The press looked anxiously on from the sidelines and, clearly inspired by leaks from the Ministry, did their best to support their ally. On 12 June a number of newspapers revealed that there was a crisis in the Ministry's affairs and that Beaverbrook had been appointed by the Prime Minister to look into the matter. The *Daily Herald* observed:

> The best informed judges, however, take the view that Mr Duff Cooper and his lieutenants will be able to hang out the bunting in celebration of 'substantial territorial gains'.
>
> It is now an open secret that Mr Duff Cooper is not prepared to continue on the basis of his present powers.
>
> The Minister of Information has found himself repeatedly in an impossible position owing to the restrictions imposed by other State departments on the release of news.[103]

The Times commented:

> The Ministry has been set a task and has been denied the effective means of carrying it out. That has been the main root of all its troubles from the beginning. It can cause no surprise if they have again approached a flash-point. The only ground for surprise can be that two successive governments have declined to set the Department in a right relation with the public and the Press, with both of which it is daily and intimately concerned, and with the war effort as a whole.[104]

The Secretary of State for War and the Foreign Secretary protested at these leaks and Churchill ordered Duff Cooper to put a stop to them.[105] As the department which had in the past shown most willingness to co-operate with the Ministry of Information, the Air Ministry's response to the situation was not reassuring:

> We are absolutely convinced . . . that the Ministry of Information cannot possibly be permitted to perform the function of controlling the issue of operational news without grave danger to security. The Ministry is notoriously dominated by the press and it would be quite impossible to guarantee that secret information would not leak out if it were supplied to the M. of I. without restrictions . . . The trouble is much too deep seated to be curable.

If any evidence were required on this point, it is provided by the fact that in the case of every crisis or proposal for reorganisation in the M. of I. the press has been fully informed of it even before the Cabinet.[106]

It is difficult to know how much justice attached to the service departments' case. Certainly the Ministry was deeply sympathetic to the press but if this constituted a 'grave danger' to security why did the service departments fail to prosecute a newspaper for breach of Regulation 3 or, after July 1940 when the power to initiate proceedings had passed out of their hands, press the Ministry to do so? Security had in fact never been seriously jeopardised by the newspapers. The difference between the defence departments and the Ministry of Information lay in the extent to which they believed the press could be trusted to act responsibly.

The Battle of Bloomsbury, as it came to be known, was joined towards the end of June 1941. Beaverbrook submitted a paper to Churchill in which he argued strongly for the Ministry to be given a far greater degree of control over publicity and the distribution of news and fuller access to information available to the defence departments, although he did not advocate as many of the Ministry's demands as might have been expected from earlier expressions of support.[107] His motives are difficult to assess. Perhaps they stemmed from memories of his own trials as Minister of Information in 1918. If he had not entirely discarded the idea of taking over the Ministry himself,[108] he would undoubtedly have preferred to assume control of something less emasculate than the existing department.

Introducing his paper, Duff Cooper put matters squarely before his Cabinet colleagues:

> The broad issue which the Cabinet has to decide is whether the Head of the Ministry of Information is to be a very important Minister charged with the conduct of political warfare and therefore having control of all propaganda and publicity, or whether he is to be a high official with the duty of carrying out the directions of other Departments.[109]

Acknowledging the supremacy of the Foreign Secretary in all questions of high policy, Duff Cooper nonetheless asserted that it should be his responsibility to disseminate all propaganda – secret and overt – and to decide on its form. Similarly, the question of deciding what news should be released and the manner of its presentation should be his alone, pending appeals by other ministers to Cabinet. All the information at the disposal of the service ministers and the Foreign Secretary should be fully supplied to the Ministry of Information and on any matter of government publicity the Ministry was to have final control. Suggesting that his department should be disintegrated and its various parts found new homes if his demands were not met, Duff Cooper concluded on a note of pathos:

> Owing to initial mistakes, many of them pre-natal, the Ministry has never enjoyed the full confidence of the public. Once a Department has incurred ridicule it has great difficulty in regaining its status. I do not think that the Ministry has lost ground in the last year, but it has a great deal of ground to make up, and unless it is given the authority which it demands there is danger of it ceasing to be an object of ridicule in order to become one only of pity.

This produced little softening in Churchill's heart. Conceding only that the Ministry should be freely supplied with departmental news and that it should conduct all government publicity, the Prime Minister reaffirmed the right of service ministers to have the final say in the censorship of news, forbade the Ministry to alter the form of communiqués unless permission of the relevant department had been obtained, and allowed the public relations and press officers in Whitehall to continue to bypass the Ministry in preserving their contacts with the press.[110] This was too much for Beaverbrook. Observing that the Prime Minister had extended to all ministers the service ministers' right of veto over news, he commented, 'The Ministry of Information comes to the Cabinet for improvement, and it gets a plan that makes things worse.' He must have experienced a strong sense of *déjà vu* for, using terms very similar to those he had employed in Lloyd George's Cabinet twenty-three years earlier when fighting for his own Ministry of Information, he said, 'I advise enlarging the powers of the Ministry of Information, or abolishing it. The Ministry cannot go on in its present form.'[111] Discussion of these papers on 30 June was a formality. Churchill was adamant in his views and assent was duly given to them.[112]

Although much was later to be made of the concessions granted by Churchill, it appeared to be a resounding defeat for the Ministry and, at one remove, for the press. Duff Cooper told the Prime Minister that had such a thing occurred in peacetime he would have felt bound to resign.[113] In the event, he did not stay long and resigned on 20 July 1941 'with a sigh of relief'[114] – only to be appointed Chancellor of the Duchy of Lancaster and to be given the even more disastrous assignment of Singapore. As for the reaction within the Ministry, Harold Nicolson summed it up thus:

> We decide (a) that we must get control of the BBC (b) that we must be short and sharp with the service ministries. All very brave and useful. But underneath it all there is the feeling that the defenders of Lucknow in a fine council of war decide that what is necessary is to capture Cawnpore.[115]

9

'The British Public Shows a Very High Degree of Common Sense'

With the advent of Brendan Bracken as Minister of Information in July 1941, and partly as a result of his own views, the deployment of morale propaganda was more or less finally abandoned. That is not to say that the Ministry also abandoned its responsibility for morale. Lord Taylor vigorously asserts the contrary:

> . . . morale was *never left to look after itself*. It was a continuous and continuing process of explanation and *education* – both of Govt. *and* the public. *Reasons* had to be given for *all* Govt. actions, so the public could judge for themselves the *merits* of the actions and their *fairness*. *Obiter dicta* were worse than useless from those with power. We did not let up at all – and truth paid off in the market-place in the end, as Justice Oliver Wendell Holmes observed.[1]

Although he could afford the luxury of offering advice without the responsibility of office, Bracken's contribution to a debate on the Ministry in July 1939 looked forward to the manner in which he would conduct the domestic activities of the department after his appointment two years later: 'I hope that the controllers of this Ministry will realise that the world is dazed and bored by propaganda . . . if the Ministry is conducted on sensible and unambitious lines – because that is very important – it will perform a useful service . . . the Ministry will do best to abjure all propaganda, which is the most discredited thing in the world.'[2]

When Bracken, still only forty years of age, succeeded Duff Cooper few people could have anticipated that this tall, red-headed and rather eccentric man would not only rescue the department from general contempt but would transform it into a Ministry of which the Official Committee on the Machinery of Government was to say less than three years later, 'There is a thoroughness and solidity, combined with flexibility and enterprise, which are the hall-marks of administrative efficiency.'[3] Widely known as a successful publisher and businessman and as Churchill's most faithful lieutenant, Bracken was at the same time a mysterious figure and all he would allow to be revealed of his more distant past was that he had been born in Ireland and had spent his adolescent years in Australia.[4] Bracken had spent a long period in the House but, apart from his business activities, he possessed no administrative experience which seemed to qualify him for the office which had sorely damaged the political reputations of his three predecessors. Why, then, did he make such a 'brilliant success'[5] of the post?

Bracken and Churchill had known each other since 1924 and during the older man's lean years in the thirties Bracken refused to desert the politician who had earned the deep suspicion of both sides of the House. When Churchill went to the Admiralty on the outbreak of war Bracken became his Parliamentary Private Secretary, keeping the post after Churchill succeeded Chamberlain and actually living at No. 10 throughout the war. But if Churchill hoped that by appointing a loyal friend to the troublesome Ministry of Information he would hear no more of it, he was disappointed. Bracken did not want the job but once there he was determined to make a go of it. Beaverbrook had no doubt that he would do so:

In the ordinary way, it would be looked on as a sarcastic or even unfriendly act to offer a man congratulations on becoming Minister of Information.

In your case this is not so. You are going to make a great success of this office. Your gifts of imagination and energy will be given a scope they have never enjoyed before.

And the glory you will win will be all the brighter because it shines in a dark and dismal sky.[6]

Unlike Duff Cooper, Bracken shrank neither from conflict with other ministers nor from confrontation with the Prime Minister himself. In June 1942, for example, Anthony Eden complained that censorship had passed a story about the Anglo-Russian negotiations then in progress and Churchill agreed to the setting up of a Cabinet subcommittee to investigate the workings of censorship. Bracken protested at not having been consulted in this decision:

241

Ten months ago, despite my strong protests, you sent me to this Ministry. It has been a post of endless anxiety, and I am most anxious to give it up.

Finally, let me say that I wish you had told me that you were dissatisfied with the management of this Ministry. You know perfectly well how glad I shall be to hand over this task to a more competent person. Why could you not have asked for my resignation instead of appointing a committee of inspection?'[7]

Exhibiting far more alacrity than he ever showed in response to the grievances of Duff Cooper, Churchill immediately abandoned any idea of constituting the subcommittee and wrote to Bracken: 'Now please leave off scolding me on paper, and if you have any griefs come and beat me up personally. You know perfectly well that you can see me almost any time.'[8]

The great advantage for the Ministry of Information of the relationship between the two men lay in Churchill's willingness to listen to Bracken's case rather than to dismiss it out of hand and award his judgement to the Ministry's opponents. In 1942, F. C. Bartlett, with the Ministry's sad history very much in mind, declared, 'Without co-ordination of policy, and without the full and willing co-operation of all other Government departments, a Ministry of Information in a democratic country is absolutely certain frequently to fail, and it is just as certain to be blamed for many failures which are not its own fault.'[9] With Bracken's arrival the conditions for the Ministry's real and assumed failures generally ceased to obtain.

Another reason for Bracken's success flowed from his handling of the House of Commons. Those members who had grown fond of exercising their wit and invective at the expense of the Ministry now had to contend with a Minister who was clearly not going to adopt an apologetic tone towards the workings of his department. Alan Hodge, one of Bracken's private secretaries, recalls the first time the Minister presented the departmental estimates:

Bracken made a speech, lasting less than half an hour, in which he pungently described the whole range of activities of his curiously assorted department. He got an ovation, and sat down to cries of 'More! More!' There was never any serious criticism of his departmental stewardship after that.[10]

When Sir Walter Monckton finally resigned in December 1941, he was replaced with Cyril Radcliffe. Bracken and his new Director

General were a good team. Radcliffe, possessed of an 'ice-cold intelligence',[11] had proved to be a first-class and fearless administrator when coping with the awesome difficulties of news and censorship, and with Bracken as a doughty fighter on the Ministry's behalf at Cabinet level he was able to pursue the task of reforming the department safe in the knowledge of full ministerial support. Although Ernest Thurtle – the Labour MP who had replaced Harold Nicolson – was hardly an asset to the Ministry, the institution was now to be run on much more energetic lines.

Of supreme importance in the rehabilitation of the Ministry were Bracken's notions of and relations with the press. He came to the department, according to Williams, 'determined to make it stand well with the newspapers and not, one felt, much interested in its other activities';[12] but if this were so, his goal was more elevated than that of merely performing a public relations exercise. 'A blind-folded democracy', he is quoted as having said, 'is more likely to fall than to fight.'[13] A neat aphorism but insofar as the Ministry was capable of achieving it, Bracken tried hard to give the press as much freedom as possible. As a press proprietor himself,* he was on good terms with other proprietors, and especially Lord Beaverbrook, and was known by journalists to be privy to Churchill's innermost thoughts. These factors together with a bluff and engaging manner assured him of the press's respect and affection. Even Claud Cockburn, who as editor of the *Daily Worker* and *The Week* had no cause to love the Ministry of Information, found it hard to resist liking Bracken.[14]

Bracken needed these advantages if he was to overcome the handi-caps peculiar to the Ministry's position as censor and bringer of news to a public hungry for information. In the first place, Churchill retained an acute sensitivity towards newspaper criticism throughout Bracken's tenure of office. In October 1943, for example, the *Sunday Pictorial* – which together with its stablemate, the *Daily Mirror*, had already come perilously close to suppression – condemned the government's reluctance to open a second front.[15] Churchill asked Bevin to see him about 'the personalities behind this sort of stuff'.[16] The Minister of Labour was clearly expected to use his position in order to conscript Cecil King, the proprietor, for in a letter to the Prime Minister Bevin explained that King had previously been medically examined and placed in the lowest category and that there was therefore 'no question of calling him up for military service'.[17]

*The Banker, The Financial News, Investors Chronicle, The Practitioner.

Churchill normally resorted to less drastic forms of rebuke. The *News Chronicle*, 'a vicious opponent of the present Coalition',[18] earned his particular displeasure for publishing a Gallup poll in which British and American citizens placed each others' country very low on a list of those nations contributing to the allied war effort. 'This is one of the worst things that has happened in the newspaper world since the war began,' Churchill expostulated to Sir Walter Layton; 'I cannot understand how you can be associated with such a thing.'[19] In September 1944 he drafted a letter to the editor of the *Manchester Guardian* objecting to its comment on his message to the Italian people. On this occasion he thought better of it and the letter was not dispatched.[20] Upon other occasions Bracken and Beaverbrook were obliged to restrain the Prime Minister's combative impulses. Lord Beaverbrook did so in January 1945 after Churchill had drafted an extremely hostile letter to Barrington-Ward about *The Times*'s editorial policy on the Greek situation:

> You told me your newspaper policy was – Square or Squash. That was a quarter of a century ago.
> You have held to it ever since.
> This letter to Barrington-Ward is a departure. It does not make any effort to 'Square' & it does not 'Squash'.
> Therefore I recommend against it.[21]

To make matters worse, the Ministry of Information could never confidently predict what Churchill's reaction might be to a given situation. Thoroughly exasperated with the *Daily Telegraph*, by far the worst offender against Regulation 3 (which forbade the publication of matter likely to be of military value to the enemy), Bracken proposed in June 1943 to proceed against it.[22] He received the following note from the Prime Minister:

> Considering what a friendly paper this is and that Camrose is a patriotic man, would it not be well to see him first and explain that we have no choice unless he can give absolute assurance for the future. However I leave it to you to decide what you think fit.[23]

The second major handicap standing in the way of Bracken's desire to provide the public with as much news and explanation as possible was, of course, the obstructiveness of the service ministries. Three days after assuming office Bracken learnt that the Admiralty had withheld an account of the last hours of the *Bismarck* from the News Division on security grounds even after giving the story to the *Evening Standard*.[24] But, armed with Churchill's decision of June 1941 that the service departments were to give the Ministry all news in their possession, Bracken gradually loosened their grip. From time to time they slipped back into their old habits. In May 1942 Bracken drew the Cabinet's attention to the fact that his department was not informed until the day before of the imminent invasion of Madagascar, and was therefore unable either to persuade the army to use the photographers and journalists attached to it at the Ministry's urging or to make its own arrangements. 'The conclusion is inescapable', Bracken minuted, 'that the Admiralty and the War Office still fail to give proper weight to the morale factor inherent in all military operations.'[25] Generally speaking, however, the Ministry of Information under Bracken was able to extract far more news than hitherto.

It was the Foreign Office which became the *bête noire* of the Ministry and the press after mid-1941. As Britain acquired powerful allies, first Russia and then the United States, and as the war moved into a phase in which the discussion of post-war boundaries and settlements became more than academic, so the Foreign Office became more than usually sensitive about press comment and open speculation on international affairs. There was also a growth of public interest in and demand for news on international developments, especially if they concerned the Soviet Union. On two issues, the creation of ill feeling between the allies and the disclosure of diplomatic negotiations, the Foreign Office and the Ministry of Information came into sharp conflict. It was a measure of the Ministry's newly discovered, if unsanctioned, authority that the press could largely ignore the strictures of the Foreign Office.

In October 1941 a Cabinet subcommittee, which included the Minister of Information, was asked to consider methods by which the publication of press articles injurious to foreign relations might be prevented. In their report, it was noted that although the Home Secretary had the power under Defence Regulation 39B(2) to suppress such articles there were too many objections to its application. One such objection was that the application of the regulation would bring with it a form of compulsory censorship which would arouse stiff opposition. The committee concluded :

During the war numerous articles have appeared in the Press which at the time appeared likely to impair the war effort either

245

by injuring foreign relations or by shaking confidence in the national Government or disrupting the national unity, but in retrospect it is seen that the effect of such articles has been comparatively insignificant.

Observations of this nature were frequently made in the War Cabinet, so it is all the more remarkable that its members should have had sudden fits of hostility to the press and endeavoured to muffle it. The subcommittee came down against the use of the regulation and advised the Prime Minister to publicly 'stigmatise' an offending newspaper by naming it in the House of Commons.[26]

This benign attitude was short-lived. After the fall of Singapore in February 1942 a number of Australian journalists sent home articles severely critical of the British government's handling of the war, which led to the disruption of the happy arrangement whereby copy bound for foreign newspapers, although compulsorily censored, was scrutinised according to the same criteria applied to the domestic press. The Ministry, against its better judgement,[27] was forced to tighten up on the censorship of articles leaving the country. Among the provisions suggested was the stopping of all messages calculated to compromise relations with foreign powers and to create ill feeling between the allies.[28] This was announced in the House of Commons on 26 March 1942 and, accordingly, the Censorship Division was obliged to judge :

> . . . whether the message goes clearly beyond the grounds of legitimate criticism of current policies, and be of a nature to sow doubt as to the basic motives and intentions of one or other of the Governments or peoples of the United Nations, and thus create suspicion as to their ultimate good faith in matters of primary importance to the war effort.[29]

Censorship of opinion and comment had manifestly arrived. British newspapers only narrowly averted a similar fate. Asked by the War Cabinet to prevent the press speculating about future operations, if necessary by compulsion, Bracken protested that such a measure would have adverse consequences in morale :

> . . . the phrase is so vague and far-reaching that it is almost impossible to operate it without precluding any public discussion or information as to the future course that the war must take. If such a wide ban is sought to be imposed the certain result will be to

preclude the public being instructed at all in the course of the war or the significance of what is happening or likely to happen. Everything that occurs will be unprepared and unexplained and there is bound to be a further increase in the public's lack of sense of actuality of the war.[30]

In reply, Churchill emphasised the necessity for restraint in such matters but watered down the strength of the Cabinet's instruction by agreeing that what was really wanted was 'reasonable consultation' with the press.[31]

Aware that a dangerous precedent had been set, the Ministry set about eroding the spirit of the provision by interpreting it as liberally as possible – so liberally, in fact, that the original Cabinet decision concerning the dispatch of stories to the foreign press was flagrantly ignored. When challenged by the Foreign Office, Bracken would go on to the offensive and tell Eden in strongly worded letters to mind his own business and let the censors get on with theirs.[32]

Bracken was encouraged by his Director General. By adhering firmly to the principle of censoring on security grounds only, explained Radcliffe, 'Censorship acquired on the whole a reputation for liberal and honest dealing that, in my view, did far more good for this country and got more favourable results out of the correspondents than has been achieved by the elaborate attempts to prevent 'indiscretions' that are now the order of the day.' He maintained that the decision of March 1942 had been a grave mistake:

It would be easy to think of one or two extreme cases in which the power would be properly exercised . . . but there is no one wise enough to say what are the proper limits of the exercise of such a power. Obviously it can be abused and made to cover the most arbitrary exercises of political censorship.[33]

By adopting the tactic of selective inattention the Ministry of Information had won more than a mere administrative squabble. Journalists were now free to report on important political developments, a fact given formal recognition when it was announced in June 1944 that outgoing messages would no longer be subjected to political censorship.

A twin source of contention, and one which poisoned relations between the Ministry of Information and the Foreign Office almost until the end of the war,[34] was the introduction in March 1942 of the following provision:

247

A message may be stopped if it contains matter dealing with diplomatic exchanges between countries of the United Nations, and neutral states, where unauthorised or premature disclosures of such discussions might tend to prejudice their outcome.[35]

This was directed at the domestic press as well as at foreign correspondents working in Britain and clearly carried serious implications for the Ministry's policy of giving the public all information short of that which was of demonstrable military value.

The situation was aggravated by the habitual neglect of the Foreign Office to inform the Ministry of the existence of diplomatic negotiations, an attitude undoubtedly strengthened by the well-founded suspicion that censorship would allow the press to tell all. It was embarrassing, too, for the Ministry's officials to be first told of diplomatic activity by journalists. A Cabinet paper was drafted on the subject:

In present circumstances, he [the Chief Press Censor] frequently receives first news . . . not from the Foreign Office but from the press correspondents themselves. Some correspondents are regularly obtaining information from the foreign Embassies which is considered to be too secret to impart to the Chief Censor.[36]

The Foreign Office was particularly touchy about the presence in Britain of Molotov in May 1942. Bracken complained of this to the Prime Minister, adding:

I could, of course, give you other edifying instances of the state of ignorance in which the Ministry has been kept. One of the most recent is that of Mr Percy Cudlipp, an editor hostile to the Government, who told me of the speeches made by the Foreign Secretary and M. Molotov on the occasion of the signing of the Treaty. He also informed me of the exchange of telegrams between you and M. Stalin. Though I do not like Mr Cudlipp, I find him far more co-operative than some of my colleagues.[37]

It was doubly annoying for the Ministry to be ignored when it was well known that the Foreign Office kept a coterie of favoured journalists who were invariably informed on matters withheld from the Ministry and the press as a whole.[38]

The American authorities, despite constant leaks from their London embassy, professed annoyance at the apparent inefficiency of

British censorship. Referring to the publication in Britain of a photograph of Churchill and Roosevelt at a secret meeting in Washington, Harry Hopkins – the President's intimate associate – wrote to Bracken in October 1943 :

> There are just too many of this type of things [*sic*] happening in London and I think you should give this business your most serious personal attention and do not for a moment underrate the effect these are having over here on Anglo-American relations. I am putting it mildly when I say the highest circles are irritated with these things.
>
> Why, in God's world, when we have a tough war to fight, do we have to cope with these unnecessary leaks, premature and otherwise ?[39]

Probably because of Hopkins's unmistakable reference to the President, Bracken was unusually contrite in response to the protest but could not resist the temptation to remind Hopkins that the Americans in the previous week had given out news of the Italian armistice before the release time mutually agreed upon.[40]

The degree to which the Ministry was prepared to ignore the Foreign Office, and even the American and Soviet governments, in permitting stories of diplomatic negotiations to be published at home and overseas is best illustrated by the dispute that centred round the deliberations of the European Advisory Committee. The Foreign Office advised Bracken in March 1944 that complaints had been lodged by the Russian and American ambassadors about press articles concerning the Commission's discussions of post-war zones of occupation in Germany and the terms of surrender. Winant, the American ambassador, insisted that such disclosures touched on operational matters because of their possible effect on Germany's continued military resistance.[41] Radcliffe had already made it plain that the Ministry resented being asked to censor stories of this type and in replying to this particular complaint, reiterated the basis of the Ministry's philosophy. The release of information likely to prolong German resistance was, he stated, of no interest to the censorship authorities since there were many items – strikes in Britain, criticism of production and rumours of allied disunity – which might have encouraged the Germans in the past but which the Ministry, as a matter of policy, would not censor. 'Surely', Radcliffe added in a telling reference to a well-known aspect of allied policy ' "unconditional surrender" leaves to the imagination little that is encouraging' to the Germans. As for Russian objections to the publication of secrets: 'Indeed, they have, of necessity, ceased to be secrets before they ever reached the Censorship . . . The Press in this country is free and it was revealing secrets, when it could discover them, long before Censorship was set up.'[42] The Ministry would not conceal from the public that which would have been revealed in time of peace. Fully suporting the views of his Director General, Bracken told Eden that the department was not designed to be and would not be 'used as a long-stop for leakages of information from allied Embassies'.[43]

In the latter half of 1941 there was a marked diminution in the Ministry's anxiety for civilian morale and by the end of the year, as one former official remembers, the department had 'relapsed into being little more than a convenient funnel through which news and publicity . . . was passed to the press and the public'.[44] This is explicable partly in terms of Britain's slowly improving war situation, but a fuller answer must be sought in the propagandists' realisation that the public were just as capable as themselves of appraising events in a relatively dispassionate manner. And it was not to be long before the department endeavoured to transform itself into a Ministry of Explanation.

'I am amazed at the intelligence of the public,' wrote Harold Nicolson in June 1941 after reading a Home Intelligence report. 'They seem to me to see the war in its real perspective.'[45] It would perhaps be unfair to say that this burst upon the Ministry with all the force of the obvious, but it led to the supplanting of exhortation by explanation. To explain rather than to overbear by emotive appeals or by distortion of one's own convictions is to treat individuals as rational beings, capable of acting sensibly on the basis of information given rather than perceiving them as unpredictable and capricious. In July 1941 Michael Balfour delivered himself of a long argument in support of a new attitude towards the public:

Departments have not only been slow to adapt themselves to popular government, and slower still to appeal for the co-operation of the public. They have been far too inclined to think that they need only tell the public what they are doing and not why they are doing it. The intelligence of the public has been underestimated (or disregarded) and far too little has been done to explain the objections against alternative courses . . . The only result has been to leave the field free for quack remedies to flourish. The public demands the adoption of a policy which the Government is not prepared to follow, but which it dare not openly oppose . . . The belief spreads that the truth is not told because the truth is too discreditable. Suspicion ensues and a breach is created between Government and people.

Confidence in leadership is therefore inextricably linked up with explanation to the public . . .

And surely we can . . . explain that policy depends on power. We can explain that what is called red tape is often only a means of preventing individuals from having uncontrolled power, or of preventing conflicting policies from being pursued at the same time . . . At all costs let us exert ourselves to convince the public that there are good and sufficient reasons why Government acts as it does or alternatively abstains from action.[46]

This was the tone of the convert turned evangelist. Balfour gained support from the Home Intelligence Division. 'The British public as a whole shows a very high degree of common-sense,' observed Stephen Taylor in October 1941. 'Given the relevant facts, they will listen to and accept explanations when they will not accept exhortations.'[47] One month later Taylor expanded on this theme in a special review of the different methods of propaganda:

B. *Exhortations*. Exhortatory campaigns aimed at producing alterations in states of mind, e.g. making the public more confident in final victory – the 'Mightier Yet' campaign; making people Empire minded – the 'Empire Crusade'. There is little evidence that these campaigns have had any appreciable effect. The public was confident in final victory before the 'Mightier Yet' campaign, and is still extremely confused on the subject of Dominion status. For many months, public opinion on the subject of the prosecution of the war has been ahead of, rather than behind, Government action. Where there is complacency it is completely untouched by advertising campaigns . . .

Exhortation is not only of very limited value. It may easily become a positive danger. To be asked to work harder by the Government when one is held up at one's work on account of lack of materials, due, one believes, (perhaps quite wrongly) to managerial or Government inefficiency, breeds cynicism about those in authority . . . *If one treats the British people as intelligent, they behave surprisingly intelligently.*[48]

The arrival of Brendan Bracken coincided with the steepening decline and eventual extinction of the Ministry's belief in inspirational propaganda. 'Brendan Bracken meets the 1922 Committee,' recorded

251

Nicolson on 10 September, 'and tells them he will have no internal propaganda.'[49] His assurance may have been no more than a device to calm the fears of those many back-bench Conservatives who looked on the Ministry of Information as a hotbed of socialism. Certainly he did nothing to halt the celebration of Britain's war effort, in such posters as 'Back Them Up !' and 'and the NAVY goes on', or the flow of ritual incantations against the Germans. But, according to Lord Radcliffe, he and Bracken were determined to have nothing to do with maintaining morale beyond keeping the public as fully informed of events as possible.[50]

During the war the public were bombarded with innumerable appeals and instructions : Dig for Victory, Make Do and Mend, Coughs and Sneezes Spread Diseases, Post Before Noon, and a host of others. There was scarcely an aspect of the individual's life on which the state did not have something to say. With the principal exception of the Ministry of Health, most departments submitted their proposals for campaigns to the Ministry of Information which, in turn, decided upon the nature and spread of the publicity. Thus, as the government's publicity agent, the Ministry was in an unexpectedly powerful position to influence the relationship between the government machine and the people. This position was reached only after a struggle. The Ministry became sharply aware of the consequences of ill-planned or unnecessary publicity and in its fight to gain ascendancy over other departments in this sphere it was motivated by more than mere *amour propre*. The Ministry's publicity role had another consequence. The lessons derived and experience gained went a long way towards clarifying the Ministry's understanding of civilian morale.

The tendency of other departments to mount their own campaigns was curbed in June 1941 when, in his comprehensive restatement of its functions, the Prime Minister instructed that departmental publicity should be conducted through the Ministry of Information. Furthermore, all public relations officers were to operate as a team under the direction of the Minister. Thereafter things worked relatively smoothly. Of its monopoly in the sphere of government publicity the Ministry was able to report in June 1944 :

This function . . . has resulted first in establishing a system of priorities and, secondly, in the provision of expert publicity advice. It has provided the newspapers with a relief from the troubles of deciding how and in what proportions their much reduced space should be allotted for Government advertisements. It has, by surveying the whole field, conserved the use of raw materials of publicity. It has effected economies in the expenditure of public funds. It has permitted a balanced use of the expert publicity manpower available. Of course, it has not satisfied everybody . . . but, on a broad survey of the last 30 months, it can safely be said that the co-ordination system gradually introduced by the Ministry of Information works.[51]

By refusing to undertake work on behalf of another department unless that department had done its homework, the Ministry exercised an oblique but real power over Whitehall. The Ministry's ultimate justification was its responsibility for civilian morale – the public had to be protected from ill-conceived appeals and from the frustration that followed publicity about measures for which administrative arrangements had been inadequately prepared. Moreover, the awareness in the Ministry of the public's habit of blaming the government for everything that appeared to go wrong made it very nervous indeed about hastily prepared appeals and instructions. The philosophy emerging from these considerations was succinctly expressed by Stephen Taylor in November 1941. Government propaganda, he asserted, is 'very largely concerned with trying to make people alter their habits and behaviour so radically that profound changes in their lives are produced'. If such attempts are to be successful the nature of the 'market' must be understood. The British people have common sense. If they are told to do something which conflicts with that common sense, such as to carry gas masks when all the evidence tells them that a gas attack is most unlikely, no amount of exhortation will make them comply. A second important characteristic, Taylor continued, is basic laziness. Publicity campaigns have the greatest chance of success when allied with compulsion and a few prosecutions : 'A 40 shilling fine does more to stop spitting than £20,000 worth of advertising does to stop indiscriminate coughing and sneezing.' Indeed, 'the attempt to use propaganda as an easy way of avoiding legislation is a waste of energy, time and money', the role of propaganda more properly being that of explaining to the public the reason for the legislation and their part in the altered situation. Appeals will have a significant effect only if massive expenditure and striking originality are used, while exhortation – whose aim is to alter states of mind – is best left to the Prime Minister and to the 'propaganda of events'. It is only in the fields of explanation, instruction and interpretation that propaganda has any real chance of achieving its object.[52]

These considerations did not prevent the Ministry from undertaking a great amount of government publicity work. In January 1941, for example, a summary of campaigns recently completed, current and projected showed sixteen separate campaigns, ranging from Rat Destruction to Health for Factory Workers, conducted on behalf of eleven departments.[53] In the year ending April 1943 campaigns were carried out for eighteen departments[54] and by D-Day this volume of work had not lessened.[55] This is to say nothing of the work of the Exhibitions Division, which during the year ending June 1944 alone mounted displays and exhibitions for a total audience exceeding 40 million.[56] With such a heavy workload, perhaps an additional reason for the careful scrutiny of every publicity proposal was a reluctance to take on any more than was absolutely necessary.

There were many instances of refusal by the Ministry to prepare and disseminate publicity, but its attitude is best illustrated by reference to two issues on which campaigns were actually undertaken: public travel and fuel economy. In July 1941 the Ministry of War Transport asked for a campaign advising people not to travel in August, especially on Bank Holiday. The Planning Committee was doubtful about the effectiveness of a short-term, as opposed to a long explanatory, campaign and wanted 'an assurance that the railway companies would make all administrative arrangements in their power to discourage additional traffic'.[57] The railways did not heed this advice, but few complaints were reported. In the following year, however, there were widespread reports of 'anger and disgust' at the muddle perpetrated by the government when it simultaneously appealed to the public to spend holidays at home and increased rail facilities by laying on special excursion trains. It was accurately observed by members of the public that 'money and effort expended on urging the absolute need for people to stay at home is utterly wasted'.[58]

Bracken brought the matter to the attention of the Cabinet as an instance of a process which never failed to irritate the public: 'appeals from the Government for a course of action on the one hand, on the other, maintenance of conditions that tend to defeat the purposes of the appeal'.[59] The subject was felt to be of sufficient moment for the Minister to raise it again a month later and to widen its implications:

This subject has been taken and fixed upon . . . as a typical example of Government muddle . . . It may be useful to record two deductions from this: (a) In its present mood the public attributes to Government action or inaction all the main incidents that affect its daily life and does not seriously attend to distinctions between various forms of responsibility. If things go right, the Government is praised; if they seem to go wrong the Government is thought to be run by incompetent people. (b) If appeals are used and things still appear to be wrong, there is a regular hostile reaction on the lines 'Why can't they say what they want, and then order everyone to do it instead of appealing to people to do things'.[60]

Of all departments of government, the Ministry of Information was well placed to know one of the more unexpected responses of the British people to wartime life. As long as their need was clearly explained and they were seen to be equitably imposed, sacrifices were not only tolerated but were welcomed as an indication of the government's singleness of purpose.

In May 1941 the Ministry of Information refused to undertake an appeal on behalf of the Petroleum Board for a voluntary reduction in petrol consumption on the ground that 'the public expected, and indeed was anxious for, administrative action to reduce the petrol rations allowed to private motorists . . . [but] it was doubtful whether publicity to procure economy (as distinct from publicity to explain) would be worth while'.[61] The petrol ration was in fact progressively reduced, without public complaint, until it was completely phased out for private motorists in March 1942. But the situation with regard to general fuel economy – coal, gas and electricity – was different. The proposal, announced in April 1942, to introduce fuel rationing was wrecked by back-bench Tories who believed its effects would be most heavily felt by owners of large houses. Gwilym Lloyd George, appointed Minister of the new department of Fuel, Light and Power in June, proposed to the Ministry of Information a massive campaign for fuel economy. But, as Radcliffe pointed out to Bracken, the Ministry far preferred to see the introduction of rationing:

1. There is already a good deal of suspicion that the Government do not really believe in the possibilities of voluntary action and that they mean all along to resort to compulsion after a show of appealing for voluntary effort . . .

2. Further, the essence of this scheme is that rationing is a bogey which the individual will want to avoid. There is abundant evidence to the effect that this is a mistaken view of public reac-

tions to rationing. Owing to the success of the food scheme, rationing is definitely popular since, in exchange for a certain amount of inconvenience, it has avoided the major inconvenience of many people getting nothing and it is regarded as guaranteeing a fair share for all . . .

4. In brief, if the idea is to be 'Every householder should act as if rationing had already been introduced', the public will believe that rationing is at hand . . . they will be disposed to say 'Why all this fuss? Put your rationing scheme into effect at once and then we will know that everyone is not merely being asked to share equally but is, in fact, being forced to do so.'[62]

But faced on the one hand by a back-bench revolt and on the other by a level of coal production below pre-war figures, the government had no recourse but to 'voluntarism' and the Ministry was forced to mount a large, expensive and, in the event, successful campaign.[63] Its success did not, however, blunt the edge of Radcliffe's objections.

On the occasions when the Ministry's advice on publicity was ignored the consequences were clear to see. If they were not, the Ministry quickly pointed them out. But there were many occasions on which its advice was heeded and campaigns abandoned or modified. It was natural for departments, most of whom had for the first time appointed public relations officers and who were therefore plunged into the heady experience of self-promotion, to seek to implement their policies by resort to propaganda rather than by the more complex process of legislation. It was equally natural for them to resent queries, not only about the need for campaigns but also about the efficiency of their administrative arrangements, from a department which claimed to know the public mind. To the extent to which the Ministry successfully persuaded them to look again at their policies, public spirits and government efficiency were very well served.

As explanation of government action came to be seen as of overwhelming importance in the maintenance of morale, so was it realised in the Ministry that the reverse process should be strengthened, that is civil servants and politicians must have explained to them the feelings and attitudes of the public. Not, as Stephen Taylor pointed out at the time, 'because the administrators ought to follow public opinion – but because only with full public co-operation could the wartime machinery of controls, affecting every aspect of civilian life, be made to operate efficiently'.[64] At the highest level of government, Bracken was the first of the four Ministers of Information to insist upon presenting a regular summary of morale and public opinion to the War Cabinet. The memoranda were in essence summaries of the weekly intelligence reports, enlivened however, by the unmistakable Bracken touch. Of the public's deep but restrained joy following El Alamein, for example, he commented : 'they are now as suspicious as the ancient Greeks of any exultation that seems to challenge fate'.[65] In his first report Bracken clearly expressed his department's attitude towards propaganda and explanation :

(i) There must be more explanation : not only about the Armed Forces and the war situation but also about production, labour, war-time restrictions and the big problems that affect the life of everyone to-day. When the public is bewildered by something new a failure to explain means the risk of driving a wedge between Government and public . . .

(ii) We must stop appealing to the public or lecturing at it. One makes it furious, the other resentful. General appeals to the public or particular sections of it to work harder should not be made. There are too many people already working to the limit of their capacity or unable to do so for reasons beyond their control.[66]

Bracken's report for November 1942 was the last of the monthly series, although it was obvious that the war would last for a good while longer. He and his advisers probably felt that after El Alamein there was no further need to trouble the Cabinet with assessments of morale, as he had earlier decided that the public should not be troubled by clumsy official attempts to maintain their spirits.

The Home Intelligence Division constantly had to guard its flanks against the hostility of other departments, whose personnel tended to interpret public criticism, as communicated in the weekly report, as attacks by the Ministry of Information. Lest this blunt the educative purpose of the reports in Whitehall, Stephen Taylor was obliged to preface each of them with the following statement :

In reading this report, it is important to bear in mind that it does not set out to record *facts*, except in so far as public opinion is itself a fact. It is a record and reflection of the public's views and feelings about the war in general. Therefore, on matters on which public opinion is ill-informed, prejudiced or inconsistent, the report does not imply any endorsement of the views which are expressed in it.[67]

257

But in April 1942 Home Intelligence came tolerably close to an early death. Churchill addressed a minute to Bracken concerning the weekly report:

> There is hardly anything in this which could not have been written by a man sitting in a London office and imagining the echoes in the country to the London press.
>
> I doubt very much whether this survey is worth its trouble. How many people are engaged upon it, and how much does it cost?[68]

The Prime Minister's intervention could have dealt a crippling blow to the vital work of Home Intelligence had it not been for the Ministry's vigorous response. Radcliffe's draft reply merits lengthy quotation since it shows the value placed on the reports:

> For the moment the important thing is that it is not written 'by a man sitting in a London office and imagining the echoes in the country to the London press' . . . The primary sources are the Intelligence Officers of each Region. They themselves work through contacts, the contacts being chosen from people reputed to be sensible and level-headed, and whose occupation brings them into contact with a large number of people every day, e.g. doctors, parsons, publicans, trade union officials. An Intelligence Officer aims at a minimum of 30 reports from these contacts every week, although some, in fact, obtain many more.
>
> He draws on two other sources when making his report: the local Information Committees . . . and the other officers of the Regional staff, meetings officers, committee officers, films officers, etc., whose job takes them about the country and in touch with numerous people.
>
> In London the various Regional reports are checked against each other and additional sources are drawn upon for checking purposes. These are the Postal Censorship Reports, the Police Duty Room Reports which come from the Home Office, and special and occasional reports, of which the most valuable are those of the BBC's large Listener Research Department . . .
>
> By this means there is really no doubt that the final summary does, in fact, proceed from the genuine collection of views and opinions from a very large number of independent non-official people from all over the country. If the result comes out to be such as might have been imagined by someone in London reading the national dailies that would seem to suggest that the national

dailies are more closely in touch with general opinion in the country than it is sometimes popular to recognise. . . .

I think it would be as large a mistake to do away with these reports as to assume that they ought to be taken at face value. They are not supposed to be an accurate survey of the total opinion in the country; but they are extremely useful pointers, and I think accurate ones, to trends of feeling and to phases of feeling in which trouble lies or is beginning to be felt. They are really of little value except to the regular reader. I think it was said of Jeremiah, 'This man is worthy of death for he hath prophesied against the city'. I should deprecate the same remedy being applied to home intelligence reports.[69]

Bracken replied to the Prime Minister in a note taken almost verbatim from Radcliffe's draft and no more was heard on the matter.

The value of the weekly report to government was given powerful testimony late in 1943. The Ministry asked all those to whom the reports were circulated whether the cessation of the service would affect their work.[70] Of 112 replies received by 11 October, only eight respondents said that the report was of little use. Violet Bonham Carter, who was then on the BBC's Board of Governors, expressed considerable enthusiasm : 'It impresses me as being an extraordinarily sane and accurate assessment of public opinion . . . My constant reflection when reading it is, "How I hope that all members of the Government receive and study this Report!" '[71] It is clear from the great majority of replies that the report was achieving its principal objective. Hugh Gaitskell at the Board of Trade said that he would regard its withdrawal 'as a serious loss';[72] the Ministry of War Transport pointed to its vital place in the making of policy;[73] while Mary Hamilton of the Reconstruction Secretariat commented, 'I think I can say without hesitation that it is found useful here : and that, in our view, it is likely to be even more useful as the period of reconstruction . . . approaches';[74] and even the Prime Minister occasionally asked for an extract on 'some controversial topic which is exciting public interest'.[75]

Not only were the reports comprehensive and detailed, delving into many apparently trivial aspects of wartime life, they were – which was more important – unbiased and accurate when tested against the quantitative findings of the British Institute of Public Opinion and the Wartime Social Survey. Their uniqueness lay in the fact that for the first time a government had at its disposal a reliable machine for testing public responses to administrative and policy decisions and for gauging the needs of the people. Goebbels, too, possessed organised means for testing public opinion but as these were in the hands of the Nazi Party and administered by local party officials, estimates of morale and public attitudes were invariably falsified or couched in euphemistic language.[76] The cynically-minded observer might be disposed to comment that it took a total war for the British governing classes to show real and practical concern for the condition of the people. But while it may be true to say that the main thrust of Home Intelligence's work was directed towards ameliorating war-time discomforts and grievances in order to buttress support for the government, it is also true that the staff of the Ministry came to regard their labours as socially useful, war or no war. Something of their enthusiasm may be glimpsed in a report by Taylor of March 1943 :

> I cannot imagine a keener team of research workers, and I have never come across, or heard of, any research organisation which tackles so many and so varied problems with such prompt and efficient results. This is due to the staff's skill at their work, but also to their universal enthusiasm. They feel that they are building up a Government social research machine unlike anything which has existed in this country, or anywhere else; and that is a machine of which the Government may feel proud – and so, I must confess, do I.[77]

Once it had settled down, the Wartime Social Survey became an extremely useful adjunct to government. In June 1941 Louis Moss, late of the BBC Listener Research unit and the British Institute of Public Opinion, was appointed as Superintendent and together with Stephen Taylor he readied the Survey for the great demands that were to be made upon it by governments. At the end of the following month all but two of the existing staff resigned when the Ministry refused to approach the National Institute of Economic and Social Research again, the Institute having earlier withdrawn its support because it objected to the Survey's study of morale as well as of public opinion. However, new staff were immediately engaged and put to work. A Scientific Advisory Panel was set up in order to guarantee and supervise the Survey's sampling and processing techniques,* the earlier suspicion of social scientists and psychologists

*Lord Moran, F. C. Bartlett, Dr H. Bradford Hill, B. Seebohm Rowntree, A. M. Carr Saunders, Cyril Burt, M. A. Hamilton, Launcelot Hogben, Dr Aubrey Lewis, A. D. K. Owen.

(Frank Pick once said of the latter, 'I am perfectly certain they give wrong advice')[78] having given way to acceptance of their expertise.

With the exception of research into the efficacy of the Ministry's publicity campaigns, the Survey devoted itself to the requirements of other departments and by October 1944 had conducted 101 surveys, involving a total of 290,000 interviews. As an indication of the scope and variety of the work undertaken, it may be useful to record here the inquiries completed, in progress and under consideration for the year ending March 1944:

Major Reports: Lighting of Dwellings, Manufactured Foods, Household Methods of Cooking Vegetables, The Battle for Fuel, Brushes, Getting to Work, Food, Oatmeal and Potato Enquiry, Schools Meals in Scotland, The Location of Dwellings in Scottish Towns, Salvage, Ministry of Information Publications.

Smaller Enquiries: Consumption of Milk, Eat More Potatoes, Knowledge of Food Values, Food Shortages, Attitude to Food Rationing, Attitude to National Wheatmeal Bread, Food of Policemen and Public Utility and Transport Workers, Growing and Buying Vegetables, Children's and Infants' Footwear, Men's Overalls, Women's Overalls, Clogs, Number of Families per House, Soup Plate Stocks, Men's Brushes, Hairdressing Difficulties and Supply of Cosmetics, First-Line Shortages, Effect of the V.D. Campaign and Attitude of the Public, Enquiry into 'Desert Victory'.

Investigations in Progress: Transport of Workers, Publicity Media – Relative Effectiveness and Coverage – for Ministry of Information, The Nursing Campaign, Effect of the New Education Act and Public Attitude of and Knowledge of Educational Services, Information Services to Farmers, Attitudes of Working Women to Post-War Occupations, Noise in Dwellings, Newsreel Census, Nutrition of Families in Stoke and Salford, Results of the V.D. Campaign, National Index of Morbidity and Ill Health, Nutrition of Expectant Mothers in Stepney and Reading, Consumption of Bought Cakes, Use of National Milk Cocoa by Young Workers, Consumption of National Wheatmeal Bread, Take-Up of Fruit Juice and Codliver Oil, First-Line Shortages.

Under Discussion: Garden Crops, Floor Loading, Domestic Inventory, Stocks of Enamelware and Hardware, Middlesbrough Town Planning Problems, Problems of the National Health Service, Samples of Cooked Vegetables, Domestic Fuel Utilisation, Fuel Stocks, Consumption of Green Vegetables in Scotland,

Herring Consumption in Scotland, Juvenile Delinquency in Scotland, Social Problems Arising from Scottish Hydro-Electricity Board.[79]

The daily press had long since tired of the 'Cooper's Snoopers' epithet and, more significantly, specialist journals such as *Nature*, *The Lancet* and the *Journal of the Royal Statistical Society* recognised and praised the contribution of the Survey to the war effort.[80] But at least one member of the Ministry was not so persuaded. R. P. Winfrey, RIO for the Eastern Region, wrote to Taylor in December 1941[81] complaining about investigators 'trundling round the staffs of certain organisations asking the women members of the staffs about the corsets they were wearing' and he doubted whether such inquiries could produce 'effects which are valuable in defeating Japan in the Pacific, Germany in Russia and the Italians in Africa'. Taylor informed Winfrey that the survey was being conducted on behalf of the Board of Trade which hoped to concentrate the corset industry, thereby enabling the release of 'tens of thousands of workers for war industry, not to mention a large amount of steel' and in order not to subject women workers to discomfort it was considered essential to have accurate data on corset habits.[82]

Although the major concern was with the immediate physical and psychological well-being of the populace in time of war, the nature and breadth of the Survey's work had obvious implications for peacetime. Never before had government involved itself so intimately with the minutiae of British, largely working-class, life. Appalled at the prospect of the loss of such a unique organisation, Taylor from as early as September 1942 urged the retention of the Survey after victory in the form of a National Institute of Opinion Studies.[83] He correctly anticipated that after the war economic and social restrictions would continue in being for some time, necessitating appropriate social research so that the government of the day might reach sound and just decisions. In the longer term, Taylor identified four virtues inherent in the activities of such an institute, which together would greatly facilitate the workings of democracy: objective research reports, especially if freely published, would offset both press misrepresentation of public opinion and the necessarily inaccurate impressions of MPs; legislators and civil servants would come to see that the public 'is far more sensible and far more reasonable than it has been given credit for in the past;[84] administrative and legislative action would be in closer accord with the needs and wants of the public; and explanation of government decisions, leading to public co-operation, would be made possible.[85] Taylor was supported by the Ministry. The unit survived and is today a valuable part of the Office of Population Censuses and Surveys.* For our purposes it is important to note that, as with the reports of Home Intelligence, the Wartime Social Survey was more than an expedient tool for the maintenance of morale. It represented a considerable widening of the ambit of government concern for the condition of the people and may be considered part of the wartime acceleration towards social reform.

The presence in Britain after January 1942 of American troops, several million of whom had passed through the country by D-Day, threw on the Ministry of Information yet another responsibility – that of smoothing and enhancing relations between this most numerous body of foreign soldiers and their civilian hosts. As Bracken pointed out two and a half years later, the task was not welcomed by the Ministry :

> I think we have far too many responsibilities. When, a few weeks before the first convoy of American troops came to this country, the Ministry of Information was asked to become responsible for arranging hospitality for them, I knew we had neither the time nor the manpower to undertake such an important task . . . but the task was forced upon us.[86]

Certain worrying questions presented themselves. How would the populace respond to the presence of soldiers whose country of origin was by no means popular in Britain? A country, moreover, which was inevitably to become the senior partner in the alliance. If resentment arose, would it affect the nature and quality of the British war effort? What of the large numbers – amounting to tens of thousands – of black American troops? The potential for friction between a strained, tired population and the well-paid, ebullient young Americans, freed of the many restraints governing their behaviour at home, was considerable.

Before Pearl Harbour three principal currents of pro-American sentiment were evident in the reports of Home Intelligence. The most substantial was the high esteem in which President Roosevelt

---

*Taylor was instrumental in saving it: in 1945, having become a Labour MP, he persuaded Aneurin Bevan to argue in Cabinet for the Survey's retention. Later, John Boyd-Carpenter was similarly persuaded. Lord Taylor to author, 2 March 1976.

was held: 'our best friend after Churchill'.[87] He was seen not only as a reforming president but as a head of state determined to overcome his fellow countrymen's isolationism and eventually to lead them into a war against the Axis.[88] Although there was disappointment at the apparent slowness with which it reached Britain, American aid was genuinely appreciated by many people.[89] Thirdly, the apprehension aroused by Japan's belligerent diplomacy in the Far East diminished to the extent that it was believed America would keep the peace or, failing that, would deal speedily with Japan if she declared war.[90] Outweighing these positive factors, in the estimation of the Ministry, were certain adverse opinions. The simple fact, in the minds of many, was the neutrality of the United States and no amount of 'big talk' about democracy could offset the conviction that she was allowing others to fight the battle for her.[91] In such a climate of opinion it was perhaps natural for people to draw parallels with America's late entry into the First World War and to comment on the lack of magnanimity underlying its present material support.[92] For all that, it was apparent to Home Intelligence that 'America is not really regarded as a foreign country, to be wooed with praise, but as a close relative to be chided freely for her shortcomings'.[93]

From this mixture of ambivalent emotions and beliefs the propagandists extracted the conclusion that the British people were hostile to such a degree that special measures were called for. Sir Kenneth Clark proposed a campaign to counter the 'average man's . . . unfavourable view' of the United States 'as being a country of luxury, lawlessness, unbridled capitalism, strikes and delays'.[94] Elaborating his proposal, Sir Kenneth suggested that the public should be reminded that the average American is 'a kindly, simple, honourable character', that his government far from being subservient to rapacious private interests was engaging in great public works such as the Boulder Dam, and that America was as concerned as Britain to defend democracy.[95] Some days later the campaign was begun.[96]

To judge from the responses of the public to Pearl Harbour, as reported by Home Intelligence, the campaign had little impact. Although the entry of the United States into the war was greeted with relief and gratitude, there were widespread reports of 'malicious delight' that at long last the Americans would have a taste of war[97] and of contempt for the 'remarkable unanimity of the Americans in going to war when they are directly threatened, after the year in which they appeared content to let other people do their fighting for democracy'.[98] A fortnight later it was reported:

While the public are prepared to make any sacrifices necessary to help Russia, it is pointed out that they have no such disposition towards America . . . America is 'too damned wealthy' . . . Americans are too mercenary-minded, and . . . the hardship and suffering of war 'will do them a lot of good'.[99]

After their experience of total war the British may perhaps be forgiven their *schadenfreude*, but it was hardly a reassuring commencement to the popular reception of the grand alliance.

Upon the arrival of US servicemen, the Ministry of Information set up an American Forces Liaison Division which was made responsible for co-ordinating what was essentially a locally based programme of smoothing relations between the public and the American forces. Only at the level of town and village could the Ministry, through the agency of RIOs, recruit the co-operation of numerous bodies and authorities. Local improvisation rather than central direction was necessary if success was to be achieved. Employing much the same tactics as were applied to stealing the thunder from the left, the Ministry remained in the background, 'fomenting spontaneous hospitality'[100] and encouraging manifestations of good will.

There were two initial difficulties. The Americans came 'self-sufficing, fully equipped, and prepared to regard Britain in much the same light as they regarded North Africa, namely, as the base from which they happened to be fighting at the moment';[101] and it was only through the efforts of General Eisenhower and the creation of a top-level British–American Liaison Board, on which the Ministry was represented, that this variant of isolationism was broken down. A number of publications prepared for distribution to American troops undoubtedly helped. One such, and probably the best, was *Welcome!* As well as providing practical information, the pamphlet accurately conveyed something of the quality of British wartime life :

A word or two about conditions here. Nearly four years of war have made us pretty realistic in our outlook. The gayer side of British life has been subordinated to the grim business of war. Nearly everybody who is physically able is doing a war job of some sort. Millions of people spend their spare time after work with the Home Guard, or in some form of civil defence. The streets are black at night and it is difficult for a stranger to find his way about. Food is plentiful, up to a point, but there are few luxuries. We have made this island into a fortress and it is important that the broad outline of the life of the population should

265

fit into this conception. Cinemas and theatres are open, of course, and indeed they flourish, but they open early and close early. You may find some of our restrictions irksome, we find them so ourselves, but we understand, as you will understand, that the shape of our lives must be altered to fit our changed conditions, and we accept this change without too much exercise of the Englishman's right to complain. If our trains are sometimes delayed, if there are few porters in the darkened station, or if the coaches are not as clean as they might be, we shrug our shoulders and use a formula which has saved our temper in the most exasperating circumstances : 'There's a war on'. You will hear the phrase until you are sick of it. We are. But it helps.[102]

The second difficulty had to do with money. The Ministry's programme languished for want of it. When the government was persuaded to allocate finance for disbursement by the department, the hospitable impulses of the areas in which US soldiers were stationed or spent their leave were given tangible form.

What was done once money became available? The Local Information Committees, which had been a cause of distress to the Ministry in the past,[103] now came into their own, for on them were represented the many interests whose co-operation was required. Hospitality Committees were set up. These comprised local authorities, the Regional Commissioner, voluntary societies and the churches, their 'ideal being to allow no American to go home again without having at least been under one British roof and made one British friend'.[104] The American Red Cross, which lodged and fed troops on leave in facilities provided by the British, was assisted by a total of 40,000 women volunteers who helped organise Red Cross Clubs. Two hundred and fifty social clubs were established by voluntary agencies such as the YMCA, Rotary, the Salvation Army and the Jewish Hospitality Committee, while the WVS ran some 200 Welcome Clubs where British civilians were able to meet American servicemen 'away from the atmosphere of the street or the pub'.[105] The Ministry encouraged and supported the British Council and the English Speaking Union in sending speakers to American establishments and aided the American Red Cross in forming clubs for the purpose of instructing some of the 60,000 'GI brides' about American life and customs. Under the department's auspices, between 3,000 and 4,000 servicemen awaiting transfer home for discharge were accepted by British universities for a term or two's academic work; and, as many of these men were destined to fill posts in the professions, industry and

politics on their return, the experience of British university life –
especially after the turmoil of war – no doubt had a lasting influence
on Anglo-American relations. Another 2,000 men entered various
trades and professions for a short period before their departure.

Care must be exercised lest the impression is given that most
Americans took their ease in church halls and Rotary clubs : it is
more likely that the majority preferred the atmosphere of the pub
and the company of 'loose women' to the amenities so earnestly and
anonymously fostered by the Ministry of Information. But insofar
as the Ministry facilitated it, the contact of hundreds of thousands
of young Americans with the kindness and warmth of ordinary
Britons undoubtedly helped to ease much confusion and loneliness.
We are, however, principally concerned with the impact of the US
troops on their hosts. It did not have the consequences which might
have been anticipated from a reading of the intelligence reports prior
to Pearl Harbour or from the fears which motivated the Ministry's
campaign to popularise the United States.

The complaints and accusations levelled at the American troops
were many. They were said to drink too heavily, to be boastful and
contemptuous of the British armed forces ('the Dunkirk Harriers'),
to be too highly paid, to corrupt young women, and to practise
discrimination against their black comrades.[106] The report for 21–28
July 1942 summarised the reactions of British civilians after six
months of the American presence :

(a) The Americans are reported to be 'settling in well and proving
to be popular' . . . The only report of 'not altogether happy
relations' comes from High Wycombe.

(b) There appears to be 'an inclination to anticipate problems
and difficulties' in places where they are expected, and 'the prospect
of an American invasion' arouses little enthusiasm.

(c) Even from places where a favourable impression is reported,
there is criticism of their behaviour with the local girls (and of the
behaviour of the local girls with them), and of their alleged hard
drinking.

(d) The arrival of American troops is said to revive the question
of the difference between their pay and conditions and those of
British soldiers, and . . . their unpopularity is said to be particularly
evident among our own Forces. In the words of a writer quoted
by Postal Censorship, 'They're too well paid and flash their money
about. What chance has a poor Tommy with a couple of bob
jingling in his pocket?'

(e) Two reports stress 'the necessity of providing information bureaux to give them practical help over such matters as money values, what goods are unrationed, transport services, etc.'

(f) It is said that the Americans seem to have been thoroughly warned what to expect in England, but that their English hosts, both military and civilian, have so far been told nothing whatever about their guests' outlook, background or use of the English language.

(g) Rumours of the 'red, white, blue and yellow' and 'as quick as you left Tobruk' variety continue to circulate. One report states that careful efforts to track down these rumours lead to the conviction that 'they are being spread by enemy agents, and have no foundation in fact'.[107]

By December 1942 such reports had considerably declined in number and in 1943 they had all but disappeared. This, together with the constant remark that the Americans were 'settling down well', may be taken as an indication of the way in which they came to be regarded as part of wartime life, albeit an exotic part. The RIO for the Southern Region described the American 'occupation' as a gigantic social experiment and asked whether it had succeeded :

> . . . in spite of fairly frequent incidents . . . annoyance and criticism lost significance as time went on. It was smothered by a growing appreciation of the Americans as a whole. Irritating and disquieting incidents continued, but there was less and less inclination to draw general and damning deductions from them. People began to realise . . . that the Americans really belong to a different nation, with different standards, customs, manners of approach'.[108]

If after actual contact the British revised their earlier notion of the Americans as close relations, how did they respond to the black American troops in their midst? Great concern was expressed in the War Cabinet. It was feared in a generally undefined way that the presence of black US soldiers would have untoward consequences for the morale of both civilians and servicemen and for Anglo–American relations. The Ministry of Information did not entertain such fears and adopted a cautious and sensible approach to this contentious matter.

In August 1942 Anthony Eden referred the War Cabinet to 'the various difficulties' likely to be encountered, including the health of coloured troops during the English winter, should the United

States continue to send the existing proportion of black troops to Britain. Cabinet agreed with the Foreign Secretary's proposal to press the Americans for a reduction in the number being sent over.[109] A month later Sir James Grigg, Secretary of State for War, submitted a memorandum in which he argued that the failure of British civilians to sympathise with the distinction drawn by white against black troops would lead to friction between white Americans and the host populace. The morale of British troops overseas would also be adversely affected should there 'be any unnecessary association between American coloured troops and British women'.[110] He therefore recommended that the lead of the US authorities should be followed and, as an example of the policy he had in mind, he appended to the memorandum a note written by the Major-General in charge of Administration, Southern Command, for the guidance of British servicemen.

Following a potted history of slavery and of the reasons for the segregation practised in the southern American states, the note spoke of the 'bond of mutual esteem' between the races and the white Southerner's sense of moral duty to the negro 'as it were to a child'. Of 'a simple mental outlook' and lacking 'the white man's ability to think and act to a plan', the negro is nevertheless capable of engaging in civil strife if allowed too much freedom and too close an association with white people. With these facts in mind, British serving men and women were advised to be sympathetic to coloured men but to avoid making intimate friends with them, women being adjured never to 'walk out, dance or drink' with coloured soldiers. As a general rule, it was thought best in such matters to emulate the behaviour of white American troops.

Grigg's recommendations were too much for Lord Cranborne who, as Secretary of State for the Colonies, was aware of the effect the adoption of such a policy might have on black colonials serving with the British forces. He protested that 'it is going too far to attempt to ask the British Army or the ATS to adopt the attitude of the American Army towards American coloured people'.[111] The Lord Chancellor, Lord Simon, warmly supported Cranborne. Although he stated that the coloured man was entitled to equal treatment only 'if he behaves himself', Simon insisted upon the maintenance of equality in service and in civilian life.[112] Herbert Morrison, despite concern for the consequences of the fascination of coloured men for some British women, also came down against Grigg's proposals: the police had already been instructed not to practise discrimination and to discourage it among others; advice to soldiers on the lines suggested

269

would certainly become known to the general public; and in any case assurances had been received from General Eisenhower that the US Army would not segregate coloured from white troops in the United Kingdom.[113]

Bracken's contribution to the debate was confined to the circulation of a letter he had written to Grigg on 16 September. Though it was desirable, the Minister of Information maintained, to avoid offending white American soldiers, it would be unwise to try to lead the British people to adopt the American social attitude to the negro:

> I do not think that the mass of the civilian population ought to be approached with any propaganda on the subject. A wrong step would be disastrous, and there is not sufficient prospect of any real success, however wise one's attitude. Incidentally, the essential agents of national hospitality are the Voluntary Societies, with whom we are working very closely. Their fundamental principles are involved in the doctrine of no racial discrimination.[114]

The Ministry's general philosophy on propaganda apart, Bracken could hardly have advised otherwise since on 20 September 1942 the *Sunday Express* had carried an article under his name, 'The Colour Bar Must Go', which, while referring to coloured British subjects, was unlikely to be divorced from the American issue in the minds of most readers.

In the light of reports reaching the Ministry of Information, Bracken's caution was well advised. The probability of antagonising the public by 'education' along the lines suggested by Sir James Grigg was high. Of all factors contributing to tension between the civil population and the Americans by far the most important was the discrimination publicly exercised by white against black, the initial puzzlement leading eventually to 'strong feeling'[115] and 'considerable indignation'.[116] British soldiers shared the civilians' feelings: one incident said to be typical was that in which a number of soldiers, upbraided by Americans for 'fraternising with negroes', commented that as both black and white troops had come 3,000 miles to help win the war they saw no reason to distinguish between one American and another.[117] Civilians took increasingly to interfering verbally and physically in disputes between black troops and white officers and military police,[118] the GOC Southern Command reporting a number of such incidents to Sir James Grigg who in turn anxiously informed the Prime Minister.[119]

Faced with a cascade of memoranda on the subject, the War

Cabinet was thrown into a lengthy discussion on 13 October 1942. While it was thought that the British people 'should avoid becoming too friendly with coloured American troops', it was also agreed that Grigg's suggestions 'went too far' and that no modification be made in respect of free access by coloured persons to canteens, pubs, cinemas and the like. The Lord Privy Seal, Sir Stafford Cripps, was asked to consult with the Home Secretary and the Secretary of State for War and to produce a revised set of instructions for the Army and an article for the Army Bureau of Current Affairs.[120]

For the man who had been chosen earlier in the year to go to India in order to conduct extremely delicate negotiations with Congress and who might therefore have been expected to possess an understanding of racial problems and communal sensitivities, Cripps made surprisingly few alterations to the instructions appended to Grigg's paper of 3 October. The offensive analysis of the negro character and the recommendation that the British should emulate the white American attitude were omitted, but there remained references to black slaves as having taken 'root and multiplied', to the capacity of their descendants for inspiring 'affection and admiration' like children, and to semi-tropical labour being more fitted to the coloured man. British servicemen and women were to be told to adopt an objective attitude in any discussions they might have with white Americans on the colour question, but the advice remained much the same as before.[121] Just what effect the issuing of these instructions had on 'other ranks' it is difficult to say, but it is doubtful whether on a matter so closely involving deeply personal beliefs and attitudes much influence was exerted. Bracken successfully vetoed the distribution of similar advice to the general public. He also expressed opposition to 'written documents' and 'the didactic approach' being inflicted on the Army, but could not prevent the scheme going ahead.[122]

Some publicity did, in fact, escape from the Ministry of Information. But it was on a small scale, aimed at specific groups in the community and exhibited rather more discretion than was shown in the final product of the War Cabinet's deliberations. Louis MacNeice, the poet, was commissioned by the Ministry on behalf of the Board of Education to write a booklet, *Meet the U.S. Army,* for the guidance of school teachers. In it he touched on the colour problem:

The American Negroes require a special comment. There are many Negro soldiers in this country, and those Britons who have met them have been very favourably impressed by their pleasant manners and their readiness to please. These Negro troops are not, on principle, separately brigaded, the U.S. War Department having rightly declined to differentiate them from other American citizens. It must be remembered, however, that . . . they are in the unique position of being descended from slaves; this memory of slavery, being still fresh, retains a psychological hold both on the Negroes themselves and on many of the white fellow-citizens . . . from this they will only gradually break free. Any American Negro who comes to Britain must be treated by us on a basis of absolute equality. And remember *never* to call a Negro a 'nigger'.[123]

The Ministry steered very cautiously between the shoals of indignant British opinion and the ingrained attitudes of many white American soldiers. The Regions were advised to seek the guidance of the commanding officer of the local American unit before encouraging hospitality for black troops and to obviate 'embarrassment' by never inviting 'negro troops to a dance at which white American troops and English girls' were present. RIOs were also asked to point out to Americans that the British people, having no colour problem of their own, could afford to take 'a more detached and seemingly more humanitarian attitude to negroes': hence their impatience at evidence of discrimination.[124] One Regional officer found this policy irksome. When asked by the American Southern Base Commander whether anything could be done to moderate the public's 'effusiveness' towards black soldiers, he replied unofficially that departmental instructions prevented him from taking such action in much the same way as US Army policy prevented 'what most American Officers would have liked to do, namely, to exclude Negro troops from this country'.[125]

A year after the thorough Cabinet discussion Sir James Grigg was still pressing for a change of 'attitude on the colour question'.[126] Failing to analyse the circumstances and the possibility of discriminatory behaviour on the part of the US military police, he cited the crime statistics relating to black troops. These showed that the incidence of sex offences was twice as heavy and of violent crimes five times as heavy as among white American soldiers; and as black troops were less inclined towards drunkenness, Grigg concluded that 'in both these classes of crime the trouble is due to the natural propensities of the coloured man'.[127] The Duke of Marlborough, who as a lieutenant-colonel was liaising between the American and British forces, also felt constrained to warn Churchill:

There is, I know, a feeling throughout parts of the country in which these negro troops are quartered that it is unwise and dangerous to go out into the roads and country lanes after dark and there is growing resentment that these conditions should be allowed to exist. I know the difficulties of the situation as they confront you and the American authorities. I do not wish to make a mountain out of a molehill but I do visualize that during the coming winter when the hours of darkness grow longer that the number of these crimes will become greater and also the possibility of their being undetected will also be facilitated.[128]

The Prime Minister considered the situation 'serious'.[129] But the Ministry of Information, in possession of no evidence to substantiate the Duke's forebodings, continued to counsel prudence. Both in the policy towards black troops and in the tactic of quietly encouraging the basically friendly and hospitable promptings of the public towards the American visitors, the department acted in accordance with the stance evolved in 1941. In these, as in other matters of morale and public opinion, the British people were trusted to behave sensibly and in a manner consistent with the nation's best interests.

For eighteen months Brendan Bracken came under pressure in Cabinet to embark on a campaign of indoctrination about the Japanese war, but such was the new-found assurance of the Ministry in basing its policies on the common sense of the public that there was no question of his agreeing to do so. Towards the middle of 1943 Wavell expressed alarm at the way in which troops in the Far East were being adversely affected by the apparent lack of interest shown by the British public in their operations. Leo Amery, Secretary of State for India, urged the formation of an interdepartmental committee 'for the purpose of considering the need for cultivating the state of morale necessary to ensure the completion of our military operations after the defeat of the Axis in Europe'.[130] As the department most affected, the Ministry of Information was strongly opposed. Pointing out to Bracken that the public would accept their obligations when the time came, Radcliffe commented, 'What I am afraid of is that this windy paper from Mr Amery will lead to the setting up . . . of one more windy committee . . . and that we shall find a silly group of Departments trying to instruct us how to do the impossible before it becomes possible'.[131] The Minister was in full agreement:

It is all very well to say 'We must educate the British public to regard the Japanese as if they were Germans, and war in the Pacific as if it were war in Europe'. But, while the Japanese remain

273

many thousands of miles away, the Germans have for 3 years been only 20 miles distant from our shore and, too often, vertically overhead. Interest and feeling follow where friends and loved ones are fighting . . . Europe is very much a home concern, whereas knowledge of or interest in the Far East is sparsely distributed in this country.

Given these conditions I do not think that any Committee could do much to alter the 'state of morale' of people in this country. The people have been left under no misapprehension by the Prime Minister that it is their duty to turn and tackle Japan when the time comes, nor, so far as my observations go, is there any general misunderstanding on the subject.[132]

As usual, Churchill agreed with Bracken. And apart from the creation of an internal committee to monitor public feeling towards the Far East, but whose real purpose seems to have been to head off the formation of an interdepartmental committee, the Ministry did little.

Public interest in and knowledge of the Japanese war remained low.[133] But a survey, conducted by the British Institute of Public Opinion at the request of the Ministry, showed that 'nearly 90% of people consider we should stay in the war until Japan is beaten' and, in support of the Ministry's contention that the stimulation of aggressive feelings was unnecessary, hatred of the Japanese 'appears to be at least as strong as hatred of the Germans'.[134] In November 1944 Leo Amery and the service ministers recommended that 'a campaign of indoctrination should now be started'. Clearly exasperated, Bracken reminded them through the Prime Minister that his department's reports on the situation had been ignored and that a campaign of explanation – for which he would not 'claim all the ponderous characteristics of a "campaign of indoctrination" ' – had in fact been in progress for a year.[135] The accompanying illustration shows that the Ministry's, and Churchill's, 'explanation' was in danger of appearing to protest too much the government's implacable determination to defeat Japan, but at least the public were not told – as they might well have been earlier in the war – '*You* must pursue the war against Japan to the very end.'

This was the last occasion on which the Ministry was obliged to defend its 'hands-off' philosophy towards morale. To some extent the North African victories, the heartening progress of the Soviet armies, the beginning of the American offensive in the Pacific and the imminence, obvious to all, of a continental invasion made government concern for morale superfluous. But what of the flying-bomb and rocket attacks of 1944–5? They raised the question of morale once again and, in the Home Secretary's mind at least, in an acute form. Four days after the first flying-bomb incident Morrison informed the War Cabinet:

> The attacks had led to a serious loss of sleep and the fact that they went on continuously meant that there was no relaxation of the strain and, in particular, made parents anxious for the safety of their children. After 5 years of war the civil population were not as capable of standing the strain of attack as they had been during the winter of 1940–41. If flying bomb attacks were supplemented by rocket attacks . . . there might be serious deterioration in the morale of the civil population.[136]

As if launched by a malicious deity, the attacks were random in nature, likely to occur at any time of the day and, especially in the case of flying bombs, most unnerving. Just on 9,000 people lost their lives. Production in the London area was disrupted for a short period, severe damage inflicted on housing and nearly $1\frac{1}{4}$ million persons took themselves from London. So the attacks were hardly in the nature of a postscript to the war experience of British civilians. But morale remained sound. At no time in Cabinet did Bracken feel constrained to warn his colleagues about morale. And any member of the government could, of course, consult the Home Intelligence reports, which in fact confirmed Bracken's confidence in the public's capacity to withstand this new form of bombardment. According to Lord Taylor, the rockets 'had no effect whatsoever on morale', although the flying bombs – owing to the tension induced by waiting for the engine to cut out – were 'very much disliked'.[137]

Because of the scattered – if extremely violent – nature of flying-bomb and rocket incidents, the Ministry's information and post-raid services were not stretched as they had been in 1940–41. The major task was that of enlisting the support of the press in preventing the Germans from gaining any information which might have served to enhance the accuracy of attacks or to overcome the British defensive measures, which included the use of jet aircraft.[138] Exhibiting that maturity and sober common sense which the Ministry had come to expect, the public were reported to be in favour of continuing the ban on publicity of rocket attacks which had been in force since the arrival of the first V2 on 8 September.[139] But as soon as the total ban became unnecessary, after the publication in America of the principal features of rocket attacks, Bracken argued for its abandonment,[140] and shortly afterwards the press were permitted to publish stories of a general character. In a very real sense, the Ministry of Information, the newspapers and the public were working smoothly in harness.

As early as November 1943 Bracken expressed the conviction that the Ministry of Information should be dissolved at the end of the European war.[141] Radcliffe agreed with him, but urged the retention of the department's publicity functions in a central agency after the war as a matter of 'administrative convenience'.[142] In this he was supported by Sir Alan Barlow of the Official Committee on the Machinery of Government:

> The Haldane Committee laid much stress on the importance of a well-informed Government: it is at least as important to the proper operation of democratic institutions that there should be a well-informed public. Therefore, though admittedly the dividing line between presenting facts and inviting particular inferences from them is sometimes thin, it can never be a misuse of the Government's resources to provide machinery by which knowledge relevant to a proper discharge of citizenship is presented accurately and attractively to as wide a public as possible.[143]

Bracken seems to have had little interest in the continuation of the Ministry in any form. It was an open secret, according to the *Evening Standard* in June 1944, that 'he would not tolerate the continuation of his Ministry at any price'.[144] Two months before the Nazi capitulation he asked Churchill for permission to dismantle the department, arguing among other things that it should no longer be seen to be involved in 'matters of acute controversy' such as post-war reconstruction.[145] The Prime Minister demurred and ordered Bracken to keep the Ministry in existence on a reduced scale until the defeat of Japan.[146] Shortly after the end of the war in Europe, in May 1945, Bracken left the Ministry to become First Lord of the Admiralty – Churchill's old post – in the caretaker government which lasted until the announcement of Labour's victory on 26 July.

The department, shorn of censorship powers and of executive authority, lingered on until March 1946, when Attlee announced the formation of the Central Office of Information.[147] This offspring of the Ministry is with us still, performing specialist publicity, research and information services for the government of the day.

Winding up an estimates debate in June 1944, in the course of which much praise had been heaped on his head, Bracken modestly explained, 'I have merely told the facts about the Ministry of

Information; and I leave it to the historians, if they have a column or two in their histories, to say whether the Ministry have done a good job in this war or not.'[148] In what respects then, did the Ministry of Information succeed in the domestic sphere, that is to say in maintaining morale? Undoubtedly the operation of news and censorship succeeded, not simply in terms of keeping valuable news from the enemy but primarily by extracting news from other departments and by operating, so to speak, as an anti-censorship agency.

Freed from peacetime constraints, the government possessed the power to impose almost any kind and degree of censorship on the press. Although mindful of the effect on parliamentary and public opinion of the exercise of this power, the War Cabinet had no hesitation in banning the *Daily Worker* and attempting to intimidate the *Daily Mirror* when the evidence provided no foundation for the charge that these newspapers were harming morale and the war effort. Had the Ministry shared the Cabinet's dark suspicions of the press there is no doubt that freedom of expression would have been another casualty of war. On the contrary, the Ministry of Information refused to act as the catspaw of government suppression. In so doing, it earned the admiration of journalists but at the same time brought a lot of trouble on its own head. It was not in the nature of things that the Ministry should have adopted such a role. Why did it do so?

'The main defect', Duff Cooper said of the Ministry, 'was that there were too few ordinary Civil Servants in it, and too many brilliant amateurs'[149] but so far as news and censorship were concerned, this 'defect' was a positive virtue. Sir Walter Monckton, Cyril Radcliffe, Admiral Thomson, Francis Williams and most of the other officers who dealt closely with press matters were none of them career civil servants. Having been recruited from outside government at the outbreak of war and for the most part with no intention of remaining in the civil service at its conclusion, they were not inclined to defer to what they took to be the unreasonable requests of other departments.[150] They brought to their arduous work a freshness of approach which, while it did not comply with the Whitehall way of doing things, prevented the application of suffocating formulae to the volatile workings of the press. Malcolm Barnes, a former officer in the Censorship Division, recalls his experiences:

The unique thing about the Ministry of Information was that it was largely run by amateurs – that is to say, people with little or no Civil Service background. Only the administrators – the

277

Treasury men in 'Establishment' – were service minded. The rest had to use their initiative as best they could within the ministerial straight-jacket . . . [the Censorship was] a very human and often comic department that on many occasions had the temerity to defend the public and the press against the service departments, the ministers and the politicians, and what's more succeeded . . . My own experience there was a happy one and my colleagues came, as they did in other departments, from all walks of life – professors and lecturers, lawyers, journalists, writers, retired men from the army and navy, even a breeder of bloodstock – and we made the thing work in an efficient and humane way, though with expected lapses.[151]

Some years after the war Radcliffe stated that freedom of information means 'that people who want to disseminate news or to put forward opinions ought to be free to do so without interference from the government in the form of censorship, licensing or suppression'.[152] Within the defined limitations of security censorship, this view was held by Radcliffe and his colleagues, and supported by successive ministers, during the war.

Was it purely adventitious that this extraordinarily talented group of men happened to possess decidedly liberal views of their tasks? Radcliffe and Monckton were lawyers and they grounded their refusals to extend censorship beyond security in a strict, if conveniently legalistic, interpretation of Defence Regulation 3; but when they believed something was wrong in principle – such as the Cabinet decision to suppress comment and news on international affairs – they had no hesitation in ignoring or side-stepping a Cabinet directive. When Francis Williams succeeded Radcliffe, as ex-editor of the *Daily Herald* he not surprisingly advocated as much freedom for the press as could be given. Sir Edwin Herbert, Director of Postal and Telegraph Censorship, said of censorship generally, 'This Frankenstein monster we have created ought to be regarded as an element of totalitarianism and its funeral should coincide with that of Germany.'[153] To some extent, then, it is true to say that the coming together of these men was a happy accident. But it is also true to say that daily contact with the press bred in the officials of the Ministry a sympathy for and friendship with journalists that fostered a willingness to combat the obscurantist tendencies of other departments and of the War Cabinet itself.

The most substantial reinforcement of the liberal promptings within the Ministry was the sure knowledge, fed by continual Home

Intelligence reports (and lent support by current empirical research)[154] that one of the most significant factors in civilian morale was news. If news was good so much the better. If the news was bad, as it so often was in the first half of the war, it should nonetheless be communicated to the public as quickly, as fully and as honestly as possible. Nothing so irritated and depressed the public as the feeling that information was being withheld from them or was being presented in unduly rosy hues. And as it became evident that the exhortations of the propagandists were largely unproductive so it was realised that the British people would bear almost any sacrifice as long as they believed they had the confidence of their leaders.

Home Intelligence and the Wartime Social Survey may also be counted as successes and, in truth, as of central importance to the functioning of the department. At the very least, as Radcliffe seems to have implied at the time of the Prime Minister's protest, they combined to act as an early warning system, enabling the government to anticipate and, where possible, to alleviate grievances. Flowing from this pragmatic function was a valuable by-product. Never before had members of a government and civil servants been given the means to apprehend the life of the population so deeply, for so long and over such a wide front. And although much of the research was concerned with war-related matters, there were numerous issues whose importance transcended wartime exigencies – health, transport, housing, social welfare, education, working conditions – and on which the administrators and policy makers gained otherwise unobtainable insights. The work of RIOs in post-raid conditions, the Ministry's co-ordination of government publicity, the protection of the BBC, the holding of thousands of public meetings may all be cited as positive contributions to morale and to popular understanding of the war and of official policy.*

Where did the Ministry fail? The repudiation of morale campaigns, accompanied as it was by the explicit admission that exhortation aroused irritation, pointed to a clear failure. It was a failure not of means but of basic comprehension. The temptation to regard morale as a sort of malleable putty stemmed from a fundamental mistrust of the British people's resilience. Similarly, while they did not actually provoke hostility, the Ministry's anti-German propaganda, its

---

*The work of the Crown Film Unit had little impact: 'A nice little flash in the cultural pan – kept the documentary film makers happy, but had almost no effect, as the films had *v. small* audiences'.[155] According to Tom Harrisson, Mass-Observation found that audiences did not respond to the films as the makers and the Ministry intended.[156]

fastidiously apolitical support of the Soviet Union and the aversion for talking about social reform rested on misinterpretations of the public's martial and ideological leanings.

Two months before he was bundled out of office Harold Nicolson ruminated in his diary:

> It is almost exactly a year ago today since I entered the Ministry. What agonies and disappointments have occurred since then! I have a feeling none the less that I have done good work and helped many people more important and creative than myself . . . I often wonder whether, if I survive this war (which seems most unlikely and almost undesirable) I shall look back upon the Ministry with pleasure or with pain. When I drive in future years from St Pancras to the Temple shall I pass that ill-designed sky-scraper with a twitch of affection or a pang of bitter memory? I have no idea. We are all dreadfully unhappy during this war – and anxious and confused . . . what will be my feelings about the Ministry? Will they be of the same texture of respect and affection which I feel for Balliol or the Foreign Office? Or will they be a compound of shame and sorrow such as I feel for Action or the Evening Standard? Somewhere between the two.[157]

Nicolson's hint at a sense of remorse for being involved in activities inimical to his true values was echoed by his former chief. 'I believe the truth of the matter to be', wrote Duff Cooper after the war, 'that there is no place in the British scheme of government for a Ministry of Information.'[158] Michael Balfour, too, has suggested that the successful creation of a centralised propaganda bureau cannot be achieved in a democracy, since there are too many different sources of authority and power, too many freely expressed points of view.[159] But this is to confuse the early, if unspoken, notion of the Ministry of Information as the British equivalent of Goebbels's propaganda machine with the role it eventually found – the agent of liaison between the public, Whitehall and Westminster.

In addition to hastening irreversible changes in British political and social life, for example in social welfare policies and the Labour Party's acceptability as an alternative government, the Second World War marked a change in the relationship between governors and governed. The Ministry of Information's responsibility for civilian morale made it an instrument of that transition. This may be seen in microcosm in the Ministry itself. The higher officers, because of their class blinkers, tended at first to look upon the mass of the population as beings to be hectored, cajoled and placated, infirm of purpose and likely to turn defeatist while their masters were resolved to stand firm against Nazism. As the war progressed, the same officers came to see that explanation and honesty were far more effective devices in the maintenance of morale and in furtherance of the war effort than were campaigns which insulted the intelligence and courage of the meanest citizen. Indeed, there was a sense in which the Ministry's internal discussions and statements represented a celebration of the common man. The permeation of this attitude, the almost pedantic insistence by the Ministry on the intelligence and fortitude of the public, persuaded government that victory hinged upon a frank and openly acknowledged partnership between government and the people.

Notes
Bibliography
Index

Notes

INTRODUCTION

1 Constantine Fitzgibbon, *The Blitz* (London, 1959).
   T. H. O'Brien, *Civil Defence* (London, 1955).
   Angus Calder, *The People's War* (London, 1971).
   Richard Titmuss, *Problems of Social Policy* (London, 1950).
   Tom Harrisson, *Living Through the Blitz* (London, 1976).
2 Unsigned memorandum to Secretary of State for Air, April 1941, AIR 2/5325.
3 Hans Speier, 'Morale and Propaganda' in Daniel Lerner (ed.), *Propaganda in War and Crisis* (New York, 1951), p. 5.
4 Lord Perth, Sir Findlater Stewart, Sir Kenneth Lee, Frank Pick, Sir Walter Monckton, Cyril Radcliffe.
5 Francis Williams, *Press, Parliament and People* (London, 1946), p. 10.
6 Beverley Baxter, *Men, Martyrs and Mountebanks* (London, 1940), p. 180.
   Norman Riley, *999 And All That* (London, 1940), pp. 12, 17, 30, 61–4, 159–60.
7 Lord Hood to author, 19 June 1976.
8 House of Commons Debates, 5 August 1943, vol. 391, col. 2587.
9 Sir Charles Webster and Noble Frankland, *The Strategic Air Offensive Against Germany, Vol. I* (London, 1961), p. 297.
10 Tom Harrisson to author, 10 October 1975.
11 J. T. MacCurdy, *The Structure of Morale* (Cambridge, 1943), p. 141.
12 R. N. Sanford and H. S. Conrad, 'Some Personality Correlates of Morale', *Journal of Abnormal and Social Psychology*, Vol. 38, 1943.
13 Irvin L. Child, 'Morale: A Bibliographical Review', *Psychological Review*, Vol. 38, 1941.
14 G. W. Allport, 'Psychological Service for Civilian Morale', *Journal of Consulting Psychology*, Vol. 5, 1941.
15 F. C. Bartlett, *Political Propaganda* (Cambridge, 1942), p. 110.
16 Ernst Kris and Nathan Leites, 'Trends in Twentieth Century Propaganda' in Lerner, op. cit., p. 40.
17 T. T. Paterson, *Morale in War and Work* (London, 1955), p. 99.
18 Jacques Ellul, *Propaganda* (New York, 1968), p. 25.
19 'Home Morale and Public Opinion', 1 October 1941, INF 1/292.
20 'The Assessment of Air-Raid Morale from the Local Press, Home Intelligence, Social Survey and Damage Reports', 24 June 1943, HO 199/456.
21 P. E. Vernon, 'A Study of War Attitudes', *British Journal of Medical Psychology*, Vol. XIX, 1942.
22 Fletcher McCord, 'A Blueprint for Total Morale', *Character and Personality*, Vol. XI, 1942–3.
23 Ernst K. Bramsted, *Goebbels and National Socialist Propaganda* (Michigan, 1965), p. 276.
24 Lord Clark to Tom Harrisson, 3 August 1973.

CHAPTER 1

1 Members of the sub-committee: John Colville MP, Parliamentary Under-Secretary of State for Scotland and Minister of Information Designate; Sir Warren Fisher, Secretary to the Treasury; Sir Russell Scott, Permanent Under-Secretary, Home Office; Sir Robert Vansittart, Permanent Under-Secretary, Foreign Office; Sir Edward Harding, Permanent Under-Secretary, Dominions Office; Lt-General J. G. Dill, Director of Military Operations and Intelligence; Rear Admiral J. A. G. Troup, Director of Naval Intelligence; Air Vice-Marshal C. L. Courtney, Deputy Chief of the Air Staff; Colonel Sir Donald Banks, Director General, Post Office; Sir John Reith, Director General, BBC.
2 Report of a sub-committee on plans for the establishment of a Ministry of Information, 27 July 1936, CAB 4/23.
3 Ibid.
4 See Beaverbrook Papers, House of Lords Library.
5 Sir Stephen Tallents to Sir Warren Fisher, 21 December 1938, Tallents Papers.
6 CID minutes, 30 July 1936, CAB 2/6.
7 D. B. Woodburn to G. C. North, 9 April 1938, INF 4/1A.
8 H. V. Rhodes to Tallents, 12 July 1938, INF 4/1A.
9 R. Kenney to H. V. Rhodes, 26 August 1938, INF 4/1A.
10 Quoted in W. P. Hildred to Tallents, 8 February 1938, INF 1/1.
11 Ibid.
12 Appendix to first annual report of CID sub-committee to prepare plans for a Ministry of Information, 4 May 1938, CAB 4/27.
13 Tallents to Lord Macmillan, 24 November 1938, Tallents Papers.
14 House of Commons Debates, 28 July 1939, vol. 350, col. 1837.
15 Draft progress report, January 1938, INF 1/1.
16 Memorandum by Tallents, 31 October 1938, INF 1/17.
17 Lord Stanhope to Tallents, 6 October 1938, Tallents Papers.
18 Tallents to Sir James Rae, 21 December 1938; Tallents to Sir Warren Fisher, 21 December 1938; Sir James Rae to Tallents, 2 January 1939; Tallents to Lord Reith, 6 October 1947: Tallents Papers.
19 Lord Reith to Tallents, 8 December 1947, Tallents Papers.
20 *The Times*, 9 September 1939.
21 J. C. W. Reith, *Into the Wind* (London, 1949), p. 341.
22 Ibid., p. 342.
23 Alfred Duff Cooper, *Old Men Forget* (London, 1957), p. 285.
24 House of Commons Debates, 28 July 1939, vol. 350, col. 1832.
25 Viscount Templewood, *Nine Troubled Years* (London, 1954), pp. 420–1.
26 Reith, op. cit., p. 353.
27 Memorandum by Stephen King-Hall, September 1938, INF 1/712; and K-H Newsletter, 5 May 1939.
28 H. V. Rhodes to Tallents, 3 September 1938, INF 1/709.
29 Appendix to report of Home Publicity Sub-Committee, 27 September 1938, INF 1/713.
30 Home Publicity Sub-Committee report, 13 September 1938, INF 1/713.
31 Home Publicity Sub-Committee report, 27 September 1938, INF 1/713.
32 Ibid.
33 A. P. Waterfield to Sir James Rae and Sir Warren Fisher, 20 February 1939, INF 1/20.
34 Bartlett, op. cit., vii.
35 Memorandum by Rohan Butler, 12 April 1939, INF 1/727.
36 Memorandum by H. V. Rhodes, 16 November 1938, INF 1/727.

37 Home Publicity Enquiry paper, 31 July 1939, INF 1/722.
38 Home Publicity Enquiry paper, 9 May 1939, INF 1/723.
39 Memorandum by H. V. Rhodes, 16 November 1938, INF 1/727.
40 Memorandum by Rohan Butler, 12 April 1939, INF 1/727.
41 Minutes of Home Publicity Enquiry, 11 May 1939, INF 1/300.
42 Memorandum by E. M. Nicholson, 12 May 1939, INF 1/723.
43 Memorandum by Rohan Butler, 12 April 1939, INF 1/727.
44 Memorandum by H. V. Rhodes, 16 November 1938, INF 1/727.
45 Memorandum by Ivison Macadam, 18 March 1939, INF 1/711.
46 Collecting Division minutes, 27 March 1939, INF 1/331.
47 MoI to Treasury, 10 June 1939, INF 1/329.
48 Home Publicity Enquiry minutes, 20 March 1939, INF 1/711.
49 John Beresford to A. P. Waterfield, July 1939, INF 1/329.
50 Beresford to A. P. Waterfield, 13 July 1939, INF 1/329.
51 Beresford to A. P. Waterfield, no date, INF 1/329.
52 'Memorandum on Press Censorship in the U.K.', INF 1/75.
53 Defence Notices, INF 1/181.
54 Beresford to Tallents, 22 October 1938, INF 1/155.
55 Minutes of a meeting between the MoI and service departments, 1 March 1939, INF 1/181.
56 Draft agreement between the MoI and service ministries on news policy, March 1940, INF 1/856.
57 T. H. O'Brien, *Civil Defence* (London, 1955), pp. 18–19, 282–83.
58 R. M. Titmuss, *Problems of Social Policy* (London, 1950), pp. 19–20. There were some dissenting voices: Maurice Wright, 'Effect of War on Civilian Populations', *Lancet*, 21 January 1939; E. Mira, 'Fear', *Lancet*, 17 June 1939; E. Mira, 'Psychiatric Experience in the Spanish War', *British Medical Journal*, 17 June 1939.
59 Memorandum by King-Hall, September 1938, INF 1/712.
60 Home Publicity Enquiry minutes, 11 May 1939, INF 1/300.
61 Home Publicity Division minutes, 1 September 1939, INF 1/316.
62 Home Publicity Division minutes, 6 September 1939, INF 1/316.
63 'The Preservation of Civilian Morale', September 1939, HO 199/434.
64 Draft reply by E. T. Crutchley to MoI, 18 September 1939, HO 199/434.
65 Home Publicity Enquiry paper, May 1939, INF 1/724.
66 Ibid.
67 Home Publicity Enquiry minutes, 4 May 1939, INF 1/300.
68 Memorandum by E. M. Nicholson, 12 May 1939, INF 1/723.
69 Home Publicity Enquiry minutes, 11 May 1939, INF 1/300.
70 Waterfield to Ivison Macadam, 17 July 1939, INF 1/226. See accompanying illustration.
71 *The Times*, 23 September 1939.
72 Information supplied by Tom Harrisson.
73 Home Publicity Division minutes, 12 September 1939, INF 1/316.
74 Home Publicity Division minutes, 19 September 1939, INF 1/316.
75 David Low, *Low's Autobiography* (London, 1956), p. 323.
76 MoI internal note, September 1939, INF 1/670.
77 Waterfield to Director General, 19 September 1939, INF 1/670.
78 Home Publicity Division minutes, 4 September 1939, INF 1/316.
79 H. V. Rhodes to D. B. Woodburn, 4 September 1939, INF 1/26.
80 A. J. P. Taylor, *Beaverbrook* (London, 1972), p. 396.

CHAPTER 2

1 Home Publicity Division paper, September 1939, INF 1/302.
2 Cabinet Home Policy Committee minutes, 6 October 1939, CAB 75/1.
3 Home Intelligence (H.I.) Daily Report, 18 May 1940, INF 1/264.
4 Memorandum by Home Secretary, 20 December 1939, CAB 67/3.
5 Memorandum by Minister of Information, February 1940, INF 1/867.
6 Sir James Grigg to A. P. Waterfield, 4 September 1939, INF 1/852.
7 G. P. Thomson, *Blue Pencil Admiral* (London, 1947), pp. 32–3.
8 War Cabinet Conclusions, 6 September 1939, CAB 65/1.
9 Note of a discussion between MoI and Admiralty, 6 September 1939, INF 1/852.
10 Thomson, op. cit., p. 12.
11 Williams, op. cit., p. 24.
12 Unsigned memorandum, 18 January 1940, INF 1/529.
13 Memorandum by A. P. Ryan, 4 June 1941, INF 1/857.
14 W. N. Ewer, 'The Ministry of Information', *Political Quarterly*, vol. XII, 1941.
15 G. P. Thomson to Director General, 10 September 1939, INF 1/852.
16 War Cabinet Conclusions, 12 September 1939, CAB 65/1; Riley, op. cit., pp. 68–72; Thomson, op. cit., pp. 21–4; Williams, op cit., pp. 3–4.
17 House of Commons Debates, 13 September 1939, vol. 351, col. 667.
18 Information supplied by Lord Radcliffe.
19 House of Commons Debates, 26 September 1939, vol. 351, col. 1209.
20 Nigel Nicolson (ed.), *Harold Nicolson Diaries and Letters 1939–45* (London, 1970), p. 27.
21 Riley, op. cit., p. 17.
22 *The Observer,* 15 October 1939.
23 *New Statesman and Nation*, 11 May 1940.
24 Interview with Malcolm Barnes, 4 November 1974.
25 R. A. Bevan to Director General, 24 May 1940, INF 1/33. Outside the Ministry, Julian Huxley deplored 'the fact that the [MoI] were not making any use of scientists or scientific method in their propaganda, either at home or abroad'. Julian Huxley, *Memories* (London, 1970), p. 255.
26 House of Lords Debates, 26 September 1939, vol. 114, col. 1129.
27 Lord Macmillan, *A Man of Law's Tale* (London, 1953), p. 166.
28 War Cabinet Conclusions, 16 September 1939, CAB 65/1.
29 Quentin Reynolds, *Only the Stars Are Neutral* (Sydney, 1942), p. 183.
30 War Cabinet Conclusions, 16 September 1939, CAB 65/1.
31 Thomson, op. cit., p. 6.
32 Ibid, p. 2.
33 Riley, op. cit., p. 61.
34 Nicolson (ed.), op. cit., p. 27.
35 Memorandum by Minister of Information, 18 September 1939, INF 1/852.
36 War Cabinet Conclusions, 19 September 1939, CAB 65/1.
37 House of Commons Debates, 11 October 1939, vol. 352, col. 388.
38 House of Commons Debates, 11 October 1939, vol. 352, col. 434.
39 House of Commons Debates, 21 September 1939, vol. 351, col. 1061.
40 Andrew Boyle, *Poor, Dear Brendan* (London, 1974), p. 265.
41 Ewer, op. cit.
42 *The Times,* 27 September 1939.
43 House of Commons Debates, 3 October 1939, vol. 351, cols 1860–61.
44 MoI Press Room Committee to Prime Minister, 28 September 1939, INF 1/852. See also letter to *The Times* from Ernest E. Hunter, Chairman MoI Press Committee, 5 October 1939.

Notes

45 David Dilks (ed.), *The Diaries of Sir Alexander Cadogan 1938–45* (London, 1971), p. 225.
46 Taylor, *Beaverbrook*, p. 399.
47 Lord Camrose to Minister of Information, 21 October 1939, INF 1/8.
48 Riley, op. cit., p. 168.
49 *Daily Express*, 20 October 1939.
50 Monckton to Home Office, 10 October 1939, INF 1/495.
51 Memorandum by Monckton, 14 October 1939, INF 1/852.
52 Ibid.
53 Monckton to Treasury, 21 December 1939, INF 1/854.
54 Monckton to Sir John Anderson, 17 November 1939, INF 1/854.
55 Ibid.
56 Memorandum by Radcliffe, 9 November 1939, INF 1/855.
57 Monckton to Treasury, 21 December 1939, INF 1/854.
58 Lord Birkenhead, *Walter Monckton* (London, 1969), pp. 176–8.
59 Monckton to Sir Horace Wilson, 3 November; and to Sir John Anderson, 17, 19 and 26 November 1939, INF 1/854.
60 Monckton to Sir John Anderson, 19 November 1939, INF 1/854.
61 Reith to Sir Horace Wilson, 31 January 1940, INF 1/856.
62 Monckton to Reith, 1 February 1940, INF 1/856.
63 *The Times*, 25 April 1940.
64 House of Commons Debates, 24 April 1940, vol. 360, col. 186.
65 Brendan Bracken to Bernard Sendall, November 1943, INF 1/941.
66 Reith to Tallents, 8 December 1947, Tallents Papers.
67 Reith, op. cit., p. 383; Andrew Boyle, *Only the Wind Will Listen* (London, 1972), pp. 305–6.
68 Memorandum by Minister of Information, December 1940, INF 1/848.
69 'Memorandum on General Policy', no date, INF 1/396.
70 John Hilton to A. P. Waterfield, 2 October 1939, INF 1/295.
71 Hoare to party agents, 1 September 1939, INF 1/295.
72 John Hilton to Waterfield, 4 September 1939, INF 1/295.
73 'Notes for Speakers', 17 September 1939, INF 1/294.
74 Home Publicity Division memorandum, 13 September 1939, INF 1/295.
75 Cabinet Home Policy Committee minutes, 15 November 1939, CAB 75/1.
76 D. B. Woodburn to Hilton, 28 November 1939, INF 1/294.
77 Co-ordinating Committee minutes, 14 September 1939, INF 1/867.
78 Information supplied by Bernard Sendall.
79 Tom Hopkinson to author, 21 August 1976.
80 Co-ordinating Committee minutes, 28 September 1939, INF 1/867.
81 Co-ordinating Committee minutes, 9 and 20 October 1939, INF 1/867.
82 See INF 1/227.
83 Memorandum by W. G. Vaughan, 26 June 1939, INF 1/721.
84 *Picture Post* to Ivison Macadam, 29 November 1939, INF 1/234.
85 MoI to *Picture Post*, 18 April 1940, INF 1/234.
86 Unsigned memorandum, 2 May 1940, INF 1/234.
87 Draft progress reports, 3–10 and 10–17 October 1939, INF 1/6.
88 *New Statesman and Nation*, 16 December 1939.
89 John Hilton to Waterfield, 7 November 1939, INF 1/47.
90 Waterfield to Director General, 13 November 1939, INF 1/47.
91 Minute by Lord Macmillan, 30 September 1939, INF 1/261.
92 Lord Macmillan to Deputy Director General, 11 October 1939, INF 1/261.
93 Ifor Evans to Waterfield, 9 November 1939, INF 1/47.
94 Memorandum by Mary Adams, 26 January 1940, INF 1/848.
95 H.I. assessment of Postal Censorship reports, February 1941, INF 1/472.
96 Mary Adams to Ivison Macadam, 6 March 1940, INF 1/262.

97 Memorandum by Richard Crossman, 26 October 1939, INF 1/261.
98 Mary Adams to Waterfield, 12 March 1940, INF 1/262.
99 Tom Harrisson to author, 19 June 1973.
100 Memorandum by Mary Adams, 26 January 1940, INF 1/848.
101 For a debate between Henry Durant of the British Institute of Public Opinion and Tom Harrisson on the relative merits of 'quantitative' and 'qualitative' methods, see *Nature*, 7 May 1942, Vol. 149.
102 Memorandum by Frederick Brown, 2 May 1940, INF 1/263.
103 H.I. memorandum, 12 May 1940, INF 1/263.
104 Memorandum by Frederick Brown, 2 May 1940, INF 1/263.
105 H.I. memorandum, 12 May 1940, INF 1/263.
106 Memorandum by John Hilton, 20 October 1939, INF 1/867.
107 Ifor Evans to Director General, 9 November 1939, INF 1/47.
108 Policy Committee minutes, 9 February 1940, INF 1/848.
109 Listener Research report, 8 March 1940, INF 1/61.
110 Memorandum by Minister of Information, no date, INF 1/867.
111 Note on anti-war movements, 22 February, 1940, Mass-Observation Archive.
112 Memorandum by Minister of Information, 27 April 1940, CAB 75/4.
113 Memorandum by Minister of Information, 30 March 1940, CAB 75/4.
114 Memorandum by Minister of Information, 27 April 1940, CAB 75/4.
115 Memorandum by Minister of Information, 29 April 1940, CAB 75/4.
116 Ministry of Home Security to Regional Commissioners, 27 July 1940, CAB 98/18.
117 'Confidential Notes on Anti-Pacifist Arguments', March 1940, INF 1/319.
118 Banner to Ivison Macadam, 21 March 1940, INF 1/319.
119 Banner to Regional Administration Division, 27 & 28 March 1940, INF 1/319.
120 D. B. Briggs to Banner, 30 March 1940, INF 1/319.
121 J. R. Scott, RIO North Western Region, to D. B. Briggs, 16 February 1940, INF 1/319.
122 RIO Southern Region to Mary Adams, 13 March 1940, INF 1/319.
123 H. V. Rhodes to Ivison Macadam, 9 March 1940, INF 1/319.
124 H.I. Weekly Report, 11–18 December 1940, INF 1/292.
125 Home Morale Emergency Committee report, 22 May 1940, INF 1/250.
126 H.I. Weekly Report, 18–24 December 1940, INF 1/292.
127 D. B. Briggs to H. V. Rhodes, 6 October 1940, INF 1/319.
128 Memorandum by Minister of Information, no date, INF 1/867.
129 'A Summary of Opinion on the Russian-Finnish Peace', no date, Imperial War Museum.
130 H.I. Daily Report, 18 May 1940, INF 1/264.
131 Reith, op. cit., pp. 374–7.
132 Director General, Sir Walter Monckton and Ivone Kirkpatrick to Minister, 29 April 1940, INF 1/989.
133 H.I. Daily Report, 18 May 1940, INF 1/264.

CHAPTER 3

1 Nicolson Diary, 11 August 1940, Balliol College.
2 H.I. Daily Report, 18 May 1940, INF 1/264.
3 Policy Committee minutes, 22 May 1940, INF 1/848.
4 Francis Williams, *Nothing So Strange* (London, 1970), pp. 164–5.
5 Home Morale Emergency Committee report, 4 June 1940, INF 1/250.
6 H.I. Daily Report, 4 June 1940, INF 1/264.
7 Home Morale Emergency Committee report, 4 June 1940, INF 1/250.

8 Planning Committee minutes, 17 June 1940, INF 1/249.
9 H. I. Daily Report, 17 August 1940, INF 1/264.
10 H. I. Daily Reports, 1, 2, 3, 22 and 30 July, 7, 16, 21, 23 and 29 August 1940, INF 1/264.
11 Sonia Orwell and Ian Angus (eds), *The Collected Essays, Journalism and Letters of George Orwell, Vol. 2* (London, 1970), p. 405.
12 Policy Committee minutes, 1 July 1940, INF 1/849.
13 Tom Clarke to Deputy Director General, 10 September 1939, INF 1/185.
14 Memorandum by S/S for Air and Minister of Home Security, 7 February 1940, CAB 67/4.
15 Internal note, June 1940, INF 1/185.
16 War Cabinet Conclusions, 3 July 1940, CAB 65/8.
17 Memorandum by Minister of Information, 9 July 1940, CAB 67/7.
18 H.I. Daily Report, 20 May 1940, INF 1/264.
19 War Cabinet Conclusions, 4 June 1940, CAB 65/7.
20 Draft memorandum, no date, INF 1/878.
21 Memorandum by Minister of Information, 3 June 1940, CAB 66/10.
22 Draft memorandum, no date, INF 1/878.
23 Nigel Nicolson (ed.), op. cit., p. 89.
24 War Cabinet Conclusions, 13 June 1940, CAB 65/7; *The Other Half* (London, 1978), p. 19.
25 *If the Invader Comes.*
26 Minister of Information to Home Secretary, 6 July 1940, INF 1/878.
27 See editorial in *Nature*, Vol. 146, 20 July 1940: it was urged that civilians be given 'a more visible, more local and more definite role in their support' of the military.
28 Nicolson Diary, 5 July 1940.
29 Planning Committee minutes, 1 July 1940, INF 1/249.
30 Note of meeting between MoI, War Office, Ministry of Home Security, Home Defence Executive, 1 July 1940, INF 1/250.
31 Mary Adams to Sir Kenneth Clark, 17 July 1940, INF 1/258.
32 Duff Cooper to Minister of Home Security, 6 July 1940, INF 1/878.
33 Memorandum by S/S for War, 8 July 1940, CAB 67/7.
34 *Stay Put.*
35 H.I. Daily Report, 18 May 1940, INF 1/264.
36 H.I. Daily Report, 20 June 1940, INF 1/264.
37 H.I. Daily Report, 24 June 1940, INF 1/264.
38 Policy Committee minutes, 27 May 1940, INF 1/848.
39 Policy Committee minutes, 29 May 1940, INF 1/848.
40 Draft Cabinet memorandum, no date, INF 1/250.
41 Note of meeting between MoI, Ministry of Supply, Ministry Home Security and Home Defence Executive, 20 June 1940, INF 1/250.
42 H. I. Daily Report, 17 June 1940, INF 1/264.
43 Planning Committee minutes, 17 June 1940, INF 1/249.
44 H. I. Daily Report, 18 June 1940, INF 1/264.
45 Planning Committee minutes, 17 June 1940, INF 1/249.
46 *Directive Letter to the Clergy and Others,* 5 July 1940, Imperial War Museum.
47 H.I. Daily Report, 30 May 1940, INF 1/264.
48 H.I. Daily Report, 24 June 1940, INF 1/264.
49 Nicolson Diary, 11 January 1940.
50 H.I. Daily Report, 18 May 1940, INF 1/264.
51 H.I. Daily Report, 15 June 1940, INF 1/264.
52 D. Cowan to Lord Davidson, 18 May 1940, INF 1/533.
53 Home Morale Emergency Committee report, 4 June 1940, INF 1/250.
54 H.I. Daily Report, 24 May 1940, INF 1/264.
55 Nicolson Diary, 27 May 1940.

56 Home Morale Emergency Committee report, 4 June 1940, INF 1/250.
57 H.I. Daily Report, 18 June 1940, INF 1/264.
58 Quoted in Angus Calder, *The People's War* (London, 1971), p. 130.
59 Nicolson Diary, 11 August 1940.
60 H.I. Daily Report, 5 June 1940, INF 1/264.
61 Policy Committee minutes, 23 May 1940, INF 1/848.
62 Planning Committee minutes, 4 July 1940, INF 1/249.
63 *The Fifth Column*, June 1940.
64 *The Observer*, 23 June 1940.
65 Home Morale Emergency Committee report, 4 June 1940, INF 1/250.
66 Annex to War Cabinet Conclusions, 3 July 1940, CAB 65/8.
67 *The Observer*, 23 June 1940.
68 Planning Committee paper, 17 June 1940, INF 1/251.
69 *Directive Letter to the Clergy and Others*, 21 June 1940.
70 H.I. Daily Report, 9 July 1940, INF 1/264.
71 H.I. Daily Report, 23 July 1940, INF 1/264.
72 H.I. Daily Report, 28 August 1940, INF 1/264.
73 H.I. Daily Report, 16 August 1940, INF 1/264.
74 H.I. Daily Report, 20 May 1940, INF 1/264.
75 H.I. Daily Report, 22 May 1940, INF 1/264.
76 H.I. Daily Report, 6 July 1940, INF 1/264.
77 Home Morale Emergency Committee report, 22 May 1940, INF 1/257
78 Charles Wilson to R. P. Stevens, 17 June 1940, INF 1/257.
79 War Cabinet Conclusions, 1 July 1940, CAB 65/8.
80 H.I. Daily Report, 24 May 1940, INF 1/264.
81 David White, 'The Power of Rumour', *New Society*, 17 October 1974; and
   G. W. Allport and L. Postman, *The Psychology of Rumour* (New York, 1965),
   pp. 2–3.
82 H.I. Daily Report, 14 August 1940, INF 1/264.
83 H.I. Daily Report, 26 July, 1940.
84 H.I. Daily Report, 7 August, 1940.
85 H.I. Daily Report, 20 August, 1940.
86 Nicolson Diary, 27 May 1940.
87 Note on rumour by Mass-Observation, no date, INF 1/251.
88 H.I. Daily Report, 22 May 1940, INF 1/264.
89 H.I. Daily Report, 27 May 1940, INF 1/264.
90 Home Morale Emergency Committee report, 4 June 1940, INF 1/250.
91 H.I. Daily Report, 24 May 1940, INF 1/264.
92 Note of rumour by Mass-Observation, no date, INF 1/251.
93 H.I. Daily Report, 5 June 1940, INF 1/264.
94 Home Morale Emergency Committee report, 4 June 1940, INF 1/250.
95 Charles Wilson to Sir Kenneth Clark, 1 July 1940, INF 1/257.
96 Quoted in Norman Longmate, *How We Lived Then* (London, 1973) p. 93.
97 Planning Committee minutes, 8 July 1940, INF 1/249.
98 'Action to Counter Rumours', 21 January 1941, INF 1/251.
99 Note on rumour by Mass-Observation, no date, INF 1/251.
100 Policy Committee minutes, 5 September 1940, INF 1/849.
101 Policy Committee minutes, 5 July 1940, INF 1/849.
102 Nicolson Diary, 20 July 1940.
103 House of Commons Debates, 1 August 1940, vol. 363, col. 1553.
104 Policy Committee minutes, 8 July 1940, INF 1/849.
105 Ibid.
106 Fougasse, *A School of Porpoises* (London, 1946), p. 38.
107 H.I. Daily Report, 16 July 1940, INF 1/264.
108 H.I. Daily Report, 20 July 1940, INF 1/264.
109 H.I. Daily Report, 16 July 1940, INF 1/264.

110 H.I. Daily Report, 22 July 1940, INF 1/264.
111 Planning Committee minutes, 15 July 1940, INF 1/249.
112 Nicolson Diary, 21 July 1940.
113 *Directive Letter to the Clergy and Others*, 19 July 1940.
114 Policy Committee minutes, 23 July 1940, INF 1/249.
115 Policy Committee minutes, 5 August 1940, INF 1/849.
116 *Daily Herald*, 25 July 1940.
117 *Daily Herald*, 26 July 1940.
118 Nicolson Diary, 28 July 1940.
119 Deputy Secretary to Director General, 21 May 1940, INF 1/273.
120 Home Intelligence memorandum, 1 March 1941, INF 1/263.
121 For a description and analysis of the Survey's methods and subjects of enquiry see Kathleen Box and Geoffrey Thomas, 'The Wartime Social Survey', *Journal of the Royal Statistical Society*, Parts III–IV, 1944.
122 House of Commons Debates, 31 July 1940, vol. 363, cols 1215–16.
123 House of Commons Debates, 1 August 1940, vol. 363, cols 1548–55.
124 House of Commons Debates, 1 August 1940, vol. 363, cols 1513–19.
125 Nicolson Diary, 1 August 1940.
126 Nicolson Diary, 3 August 1940.
127 Nicolson Diary, 4 August 1940.
128 See Tom Harrisson, 'What is Public Opinion?', *Political Quarterly*, Vol. XI, 1940.
129 H.I. Daily Report, 5 August 1940, INF 1/264.
130 Report of Select Committee on National Expenditure on the Wartime Social Survey, 17 February 1942.
131 Mary Adams to Sir Wyndham Deedes, 29 July 1940, INF 1/697.
132 Home Intelligence memorandum, 15 August 1940, INF 1/263.
133 Memorandum by Winifred Holmes, August 1940, INF 1/697.
134 Memorandum by H. V. Rhodes, 17 August 1940, INF 1/79.
135 Nicolson Diary, 18 August 1940.
136 Memorandum by Director General, 19 September 1940, INF 1/273.
137 Home Intelligence note, 1 March 1941, INF 1/263.
138 Policy Committee minutes, 31 May 1940, INF 1/848.
139 Barrington-Ward to Ministry of Information, 30 May 1940, INF 1/848.
140 Policy Committee minutes, 31 May 1940, INF 1/848.
141 War Cabinet Conclusions, 3 June 1940, CAB 65/7.
142 Chief of Naval Staff to P.M., 9 June 1940, PREM 4/66/2.
143 Memorandum by Minister of Information, 11 June 1940, CAB 67/6.
144 Minister of Information to P.M., 2 July 1940, PREM 4/99/4A.
145 Minister of Information to Lord President of the Council, 17 July 1940, PREM 4/66/2.
146 War Cabinet Conclusions, 18 July 1940, CAB 65/8.
147 Memorandum by Minister of Information, 11 June 1940, CAB 67/6.
148 Duff Cooper, op. cit., p. 286.
149 Director General's Order No. 32, 22 December 1939, INF 1/190.
150 Sir Kenneth Clark to Sir Walter Monckton, 15 June 1940, INF 1/256.
151 Sir Walter Monckton to Sir Horace Wilson, 3 November 1939, INF 1/854.
152 Ministry of Information to editors, 5 May 1941, HO 199/381.
153 Thomson, op. cit., p. 26 and p. 40.
154 Memo by Brebner, no date, INF 1/64.
155 'As I Please', 7 July 1944 in Orwell and Angus, Vol. 3, op. cit., pp. 211–12.
156 Home Morale Emergency Committee Report, 4 June 1940, INF 1/250.
157 H.I. Daily Report, 18 June 1940, INF 1/264.
158 Phyllis Ord to E. C. Cobb MP, 30 June 1940, INF 1/252.
159 H.I. Daily Report, 20 June 1940, INF 1/264.
160 Planning Committee paper, 'Home Morale Campaign', 21 June 1940, INF 1/849.

161 Home Morale Emergency Committee report, 4 June 1940, INF 1/250.
162 Macadam to Clark, 22 July 1940, INF 1/250.
163 Sir Kenneth Clark to Ivison Macadam, 2 August 1940, INF 1/250.
164 H.I. Daily Report, 16 July 1940, INF 1/264.
165 War Cabinet Conclusions, 1 July 1940, CAB 65/8.
166 H.I. Daily Report, 16 July 1940, INF 1/264.
167 H.I. Daily Report, 3 August 1940, INF 1/264.
168 H.I. Daily Report, 18 May 1940, INF 1/264.
169 H.I. Daily Report, 25 May 1940, INF 1/264.
170 H.I. Daily Report, 20 July 1940, INF 1/264.
171 H.I. Daily Reports, 20 and 25 May, 15 June, 25 July 1940, INF 1/264.
172 H.I. Daily Report, 2 July 1940, INF 1/264.
173 Bartlett, op. cit., p. 143.
174 Robert Rhodes James, *Memoirs of a Conservative*: *J. C. C. Davidson's Memoirs and Papers* (London, 1969), p. 425.
175 Nicolson Diary, 27 May 1940.
176 Nicolson Diary, 8 June 1940.
177 Nicolson Diary, 21 October 1940.
178 Policy Committee minutes, 14 June 1940, INF 1/849.
179 Nicolson Diary, 3 July 1940.
180 A. P. Waterfield to Deputy Director General, 4 May 1940, INF 1/37.
181 Nicolson Diary, 21 January 1941.
182 Draft of paper given by Michael Balfour to Imperial War Museum conference on 'Film Propaganda and the Historian', July 1973.
183 Ibid.
184 H.I. Daily Report, 15 June 1940, INF 1/264.
185 Nicolson Diary, 11 November 1940.
186 Nicolson Diary, 20 October 1940.
187 Planning Committee minutes, 10 July 1940, INF 1/249.
188 Memorandum by Sir Kenneth Clark, 30 August 1940, INF 1/251.
189 *Directive Letter to the Clergy and Others*, 21 June 1940.
190 Harry Stack Sullivan, 'Psychiatric Aspects of Morale' in A. H. Stanton and S. E. Perry (eds), *Personality and Political Crisis* (New York, 1951).
191 MacCurdy, op. cit., p. 142.
192 Daniel Lerner, 'Effective Propaganda' in Lerner (ed.), op. cit.
193 Home Morale Emergency Committee report, 4 June 1940, INF 1/250.
194 Policy Committee minutes, 18 June 1940, INF 1/849.
195 Nicolson Diary, 3 July 1940.
196 Policy Committee minutes, 8 July 1940, INF 1/849.
197 Policy Committee minutes, 18 July 1940, INF 1/849.
198 Nicolson Diary, 16 July 1940.
199 Policy Committee minutes, 17 July 1940, INF 1/849.
200 H.I. Daily Report, 20 May 1940, INF 1/264.
201 H.I. Daily Report, 6 August 1940, INF 1/264.
202 H.I. Daily Report, 10 August 1940, INF 1/264.
203 H.I. Daily Report, 5 September 1940, INF 1/264.
204 Ibid.
205 H.I. Daily Report, 20 July 1940, INF 1/264.
206 H.I. Daily Report, 22 July 1940, INF 1/264.
207 Memorandum by Minister of Information, 20 July 1940, CAB 66/10.
208 War Cabinet Conclusions, 26 July 1940, CAB 65/8.
209 Minister of Information to Foreign Secretary, 29 July 1940, INF 1/862.
210 Minister of Information to Sir Alexander Cadogan, 27 July 1940, INF 1/862.
211 Nicolson Diary, 2 September 1940.
212 Minister of Information to Sir Alexander Cadogan, 27 July 1940, INF 1/862.

213 Lord Halifax to Duff Cooper, 30 July 1940, INF 1/862.
214 William Armstrong (ed.), *With Malice Towards None: A War Diary by Cecil H. King* (London, 1970), p. 65.
215 War Cabinet Conclusions, 23 August 1940, CAB 65/8.
216 Ibid.
217 Nicolson Diary, 4 November 1940.
218 Memorandum by War Aims Committee, no date but evidence suggests early September 1940, INF 1/863.

CHAPTER 4

1 H.I. Daily Reports, 18 May–10 August 1940, INF 1/264.
2 Memorandum by Minister of Home Security, 7 September 1940, CAB 68/7.
3 Dr Felix Brown, 'Civilian Psychiatric Air-Raid Casualties', *Lancet*, 31 May 1941.
4 P. E. Vernon, 'Psychological Effects of Air Raids', *Journal of Abnormal and Social Psychology*, 1941, Vol. 36. See also R. J. Bartlett, 'The Civilian Population under Bombardment', *Nature*, 7 June 1941, Vol. 147.
5 H.I. Weekly Report, 14–21 October 1940, INF 1/292.
6 H.I. Weekly Report, 28 October–4 November 1940, INF 1/292.
7 Note by Ministry of Home Security Intelligence Branch, 19 September 1940, HO 199/316.
8 H.I. Daily Report, 9 September 1940, INF 1/264.
9 Nicolson Diary, 17 and 21 September 1940.
10 Nicolson Diary, 1 October 1940.
11 H.I. Weekly Report, 21–28 October 1940, INF 1/292.
12 Nicolson Diary, 21 October 1940.
13 H.I. Weekly Report, 7–14 October 1940, INF 1/292.
14 H.I. Weekly Report, 9 September 1940, INF 1/264.
15 Ibid.
16 H.I. Daily Report, 20 September 1940, INF 1/264.
17 H.I. Daily Report, 21 September 1940, INF 1/264.
18 H.I. Daily Report, 19 and 20 September 1940, INF 1/264.
19 H.I. Weekly Report, 30 September–9 October 1940, INF 1/292.
20 H.I. Daily Report, 21 September 1940, INF 1/264.
21 H.I. Weekly Report, 7–14 September 1940, INF 1/292.
22 H.I. Weekly Report, 4–11 November 1940, INF 1/292.
23 Memorandum by Minister of Home Security, 5 May 1941, CAB 67/9.
24 H.I. Daily Report, 12 September 1940, INF 1/264.
25 War Cabinet Conclusions, 15 October 1940, CAB 65/9.
26 H.I. Weekly Report, 18–25 November 1940, INF 1/292.
27 H.I. Weekly Report, 14–21 October 1940, INF 1/292.
28 H.I. Daily Reports, 17 and 19 September 1940, INF 1/264.
29 H.I. Daily Report, 10 September 1940, INF 1/264.
30 H.I. Daily Report, 19 September 1940, INF 1/264.
31 H.I. Daily Report, 9 September 1940, INF 1/264; H.I. Weekly Reports, 30 September–7 October, 21–28 October 1940, INF 1/292.
32 H.I. Weekly Report, 14–21 October 1940, INF 1/292.
33 H.I. Weekly Report, 4–11 November 1940, INF 1/292.
34 Bernard Donoghue and G. W. Jones, *Herbert Morrison: Portrait of a Politician* (London, 1973), p. 291.
35 H.I. Weekly Report, 7–14 May 1941, INF 1/292.
36 Dr R. H. Thouless, 'Psychological Effects of Air Raids', *Nature*, 16 August 1941, Vol. 148.

37 H.I. Report on Coventry, 19 November 1940, INF 1/292.
38 H.I. Weekly Report, 4–11 December 1940, INF 1/292.
39 H.I. Weekly Report, 12–29 March and 16–23 April 1941, INF 1/292.
40 H.I. Report on Portsmouth, May 1941, INF 1/292.
41 H.I. Weekly Report, 21–28 May 1941, INF 1/292.
42 Donoghue and Jones, op. cit., p. 292; Nicolson Diary, 7 May 1941.
43 H.I. Reports on Coventry, 19 November 1940, and on Plymouth, 9–16 April 1941, INF 1/292. This phenomenon was noted in all combatant nations subjected to air attacks: see I. L. Janis, *Air War and Emotional Stress* (New York, 1951), p. 89.
44 H.I. Weekly Report, 5–12 March 1941, INF 1/292.
45 H.I. Report on Hull, 28 July 1941, INF 1/292.
46 H.I. Weekly Report, 30 June–7 July 1942, INF 1/292.
47 H.I. Weekly Report, 4–11 November 1940 INF 1/292.
48 H.I. Report on Coventry, 19 November 1940, INF 1/292.
49 H.I. Weekly Report, 25 November–4 December 1940, INF 1/292.
50 H.I. Weekly Report, 16–23 April 1941, INF 1/292.
51 H.I. Daily Report, 11 September 1940, INF 1/264.
52 H.I. Weekly Report, 2–9 July 1941, INF 1/292.
53 Janis, op. cit., p. 127.
54 Titmuss, op. cit., pp. 327–8.
55 H.I. Weekly Report, 1–8 January 1941, INF 1/292.
56 H.I. Report on Portsmouth, May 1941, INF 1/292.
57 Titmuss, op. cit., pp. 307–9.
58 H.I. Weekly Report, 7–14 May 1941, INF 1/292.
59 H. I. Report on Portsmouth, May 1941, INF 1/292.
60 'Home Morale and Public Opinion', 1 October 1941, INF 1/292.
61 'The Assessment of Air-Raid Morale from the Local Press, Home Intelligence, Social Survey and Damage Reports in Britain' by Dr C. W. Emmens, 24 June 1943, HO 199/456.
62 'Home Morale and Public Opinion', 1 October 1941, INF 1/292.
63 Report on Coventry, 19 November 1940, HO 199/442.
64 United States Strategic Bombing Survey, 'Social and Psychological Factors Affecting Morale' in Lerner, op. cit., p. 355.
65 H.I. Weekly Report, 12–19 February 1941, INF 1/292.
66 Titmuss, op. cit., pp. 339–40.
67 Janis, op. cit., pp. 75–6.
68 H.I. Report on Portsmouth, May 1941, INF 1/292.
69 H.I. Weekly Report, 23–30 April 1941, INF 1/292.
70 Summary version of 'The Total Effects of Air Raids', May 1942, HO 199/453.
71 Titmuss, op. cit., pp. 341–2; Emmens's report, op. cit.
72 H.I. Report on Portsmouth, May 1941, INF 1/292.
73 See also Longmate, op. cit., p. 134.
74 Emmens' report, op. cit.
75 Janis, op. cit., p. 148.
76 H.I. Report on Merseyside, 2–9 July 1941, INF 1/292.
77 Emmens' report, op. cit.
78 'Home Morale and Public Opinion', 1 October 1941, INF 1/292.
79 See *New Statesman*, 23 January 1943: 'The notion that Germans would suddenly collapse because they were bombed, whereas British morale would be toughened by the same process, has been one of those mystical illusions which beset otherwise sane people in time of war.'
80 Air Ministry to Ministry of Home Security, 11 October 1941, HO 199/453.
81 Summary version of 'The Total Effects of Air Raids', op. cit.
82 Ibid.

83 See David Irving, *The Destruction of Dresden* (New York, 1965).
84 Webster and Frankland, op. cit., vol. 1, pp. 331 and 492; vol. 2, pp. 224, 225, 235–43; vol. 3, p. 302.
85 Planning Committee minutes, 30 December 1940, INF 1/249.
86 Unsigned minute to Sir George Gater and Minister of Home Security, 27 January 1941, HO 199/442.
87 Unsigned minute, 21 January 1941, HO 199/442.
88 Sullivan, op. cit., p. 49.
89 Note by Winifred Holmes, August 1940, INF 1/697.
90 See INF 1/285.
91 Mary Adams to RIOs, 25 February 1941, INF 1/697.
92 Policy Committee minutes, 17 October 1940, INF 1/849.
93 Policy Committee minutes, 24 October 1940, INF 1/849.
94 Planning Committee minutes, 21 April 1941, INF 1/249.
95 Planning Committee minutes, 4 December 1940, INF 1/249.
96 Planning Committee minutes, 26 December 1940, INF 1/249.
97 Mary Adams to Ivison Macadam, 28 February 1941, INF 1/174A.
98 Ivison Macadam to Radcliffe, 4 March 1941, INF 1/174A.
99 Preparation of Air Raid Commentaries, 31 March 1941, INF 1/174A.
100 INF 1/297.
101 Hubert S. Banner, *Kentish Fire* (London, no date).
102 Mass-Observation report on Coventry, 19 November 1940, HO 199/442.
103 Tom Harrisson, 'Blitzinformation', *Local Government Service*, vol. 21, no. 8, August 1941.
104 Planning Committee minutes, 9 January 1941, INF 1/249.
105 Note on the work of MoI loudspeaker vans, February 1941, INF 1/296.
106 Harrisson, 'Blitzinformation', op. cit.
107 Emmens's report, op. cit.
108 Titmuss, op. cit., p. 307.
109 Regional Administration Division to RIOs, 31 March 1941, INF 1/323.
110 Editorial in *Local Government Service,* op. cit.
111 O'Brien, op. cit., scarcely refers to the MoI. For a favourable contemporary view, see Metropoliticus, 'The Ministry of Information and Public Morale', *Political Quarterly*, vol. XIII, 1942.
112 For a detailed review of these, based on research findings, see Janis, op. cit., pp. 177–8; and Vernon, 'Psychological Effects of Air Raids', op. cit.

CHAPTER 5

1 Hans Speier, 'Morale and Propaganda' in Lerner (ed.), op. cit.
2 Joseph Geoghegan, 'Morale', *Nature*, 4 July 1942.
3 'Aims of Home Publicity', 28 September 1939, INF 1/302.
4 Diary entry, 14 March 1942, in Orwell and Angus, vol. 2, op. cit., p. 465.
5 E. H. Henderson, 'Towards a Definition of Propaganda', *Journal of Social Psychology*, August 1943.
6 Nicolson Diary, 1 April 1941.
7 Prime Minister to Minister of Information, 12 June 1940, PREM 4/83/1A.
8 Prime Minister to Resident Minister in Algiers, 4 April 1943, PREM 4/66/2.
9 Memorandum by Stephen King-Hall, 11 July 1938, INF 1/712.
10 *Why We Are Fighting Germany*, August 1939.
11 *Assurance of Victory*, September 1939.
12 *Hitler and the Working Man*, October 1939.
13 Memorandum by Minister of Information, 20 September 1939, CAB 75/2.
14 Memorandum by Minister of Information, 22 December 1939, CAB 67/3.

15 War Cabinet Conclusions, 16 January 1940, CAB 65/5.

16 Memorandum by Minister of Information, 26 January 1940, CAB 67/4.

17 War Cabinet Conclusions, 30 January 1940, CAB 65/5.

18 Memorandum by Minister of Information, 26 January 1940, CAB 67/4.

19 See Bramsted, op. cit., p. 310: 'At first the official British attitude was inclined to make a distinction between the National-Socialists and the Military in Germany on the one hand and the millions of mere subjects . . . on the other . . . It was only after the bitter and dramatic events in the summer and autumn of 1940 . . . that British propaganda took a more drastic line.'

20 Policy Committee minutes, 2 May 1940, INF 1/848.

21 Policy Committee minutes, 4 June 1940, INF 1/848.

22 'Anger Campaign', 17 June 1940, INF 1/849.

23 Memorandum by Lord Macmillan, 20 September 1939, CAB 75/2.

24 H.I. Daily Report, 11 June 1940, INF 1/264.

25 H.I. Daily Reports, 4, 5, 13 and 19 September 1940, INF 1/264.

26 Nicolson Diary, 20 July 1940.

27 Major R. F. Barbour in a discussion of morale at Shaftesbury Military Hospital on 4 February 1941, 'Morale', *Lancet,* 22 March 1940; Isidor Chein, 'The Meaning of "Morale" in Relation to Morale Building and Morale Research', *Psychological Review*, vol. 50, 1943.

28 Dr R. H. Thouless, 'Mental Attitudes in War-Time', *Nature*, 19 June 1943, vol. 151.

29 See R. Money-Kyrle, 'The Psychology of Propaganda', *British Journal of Medical Psychology*, 1943, vol. 19: 'First fear is stirred up, then hate to keep it in check; but the hate expects retaliation and thus increases fear, which has to be drowned by more hate and so on. The system needs effective hate—hate which can not be satisfied.'

30 Memorandum by Stephen King-Hall, September 1938, INF 1/712.

31 *Assurance of Victory*, September 1939; and *Hitler and the Working Man*, October 1939.

32 *What Would Happen if Hitler Won*, 1940.

33 *Directive Letter to the Clergy and Others*, 5 July 1940.

34 Planning Committee minutes, 23 June 1940, INF 1/249.

35 J. M. Keynes to Harold Nicolson, 20 November 1940, INF 1/871.

36 Nicolson Diary, 24 November 1940.

37 H.I. Weekly Report, 2–9 March 1942, INF 1/292.

38 Memorandum by Minister of Information, December 1939, INF 1/848.

39 Memorandum by Francis Williams, 21 May 1941, INF 1/251.

40 See introduction to Alan Bullock and Maurice Shock (eds), *The Liberal Tradition* (London, 1967), liv.

41 Draft War Cabinet memorandum, 17 July 1940, INF 1/862.

42 Policy Points for Regional Information Officers, 22 August 1940, INF 1/672.

43 Memorandum by Minister of Information, December 1939, INF 1/848.

44 Note on organisation of Religions Division, 6 September 1939, INF 1/38.

45 Memorandum by Kenneth MacLennan, February 1940, INF 1/396.

46 Summary of Religions Division functions, July 1940, INF 1/396.

47 Rev. Hugh Martin to R. H. Parker, 24 June 1941, INF 1/414.

48 Memorandum for meeting with church leaders, 12 September 1939, INF 1/403.

49 *The Times*, 21 December 1940.

50 *Directive Letter to the Clergy and Others*, 5 July 1940.

51 'Religious Propaganda at Home', 1941, INF 1/251.

52 *Hitler's War on the Catholic Church*, 1942.

53 *Personality in War Time*, October 1940.

54 *Freedom and the Individual*, October 1940.

55 Memorandum by Francis Williams, 21 May 1941, INF 1/251.

56 *Eve in Overalls*, no date.
57 *The Battle for Civilisation*, 1942.
58 *Freedom and the Individual*, October 1940.
59 *Faith in the Fight*, no date.
60 Report of meeting of British Psychological Society, 13 March 1940, *Lancet*, 23 March 1940.
61 'Mental Attitudes in War-Time', *Nature*, 19 June 1943, vol. 151.
62 Planning Committee minutes, 2 January 1941, INF 1/249.
63 Memorandum by Sir Kenneth Clark, 22 January 1941, INF 1/849.
64 Planning Committee minutes, 23 January 1941, INF 1/249.
65 H.I. Weekly Report, 25 November–4 December 1940, INF 1/292.
66 H.I. Weekly Report, 18–26 May 1942, INF 1/292.
67 *The Same Aggressor*, August 1941.
68 *Children into Ruffians*, 1941.
69 Executive Board minutes, 28 August 1941, INF 1/73.
70 Memorandum by Deputy Director General, 29 August 1941, INF 1/672.
71 *Japan: The Place and the Population*, April 1942.
72 *The Japanese People*, 1943.
73 *A Diagnosis of Japanese Psychology*, April 1945.
74 *The Japanese People*, 1943.
75 Noble Frankland, *The Bombing Offensive Against Germany* (London, 1965), p. 97.
76 Planning Committee minutes, 4 November 1940, INF 1/249.
77 Note for Regional Information Officers, 4 February 1941, INF 1/73.
78 Policy Points for Regional Information Officers, 12 April 1941, INF 1/672.
79 Sir Wyndham Deedes to Ministry, 16 April 1941, INF 1/672.
80 Unsigned note to H. V. Rhodes and R. H. Parker, 21 April 1941, INF 1/672.
81 Policy Points for RIOs, 26 May 1941, INF 1/672.
82 H.I. Weekly Report, 10–17 November 1941, INF 1/292.
83 *As Hitler Sows*, 1942.
84 H.I. Weekly Report, 26 May–2 June 1942, INF 1/292.
85 Air Chief Marshal Sir Arthur Harris to Air Ministry, 25 October 1943, AIR 2/7852.
86 S/S for Air to Chief of the Air Staff, 28 October 1943, AIR 2/7852.
87 Minute by Deputy Chief of the Air Staff, 5 November 1943, AIR 2/7852.
88 Sir Arthur Street to Harris, 15 December 1943, AIR 2/7852.
89 Harris to Street, 23 December 1943, AIR 2/7852.
90 Street to Harris, 2 March 1944, AIR 2/7852.
91 Harris to Street, 7 March 1944, AIR 2/7852.
92 H.I. Weekly Report, 11–18 May 1943, INF 1/292.
93 H.I. Weekly Report, 4–11 August 1942, INF 1/292.
94 *Daily Telegraph*, 21 October 1943.
95 H.I. Weekly Reports, 12–19, 19–26 January, 2–9 March, 30 March–6 April, 13–20 April, 27 April–4 May 1943, INF 1/292.
96 H.I. Weekly Report, 20–27 October 1942, INF 1/292.
97 H.I. Weekly Report, 19–26 January 1943, INF 1/292.
98 H.I. Weekly Report, 9–16 March, 1943, INF 1/292.
99 H.I. Weekly Report, 30 March–6 April 1943, INF 1/292.
100 H.I. Weekly Report, 27 April–4 May 1943, INF 1/292.
101 Air Ministry to Radcliffe, 19 July 1941, AIR 2/5325.
102 *Aerial Bombing – The Facts*, 1944.
103 *The Same Aggressor*, 1942.
104 *The Real Struggle*, October 1941.
105 Planning Committee memorandum, 25 July 1941, INF 1/251. My italics.
106 Andrew Sharf, *The British Press and Jews under Nazi Rule* (London, 1964). p. 193.

107 H.I. Daily Reports, 19 and 24 June 1940, INF 1/264.
108 H.I. Daily Reports, 9 and 11 September 1940, INF 1/264.
109 H.I. Weekly Reports, *passim*, INF 1/292.
110 H.I. Weekly Report, 18–26 May 1942, INF 1/292.
111 H.I. Weekly Report, 8–15 December 1942, INF 1/292.
112 H.I. Weekly Report, 15–22 December 1942, INF 1/292.
113 H.I. Weekly Report, 29 December–5 January 1943, INF 1/292.
114 H.I. Weekly Report, 2–9 March 1943, INF 1/292.
115 Note on proposal to establish Jewish Section, 27 May 1942, INF 1/770.
116 Memorandum by Robert Fraser, 10 February 1942, INF 1/251.
117 H.I. Weekly Report, 5–12 January 1942; and 'Home Morale and Public Opinion', 11 February 1942, INF 1/292.
118 'Atrocity Propaganda in the Press', 25 February 1942, INF 1/292.
119 H.I. Weekly Report, 2–9 February 1943, INF 1/292.
120 B.I.P.O. survey, April 1943, INF 1/292.
121 H.I. Weekly Report, 17–24 November 1942, INF 1/292.
122 *A Catalogue of Crime*, September 1944.
123 House of Commons Debates, 25 April 1945, vol. 410, col. 820.
124 Memorandum by Prime Minister, 9 November 1943, CAB 66/42; and draft telegrams for Stalin and Roosevelt, 3 October 1944, CAB 66/56.
125 Lord Taylor to author, 17 April 1976.

CHAPTER 6

1 Metropoliticus, op. cit.
2 Daniel Lerner, 'Effective Propaganda', op. cit.
3 Duff Cooper to Attlee, 4 December 1940, INF 1/863.
4 Nicolson Diary, 4 November 1940.
5 Nicolson Diary, 21 and 26 October 1940.
6 Nicolson Diary, 3 December 1940.
7 'Declaration of War Aims', 5 December 1940, PREM 4/100/4.
8 Duff Cooper to Attlee, 4 December 1940, INF 1/863.
9 Memorandum by Foreign Secretary, 7 January 1941, CAB 67/9.
10 War Cabinet Conclusions, 20 January 1941, CAB 65/17.
11 Nicolson Diary, 22 January 1941.
12 Memorandum by S. G. Gates, 21 April 1942, INF 1/864.
13 Nicolson to Duff Cooper, 15 January 1941, INF 1/177.
14 Nicolson to Duff Cooper, 21 January 1941, INF 1/177.
15 Nicolson to Duff Cooper, 28 January 1941, INF 1/177.
16 Duff Cooper to Greenwood, 30 January 1941, INF 1/177.
17 House of Commons Debates, 8 April 1941, vol. 370, cols. 1529–31.
18 Greenwood to Duff Cooper, 1 July 1941, INF 1/177.
19 Executive Board minutes, 22 July 1941, INF 1/73.
20 *Picture Post* to Sir Kenneth Clark, 19 November 1940, INF 1/234.
21 Tom Hopkinson to Robert Fraser, 14 March 1941, INF 1/234.
22 Planning Committee minutes, 3 February 1941, INF 1/249.
23 Tom Hopkinson to Robert Fraser, 14 March 1941, INF 1/234.
24 INF 1/234.
25 Robert Fraser to Lord Davidson, 19 March 1941, INF 1/234.
26 Memorandum by Lord Davidson, 20 March 1941, INF 1/73.
27 H.I. Weekly Report, 14–21 October 1940, INF 1/292.
28 H.I. Weekly Reports, 21–28 October and 28 October–4 November 1940, INF 1/292.

29 H.I. Weekly Report, 4–11 June 1941, INF 1/292.
30 H.I. Weekly Report, 6–13 October 1941, INF 1/292.
31 H.I. Weekly Reports, 27 August–3 September and 29 September–6 October 1941, INF 1/292.
32 H.I. Weekly Reports, 13–20 April and 28 July–4 August 1942, INF 1/292.
33 H.I. Weekly Report, 7–14 May 1941, INF 1/292.
34 H.I. Weekly Report, 16–23 March 1942, INF 1/292.
35 H.I. Weekly Report, 25 August–1 September 1942, INF 1/292.
36 H.I. Weekly Report, 2–9 March, INF 1/292.
37 Memorandum by S. G. Gates, 21 April 1942, INF 1/864.
38 H.I. Weekly Report, 26 February–5 March 1941, INF 1/292.
39 H.I. Weekly Report, 24 November–1 December 1941, INF 1/292.
40 H.I. Weekly Report, 11–18 May 1942, INF 1/292.
41 H.I. Weekly Report, 17–24 August 1942, INF 1/292.
42 Memorandum by Minister of Information, 9 October 1942, CAB 66/29.
43 H.I. Weekly Report, 27 October–3 November 1941, INF 1/292.
44 H.I. Weekly Report, 26 May–2 June 1942, INF 1/292.
45 H.I. Weekly Report, 25 November–4 December 1940, INF 1/292.
46 H.I. Weekly Report, 8–15 January 1941, INF 1/292.
47 H.I. Weekly Report, 6–13 April 1942, INF 1/292.
48 H.I. Weekly Reports, 25 November–4 December 1940 and 9–16 February 1942, INF 1/292.
49 H.I. Weekly Report, 9–16 February 1942, INF 1/292.
50 H.I. Weekly Report, 20–27 October 1941, INF 1/292.
51 Mass-Observation, 'Social Security and Parliament', *Political Quarterly*, vol. XIV, 1943.
52 H.I. Weekly Report, 27 November–1 December 1941, INF 1/292.
53 H.I. Weekly Report, 16–23 June 1942, INF 1/292.
54 Sir Arthur Willert to headquarters, 28 April 1942, INF 1/679.
55 S. A. Heald to Director General, 17 June 1942, INF 1/683.
56 R. H. Parker to Regional Information Officers, 3 November 1942, INF 1/301.
57 Williams, op. cit., pp. 82–3.
58 Ibid., p. 82.
59 Calder, op. cit., p. 613.
60 Paul Addison, *The Road to 1945* (London, 1975), p. 217.
61 Sir John Anderson to Brendan Bracken, 6 March 1943, INF 1/864.
62 H.I. Weekly Report, 8–15 December 1942, INF 1/292.
63 H.I. Weekly Report, 1–8 December 1942, INF 1/292.
64 H.I. Weekly Report, 29 December 1942–5 January 1943, INF 1/292.
65 H.I. Weekly Report, 16–23 February 1943, INF 1/292.
66 Ibid.
67 H.I. Weekly Report, 1–8 December 1942, INF 1/292.
68 H.I. Weekly Report, 8–15 December 1942, INF 1/292.
69 H.I. Weekly Reports, 16–23 February and 30 March–6 April 1943, INF 1/292.
70 H.I. Weekly Report, 1–8 December 1942, INF 1/292.
71 H.I. Weekly Report, 11–18 May 1943, INF 1/292.
72 Memorandum by Prime Minister, 12 January 1943, CAB 66/33.
73 Executive Board Minutes, 18 March 1943, INF 1/73.
74 Minutes of meeting between representatives of MoI and Reconstruction Secretariat, 5 July 1943, INF 1/683.
75 *Post-War Reconstruction in Britain*, June 1943.
76 H.I. Special Report, 31 May 1944, INF 1/293.
77 H.I. Special Report, 14 March 1944, INF 1/293.

CHAPTER 7

1 Home Office to Sir Kenneth Lee, 1 March 1940, INF 1/909; Sir Alexander Cadogan to Lee, 9 March 1940, INF 1/909; Lord Halifax to Sir John Reith, 16 April 1940, INF 1/909; Cabinet Home Policy Committee minutes, 30 April 1940, CAB 75/4.
2 Director General to Ivison Macadam, 29 May 1940, INF 1/909.
3 Radcliffe to E. T. Wiltshire, September 1940, INF 1/910.
4 Memorandum by Frank Pick, 27 September 1940, INF 1/849.
5 Foreign Office to MoI, 30 October 1940, INF 1/910.
6 Roger Hollis to Foreign Office, 25 October 1940, INF 1/910.
7 Memorandum by N. G. Scorgie, 11 November 1940, INF 1/849.
8 Ibid.
9 Memorandum by Radcliffe, 15 January 1941, INF 1/910.
10 Extract from Executive Board minutes, 21 January 1941, INF 1/910.
11 Memorandum by Lord Swinton, 16 January 1941, CAB 98/18.
12 Memorandum by Minister of Labour, 29 January 1941, CAB 98/18.
13 Minutes of Committee on Communist Activities, 20 January 1941, CAB 98/18.
14 Ibid., and memorandum by Minister of Labour, 29 January 1941, CAB 98/18.
15 Memorandum by Home Secretary, 17 January 1941, CAB 98/18.
16 Minutes of Committee on Communist Activities, 5 February 1941, CAB 98/18.
17 ibid.
18 MoI to Home Office, 18 March 1941, INF 1/910.
19 See INF 1/910 and INF 1/911.
20 Note by Mary Adams, September 1940, INF 1/910.
21 War Cabinet Conclusions, 4 July 1940, CAB 65/8.
22 War Cabinet Conclusions, 5 July 1940, CAB 65/8.
23 Sir Alexander Maxwell to Regional Commissioners, 27 July 1940, CAB 98/18.
24 Memorandum by Home Secretary, 23 December 1940, CAB 66/14.
25 Nicolson Diary, 27 January 1941.
26 H.I. Weekly Report, 22–29 January 1941, INF 1/292.
27 Scottish Region Intelligence report, 2 December 1940, INF 1/673.
28 N. F. McNicoll to H. V. Rhodes, 26 November 1940, INF 1/673.
29 N. F. McNicoll to H. V. Rhodes, 17 December 1940, INF 1/673.
30 Report on Industrial Areas Campaign, 15 February 1941, INF 1/673.
31 N. F. McNicoll to H. V. Rhodes, 10 January 1941, INF 1/673.
32 Appendix to H.I. Weekly Report, 28 May–4 June 1941, INF 1/292.
33 N. F. McNicoll to Regional Administration Division, 28 December 1940, INF 1/673.
34 Ibid.
35 Report of a meeting in Clydebank on 18 February 1941, INF 1/673.
36 Report on Industrial Areas Campaign, 24 April 1941, INF 1/673.
37 Report by William Roberts, 5 June 1941, INF 1/673.
38 H.I. Weekly Report, 19–26 March 1941, INF 1/292.
39 Memorandum by Harold Nicolson, 17 June 1941, INF 1/913.
40 War Cabinet Conclusions, 19 June 1941, CAB 65/18.
41 Nicolson Diary, 22 June 1941.
42 H.I. Weekly Report, 18–25 June 1941, INF 1/292.
43 Eden to Cooper, 26 June 1941, INF 1/913.
44 Cooper to Eden, 28 June 1941, INF 1/913.
45 Policy Committee minutes, 26 June 1941, INF 1/849.

46 Nicolson Diary, 11 July 1941.
47 Ibid.
48 Cooper to Eden, 12 July 1941, INF 1/913.
49 H.I. Weekly Report, 16–23 July 1941, INF 1/292.
50 Note by Director General, 22 January 1942, INF 1/849.
51 Nicolson Diary, 28 June 1941.
52 Memorandum by Alexander Werth, no date, INF 1/913.
53 R. H. Parker to Director General, 15 July 1941, INF 1/676.
54 Memorandum by R. H. Parker, 12 August 1941, INF 1/676.
55 R. H. Parker to Director General, 19 August 1941, INF 1/676.
56 Desmond Morton to Prime Minister, 31 August 1941, PREM 4/64/5.
57 Policy Committee minutes, 4 September 1941, INF 1/849.
58 Minister of Information to Prime Minister, 8 September 1941, PREM 4/64/5.
59 A. P. Ryan to Director General, 4 September 1941, INF 1/676.
60 Quoted in A. J. P. Taylor, *English History 1914–1945* (London 1970), p. 641.
61 Memorandum by H. P. Smollett, 7 October 1941, INF 1/147.
62 Ibid.
63 Ibid.
64 Peter Smolka (H. P. Smollett) to author, 25 May 1976.
65 Anglo-Soviet Publicity for September 1943, INF 1/678.
66 Memoranda by Minister of Information, 24 November 1943, CAB 66/43 and 4 February 1944, CAB 66/46.
67 H.I. Weekly Report, 16–23 February 1943, INF 1/292.
68 George Orwell, 'The Freedom of the Press', *Times Literary Supplement*, 15 September 1972.
69 H.I. Weekly Report, 27 August–3 September 1941, INF 1/292.
70 Home Division to RIOs, September 1941, INF 1/676.
71 Radcliffe to Harry Pollitt, 7 October 1941, INF 1/676.
72 Memorandum by Maureen Church, no date, INF 1/678.
73 Home Division to RIOs, September 1941, and D. B. Briggs to R. H. Parker, 10 October 1941, INF 1/676.
74 D. B. Briggs to RIOs, 20 October 1941, INF 1/676.
75 Ibid.
76 Note by D. B. Briggs, October 1941, INF 1/676.
77 London Regional Information Officer to Home Division, no date, INF 1/676.
78 R. H. Parker to Regional Information Officers, 10 February 1942, INF 1/677.
79 Henry Pelling, *The British Communist Party* (London, 1958), pp. 120–21.
80 H.I. Weekly Report, 26 January–2 February 1942, INF 1/292.
81 H.I. Weekly Report, 3–10 September 1941, INF 1/292.
82 H.I. Weekly Report, 2–9 February 1942, INF 1/292.
83 See Ralph Ingersoll, *Covering All Fronts* (London, 1942), p. 239: 'As the aid-to-Russia movement grew it began to become apparent that there was much more to it than simply special pleading for a diversion front. It began to sound like an incipient nation-wide rebellion – a rebellion against inaction . . . They didn't care what sacrifices it entailed.'
84 H.I. Weekly Reports, 16–23 July and 8–15 September 1941, INF 1/292.
85 H.I. Weekly Report, 11–18 May 1942, INF 1/292.
86 Ibid.
87 BBC Listener Research Report, September 1942.
88 H.I. Weekly Report, 2–9 March 1942, INF 1/292.
89 H.I. Weekly Report, 10–17 November 1941, INF 1/292.
90 H.I. Weekly Report, 2–9 June 1942, INF 1/292.

91 H.I. Weekly Report, 18–26 May 1942, INF 1/292.
92 'Home-Made Socialism', 24 March 1942, INF 1/292.
93 H.I. Weekly Report, 19–26 January 1943, INF 1/292.
94 H.I. Weekly Report, 26 January–2 February 1943, INF 1/292.
95 Ibid.
96 H.I. Weekly Report, 9–16 March 1943, INF 1/292.
97 Desmond Morton to Lord Swinton, 11 November 1941, INF 1/913.
98 Desmond Morton to Prime Minister, 12 November 1941, INF 1/913.
99 R. H. Parker to S. G. Gates, 25 November 1941, INF 1/913.
100 S. G. Gates to Radcliffe, 11 December 1941, INF 1/913.
101 Note by Radcliffe, 11 December 1941, INF 1/913.
102 Unsigned memorandum, 1944, INF 1/678.
103 BBC Listener Research Report, July 1942.
104 Memorandum by Richard Hope, 20 July 1940, INF 1/849.
105 Policy Committee minutes, 21 July 1940, INF 1/790.
106 Memorandum by Religions Division, 5 July 1941, INF 1/790.
107 Sir Stafford Cripps to MoI, 30 July 1941, INF 1/790.
108 Memorandum by Religions Division, 1 October 1941, INF 1/790.
109 Richard Hope to Hugh Martin, 25 April 1942, INF 1/787.
110 H. P. Smollett to Radcliffe and Kenneth Grubb, 7 October 1941, INF 1/147.
111 H. M. Waddams to Hugh Martin, 22 October 1942, INF 1/790.
112 Ibid.
113 Hugh Martin to Foreign Office, 2 December 1942, INF 1/792.
114 Note by H. M. Waddams of conversation with Archbishop of York, 24 June 1943, INF 1/792.
115 Archbishop of Canterbury to Hugh Martin, 27 May 1943, INF 1/792.
116 Home Division to RIOs, 16 June 1943, INF 1/790.
117 Note of Dr Garbett's press conference of 11 October 1943, INF 1/792.
118 Calder, op. cit., p. 559.
119 Note on visit of Russian Orthodox Church delegation to England, June 1945, INF 1/793.

CHAPTER 8

1 Orwell and Angus, op. cit., p. 168.
2 Lord Clark to author, 30 May 1974.
3 Lord Taylor to author, 2 March 1976.
4 H.I. Daily Report, 6 July 1940, INF 1/264; *Daily Mail* and *Daily Express*, 13 July 1940.
5 Memorandum by Minister of Information, 25 November 1940, CAB 67/8.
6 Minister of Information to S/S for Air, 28 November 1940, INF 1/845.
7 S/S for Air to Minister of Home Security, 2 January 1941, INF 1/846.
8 War Cabinet Conclusions, 18 November 1940, CAB 65/10.
9 Minister of Information, Minister of Home Security and S/S for Air to Prime Minister, 4 March 1941, INF 1/846.
10 Prime Minister to Minister of Information, 7 March 1941, INF 1/846.
11 Planning Committee minutes, 20 March 1941, INF 1/249.
12 Nicolson to Monckton, 13 May 1941, INF 1/912.
13 Williams to Monckton, 14 May 1941, INF 1/912.
14 Nicolson Diary, 15 May 1941.
15 Ronald Tree, 'Churchill's Secret Retreat', *The Observer*, 1 December 1974.
16 James Douglas-Hamilton, *Motive for a Mission* (London, 1971), p. 173.

17 Calder, op. cit., p. 249.
18 Douglas-Hamilton, op. cit., p. 173–4.
19 H.I. Weekly Report, 7–14 May 1941, INF 1/292.
20 War Cabinet Conclusions, 15 May 1941, CAB 65/18.
21 Nicolson Diary, 16 May 1941; Armstrong (ed.), op. cit., p. 129.
22 Boyle, *Poor, Dear Brendan*, p. 264.
23 Minister of Information to Prime Minister, 15 May 1941, INF 1/912.
24 War Cabinet Conclusions, 19 May 1941, CAB 65/18.
25 H.I. Weekly Report, 14–21 May 1941, INF 1/292.
26 Prime Minister to S/S for Air, 7 April 1945, INF 1/192.
27 Monckton to Minister of Information, 27 May 1941, INF 1/857.
28 MoI to Air Ministry, 26 May 1941, INF 1/912.
29 E. S. Herbert to Monckton, 26 May 1941, INF 1/912.
30 MoI to Air Ministry, 26 May 1941, INF 1/912.
31 S/S for Air to Minister of Information, 22 May 1941, INF 1/912.
32 Memorandum by Harold Nicolson, 'The Alleged Letter from Hess to the Duke of Hamilton', 13 June 1941, INF 1/73.
33 *Evening Standard*, 22 May 1941.
34 Monckton to Minister of Information, 27 May 1941, INF 1/857.
35 Minister of Information to Monckton, 27 May 1941, INF 1/857.
36 House of Commons Debates, 27 May 1941, vol. 371, col. 1702.
37 Nicolson Diary, 28 May 1941.
38 Memorandum by H. V. Hodson, 27 September 1940, INF 1/849.
39 Nicolson Diary, 1 October 1940.
40 Policy Committee minutes, 1 October 1940, INF 1/849.
41 *The Observer*, 13 October 1940.
42 Memorandum by H. V. Hodson, 19 November 1940, INF 1/251.
43 'Home Propaganda', *Change*, No. 2, 1941.
44 Peter Cromwell, 'The Propaganda Problem', *Horizon*, vol. III, No. 13, January 1941.
45 Planning Committee minutes, 27 February 1941, INF 1/249.
46 Planning Committee minutes, 2 January 1941, INF 1/249.
47 House of Commons Debates, 7 May 1941, vol. 371, col. 838.
48 Planning Committee minutes, 5 May 1941, INF 1/249.
49 Memorandum by Sir Kenneth Clark, 10 June 1941, INF 1/73.
50 Executive Board minutes, 27 June 1941, INF 1/73.
51 Report by Duty Room Committee, December 1940, INF 1/251.
52 Nicolson Diary, 2 March 1941.
53 Nicolson Diary, 5 April, 1941.
54 Nicolson Diary, 3 May 1941.
55 Nicolson Diary, 8 May 1941.
56 Nicolson Diary, 10 June 1941.
57 House of Commons Debates, 3 July 1941, vol. 372, cols. 1611–12.
58 Nicolson Diary, 2 March 1941.
59 Nicolson Diary, 13 April 1941.
60 Planning Committee minutes, 17 April 1941, INF 1/249.
61 Memorandum by Nicolson, April 1941, INF 1/251.
62 Williams to Sir Kenneth Clark, 16 April 1941, INF 1/251.
63 Memorandum by Williams, 21 May 1941, INF 1/251.
64 Planning Committee minutes, 30 May 1941, INF 1/249; Executive Board minutes, 10 June 1941, INF 1/73.
65 Balfour's conference paper, op. cit.
66 Memorandum by committee public relations officers of defence departments, 18 January 1941, INF 1/849.
67 Executive Board minutes, 1 February 1941, INF 1/73.
68 Memorandum by Nicolson, 16 January 1941, INF 1/849.

69 Nicolson to Sir Kenneth Clark, 5 March 1941, INF 1/252.
70 H. V. Rhodes to Sir Wyndham Deedes, 1 May 1941, INF 1/697.
71 Planning Committee Minutes, 8 May 1941, INF 1/249.
72 Asa Briggs, *The History of Broadcasting in the United Kingdom: The War of Words* (Oxford, 1970), pp. 164–5.
73 Prime Minister to Minister of Information, 17 May 1940, INF 1/869.
74 Minister of Information to Prime Minister, 20 May 1940, INF 1/869.
75 Lord Hood to Duff Cooper, 24 October 1940, INF 1/869.
76 Lord Hood to Duff Cooper, 27 November 1940, INF 1/869.
77 Memorandum by Director General, 3 November 1940, INF 1/869.
78 Duff Cooper to Hugh Dalton, 23 January 1941, INF 1/869.
79 N. G. Scorgie to Director General, 10 May 1941, INF 1/869.
80 Lord Normanbrook to Director General, 9 July 1941, INF 1/869.
81 Director General to Lord Normanbrook, 11 July 1941, INF 1/869.
82 Director General to Minister of Information, 1 November 1943, INF 1/941.
83 Nicolson Diary, 31 March 1941.
84 *New Statesman and Nation*, 21 June 1941.
85 Minister of Information to S/S for Air, 28 April 1941, AIR 2/5325.
86 Memorandum by Air Vice-Marshal Peck, April 1941, AIR 2/5325.
87 Nicolson Diary, 5 June 1941.
88 Duff Cooper, op. cit., p. 280.
89 House of Commons Debates, 28 May 1940, vol. 360, col. 453.
90 Armstrong (ed.), op. cit., p. 55.
91 Ibid., p. 75.
92 Nicolson Diary, 27 March 1941.
93 Nicolson Diary, 15 April 1941.
94 Williams, *Nothing So Strange*, pp. 164–5.
95 Memorandum by Sir Walter Monckton and Cyril Radcliffe, 21 May 1941, INF 1/857.
96 Monckton to Beaverbrook, 24 May 1941, INF 1/857.
97 Duff Cooper to Monckton, 28 May 1941, INF 1/857.
98 Brendan Bracken to Monckton, 5 June 1941, INF 1/857.
99 Minister of Information to Prime Minister, 6 June 1941, PREM 4/99/3.
100 Nicolson Diary, 12 June 1941.
101 Monckton to Bracken, 21 June 1941, INF 1/857.
102 Armstrong (ed.), op. cit., p. 124.
103 *Daily Herald*, 12 June 1941.
104 *The Times*, 16 June 1941.
105 S/S for War to Prime Minister, 12 June 1941, PREM 4/99/3.
106 Memorandum by Wing Commander Heald, 11 June 1941, AIR 2/5322.
107 Minister of Supply to Prime Minister, 21 June 1941, CAB 66/17.
108 See Taylor, *Beaverbrook*, p. 399.
109 Memorandum by Minister of Information, 24 June 1941, CAB 66/17.
110 Memorandum by Prime Minister, 26 June 1941, CAB 66/17.
111 Memorandum by Minister of Supply, 28 June 1941, CAB 66/17. See memoranda by Lord Beaverbrook, 13 and 22 July 1918, Beaverbrook Papers.
112 War Cabinet Conclusions, 30 June 1941, CAB 65/18.
113 Nicolson Diary, 1 July 1941.
114 Duff Cooper, op. cit., p. 288.
115 Nicolson Diary, 4 July 1941.

CHAPTER 9

1 Lord Taylor to author, 2 March 1976.
2 House of Commons debates, 28 July 1939, vol. 350, cols 1892–3.

Notes

3 Draft report of the Official Committee on the Machinery of Government on the post-war plans for the MoI, 28 March 1944, INF 1/941.

4 Boyle, *Poor, Dear Brendan, passim.*

5 Lord Birkenhead in *Brendan Bracken 1901–1958* (privately published, London, 1958), p. 41.

6 Beaverbrook to Bracken, 21 July 1941. I am indebted to Mr Charles Lysaght for permission to quote this letter.

7 Bracken to Churchill, 2 June 1942, INF 1/859.

8 Churchill to Bracken, 2 June 1942, INF 1/859.

9 Bartlett, *Political Propaganda*, p. 142.

10 Alan Hodge in *Brendan Bracken 1901–1958*, p. 4.

11 Sir Robert Marett quoted in Sir Kenneth Grubb, *Crypts of Power: An Autobiography* (London, 1971), p. 118.

12 Williams, *Press, Parliament and People*, p. 28.

13 Maurice Edelman, *The Mirror: A Political History* (London, 1966), p. 121.

14 Claud Cockburn, *I, Claud* (London, 1967), p. 234.

15 *Sunday Pictorial*, 24 October 1943.

16 Prime Minister to Minister of Labour, 25 October 1943, PREM 4/66/4.

17 Minister of Labour to Prime Minister, 3 November 1943, PREM 4/66/4.

18 Prime Minister to Dominions Secretary and Minister of Information, 2 April 1944, PREM 4/66/6A.

19 Churchill to Sir Walter Layton, 17 July 1943, PREM 4/66/2.

20 Draft letter to *Manchester Guardian*, 1 September 1944, PREM 4/66/4.

21 Beaverbrook to Churchill, 2 January 1945, PREM 4/66/4.

22 Note by Alan Hodge, 12 June 1943, PREM 4/66/2.

23 Prime Minister to Minister of Information, 14 June 1943, PREM 4/66/2.

24 Radcliffe to Monckton, 23 July 1941, INF 1/858.

25 Memorandum by Minister of Information, 14 May 1942, CAB 66/24.

26 Memorandum by Home Secretary, Foreign Secretary and Minister of Information, 12 November 1941, CAB 66/19.

27 Williams, *Press, Parliament and People*, p. 67.

28 War Cabinet Conclusions, 18 March 1942, CAB 65/25.

29 'Press Censorship in the U.K.', April 1943, INF 1/75.

30 Minister of Information to Prime Minister, 20 March 1942, PREM 4/99/4A.

31 Prime Minister to Minister of Information, 22 March 1942, PREM 4/99/4A.

32 Minister of Information to Foreign Secretary, 22 February and 18 May 1944, INF 1/859.

33 Memorandum by Director General, February 1944, INF 1/859.

34 Williams, *Press, Parliament and People*, p. 75.

35 'Press Censorship in the U.K.', April 1943, INF 1/75.

36 Draft Cabinet paper, 8 June 1942, INF 1/859.

37 Minister of Information to Prime Minister, 13 June 1942, INF 1/859.

38 Francis Williams to Director General, 17 February 1944, INF 1/859.

39 Harry Hopkins to Bracken, 16 October 1943, PREM 4/99/4A.

40 Bracken to Harry Hopkins, 20 October 1943, PREM 4/99/4A.

41 Foreign Office to Director General, 31 March and 6 April 1944, INF 1/859.

42 Director General to Foreign Office, 7 April 1944, INF 1/859.

43 Minister of Information to Foreign Secretary, April 1944, INF 1/859.

44 Balfour's conference paper, op. cit.

45 Nicolson Diary, 5 June 1941.

46 Memorandum by Balfour, 7 July 1941, INF 1/251.

47 'Home Morale and Public Opinion', 1 October 1941, INF 1/292.

48 'Home Front Propaganda', November 1941, INF 1/251. My italics.

49 Nicolson Diary, 10 September 1941.

50 Interview with Lord Radcliffe, 2 October 1974.

51 Report on the work of the Productions Division, 23 June 1944, INF 1/76.

52 'Home Front Propaganda', November 1941, INF 1/251.
53 Note on publicity campaigns, January 1941, INF 1/310.
54 Report by Campaigns Division, April 1943, INF 1/75.
55 Report by Campaigns Division, June 1944, INF 1/76.
56 Report by Exhibitions Division, June 1944, INF 1/76.
57 Planning Committee minutes, 22 July 1941, INF 1/249.
58 H.I. Weekly Report, 7–14 and 14–21 July 1942, INF 1/292.
59 Memorandum by Minister of Information, 17 July 1942, CAB 66/26.
60 Memorandum by Minister of Information, 28 August 1942, CAB 66/29.
61 Planning Committee minutes, 20 May 1941, INF 1/249.
62 Director General to Minister of Information, 1 August 1942, INF 1/921.
63 See Longmate, op. cit., pp. 321–34.
64 Memorandum by Taylor, no date, INF 1/290.
65 Memorandum by Minister of Information, 27 November 1942, CAB 66/31.
66 Memorandum by Minister of Information, 10 April 1942, CAB 66/23.
67 First appended to H.I. Weekly Report, 23–30 April 1941, INF 1/292.
68 Prime Minister to Minister of Information, 4 April 1942, INF 1/282.
69 Director General to Minister, 9 April 1942, INF 1/282.
70 MoI to government departments, Dominion High Commissioners, U.S. Ambassador, BBC Governors, 10 September 1943, INF 1/285.
71 Violet Bonham Carter to MoI, 14 September 1943, INF 1/285.
72 Hugh Gaitskell to MoI, 13 September 1943, INF 1/285.
73 F. C. Pritchard to MoI, 11 September 1943, INF 1/285.
74 Mary Hamilton to MoI, 13 September 1943, INF 1/285.
75 J. H. Peck to MoI, 30 September 1943, INF 1/285.
76 Aryck L. Unger, 'The Public Opinion Reports of the Nazi Party', *Public Opinion Quarterly*, Winter, 1965/66.
77 Memorandum by Taylor, 6 March 1943, INF 1/263.
78 Frank Pick to Harold Nicolson, 29 November 1940, INF 1/318.
79 Report to WTSS Scientific Advisory Committee, 5 December 1944, INF 1/273.
80 Edward Glover, 'The Birth of Social Psychiatry', *Lancet*, 24 August 1940; 'The Wartime Social Survey', *Nature*, vol. 149, 21 February 1942; Box and Thomas, op. cit.
81 R. P. Winfrey to Taylor, 30 December 1941, INF 1/273.
82 Taylor to Winfrey, 31 December 1941, INF 1/273.
83 Memorandum by Taylor, 7 September 1942, INF 1/263.
84 Ibid.
85 Stephen Taylor, 'The Study of Public Opinion', *Public Administration*, October/December 1943; Taylor to Professor A. V. Hill, 30 May 1944, INF 1/263.
86 House of Commons Debates, 29 June 1944, vol. 401, col. 832.
87 H.I. Weekly Report, 17–24 November 1941, INF 1/292.
88 H.I. Weekly Reports, 11–18 November 1940, 11–18 June, 8–15 September, 15–22 September and 17–24 November 1941, INF 1/292.
89 H.I. Weekly Reports, 15–22 January, 12–19 February, 19–26 March, 26 March–2 April, 20–27 August and 27 August–3 September 1941, INF 1/292.
90 H.I. Weekly Report, 3–10 November 1941, INF 1/292.
91 H.I. Weekly Reports, 12–19 February, 14–21 May 1941, INF 1/292.
92 H.I. Weekly Reports, 15–22 January, 17–25 November 1941, INF 1/292.
93 'Public Attitudes Towards the U.S.A.', 24 December 1941, INF 1/292.
94 Planning Committee minutes, 4 June 1941, INF 1/249.
95 Memorandum by Sir Kenneth Clark, 21 June 1941, INF 1/312.
96 Executive Board minutes, 25 June 1941, INF 1/73.
97 H.I. Weekly Report, 1–8 December 1941, INF 1/292.
98 H.I. Weekly Report, 8–15 December 1941, INF 1/292.

99 'Public Attitudes Towards the U.S.A.', 24 December 1941, INF 1/292.
100 Southern Region report, no date, INF 1/327B.
101 Midland Region report, no date, INF 1/327B.
102 *Welcome!*, 1942.
103 In a special report on LICs in January 1941, of which there were then 394, Harold Nicolson regretted their formation: 'Few of them possess any loyalty towards the Ministry and there are many members who believe they can exert pressure on us by threats of resignation or gain personal publicity by revelations to the Press. I am appalled by the general atmosphere of irresponsibility which exists.' 16 January 1941, INF 1/849.
104 'Liaison with the United States Forces in the U.K. 1942–45', 4 September 1945, INF 1/327B.
105 Ibid.
106 H.I. Weekly Reports, March–December 1942, INF 1/292, *passim.*
107 H.I. Weekly Report, 21–28 July 1942, INF 1/292.
108 Southern Region report, no date, INF 1/327B.
109 War Cabinet Conclusions, 31 August 1942, CAB 65/27.
110 Memorandum by S/S for War, 3 October 1942, CAB 66/29.
111 Memorandum by S/S for Colonies, 9 October 1942, CAB 66/29.
112 Memorandum by Lord Chancellor, 9 October 1942, CAB 66/29.
113 Memorandum by Home Secretary, 10 October 1942, CAB 66/29.
114 Memorandum by Minister of Information, 12 October 1942, CAB 66/29.
115 H.I. Weekly Report, 25 August–1 September 1942, INF 1/292.
116 H.I. Weekly Report, 1–8 September 1942, INF 1/292.
117 H.I. Weekly Report, 14–21 July 1942, INF 1/292.
118 Southern Region report, no date, INF 1/327B.
119 S/S for War to Prime Minister, 21 October 1943, PREM 4/26/9.
120 War Cabinet Conclusions, 13 October 1942, CAB 65/28.
121 Memorandum by Lord Privy Seal, 17 October 1942, CAB 66/30.
122 Memorandum by Minister of Information, 12 October 1942, CAB 66/29.
123 *Meet the U.S. Army*, 1943.
124 'Liaison with the United States Forces in the U.K. 1942–45', 4 September 1945, INF 1/327B.
125 Southern Region report, no date, INF 1/327B.
126 S/S for War to Prime Minister, 21 October 1943, PREM 4/26/9.
127 S/S for War to Prime Minister, 2 December 1943, PREM 4/26/9.
128 Duke of Marlborough to Prime Minister, 21 October 1943, PREM 4/26/9.
129 Prime Minister to S/S for War, 22 October 1943, PREM 4/26/9.
130 Memorandum by S/S for India, 3 June 1943, CAB 66/37.
131 Director General to Minister, 1 June 1943, INF 1/966.
132 Memorandum by Minister of Information, 11 June 1943, CAB 66/37.
133 First Quarterly Report of the MoI Far-Eastern War Committee, April 1944, INF 1/966.
134 H.I. Special Report, 11 July 1944, INF 1/293.
135 Minister of Information to Prime Minister, 15 November 1944, INF 1/966.
136 War Cabinet Conclusions, 16 June 1944, CAB 65/42.
137 Lord Taylor to author, 20 December 1976.
138 War Cabinet Conclusions, 13 June 1944, CAB 65/42; 28 July and 28 August 1944, CAB 65/43. See also Thomson, op. cit., pp. 196–207.
139 War Cabinet Conclusions, 18 September 1944, CAB 65/43.
140 War Cabinet Conclusions, 16 October 1944, CAB 65/43.
141 Bracken to Bernard Sendall, November 1943, INF 1/941.
142 Radcliffe to Bracken, 1 November 1943, INF 1/941.
143 Sir Alan Barlow to Radcliffe, 28 March 1944, INF 1/941.
144 *Evening Standard*, 28 June 1944.
145 Minister of Information to Prime Minister, 2 March 1945, INF 1/942.

146 Prime Minister to Minister of Information, 5 March 1945, INF 1/942.
147 House of Commons Debates, 7 March 1946, vol. 420, cols. 520–21.
148 House of Commons Debates, 29 June 1944, vol. 401, col. 929.
149 Duff Cooper, op. cit., p. 285.
150 Interview with Lord Radcliffe, 2 October 1974.
151 Information supplied by Malcolm Barnes, October 1974.
152 'Freedom of Information: A Human Right', Montague Burton Foundation Lecture, Glasgow University, 6 March 1953, in Lord Radcliffe, *Not in Feather Beds* (London, 1968), p. 18.
153 E. S. Herbert to Minister of Information, 1 November 1943, INF 1/941.
154 See, for example, R. N. Sanford and R. R. Holt, 'Psychological Determinants of Morale', *Journal of Abnormal and Social Psychology*, vol. 38, 1943.
155 Lord Taylor to author, 17 April 1976.
156 Paper given to Imperial War Museum conference on 'Film Propaganda and the Historian', 11 July 1973.
157 Nicolson Diary, 18 May 1941.
158 Duff Cooper, op. cit., pp. 287–8.
159 Balfour's conference paper, op. cit.

Bibliography

MANUSCRIPT SOURCES

Beaverbrook Papers (Beaverbrook Library).
Mass-Observation Archive (University of Sussex).
Nicolson Diary (Balliol College, Oxford).
Public Record Office – Ashridge Repository:
INF 1: Ministry of Information committee minutes and memoranda, internal notes, general correspondence, draft Cabinet memoranda, research reports and draft propaganda material.
INF 2: original art work for posters, cartoons, books and magazines; printed propaganda and publicity material.
Public Record Office – Chancery Lane and Portugal Street Repositories:
AIR 2: Air Ministry correspondence with Ministry of Information, correspondence and memoranda on publicity matters.
CAB 2: Minutes of the Committee of Imperial Defence.
CAB 4: Memoranda and reports of the Committee of Imperial Defence.
CAB 65: War Cabinet Conclusions.
  CAB 66.
CAB 67: War Cabinet memoranda of a less secret nature than those found in CAB 66.
CAB 68: Reports by various government departments to the War Cabinet.
CAB 75: Minutes and memoranda of the War Cabinet Home Policy Committee.
CAB 98/18: Minutes and memoranda of Committee on Communist Activities.
HO 199: Ministry of Home Security correspondence with Ministry of Information, intelligence reports, publicity matters, research reports on air raids and civilian morale.
INF 4: research reports and memoranda by Ministry of Information planners on propaganda, news and censorship agencies in First World War.
PREM 4: Churchill's prime-ministerial correspondence.
Tallents Papers (by courtesy of Mr. T. W. Tallents).

PRINTED SOURCES

House of Commons Debates.
House of Lords Debates.
Imperial War Museum: printed and visual propaganda produced by the Ministry of Information.
Newspapers: *Daily Express*
               Daily Herald

Daily Mail
Daily Telegraph
Evening Standard
Manchester Guardian
News Chronicle
Sunday Pictorial
The Observer
The Times

Memoirs and Diaries

Armstrong, William (ed.), *With Malice Towards None: A War Diary by Cecil H. King* (London, 1970).

Banner, Hubert S., *Kentish Fire* (London, no date).

Clark, Kenneth, *The Other Half* (London, 1978).

Cockburn, Claud, *I Claud* (London 1967).

Dilks, David (ed.), *The Diaries of Sir Alexander Cadogan 1938–45* (London, 1971).

Duff Cooper, Alfred, *Old Men Forget* (London, 1957).

Fougasse, *A School of Porpoises* (London, 1946).

Grubb, Kenneth, *Crypts of Power: An Autobiography* (London, 1971).

Huxley, Julian, *Memories* (London, 1970).

Ingersoll, Ralph, *Covering All Fronts* (London, 1942).

Low, David, *Low's Autobiography* (London, 1956).

Macmillan, Lord, *A Man of Law's Tale* (London, 1953).

Nicolson, Nigel (ed.), *Harold Nicolson Diaries and Letters 1939–45* (London, 1970).

Orwell, Sonia and Angus, Ian (eds), *The Collected Essays, Journalism and Letters of George Orwell* (London, 1970).

Reith, J. C. W., *Into the Wind* (London, 1949).

Reynolds, Quentin, *Only the Stars Are Neutral* (Sydney, 1942).

Templewood, Viscount, *Nine Troubled Years* (London, 1954).

Thomson, G. P., *Blue Pencil Admiral* (London, 1947).

Thurtle, Ernest, *Time's Winged Chariot* (London, 1945).

Williams, Francis, *Nothing So Strange* (London, 1970).

Biographies

Birkenhead, Lord, *Walter Monckton* (London, 1969).

Boyle, Andrew, *Only the Wind Will Listen* (London, 1972).

Boyle, Andrew, *Poor, Dear Brendan* (London, 1974).

Brendan Bracken 1901–1958 (privately published, London, 1958).

Donoghue, Bernard and Jones, G. W., *Herbert Morrison: Portrait of a Politician* (London, 1973).

Taylor, A. J. P., *Beaverbrook* (London, 1972).

Secondary works

Addison, Paul, *The Road to 1945* (London, 1975).

Allport, G. W. and Postman, L., *The Psychology of Rumour* (New York, 1965).

Bartlett, F. C., *Political Propaganda* (Cambridge, 1942).

Baxter, Beverley, *Men, Martyrs and Mountebanks* (London, 1940).

Bramsted, Ernst K., *Goebbels and National Socialist Propaganda* (Michigan, 1965).

Bibliography

Briggs, Asa, *The History of Broadcasting in the United Kingdom: The War of Words* (Oxford, 1970).

Calder, Angus, *The People's War* (London, 1971).

Clark, Sir Fife, *The Central Office of Information* (London, 1970).

Doob, Leonard W., 'Goebbels' Principles of Propaganda' in Daniel Katz (ed.), *Public Opinion and Propaganda* (New York, 1965).

Douglas-Hamilton, James, *Motive for a Mission* (London, 1971).

Edelman, Maurice, *The Mirror: A Political History* (London, 1966).

Ellul, Jacques, *Propaganda* (New York, 1968).

Frankland, Noble, *The Bombing Offensive Against Germany* (London, 1965).

Irving, David, *The Destruction of Dresden* (New York, 1965).

Janis, I. L., *Air War and Emotional Stress* (New York, 1951).

Kris, Ernst and Leites, Nathan, 'Trends in Twentieth Century Propaganda' in Daniel Lerner (ed.), *Propaganda in War and Crisis* (New York, 1951).

Lerner, Daniel, 'Effective Propaganda' in Daniel Lerner (ed.), *Propaganda in War and Crisis* (New York, 1951).

Longmate, Norman, *How We Lived Then* (London, 1973).

MacCurdy, J. T., *The Structure of Morale* (Cambridge, 1943).

Ogilvy-Webb, Marjorie, *The Government Explains: A Study of the Information Services* (London, 1968).

O'Brien, T. H., *Civil Defence* (London, 1955).

Paterson, T. T., *Morale in War and Work* (London, 1955).

Pelling, Henry, *Britain and the Second World War* (London, 1970).

Pelling, Henry, *The British Communist Party* (London, 1958).

Radcliffe, Lord, *Not in Feather Beds* (London, 1968).

Riley, Norman, *999 And All That* (London, 1940).

Sharf, Andrew, *The British Press and the Jews Under Nazi Rule* (London, 1964).

Speier, Hans, 'Morale and Propaganda' in Daniel Lerner (ed.), *Propaganda in War and Crisis* (New York, 1951).

Sullivan, H. S., 'Psychiatric Aspects of Morale' in A. H. Stanton and S. E. Perry (eds), *Personality and Political Crisis* (New York, 1951).

Taylor, A. J. P., *English History 1914–1945* (London, 1970).

Titmuss, R. M., *Problems of Social Policy* (London, 1950).

Webster, Sir Charles and Frankland, Noble, *The Strategic Air Offensive Against Germany* (London, 1961).

Williams, Francis, *Press, Parliament and People* (London, 1946).

United States Strategic Bombing Survey, 'Social and Psychological Factors Affecting Morale' in Daniel Lerner (ed.), *Propaganda in War and Crisis* (New York, 1951).

Journal articles

Allport, G. W., 'Psychological Service for Civilian Morale', *Journal of Consulting Psychology*, Vol. 5, 1941.

Barbour, R. F., 'Morale', *Lancet*, 22 March 1940.

Bartlett, R. J., 'The Civilian Population Under Bombardment', *Nature*, Vol. 147, 7 June 1941.

Box, Kathleen and Thomas, Geoffrey, 'The Wartime Social Survey', *Journal of the Royal Statistical Society*, Parts III–IV, 1944.

Brown, Felix, 'Civilian Psychiatric Air-Raid Casualties', *Lancet*, 31 May 1941.

Chein, Isidor, 'The Meaning of "Morale" in Relation to Morale Building and Morale Research', *Psychological Review*, Vol. 50, 1943.

Child, Irvin L., 'Morale: A Bibliographical Review', *Psychological Review*, Vol. 38, 1941.

Cromwell, Peter, 'The Propaganda Problem', *Horizon*, Vol. III, No. 13, 1941.

Editorial, *Nature*, Vol. 146, 20 July 1940.

Ewer, W. N., 'The Ministry of Information', *Political Quarterly*, Vol. XII, 1941.

Geoghegan, Joseph, 'Morale', *Nature*, Vol. 150, 4 July 1942.

Glover, Edward, 'The Birth of Social Psychiatry', *Lancet*, 24 August 1940.

Harrisson, Tom, 'Blitzinformation', *Local Government Service*, Vol. 21, No. 8, August 1941.

Harrisson, Tom, 'What is Public Opinion?', *Political Quarterly*, Vol. XI, 1940.

Henderson, E. H., 'Towards a Definition of Propaganda', *Journal of Social Psychology*, August 1943.

Hopkin, Deian, 'Domestic Censorship in the First World War', *Journal of Contemporary History*, Vol. 5, No. 4, 1970.

Mass-Observation, 'Home Propaganda', *Change*, No. 2, 1941.

Mass-Observation, 'Social Security and Parliament', *Political Quarterly*, Vol. XIV, 1943.

McCord, Fletcher, 'A Blueprint for Total Morale', *Character and Personality*, Vol. XI, 1942–3.

Metropoliticus, 'The Ministry of Information', *Political Quarterly*, Vol. XIII, 1942.

Mira, E., 'Fear', *Lancet*, 17 June 1939.

Mira, E., 'Psychiatric Experience in the Spanish War', *British Medical Journal*, 17 June 1939.

Money-Kyrle, R., 'The Psychology of Propaganda', *British Journal of Medical Psychology*, Vol. 19, 1943.

Report of a debate between Tom Harrisson and Henry Durant, *Nature*, Vol. 149, 7 May 1942.

Report of a meeting of the British Psychological Society, *Lancet*, 23 March 1940.

Sanford, R. N. and Holt, R. R., 'Psychological Determinants of Morale', *Journal of Abnormal and Social Psychology*, Vol. 38, 1943.

Sanford, R. N. and Conrad, H. S., 'Some Personality Correlates of Morale', *Journal of Abnormal and Social Psychology*, Vol. 38, 1943.

Taylor, Stephen, 'The Study of Public Opinion', *Public Administration*, October/December 1943.

Thouless, R. H., 'Mental Attitudes in War-Time', *Nature*, Vol. 151, 19 June 1943.

Thouless, R. H., 'Psychological Effects of Air Raids', *Nature*, Vol. 148, 16 August 1941.

Tree, Ronald, 'Churchill's Secret Retreat', *Observer*, 1 December 1974.

Unger, Aryck L., 'The Public Opinion Reports of the Nazi Party', *Public Opinion Quarterly*, Winter 1965–66.

Vernon, P. E., 'A Study of War Attitudes', *British Journal of Medical Psychology*, Vol. XIX, 1942.

Vernon, P. E., 'Psychological Effects of Air Raids', *Journal of Abnormal and Social Psychology*, Vol. 36, 1941.

White, David, 'The Power of Rumour', *New Society*, 17 October 1974.

Wright, Maurice, 'Effect of War on Civilian Populations', *Lancet*, 21 January 1939.

Index

Index

Other Half, The 68
'Our Fighting Men Depend on You' 54

Pacifism 55–6, 57–8
Parker, R. H. 183–4, 210, 225; on dangers of communism 199–200; satisfied with progress of Stealing the Thunder campaign 206
Peace News 58
Pear, T. H., condemns Black Record 155
Peck, Air Vice-Marshal 233
People's Convention 58, 175
Perth, Lord 16
Petain 70, 74, 149, 212
Pick, Frank 87; wants complete control of BBC 230; suspicious of psychologists 261
Picture Post, co-operation with M.O.I. 48–9; changed relationship with M.O.I. 174–76
Planning Committee 69, 72, 77, 81, 84, 125, 138, 148, 156, 166, 219, 227, 230, 254
Plant, Arnold 85
Plymouth 114, 118, 131, 134
Policy Committee 50, 55, 63, 74, 84, 88, 90, 101, 102, 128, 138, 142, 143, 187, 200, 211, 227
Political Quarterly 171
Political Warfare Executive 3
Pollitt, Harry 198, 204
Portsmouth 114, 118, 120
Postal and Telegraph Censorship 222, 258, 278; transferred to M.O.I. 44; reports of passed on to M.O.I. 52
Posters 76, 183; design for initial poster 21; importance of to morale 30; 'Your courage, your cheerfulness, your resolution will bring us victory' 31; country festooned with 54
Powell, Sir Allan 231
Press, The 83, 86, 95, 221; Duff Cooper alienates 6; left by Defence Notices with nothing to talk about 25; delighted with Senate House facilities 35; assured by M.O.I. no censorship of opinion 36; furious at M.O.I. 38; opposes formation Press and Censorship Bureau 38; contemptuous of censorship rulings 43; attacks Cooper's Snoopers 85; on compulsory censorship 88–90; behaves well 89; Sir Kenneth Clark urges opinion censorship of 91; and M.O.I. influence 91–3; Bracken's

good relations with 243; Churchill's sensitivity to criticism by 243–4. Press and Censorship Bureau 3, 41, 42–3. Press Censorship, voluntary principle of 24–5; early difficulties of 36–41; near collapse of voluntary system 43; M.O.I. considers making compulsory 88–90; of material damaging to allied unity and of disclosure of diplomatic negotiations 245–50
Priestley, J. B. 99, 146
Pritt, D. N. 41
Public meetings 47, 48

Radcliffe, Cyril 7, 38, 129, 192, 210, 231, 252, 273, 276, 277, 279; defines censorship principles 36; on War Office 43; and censorship 88; receives daily summary air operations 164; opposes ban on export of certain publications 187; on militant socialism 212; threatens resignation 233–4; qualities of 243; defends censorship on security grounds only 247; against censorship of diplomatic negotiations 249; wants compulsory fuel rationing 255–6; defends Home Intelligence reports 258–9; on freedom of information 278
Red Army Day 203
Regional Information Officers 22–3, 29, 42, 46, 48, 51, 54, 57–8, 59, 65, 125, 126, 127, 131, 133, 134, 135, 154, 160, 176, 180, 192, 204–5, 208, 228, 262, 265, 268, 272, 279
Reith, Sir John 4, 16, 17, 42, 55, 60, 62, 100; reluctant to force Chamberlain's hand 6; on Chamberlain 18; on public boredom 35; wants Monckton in Commons 44; dumped from office 45; domestic propaganda policy of 45–6; on communists 56; on social reform 59; on principles of propaganda 141; on ruthlessness of Germans 142
Religions Division 4, 56, 151, 152, 153, 168, 213–16
Return-to-work rate 122–3
Reynolds, Quentin 40
Rhodes, H. V. 18, 229–30; on rumours 21; wants Home Intelligence transferred to Ministry of Home Security 87
Riley, Norman, 999 and All That 6; on M.O.I. staffing 39; on censorship bungles 40

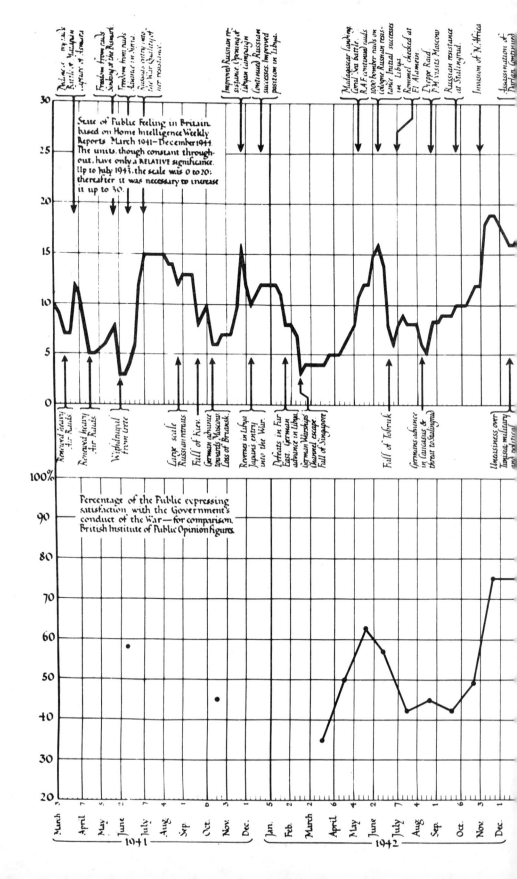

CLOSING COMMENTS

I love simplicity. As Da Vinci *said simplicity is the ultimate sophistication*. So let us try five simple statements.

One. We are all curious beings at different stages in our life. Would you agree? *Two*. We all seek happiness. No one wants to be sad. Right? *Three*. We all seek meaning, in some shape or form. Yes? *Four*. We all crave to be understood and liked. True? *Five*. We all 'hope' for something. Agree?

If you do agree to the above, I know I have your consent on the closing section of my book. Be tireless and prolific. Just as there is a *survivor and an artist* in each one of us, there is also a *creator and leader* in each one of us too. Believe in it and ...let it out.

We live in a society which can catapult us into the galaxy of success and bring us right down with a thud. Success is never permanent, neither is failure. But belief is. So, control the controllable, and be prepared for the uncontrollable. Years of preparation for a 90 seconds win at the Olympics matters just as much – you know why? Because it is worth it. That 90 seconds changes history. Find your 90 seconds. It could be 90 minutes, 90 hours or 90 days. Or more. But find your passion.

Think of the cinema. When you are sitting in a dark hall, staring at a screen, bigger than a football field, looking at a hero larger than life, your experience of everything the actor goes through is exaggerated. Likewise, when you are in a stadium watching eleven players, amongst 50,000 fans chasing a goal, you feel the blood in your legs rise. Or, when you sit amongst a thousand people listening to a CEO tell visionary story, you feel the heart race – you want to meet the man on stage. Why? Because we are inspired by meaning, success, and victory. We are born to identify with heroes. We are wired to crave inspiration.

Every time I have got on *any form of stage* I have felt the highs of inspiring others. It is like a hundred cups of coffee shooting through the veins. Do you know why? There is something about a 'crowd of people' looking to you for something special. That crowd could be big (generation, nation, stadium) or small (team, group, class, family). But the crowd matters. And the 'special something' you can give them matters even more. 90 seconds or 90 minutes or ninety days.

From time immemorial, across cultures and generations, society creates leaders to escape the looming inevitability of 'the end'. Leaders live legacies, which outlasts them. Society defines three types of leaders. The traditional one which comes from lineage – the 'kings and princes' type.

The bureaucratic one which comes from official power – the 'politicians' type. The charismatic one which comes from being a star – the 'stars' type. But I urge you to be the "be better than yesterday" type. I mean, if every day you aspire to be better and fresher than yesterday, you will naturally become a leader. And then you will see yourself inspiring many others and redefining the demands, desires and drivers of your era.

Don't depend on a big leader – Presidents, CEOs – to solve your problems. You solve them. Don't rely on big heroes to follow your way. You find it.

If the ordinary people in this book – *6 chairmen, 16 CEOs, 5 leading musicians, 2 sporting athletes, 2 world famous chefs, a policewoman, young Gen Y bright students, young rising stars, high potential managers, principals/teachers, ministers, social workers, a priest, a poet and film maker and me* – can find their way, so can you.

The world has given me its best and also some of its worst. I did not read books to know the theme of life was *tests*. Through a series of tests, we grow. Though these tests we realise life is about happiness, and sadness, trouble and ...getting out of trouble. Good and Bad drift upon us like clouds, but the sun never quits, although it may hide. The sun is in you. Find it. *Leadership is in your DNA*, release it. Instinctively all my life, work and writing is based on this principle: the process of getting out of people what they may not know they have within.

Imagine the following people who have inspired us. Michael Jackson as a *boxer*? Muhammad Ali as a *musician*? Tiger Woods as a *footballer*? Steve Jobs as a *politician*? Roger Federer as a *lead singer*? You can't, right? Well, ordinary people just found their one passion in their DNA that then became their inspiration, and made them extraordinary. Keep it simple. I leave you with my ten ingredients entwined together as a poem.

- *Know your self. Seek in your **Self** and you shall find*
- *An **Expression** that is, you could say, your authenticity.*
- *Tune in to your **Emotions** and be guided by your **Instincts***
- *Unleash your **Creativity** with a belief so bright*
- *It shadows the **Dark Side** away into the night*
- ***Fear** not then as you sail through this turbulence*
- *For out of it will come steadfast **Resilience***
- ***Focus** instead on what lies within you,*
- *And **Luck** will be with you from the moment you believe in you.*

Discovery, Hope and Inspiration never go out of fashion. Something always needs to be discovered, achieved, or made sense of. What's classic today was norm-breaking a few years ago. There is a way of tapping into the infinite possibilities that await us in this incredible age of re-defining norms. We are lucky to be born at this time and to witness the world rebuild its own DNA in a whole, new way. You can't control the changes. But you can read the pulse of your time and try to strike a resonance in your world. You may lead or leave a legacy or just inspire someone next to you, or a team or an entire nation. Leadership is an attitude.

Everyone asks me "what will be the next big thing?"

I say it is **YOU**.

Your ability to develop and, yes, reinvent yourself will be the next biggest thing that matters.

The best things are really simple. Have a dream that will leave this world an inspired place. Never quit that dream. Don't chase leadership. Chase *inspiration* every day and *inspire* to be stronger and better than you were yesterday. Leadership will be a natural outcome, for after all *Leadership: It's in your DNA.*

It is with these words, that I now turn this book to you. Dare. Be different. Be YOU.

You can do anything if you really want to.